EERATIVE
STRATEGIES IN
INTERNATIONAL
BUSINESS EXPANSION

ENTRY AND COOPERATIVE STRATEGIES IN INTERNATIONAL BUSINESS EXPANSION

Yadong Luo

QUORUM BOOKS
Westport, Connecticut • London

Library of Congress Cataloging-in-Publication Data

Luo, Yadong.
    Entry and cooperative strategies in international business
expansion / Yadong Luo.
      p.   cm.
    Includes bibliographical references and index.
    ISBN 1–56720–161–X (alk. paper)
    1. International business enterprises. 2. Cooperation.
3. Competition, International. I. Title.
HD62.4.L86   1999
658'.049—dc21   98–48946

British Library Cataloguing in Publication Data is available.

Library of Congress Catalog Card Number: 98–48946
ISBN: 1–56720–161–X

First published in 1999

Quorum Books, 88 Post Road West, Westport, CT 06881
An imprint of Greenwood Publishing Group, Inc.
www.quorumbooks.com

Printed in the United States of America

The paper used in this book complies with the
Permanent Paper Standard issued by the National
Information Standards Organization (Z39.48–1984).

10 9 8 7 6 5 4 3 2 1

Contents

Illustrations

Preface

Over the past decade or so the nature of competition has been fundamentally altered by increasing technological advancements and the globalization of business. The need to balance the dynamic tension between multiple forces that need to be managed simultaneously — geographic, product, market, and technological — has resulted in firms extending their presence all over the globe for a multitude of purposes and through a multitude of forms. Correspondingly, international expansion decisions and strategies have acquired increasing strategic significance.

This book is written for international executives who are actively pursuing international market opportunities or want to do so and for scholars and students of international business or global management. It is intended to provide conceptual backgrounds, analytical frameworks, managerial insights, business guidance, and practical evidence for managers active or interested in international expansion. The grand theme is the need for international managers to formulate appropriate international expansion strategies that aim to achieve a sustainable and successful presence in the global marketplace.

In the course of writing this book, I have benefitted from financial support from the University Research Council, the College of Business Administration, and the Center for International Business Education and Research, all at the University of Hawaii. This book is dedicated to my family in recognition of their patience and support throughout this project.

I

THEORETICAL PERSPECTIVES OF INTERNATIONAL EXPANSION

1

Concept and Importance

Globalization has become a permanent and irreversible part of economic life. It provides firms with both tremendous opportunities and daunting challenges. International expansion has become a pervasive and prominent strategic response to global economic dynamics for a large array of companies. This chapter begins with an introduction to the definition and scope of international expansion, followed by a presentation on its benefits and importance. The third section outlines the challenges, uncertainties, and risks involved in international expansion. The last section illustrates major trends and patterns of global economy and international expansion activities, particularly focusing on recent foreign direct investment (FDI) flow.

DEFINITION AND SCOPE

Over the past decade or so competition has been fundamentally altered by technological advancements and the globalization of business. The need to balance simultaneously the dynamic tension between multiple forces (geographic, product, market, and technological) has resulted in firms extending their presence all over the globe for a multitude of purposes and through a multitude of forms. Correspondingly, international expansion decisions and strategies have acquired increasing strategic significance.

In this book international expansion is defined as the process by which a multinational enterprise (MNE) enters and invests in a target foreign

country in pursuit of the MNE's strategic objectives. This working definition contains several attributes that differentiate international expansion
from other concepts, such as international business, international operations, or international investment. First, we are concerned specifically
with MNEs, rather than all companies involved in international business
activities. The firm under consideration must have substantial direct
investments in foreign countries; it cannot be just an export business.
Moreover, the firm should be actively managing its offshore assets rather
than simply buying raw materials offshore, licensing technologies
abroad, exporting products into foreign markets, or holding a small
minority ownership position in a foreign joint venture without any management participation.

Second, we focus on FDI rather than indirect investment. In other
words, issues of investing and maintaining a financial portfolio are not
our concern. Although security investment is a part of international
business, it is not a major aspect of global strategic management, the
primary perspective employed in this book. Nevertheless, we do not
rule out the importance of several international finance issues, such as
foreign exchange risk, operational exposure, and financial management,
in affecting international expansion processes and consequences. These
issues are incorporated in several analytical frameworks for international
expansion.

Third, we emphasize overseas expansion, rather than operations
abroad. Put most simply, international business equals international
expansion plus international operations. International expansion mainly
concerns antecedent investment decisions about how, what, where, and
when an MNE should expand during the internationalization process,
whereas international operations are associated largely with how to operate successfully in a country where an investment has been established.
Thus, international operations are important but subsequent to international expansion decisions. From the strategy formulation point of view,
most international expansion decisions are made within the domain of
corporate level strategy, but a large number of international operation
decisions fall within business or functional level strategies.

Last, international expansion differs from international investment or
FDI, although they are related. The common ground between international expansion and international investment resides in international
entry strategies (e.g., what, where, when, and how) and some cooperative
strategy issues (e.g., partner selection and sharing arrangement). As a
result of a shift from international development (using multidomestic
strategy) to transnational development (using hybrid or transnational
strategy) by most MNEs today, firms have to attach paramount value to
such issues as dynamic capability, global integration and control, and
cooperative strategies. These issues constitute key concerns underlying

international expansion decisions and directly affect the success of transnational development. These issues, however, are not the primary concerns of conventional wisdom of FDI.

Broadly, the strategic objectives of international expansion include: efficiency enhancement from location advantages; return improvement from ownership advantages; integration economies from internalization advantages; and learning and experience benefits from expansion, adaptation, and partnerships. Ideally, MNEs will simultaneously focus on all four strategic goals, which would promote the maximum possible economic rents gained through international expansion. Because international expansion is an evolutionary process, during which firms face dynamic industry life cycles and contextual changes, individual MNEs may place varying weight on different objectives to cope with environmental and organizational dynamics. Such weight also varies according to firm and time period. These objectives and advantages will be further discussed in the next section.

Firms often expand internationally because of both pull and push factors. Firms are pulled or attracted by the cost and revenue benefits derived from host country dynamics. Cost benefits are generated from low cost production factors and operational expenses. Of these, cheap labor costs and low prices for raw materials and natural resources are the most prominent cost-related factors. Revenue benefits result from market demand growth in a foreign country. Although facing liabilities of foreignness, an MNE's competitive advantages, manifested in strong technological and organizational skills, may enable the firm to preempt emerging investment opportunities and explore market potential. Other revenue-related benefits include accessibility to scarce resources, preferential treatment for FDI, and learning or experience accumulation. Unlike the pull factors, which are host country-related, push factors are associated with the home or source country environment. Source country contextual factors act either as stimuli or impediments to the outflow of FDI. Home country conditions affect FDI outflow decisions by offering a frame of reference by which MNEs judge and evaluate host country factors. The degree of attractiveness of a given foreign investment environment lies in the relative differences of contextual factors, as judged by MNEs, between home and host countries.

International expansion offers several advantages to firms. It provides the opportunity to exploit the benefits of internalization, such as economies of scale, scope, and learning, exploitable relationships between business segments and geographic areas, shared distinctive firm capabilities or core competencies among business units, and differences in factor markets. In addition, MNEs have the opportunity to integrate across country borders by standardizing products, rationalizing production, and coordinating critical resource functions. Thus, international expansion provides greater opportunity to achieve optimal economic scale and amortize investments in critical functions. Moreover, international expansion can gain competitive advantages by exploiting market imperfections and cross-border transactions and can also gain the increased flexibility and greater bargaining power that result from a multinational network and larger economies of scale, scope, and learning. Economies of scale allow firms to increase efficiency. Increased learning and innovation result from economies of scope. The competitive advantages that produce greater profitability in domestic markets can be applied in international markets to enhance further a firm's profitability. Resource sharing among multiple international operations in turn facilitates exploitation of common sets of core competencies to produce synergy.

International expansion as defined in this book is broadly threefold in scope. First, international expansion imperatives, such as dynamic capabilities, evolutionary development, and global integration, are the fundamental building blocks on which a wide variety of international expansion strategies, decisions, and policies are based. They are imperatives because they cannot be unlinked from the decision-making process during international expansion. Each of these issues independently represents an important perspective, and collectively they constitute the core of international expansion theory. Specifically, capability exploitation (rent-generating resources) and capability building (organizational learning), the two key components of dynamic capability, have become increasingly fundamental to international expansion. Firm-specific strategic resources are critical to both competitive advantage and the determination of a firm-level strategy for exploiting such an advantage. Dynamic learning capability is critical because it ensures the evolutionary development of a sustainable advantage and generation of new bundles of resources. International expansion is a dynamic, evolutionary process shaped by an MNE's international experience, organizational capabilities, strategic objectives, and environmental dynamics. A firm's strategic behavior during this process is generally mirrored in market commitment, resource contributions, investment size, product relatedness, and entry mode selection. Furthermore, international expansion requires coordinating subsidiary activities across country locations. With increasing globalization of the competitive environment, the dual imperatives of global integration and local responsiveness are becoming more critical than ever before for MNEs' survival and growth.

The second major part tackles international entry strategies. Unlike previous studies, which have narrowly defined entry strategies as only involving entry mode selection (how), we address not only how but also where (location selection), when (timing of entry), and what (industry selection). Location selection for FDI projects is critical because it affects both investment efficiency and effectiveness. Cultural distance, business atmosphere, government policies, foreign business treatment, stage of economic development, and degree of openness all vary substantially across different countries and even different regions within countries. In addition, timing of international expansion plays a critical role in shaping transnational firm behavior and represents an important source of competitive advantage in international settings. It is associated with the height of entry barriers, evolving industry and market structures in the host country, and degree of access to various indigenous resources. In today's increasingly integrated global marketplace where demand level, consumption sophistication, factor costs, input characteristics, and rivalry intensity are all changing drastically, the decision of when to embark on international expansion is critical to transnational operations. Finally, as industry structure is partially exogenous, industry selection will have a strong impact on international expansion performance. It determines the industrial environment and market demand that the firm will face abroad, which in turn affect the firm's profitability, stability, sales growth, and competitive position in the host country.

The third domain of international expansion lies in international cooperative strategies. These include partner selection, sharing arrangement and control, and joint venture negotiation, cooperation, and termination. The success of international cooperative ventures largely depends on the selection of local partners. Sharing arrangement and its corresponding ownership control have critical implications in risk sharing, resource allocation, knowledge commitment, environment vulnerability, strategic flexibility, and organizational control. Further, knowledge about determinants, processes, and outcomes of negotiation, cooperation, and termination can help international business managers employ appropriate collaborative strategies that will result in maximum payoff. International managers must attach a pivotal importance to making the right decisions about three critical issues in joint venture development: negotiations during the formation stage, cooperation during the operational stage, and termination at the concluding stage.

BENEFITS AND IMPORTANCE

A major challenge for global strategic management today is improving the competence and sustaining the superior performance of MNEs. International expansion seeks to use internal resources and capabilities to exploit market imperfections existing across global regions and countries. Firms experience increasing transaction costs with greater international diversification, however. For example, coordinating units in different geographic regions is necessary for exploiting potential economies of scope. At some point, however, the coordination required costs more than the benefits derived from sharing resources and exploiting market opportunities. These transaction costs begin to produce diminishing returns from international expansion. In addition, knowledge development or organizational learning may be more important rationales for FDI than market opportunities. MNEs have incentives to build and maintain the dynamic capabilities needed to become more innovative and adaptable.

Firms expand globally to increase and use the value of intangible assets. Firms have more opportunities to gain high returns on intangible resources, use market power, spread their market risks, and seek less expensive inputs and price-sensitive markets. They can benefit across factor markets and utilize their market power to both reduce input costs and control output markets. A firm with profit-making internal capabilities (ownership advantages) will seek additional profits in international market locations. If these capabilities are embedded in the firm's structure, these international markets will be internalized by FDI, ensuring the best application of these capabilities while protecting them from compromise. So long as the ownership factors can be applied profitably, the firm will expand its international scope.

Some other benefits may include volume economies, intelligence gathering, product improvement, operational flexibility and stability, tax differential, and organizational advantages. Firms that realize such advantages will achieve superior overall performance and perform well in their own home market and key markets throughout the world. Leverage and economies of scope and scale gained by applying resources across national markets should enable MNEs to improve their returns on resource investments while reducing variance in their cash flows. Although external influences are more varied than in the domestic expansion in a single market, gradual expansion through related markets or marketing of global products can reduce external uncertainties. Morck and Yeung (1991) found that when expanding internationally, MNEs tend to achieve higher performance than domestic firms because they benefit from national differences in market structure, product life cycle, and other environmental resources by utilizing monopolistic advantages or internalizing markets.

This introduction outlines some general benefits of international expansion. These benefits also suggest the importance of international expansion. The following discussions illustrate the detailed match between international expansion advantages (benefits) and strategic goal accomplishment (importance). MNEs undergoing international expansion can benefit from country-specific (location) advantages that enhance economic efficiency; structural discrepancies that spur market power; firm-specific (ownership) advantages that inflate investment return; internalization (network) advantages that increase integration synergy; and cross-border and interfirm learning that improve organizational capabilities, such as innovation, experience, and adaptability. The second objective of this discussion is to integrate the global strategy paradigm with major MNE theories because these are inadequately combined in the literature.

Enhancing Efficiency from Location Advantages

In Dunning's eclectic paradigm (1981, 1988), host country-specific advantages are one of the three types of dominant forces that trigger international expansion. Firms are prompted to invest abroad to acquire particular and specific resources at lower real costs than could be obtained in their home country. The motivation for expansion internationally is to make the investing firm more profitable and competitive in the markets it serves or intends to serve. Similarly, Porter's diamond model (1990) shows that factor conditions are one of the four components determining a nation's competitive advantage. Competitive advantages abroad affect the business potential and usefulness of FDI as perceived by MNEs. With increasing integration of the world economy and growing importance of developing countries in shaping international trade, many MNEs with high labor costs are finding that their products are at a competitive disadvantage compared to imports.

In addition to natural endowments (cost and availability), location-specific advantages also include created endowments, such as economic systems, cultural distance, language barriers, and investment incentives. These created resource endowments can be a strong trigger for internationalization. The economic perspective of MNE theories predicts that a company investing in production facilities will choose the location that minimizes total costs, given a distribution of demand in local (national) markets. Labor cost differentials, transportation costs, the existence of tariff and non-tariff barriers, as well as governmental policies (e.g., taxes affecting the investment climate in a given host country) are generally held to be important determinants of location choice. It should be noted that location-specific advantages in MNE theories refer not only to national endowments, but also to gains arising from an MNE's ability to position itself properly geographically. MNEs use their superior knowledge and information scanning ability to locate manufacturing activities in countries that are the most advantageous from the standpoint of cost considerations.

Improving Performance from
Structural Discrepancies

A widely accepted conceptual framework for industrial organization holds that structural conditions determine the behavior and subsequent performance of a firm. In an economy unfettered by structural imperfection of output, profit rates across industries should fall to an equilibrium reflecting the risk-adjusted marginal efficiency of capital. In the presence of structural imperfection, however, inter-industry variations in profitability abound because entry barriers prevent new competition and expanded output. When expanding globally, MNEs are likely to achieve higher performance than firms operating domestically because the former benefit from structural variance between host and home country industries by investing those distinct resources that can enhance a firm's competitive advantages vis-à-vis its rivals in indigenous markets. It is recognized that industry structure imperfections in foreign markets constitute a dominant factor that not only makes FDI preferable to trade or licensing but also determines the relative attractiveness of some host countries over other host countries and the home country itself. When industry structure of a host country is imperfect, FDI will flow in as a direct response if entry barriers are low. Firms in oligopolistic industries in the host country enjoy the advantages of economies of scale and supply control that give them market power. This power allows them to overcome the disadvantages of being foreign so they can compete with local competitors. Direct investment tends to involve market conduct that extends the recognition of mutual market dependence — the essence of oligopoly — beyond national boundaries. Likewise, it tends to equalize the rate of return on capital (equity) broadly throughout a given industry in all the countries where production actually takes place. This common profit rate, however, may exceed a normal or competitive one because a persistent oligopoly, whether national or worldwide, is marked by various barriers to entry by new firms and, perforce, to the inflow of capital.

Apart from industry structural difference, another aspect of structural discrepancies lies in market structure idiosyncrasies between home and host countries. Firms can expand the size of their potential market, sometimes dramatically, by moving into international markets. Such international expansion is a particularly attractive strategy to firms operating within domestic markets that have growth limitations. MNEs benefit from greater market demand and market opportunity. These benefits in turn increase financial returns, market power in the host country, and competitive position with rivals in the local industry. Because national markets vary in industry life cycle stages, consumer utility functions, and purchasing power, market demand and sophistication are heterogenous across national markets. Many emerging economies in recent years, for instance, present vast market opportunities for MNEs to attain above average returns from pent-up demands long stifled by ideologically based government interventions. In addition to market size and growing demand factors, there are several other reasons leading to market-seeking international expansion. First, MNEs may consider it necessary as part of their global production and market strategy to have a physical presence in the leading markets served by their competitors. Second, a firm's products need to be adapted to local tastes or needs and to indigenous resources and capabilities. In addition, without familiarizing themselves with local language, business customs, legal requirements, and marketing procedures, foreign firms might find themselves at a disadvantage vis-à-vis local firms in operations and marketing activities. Last, when an MNE's main suppliers or customers have set up producing facilities abroad, the firm needs to follow them overseas to attain its business.

Increasing Return from Ownership Advantages

Ownership-specific endowments have long been recognized as relevant to an understanding of international expansion. In MNE theories, the possession of proprietary intangible assets, such as technological expertise or organizational skills, confers on their foreign owners oft-cited advantages. Monopolistic power arises in part from the property rights granted to firms to protect their assets and is translated into high rates of return on invested capital. Further, international expansion is an instrument that allows business firms to transfer capital, technology, and organizational skills from one country to another. Common governance of cross-border, value-added activities can increase the wealth-creating capacity of a firm and, hence, the value of its assets.

The monopolistic power view of MNE theories corroborates the core competence notion in global strategic management. The term "core competence" refers to skills within the firm that competitors cannot easily match or imitate. These skills may exist in any of the firm's value-creation activities, such as production, marketing, research and development, human resources, general management, and the like. Such skills are typically expressed in product or service offerings that other firms find difficult to imitate; the core competencies are thus the bedrock of a firm's competitive advantage. They enable an MNE to reduce the costs of value creation or to create value in such a way that premium pricing is possible from product differentiation. International expansion is, hence, a way of further exploiting the value-creation potential of skills and product offerings by applying them in new markets. The potential for adding value from international expansion is greater when the core competencies or strategic assets are unique, when the value placed on them by consumers is high, and when there are few capable rivals with similar competencies.

Heightened Synergies from Internalization Advantages

An MNE consists of a group of geographically dispersed and goal-disparate organizations that include its headquarters and different national subsidiaries. The internalization perspective of MNE theories suggests that internalization implements contracting through a unified, integrated intrafirm governance structure. It takes place either because there is no market for the intermediate products needed by MNEs or because the external market for such products is inefficient. The costs of transactions conducted at an arm's length in an external market are higher than transactions within an internal market or hierarchy. In other words, intermediate product markets are difficult to organize because of their imperfections. Creation of internal markets brings activities that are linked by the market under common ownership and control. The incentives to internalize activities are to avoid the disadvantages or capitalize on the advantages of imperfections in external mechanisms of resource allocation. In an internally integrated network, different stages of the value chain are dispersed to locations around the globe where additions are maximized or the costs of value creation are minimized.

According to Dunning (1988), there are two different kinds of market imperfections that may influence the expansion and performance of MNEs. Structural market distortions, arising from some (but not all) kinds of government intervention that affect costs or revenues of production, may encourage or discourage inward FDI. Even without such distortions, however, MNE activity would still occur wherever the common governance of activities in different locations is likely to result in transaction gains. Such advantages include enhanced arbitrage and leverage opportunities, reduction of exchange risks, better coordination of financial decision making, the protection afforded by a hedged marketing or multiple sourcing strategy, and gains through transfer price manipulation, leads and lags in payments, and so on. The ability to generate and sustain such ownership advantages itself strengthens the competitive position of MNEs vis-à-vis local firms.

Increasing globalization has captured the attention of practitioners who are increasingly searching for sustained competitive advantages in an ever-changing world. For managers the message seems clear: markets are fast becoming borderless; strategies that fail to recognize the integration of the global marketplace are shortsighted and misguided. International managers competing in a global environment face the central issue of how to integrate their operations strategically in various countries in the presence of forces for national responsiveness that cause fragmentation. Increasing economies of scale in many industries, improvements in transportation and communications, increasing homogenization of tastes and market structures among countries, and rapid technological development have all contributed to market globalization. In such a context, MNEs can attain a sustainable competitive advantage by integrating the value chain activities performed in their subsidiaries around the world. Integrating these activities means raising the level of interdependence among subsidiaries by designing narrow product lines to be sold worldwide, concentrating production in a few plants to capture economies of scale, reducing input sources to the most efficient ones, and the like. Within many industries, MNEs are no longer able to compete as a collection of nationally independent subsidiaries. Rather, competition is based in part on the ability to link or integrate MNEs' subsidiary activities across geographic locations. Although an MNE headquarters has global responsibility for activities that cross national boundaries, it must also address the need for differentiation in local markets. This varies substantially across host countries because subsidiary capabilities and environments are typically diverse. An asymmetrical treatment of overseas subsidiaries is necessary while coordinating worldwide businesses within a network. The transnational solution seems a better choice where the roles and responsibilities of subsidiaries are selectively varied to reflect explicit differences in external environments and internal capabilities.

Through global integration during international expansion, global competitive advantages are developed through international economies of scale and scope and organizational learning across national markets. Operational flexibility can affect the degree of integration. Resource allocation and dispersal (both tangible and intangible) are primary devices for maintaining operational flexibility in global business activities. Essentially, by directing resource flows an MNE may shift its activities in response to changes in tax structures, labor rates, exchange rates, governmental policy, competitor moves, or other variables. Thus, resource flows are a necessary condition for achieving either location-specific or competitive advantages in global business. Resource flow requires extensive coordination within an MNE network because it creates interdependency among subsidiaries. Coordination, in turn, is thought to require centralized decision-making responsibility and authority, particularly in the context of reciprocal interdependencies. Centralized control is important for making trade-off decisions between subsidiaries. However, control should be segmented by product line and distributed among different subsidiaries, depending on particular capabilities and environmental contingencies.

Ensuring Growth from Organizational Learning

A key asset of the MNE is the diversity of environments in which it operates. This diversity exposes the MNE to multiple stimuli, allows it to develop diverse capabilities, and provides it with broader learning opportunities than are available to a purely domestic firm. The enhanced organizational learning that results from internalized diversity explains its ongoing growth and flourishing, while its initial stock of knowledge may well be the strength that allows it to create such organizational diversity in the first place. To exploit such potential, the MNE must consider learning as an explicit objective of international expansion and must create mechanisms and systems by which such learning can take place.

Organizational learning has long been a key building block and major source of competitive advantages. Sustainable competitive advantages are only possible when firms continuously reinvest in building resources. New inputs to the resource base of the firm are imperative to permit the development of a resource pool that can respond to a changing environment. Thus, a dynamic resource mix and organizational learning are crucial for the growth of firms. The necessity for dynamic learning is even more magnified during international expansion. Organizational learning helps a firm overcome the liability of foreignness when operating abroad. On one hand, international expansion provides learning opportunities through exposure to new markets, internalization of new concepts, ideas from new cultures, access to new resources, and exposure to new competitors and terms of competition. These opportunities can result in the development of new capabilities that may be applicable to both old and new locations and, thus, the evolution of the firm's strategic configuration. On the other hand, learning does not take place in a vacuum; rather, it has to cope with experience in specific environments. Host country environments are often characterized by both market opportunities and tremendous uncertainties. These force MNEs to learn how to respond to local settings. Although rent-generating resources are indispensable for MNEs exploring market opportunities, learning capabilities are imperative for firms that need to reduce their vulnerability to contextual variability.

Interfirm learning is another aspect of knowledge acquisition. Firms expand internationally in order to acquire distinctive skills that are critical to their global success but are only available from foreign businesses or rivals. Global competitiveness is largely a function of the firm's pace, efficiency, and extent of knowledge accumulation. Core competencies and value-creating disciplines are not distributed equally among international companies. International collaborations can lead to an increase in knowledge. For the partners, an alliance may be not only a means for trading access to each other's skills (quasi-internalization) but also a mechanism for actually acquiring a partner's skills (de facto internalization). A global alliance can provide a firm with low cost, fast access to new markets by borrowing a partner's existing core competencies, innovative skills, local infrastructure, and country-specific knowledge.

CHALLENGE AND UNCERTAINTY

The benefits discussed earlier are by no means guaranteed because MNEs face the liability of foreignness. MNEs also encounter many other challenges and risks in international expansion. Great costs arise from unfamiliarity with cultural, political, and economic dimensions of a new environment. The necessity to coordinate business at a distance can also be expensive. International operations are usually more difficult and costly to manage than economic activities in a single country. Benefits might not be realized if an MNE's managers cannot run a complex firm effectively. Transferring intangible assets is often costly and uncertain, so product development, production, and marketing cross-fertilization among several national operations might not occur if organizational complexity creates confusion and management difficulties. Organizational inertia may disrupt attempts to change the structure of the firm, and standard operating procedures and other organizational routines may be difficult and costly to change. The cultural diversity encountered when operating in several countries may create major problems of communication, coordination, and motivation. The aggregate effect of such disadvantages sometimes outweighs the advantages of international operations.

MNEs and domestic firms diverge in terms of the environmental homogeneity or heterogeneity they face. A domestic firm operates within a single regulatory-industrial system, but an MNE faces conditions that are heterogeneous with its home base. This makes MNE management tasks enormously complicated. Heterogeneity in the regulatory segment of a foreign country environment is generally reflected in ownership, foreign exchange balance and remittance, inflow performance requirements (e.g., import restrictions, local content requirements), and outflow performance requirements (e.g., export requirements, incentives contingent on export). Within the open systems view of organizations, an MNE should adopt idiosyncratic strategies compared to a local firm because it faces vastly different environmental and resource contingencies.

Unlike domestic firms, the strategy of an MNE subunit is also influenced by the role the business intends to play in a global network. FDI occurs predominantly because of the desire to internalize the transfer of proprietary assets. These assets can be transferred more effectively and efficiently through internal organizational mechanisms rather than through external market transactions because the latter are susceptible to market imperfection. Thus, although a local firm is relatively freestanding, an MNE subunit has to keep an eye on its degree of integration with a whole global network. International sales, production, and research and development activities may have to be responsive not only to the local market and context but also to the demands of other subunits within a network. By contrast, domestic firms do not face such integration restrictions. At the corporate level, the purely domestic company can respond to competitive challenges only within the context of a single market. The MNE often must play a much more complex competitive game. Global scale or low cost sourcing may be necessary to achieve a competitive position, implying the need for complex logistical coordination. Additionally, an MNE is intrinsically more complex in terms of organizational structure and management systems because it must provide for management control over its product and functional and geographic diversity.

Apart from the above challenges, firms participating in international expansion also face more risks than domestic companies. Broadly, risk refers to unpredictability of financial and operational outcome variables. Uncertainty refers to the unpredictability of environmental or organizational variables that affect firm performance and the inadequacy of information about these variables. Uncertainty about environmental and organizational variables reduces the predictability of corporate performance and, therefore, increases risk. A third related term is "exposure." Exposure refers to the sensitivity of a firm or a project's cash flows to changes in any of a number of interrelated uncertain variables. An MNE's strategic choices determine its exposure to uncertain environmental and organizational components that impact firm performance.

Risks and uncertainty largely derive from the external environment facing an MNE. The environment may be perceived along two dimensions: the source of impact (e.g., regulatory, competitors, suppliers, and customers) and the nature of impact (complexity, dynamism, and hostility). These dimensions virtually represent the host societal profile, which is fairly tacit, ambiguous, complex, cumulative, and history dependent. Their influence is thus highly sustainable. Moreover, the above dimensions depend upon and reinforce each other in a complex way. Impact sources constitute the environmental segments. In each of these segments, environmental complexity, dynamism, and hostility may be identified.

The impact of host regulatory and industrial environments on an MNE's decision characteristics and organizational behavior is fairly vigorous and direct. In an uncertain host environment, regulatory factors (e.g., FDI policies, taxation and financing regulations, foreign exchange administration rules, threat of nationalization, earnings repatriation, and price controls) may outweigh macroeconomic and technological factors. Regulatory environment should also include the threats and opportunities associated with potential or actual changes in the political system because changes in governments do not necessarily result in changes in government policies affecting foreign business operations, nor does political stability preclude policy uncertainty. The effect of such policy uncertainty may be significant in formerly centrally-planned economies undergoing transition, such as the former Soviet republics, Eastern European countries, and China. At the industry level, Porter's five forces model clearly addressed that customer, suppliers, and competitors (i.e., existing and potential competitors in the same and substitute industries) all shape competition in the industry. Similarly, in his integrated environment management framework, Miller (1992) categorizes industry environment into input dimension (suppliers), product dimension (customer), and competitive dimension (competitors).

Uncertainty perceived about general environment, industry, and organizational contingencies increases risk. The general environmental uncertainties correspond to factors that affect the business context across industries. General environmental uncertainties include political instability, government policy instability, macroeconomic uncertainties, social uncertainties, and natural uncertainties (Miller, 1992). Industry uncertainties are manifested in input market uncertainty (uncertainties surrounding the acquisition of adequate quantities and qualities of inputs into the production process), product market uncertainty (unexpected changes in the demand for an industry's output), and competitive uncertainty (unpredictabilities associated with rivalry among existing firms and potential entrants into the industry). At the firm level, organizational unpredictabilities include operating, liability, and accounts receivable uncertainties. Operating uncertainty is often mirrored in labor uncertainty, input supply uncertainty, and production uncertainty. Liability uncertainties are associated with unanticipated harmful effects caused by the production or consumption of a firm's product. Accounts receivable uncertainty involves the possible default by clients on their debts, which can be a direct cause of variation in the firm's cash flow and liquidity position. Because MNEs confront much more complicated general, industrial, and operational environments in international expansion, uncertainties at these three levels are considerably greater than those facing domestic businesses. The heterogeneity of such multilevel environments between host and home countries and across different nations where subsidiaries are located further magnifies such uncertainties.

PATTERNS AND TRENDS

Global Economy

Today globalization has become a permanent and irreversible part of economic life. This global economy is characterized by tremendous opportunities and daunting challenges. In recent years we have witnessed declining trade and investment barriers, opening of formerly centrally planned economies, and globalization of industries. At the same time, however, worldwide competition is magnified, environmental uncertainty is intensified, and competitive advantage requirement is reinforced. Increasing integration of the global economy and growing technological changes, the twin forces interacting with each other, are both antecedent and consequent factors propelling transformation of globalization of markets and products.

Since 1992 we have been experiencing global economic expansion. This expansion resulted in a 3.6 percent average annual growth rate in the world's real output and an upswing in the volume of world trade, which increased by an average annual rate of 7 percent. This is the fourth global expansion since 1970 and has been underpinned by three factors: the democratization and economic transformation of transitional economies, industrialization of mini-dragons, and global and regional economic integration, which leads to trade liberalization and globalization of financial markets. Economic integration has been intensified during the past seven years. The global economy witnessed an enlargement of the European Union with prospects of monetary unification, the creation of the North American Free Trade Agreement with trade arrangements for inclusion of Chile, Brazil, and other South American countries, the establishment of the World Trade Organization, and the strengthening of trade and investment links between Japan and the dynamic Southeast Asia economies.

There are several factors that characterize global economy integration. The first positive factor is the enhancement of growth opportunities associated with increased investment, improved technology, economies of scale, and specialization. The second positive factor is that trade liberalization among member countries expands markets, stimulates exports, and creates new jobs. The third positive factor for integration, especially on a regional basis, is noneconomic and related to the strengthening of political cohesion, management of immigration laws, and promotion of political security. The fourth factor is negative and concerns the likelihood of increased instability resulting from economic and financial integration. In particular, the growing interdependence among member countries in a trading or economic bloc increases the likelihood that political, economic, or financial problems in one country may spread to other countries. As a result, the dynamics of financial and trade integration among member countries would result in the persistence of the problem within the economic bloc and an escalation of the adverse effects of the original problem.

The increasing rate of technological change and diffusion is one of the major forces transforming the international economy. The shorter product life cycles resulting from this rapid change place a competitive premium on being able to introduce new goods and services into the marketplace quickly. Along with this trend, a dramatic development in information technology has occurred in recent years. An important outcome of this development is that the ability to access and effectively use information has become an importance source of competitive edge in virtually all industries. Further, knowledge (information, intelligence, and expertise) has become an increasingly critical resource and competitive advantage. Because of this, many firms now strive to transmute the accumulated knowledge of individual employees into a corporate asset. The probability of achieving strategic competitiveness in the new competitive landscape is enhanced for the firm that realizes that its survival depends on its ability to capture intelligence, transform it into usable knowledge, and diffuse it rapidly throughout the company. Companies that accept this challenge shift their focus from obtaining to exploiting information to gain a competitive edge.

Indeed, one of the distinctive features of the globalizing economy is the extent to which the cross-border movement of created assets, particularly technological and organizational capabilities, is internalized either within multinational hierarchies or between two or more separately owned but interrelated firms located in different countries. For most of the past century, the uneven spatial distribution of natural resources has been the primary trigger for international specialization of value-added activities. Today, however, the competitive and comparative advantages of different countries are increasingly determined by the ability of governments and firms to create and deploy created assets and from the trade in FDI arising from these assets. At the same time the significance of intrafirm and interalliance trade is also increasing. Those involved in the most dynamic sectors of the international economy are most likely to be part of a business district or cross-border network of activities in which the pivotal role is played by large multi-activity and multi-locational corporations. FDI plays a major part in boosting both the integration of global economy and the international expansion of firms.

Foreign Direct Investment: Worldwide Overview

FDI has been growing rapidly in recent years. It is increasing even faster than international trade, which has been the primary mechanism linking national economies. In 1995 FDI inflows increased by 40 percent worldwide to an unprecedented $315 billion. Developed countries were the key generators of these record FDI inflows, investing $270 billion and receiving $203 billion (Table 1.1). FDI by developed countries in developing countries reached $100 billion in 1995, setting another record. Developed countries increased their share of world FDI inflows from 59 percent in 1994 to 65 percent in 1995, while outflows rose from 83 percent to 85 percent (Table 1.1).

FDI inflows are concentrated in a few countries. The largest host countries received two thirds of total inflow in 1995, while the smallest 100 recipient countries received only 1 percent (United Nations Conference on Trade and Development, 1996). Similarly, the United States, Germany, the United Kingdom, Japan, and France represent the five largest home countries, which collectively accounted for about two-thirds of all outflows in 1995 (United Nations Conference on Trade and Development, 1996).

The United States remains both the world's largest host and home country. Receiving $60 billion in 1995, the United States inflows were

TABLE 1.1
Foreign Direct Investment Inflows and Outflows: 1983–95

Year	Developed Countries		Developing Countries		All Countries*	
	Inflows	Outflows	Inflows	Outflows	Inflows	Outflows
Value ($ billion)						
1983–87	58.7	72.6	18.3	4.2	77.1	76.8
1988–89	139.1	193.3	36.8	15.2	177.3	108.5
1990	169.8	222.5	33.7	17.8	203.8	204.3
1991	114.0	201.9	41.3	8.9	157.8	210.8
1992	114.0	181.4	50.4	21.0	168.1	203.1
1993	129.3	192.4	73.1	33.0	207.9	225.5
1994	132.8	190.9	87.0	38.6	225.7	230.0
1995	203.2	270.5	99.7	47.0	314.9	317.8
Share in total (%)						
1983–87	76	95	24	5	100	100
1988–92	78	93	21	7	100	100
1993	62	85	35	15	100	100
1994	59	83	39	17	100	100
1995	65	85	32	15	100	100
Growth rate (%)						
1983–87	37	35	9	24	29	35
1988–92	–4	3	15	16	1	4
1993	13	6	45	52	24	11
1994	3	–1	19	17	9	2
1995	53	42	15	22	40	38

*The difference between All Countries and combined Developed and Developing Countries is Central and Eastern Europe.

Source: Adapted from World Investment Report, 1996, p. 23.

twice that of the United Kingdom, which is the second largest recipient of FDI among developed countries. Reflecting high levels of merger and acquisition related investments by Western European MNEs, equity flow to the United States rose by 50 percent in 1995.

Most Japanese FDI has recently gone to East and Southeast Asian countries and developed countries, aiming at establishing regional or global networks or supplying local markets. To increase international competitiveness, Japanese MNEs are establishing second generation affiliates abroad. For example, 47 percent of Japanese affiliates in Hong Kong have already established their own foreign affiliates (United Nations Conference on Trade and Development, 1996).

FDI flow has doubled between 1980 and 1994 relative to both global gross fixed capital formation and world gross domestic product (GDP). The value added of all foreign affiliates accounted for 6 percent of world GDP in 1991, compared with 2 percent in 1982 (Table 1.2). As Table 1.2 shows, the outward FDI stock that the 39,000 or so parent firms invested in their approximately 270,000 foreign affiliates reached $2.7 trillion in 1995. Table 1.3 demonstrates that some MNEs have invested half of their total assets overseas and sent half of their total employees abroad. As a result, more than half of total sales are created by foreign affiliates. This evidence indicates that FDI plays a critical part in shaping economic globalization.

TABLE 1.2
Major Indicators of World Foreign Direct Investment: 1986–95

Indicators	Value at Current Prices 1995 (in billions of dollars)	Annual Growth Rate 1986–90 (in percent)	1991–94 (in percent)
FDI inflows	315	24.7	12.7
FDI outward stock	2,730	19.8	8.8
Sales of foreign affiliates	6,022	17.4	5.4
Royalties and fees receipts	41	21.8	10.1
GDP at factor cost	24,948	10.8	4.3
Gross output of foreign affiliates	1,410	11.0	11.4
Gross fixed capital formation	5,681	10.6	4.0
Exports of goods and non-factor services	4,707	14.3	3.8

Source: Adapted from World Investment Report, 1996, p. 27.

Investment from developing countries to other developing countries is also increasing. For example, more than half of the FDI flows from Asian developing countries were invested in the same region in 1994. Total FDI coming from developing countries rose to $47 billion in 1995. The 50 largest MNEs in developing countries, ranked by foreign assets, accounted for about 10 percent of the combined outward FDI stock of firms in their countries of origin. These firms' ratio of foreign to total sales is high (about 30 percent), but their ratio of foreign to total assets is low (about 9 percent). According to the World Investment Report

(1996), their overall index of transnationality is about 21 percent, only about half of 42 percent for the world's top 100 MNEs.

Driven by privatization and economic recovery in Central and Eastern Europe, FDI inflows to these regions nearly doubled to $12 billion in 1995, after stagnating in 1994. The region accounted for 5 percent of world inflows in 1995, compared with only 1 percent in 1991. Investment inflow in Hungary, the Czech and Slovak republics, and the Russian Federation were all doubled in the last two years. This reflects the recognition by MNEs that Central and Eastern European countries, particularly those in Central Europe, are well on the way to becoming market economies.

South, East, and Southeast Asia continue to be the largest developing host region, accounting for two thirds of all FDI in developing countries. The size and dynamism of emerging economies in Asia have made it increasingly important for MNEs from all countries to serve expanding markets rapidly or to tap the tangible and intangible resources of that region for global production networks. Since 1992 China has been the largest developing country recipient of FDI. Although inflows are soaring in other countries as well, China is driving Asia's current investment boom.

REFERENCES

Dunning, J. H. 1988. The eclectic paradigm of international production: A restatement and some possible extensions. *Journal of International Business Studies*, 19, pp. 1–31.

Dunning, J. H. 1981. *International production and the multinational enterprise*. London: Allen and Unwin.

Miller, K. D. 1992. A framework for integrated risk management in international business. *Journal of International Business Studies*, 23(2): 311–332.

Morck, R. and B. Yeung. 1991. Why investors value multinationality. *Journal of Business*, 64(2): 165–187.

Porter, M. E. 1990. The competitive advantage of nations. *Harvard Business Review*, March–April, pp. 73–93.

United Nations Conference on Trade and Development. 1996. *World investment report*. New York: United Nations.

FURTHER READINGS

Bartlett, C. A. and S. Ghoshal. 1989. *Managing across borders: The transnational solution*. Boston, MA: Harvard Business School Press.

Buckley, P. J. 1988. The limits of explanation: Testing the internalization theory of the multinational enterprise. *Journal of International Business Studies*, 19: 181–194.

Dunning, J. H. 1995. *Multinational enterprises and the global economy*. New York: Addison-Wesley.

Geringer, J. M., P. W. Beamish, and R. C. da Costa. 1989. Diversification strategy and internationalization: Implications for MNE performance. *Strategic Management Journal*, 10: 109–119.

Ghoshal, S. 1987. Global strategy: An organizing framework. *Strategic Management Journal*, 8: 425–440.

Grant, R. M. 1987. Multinationality and performance among British manufacturing companies. *Journal of International Business Studies*, 18: 79–89.

Hitt, M. A., R. E. Hoskisson, and H. Kim. 1997. International diversification: Effects on innovation and firm performance in product-diversified firms. *Academy of Management Journal*, 40: 767–798.

Kim, W. C., P. Hwang, and W. P. Burgers. 1993. Multinational's diversification and the risk-return trade-off. *Strategic Management Journal*, 14: 275–286.

Kim, W. C., P. Hwang, and W. P. Burgers. 1988. Global diversification strategy and corporate profit performance. *Strategic Management Journal*, 10: 45–57.

Luo, Y. and J. J. Tan. 1998. A comparison of multinational and domestic firms in an emerging market: A strategic choice perspective. *Journal of International Management*, 4(1): 68–87.

Michel, A. and I. Shaked. 1986. Multinational corporations vs. domestic corporations: Financial performance and characteristics. *Journal of International Business Studies*, 16: 89–106.

Mitchell, W., M. Shaver, and B. Yeung. 1993. Performance following changes of international presence in domestic and transition industries. *Journal of International Business Studies*, 24(4): 647–670.

Ohmae, K. 1989. Managing in a borderless world. *Harvard Business Review*, May–June: 16–25.

Tallman, S. and J. T. Li. 1996. Effects of international diversity and product diversity on the performance of multinational firms. *Academy of Management Journal*, 39: 179–196.

TABLE 1.3
Top Ten Multinational Enterprises in 1994

Rank		Country	Industry	Assets (billion $)		Sales (billion $)		Employment		Trans-nationality*
				Foreign	Total	Foreign	Total	Foreign	Total	
1	Royal Shell	Holland	Petroleum	63.7	102.0	51.1	94.8	79.00	106.00	63.6
2	Ford	United States	Motor & parts	60.6	219.4	38.1	128.4	96.73	337.79	28.6
3	Exxon	United States	Petroleum	56.2	87.9	72.3	113.9	55.00	86.00	63.8
4	GM	United States	Motor & parts	na	198.6	44.0	152.2	177.70	692.80	25.7
5	IBM	United States	Computer	43.9	81.1	39.9	64.1	115.60	219.84	56.4
6	Volkswagen	Germany	Motor & parts	na	52.4	29.0	49.3	96.55	242.32	60.4
7	GE	United States	Electronics	33.9	251.5	11.9	59.3	36.17	216.00	16.7
8	Toyota	Japan	Motor & parts	na	116.8	37.2	91.3	27.57	172.68	28.1
9	Daimler-Benz	Germany	Transport	27.9	66.5	46.3	74.0	79.30	330.55	42.8
10	Elf Aquitaine	France	Petroleum	na	48.9	26.2	38.9	43.95	89.50	56.7

*Ranked by foreign assets. Transnationality index is calculated as the average of foreign assets to total assets, foreign sales to total sales, and foreign employment to total employment (in 1,000).

Source: Adapted from World Investment Report, 1996, p. 65.

2

Dynamic Capability
Perspective

Capability exploitation (rent-generating resources) and capability building (organizational learning) have become increasingly fundamental to
international expansion. Firm-specific strategic resources are critical to
both competitive advantages and determining firm-level strategies that
can exploit such advantages. Dynamic learning capability is critical as it
ensures the evolutionary development of sustainable advantages and
generates new bundles of resources. This chapter outlines the conceptual
background and key notions surrounding the dynamic capabilities
involved in international expansion. Various manifestations include technological, strategic, organizational, and financial capabilities. This chapter further articulates the issue of transferability. International expansion
success depends on not only the creation of dynamic capabilities but also
their diffusion among geographically dispersed subunits within a globally integrated network.

CONCEPTUAL BACKGROUND

The ability of a multinational enterprise (MNE) to survive and succeed in
today's turbulent international environment largely depends on its
dynamic capabilities during international expansion. Firm-specific strategic resources are critical to gaining a competitive advantage and determining the firm-level strategies used to exploit such an advantage.
Dynamic capabilities refer to a firm's ability to diffuse, deploy, and
use tacit, organizationally embedded resources to attain a competitive

advantage. Such abilities are difficult to copy or replace. They can be bundled with a variety of hard assets and skills to encourage and permit the growth of a firm. Dynamic capability requires a capacity to learn and develop new capabilities or extract rents from current resources. In other words, dynamic capabilities take organizational resources beyond their role as static sources of inimitable advantages; instead, they become important aspects of sustainable, evolving advantage.

An MNE must develop certain strategic and organizational assets before expanding internationally. In each national market a foreign firm suffers from some disadvantages relative to local competitors. Familiar with the national culture, industrial structure, governmental requirements, and other aspects of doing business in their country, indigenous businesses have enormous natural advantages. Their existing relationships with relevant customers, suppliers, regulators, and the like provide additional advantages that the foreign firm must either match or counteract. MNEs must have some strategic competencies to mitigate the disadvantages of relatively unfamiliar foreign markets. Most often these strategic advantages are found in an MNE's superior knowledge or skills, typically in the form of advanced technological expertise or marketing skills. At other times economies of scale in research and development (R&D), production, or some other part of the value chain become main sources of advantage over domestic businesses. Such knowledge- or scale-based strategic advantages are, however, insufficient for justifying international expansion. An MNE must also have some organizational capabilities that will provide better returns if it is leveraging its strategic strengths internally rather than through external market mechanisms such as contracts or licenses. If superior knowledge is the main source of an MNE's competitive advantage, it must have an organizational system that allows better returns from extending and exploiting its knowledge through direct foreign operations than it could get by selling or licensing that knowledge.

Capability exploitation (rent generation) and capability building (organizational learning) are two critical aspects of the dynamic capability perspective. Resource-based theory describes the process of economic rent generation through the exploitation of complex firm-specific resources or capabilities (e.g., financial, technological, operational, or organizational resources). It formalizes the role of invisible resources, resources based on know-how, or routines for providing competitive advantages to individual firms (Barney, 1991; Wernerfelt, 1984). Rent-yielding resources in MNEs, which derive from unique firm endowments, home country experiences, or experiences in international operations, provide competitive advantages and cash flow. These can be used to drive subsequent strategy and fund continued development of new capabilities needed for international expansion. Resources do not generate advantages in a vacuum (Wernerfelt, 1984); they must be applied through a business strategy in a competitive environment to have any effect. Even a global business must anticipate strategic variations across international markets and over time (Tallman, 1992).

Similarly, the monopolistic advantage theory argues that firms are motivated to go overseas to exploit monopolistic, firm-specific advantages. Rent-yielding, intangible assets such as technology and marketing skills encourage firms to invest abroad, as does the opportunity to exploit underutilized resources in new markets. This in turn generates extra profits in foreign markets, thus giving rise to greater monopolistic advantages. More importantly, rent-generating resources create a need for internalization because renting or licensing them involves high costs. Often these resources are information-intensive, tacit, and embedded in individuals or the organization. Firms decide to use such resources through expansion rather than by renting or selling them. In fact, the internalization theory sees MNEs as efficient agents for transferring resources (Buckley & Casson, 1998). An MNE minimizes transactions cost not only by internalizing its distinctive skills or know-how but also by internalizing the sourcing of raw materials and intermediate goods. Rent-generating resources may impact an MNE's governance structure directly, particularly if they are tacit, organizational resources or capabilities (Teece, 1982) that cannot be transmitted through markets. More embedded, diffuse resources result in greater use of internal control of transactions. Although host country characteristics also affect an MNE's strategy and structure, strategic assets that are essential to the rent-earning potential of strategic resources in the compound asset bundle have a major impact on entry, investment, and operational strategies during international expansion.

Organizational learning has long been a key building block in the behavioral theory of the firm. More recently organizational learning has been incorporated into the resource-based view of the firm in the strategic management literature, which conceptualizes the firm as a collection of knowledge and the firm's learning capability as a major source of competitive advantage. Levitt and March (1988) define organizational learning as "the process by which organizations encode experiential inferences into behavioral routines." Because an equilibrium environment is never reached, an equilibrated resource bundle can not generate sustained advantages (Nelson & Winter, 1982). The assumption that a sustainable competitive advantage can come from an unchanging resource bundle is inherently at odds with operating in a dynamic environment (Collis, 1991). Sustainable competitive advantages are only possible when firms continuously reinvest in building resources. New inputs to the resource base of the firm are imperative to permit flexible responses to a changing environment (Dierickx & Cool, 1989). Thus, a dynamic resource mix and organizational learning are crucial for the growth of firms in a dynamic, complex environment.

The necessity for such dynamic learning is magnified during international expansion. Expansion is always challenging, calling for organizational learning to overcome the liability of foreignness when operating abroad. On one hand, international expansion provides learning opportunities through exposure to new markets, internalization of new concepts, ideas from new cultures, access to new resources, and exposure to new competitors and terms of competition. These opportunities can result in the development of new capabilities that may be applicable to both old and new locations, and, by extension, the evolution of the firm's strategic configuration. On the other hand, learning does not take place in a vacuum but rather has to cope with experience in specific environments. Host country environments are often characterized by both market opportunities and tremendous uncertainty. This in turn forces MNEs to learn in response to local settings. Although rent-generating resources are indispensable for MNEs exploring market opportunities, learning capabilities are imperative for firms trying to reduce their vulnerability to contextual variabilities. Combinative capability, a firm's ability to integrate and synthesize internal resources and external learning and apply both to the competitive environment, is vital to the firm's survival and growth in a foreign market (Kogut & Zander, 1992). These capabilities are the basis for the evolution of new strategies and structures in the firm as it continues to learn about the international competitive environment.

To fulfill this process, MNEs need to continuously improve their dynamic capabilities and institutionalize innovation, learning, and information transfer. MNEs with limited managerial capabilities are less likely to seek new opportunities in the uncertain international marketplace, but an MNE with a well-developed repertoire of managerial routines should have both the rent-generating potential and the ability to deal with uncertainty that would make international markets attractive. The simultaneous effort needed to extract rents from current resources while pursuing new capabilities for their future rent-earning potential appears to affect the accomplishment of sustained competitive advantages in international expansion. Firms with high levels of motivation and capacity to learn should be more open to gaining experience from different situations; this makes them more likely to do business abroad than more defensive firms using a static resource exploitation strategy.

Although not all MNEs adopt a common strategy because of differences in their industrial characteristics and administrative heritages, many are making the transition from multinational, international, or global strategies to transnational ones. Managing across borders has become a common task for all MNEs. To respond to the complexity, diversity, and dynamism of the external environment with the multidimensional strategic postures required for international expansion, transnational firms must build a multifaceted organization capable of developing new competencies while protecting existing strengths.

In the emerging economic environment, it is becoming increasingly important for MNEs to capture and interpret information and use the resulting knowledge and skills on a global basis. The growing sophistication of global competitive strategies means that the knowledge one subsidiary gains about a competitor and the skills the subsidiary develops in response to its activities in one market may be of vital importance for company units elsewhere in the world. Furthermore, with more markets becoming more sophisticated worldwide, rapidly changing technology, and shorter product life cycles, rich rewards accrue to companies that can develop and diffuse successful innovations abroad. The increasing need for efficiency and integration is driven by soaring R&D costs that can only be supported through global volume and better scale economies in component production. A firm's worldwide organizational learning capability is quickly becoming an essential strategic asset (Bartlett & Ghoshal, 1987). Today there are fewer and fewer examples of industries that are purely global or international. Instead, more and more businesses are being driven by simultaneous demands for global efficiency, national responsiveness, and worldwide learning. Those companies traditionally operating in an international strategic mode (with responsiveness as their dominant posture) need to develop global efficiency and improve their ability to develop and diffuse knowledge and skills throughout the organization. Firms having previously adopted a global strategic posture need more national responsiveness and improved access to worldwide innovative resources and stimuli.

MNEs need to realize not only the importance of dynamic capability but also how to build capability during international expansion. Miner and Mezias (1996) describe four general learning styles representing increasing degrees of sophistication in organizational learning capability: trial and error, inferential, vicarious, and generative. Trial and error involves the use of standard operating procedures and the repetition of successful routines. Inferential learning entails more informed observation and experimentation within the firm together with active information acquisition. Firms that engage in vicarious learning tend to observe and copy the successful routines of other organizations. Last, generative learning necessitates that the firm be fully involved in a dynamic, creative learning process that goes beyond discovering already existing alternatives to include substantial knowledge creation. Within a diversified MNE that has geographically dispersed multiple products and markets, different subunits may use different learning processes.

March (1991) distinguishes between exploration and exploitation in organizational learning. Explorative learning is characterized by seeking out variation, risk taking, experimentation, flexibility, discovery, and innovation, but exploitation focuses more on making and refining choices, increasing production efficiency, and implementing and executing strategies. Both kinds of organizational learning activities are important, but there is a trade-off between the two. Exploration of new alternatives reduces the speed with which existing skills are improved and vice versa. Organizational learning by MNEs in internationalization involves both exploration and exploitation. A balance of the two approaches is also necessary for competitive advantage. Learning that leans too heavily toward exploitation will result in below-average performance, but too much exploration without exploitation may produce interesting but unproductive experiments.

International expansion entails both exploration and exploitation. One way to conceptualize these activities is to regard them as option windows permitting MNEs wider strategic choices. An initial option involves a small amount of investment in a host country; the MNE can use this option to explore emerging opportunities. Once enough experience is gained and the option calls for further investment, the MNE increases its commitment to exploit more opportunities in a more massive and determined way. These learning options serve as means for MNEs to gain more host country experience and organizational learning. Although initial learning may enable the first-mover firm to explore new opportunities, over time exploitation tends to drive out exploration; the firm's operations gradually concentrate on a set of routinized exploitation activities that tend to discourage new exploratory learning. Competitors, in contrast, may not be burdened with such learning inertia and continue to engage in exploration; at some time they may neutralize the learning-based advantages of the first-mover. This process by which exploitation gradually drives out exploration is consistent with the pattern of MNE expansion. For instance, during the 1980s the first generation of MNEs in China engaged in exploratory learning by establishing a small number of subunits mostly as joint ventures. Since the 1990s an increasing number of second generation MNEs have shifted to exploitive learning by consolidating multiple subunits, converting joint ventures into wholly owned subsidiaries, and bringing the China operations up to global standards. In the language of option theory, with enough exploratory learning, the call option becomes exercised and exploration is gradually phased out by exploitation.

MANIFESTATION OF CRITICAL CAPABILITIES

Critical capabilities can be defined as an MNE's business and organizational competencies as well as various forms of intellectual property, such as patents, trademarks, software technology, and other non-patented but exclusive technological products and processes. Economic rents are created when the business, organizational, and technological process skills of a firm are enhanced by or interwoven with key industrial or intellectual property, such as brands or patents. Examples of technological capabilities may include design for manufacturing, time to market, patents and intellectual property, low cost manufacturing, quality management, and technology in general. Examples of strategic capabilities include fully exploiting worldwide capabilities, acting on changing globalization drivers, product life cycle management, customer service, speed and flexibility, and making moves against competitors around the world. Financial capabilities may include transfer pricing, capital structure optimization, cash flow management, foreign exchange risk reduction, economic exposure reduction, tax avoidance, and the like. Last, examples of organizational capabilities include developing talent and leadership for innovation and renewal, using global capabilities effectively, partnering and alliance skills, hiring and developing international managers, structuring optimal global performance, nurturing global management talent, transferring excellent practices, stimulating transfer of critical capabilities, international negotiating, contract building, and relationship cultivation. The resource-based view suggests that MNEs make strategic choices based on their ability to exploit firm-specific resources or capabilities in international environments. Firm-specific resources must fulfill the requirements of value, rarity, inimitability, and non-substitutability and be operationalized at the level of the firm.

Technological Capabilities

A recent survey shows that MNE chief executive officers identify new product development and technology as their companies' most critical capabilities (Conn & Yip, 1997). One important feature of the cross-border network is transfer of product development and design capabilities in addition to the conventional transfer of production facilities. Capability transfer goes beyond the usual technology transfer. It involves transfer of human capacities that generate dynamic technological changes. In addition, the cross-border network facilitates transfer of procurement and coordination capabilities. Coordination and control of information are carried out within a region in response to a corporate strategy of setting up autonomous regional headquarters or centers. Organizational arrangements are critical to generating dynamic capability.

Technological capabilities, such as patents or proprietary designs, are more difficult to diffuse across national and cultural borders than within a national industry and are greatly affected by differences in supporting industries and demand patterns. Therefore, this type of capability is more likely to yield a sustainable advantage internationally than in a purely domestic context. Sharing technologies is difficult, which suggests that strategies that rely on shared resources, such as mergers, acquisitions, or joint ventures, will not be used. Much of the rationale for such strategies is based on the possible synergies, often technological, that may be achieved by combining the resources of two or more firms. If such synergies are technically incompatible, the incentives to use such arrangements are limited. Therefore, the greater the dependence on home country specific technologies, the more likely it is that firms will either rely on market (export or licensing) arrangements or expand through wholly-owned greenfield ventures. Export arrangements allow firms to avoid substantial technological makeovers, licenses place development burdens on the licensee, and the wholly-owned greenfield operations permit firms to transfer technology internally that has already been tested.

The process of creating an industrial product involves both technological accumulation and technical change. Technical change involves both the introduction of technology embodied in new products or new plants through major investment projects and incremental adaptation and improvement of existing production capacity. The first involves incorporation of new technology in relatively large lumps through investments in new production facilities. The second incorporates strands of new technology into existing facilities through incremental changes. To bring about technical change, technological capability is a significant factor. Technological capability is a resource needed to generate and manage technical change. It comprises knowledge, skills, and experience, and institutional structures and linkages within a firm, between firms, and outside firms. Technical capabilities have to be acquired and accumulated through learning.

There are several forms of technical accumulation that create technological capability:

some is derived from trial and error and experience rather than formal R&D;

some is tacit, uncodified, and embodied in people or institutions; it is acquired and improved only with experience;

some is centered in firms by learning from operating experience and development of production systems; technological accumulation may be a part-time activity in a smaller firm, under the name of design or production engineering;

some technological accumulation is generated out of the complex interactions of firms, suppliers, and customers; the process of acquiring technological capability involves building various kinds of institutional structures within which firms can interact in creating and improving the technology they use; and

technical learning is cumulative; there are cross-country differences regarding technological efficiency; it cannot be changed rapidly, and it has long-term implications for competitiveness and comparative advantage.

Strategic Capabilities

A firm's marketing competencies in distribution channels, promotional skills, knowledge about local business practices, and relationships with major buyers, wholesalers, and relevant governmental authorities are fundamentally important for foreign companies seeking market position and power in the host country. Foreign companies can gain an edge over their competitors in the host country if they have superior relationships within the business community of suppliers, buyers, and distributors. Networking with other players in the business community affects value creation and profit margin. The costs of establishing distribution channels or business networks in a host country market are often likely to outweigh the potential benefits. Moreover, establishing such networks can be such a long process that foreign companies may be unable to seize market opportunities or align with contextual changes in a timely fashion. Comparatively, indigenous firms have natural advantages in networking with the local business community. Thus, MNEs need to strive either to establish their own supply and distribution networks in the local context or to build up strategic alliances with local firms. Relationships with various government authorities are also critical to gaining a competitive advantage in a foreign country. Governmental regulations concerning market activity, such as antitrust laws, significantly affect the degree of competition among firms. The intense competition of multiple competitors in Japan compared with the stagnation of government-supported or -owned national champions in Europe provides an example of how national policies influence global competition. The role of political actors, such as the Ministry of International Trade and Industry, in influencing business to focus on new technologies of national significance has been widely described as critical to the rapid development of Japanese multinational firms. A good relationship with host and home country governments usually enhances a firm's market and financial performance.

Because a major objective of international expansion is to preempt market opportunities and business potential overseas, a firm's market power in the global marketplace is a key asset. This power is often represented by the firm's industrial and business background, market position, and established marketing and distribution networks. Market power also enables the firm to influence some industry-wide restrictions on output, increase bargaining power, and offer the advantages of economies of scale. Market power in the global marketplace propels the firm's ability to preempt emerging opportunities in some foreign countries, coordinate vertical integration among geographically dispersed subunits, and increase profit margins from economies of scale, transfer pricing, and reductions of communication, transportation, and transaction costs.

Organizational Capabilities

Organizational capabilities are developed from diverse legal, political, and cultural traditions, which create different administrative heritages among firms from different nations. Organizational capabilities include a firm's reporting structure, formal and informal planning systems, controlling and coordinating systems, and informal relations among groups within a firm and among different firms. Organizational resources involve firm-specific routines, that is, regular and predictable behavioral patterns rather than specific product skills or knowledge.

The historical development of different routines and systems in firms from different nations is important for understanding why firm-specific invisible resources vary. Even within a culturally similar setting, such resources are generally difficult to substitute or imitate because of the socially complex nature of their development. At the international level, given widely varying firm cultures, organizational resources are particularly insulated. Consequently, these resources are considered to be a major source of sustainable competitive advantages. Organizational resources affect strategic choices concerning the product market and the ability to coordinate globally dispersed operations and use of alliance arrangements.

Broadly, an MNE's human resource system is also part of organizational resources. In many foreign subunits of an MNE people with different cultural backgrounds, career goals, compensation systems, and other human resource baggage often have to begin working together with little preparation. Because of the existence of cultural barriers, the use of a large workforce, and the reliance on local managers, human resource management skills are key to the goal accomplishment of foreign companies. These skills are reflected not only in blending with the cultures and management styles of foreign colleagues but also in job design, recruitment and staffing, orientation and training, performance appraisal, compensation and benefits, career development, and labor-management relations. Among these attributes, the abilities to surpass cultural barriers, recruit qualified employees, and establish incentive structures are particularly imperative. Building and maintaining a multinational cadre of senior executives and middle managers strongly boosts a firm's competitive edge. International development and rotation of managers will increase their adaptability to the value systems of other cultures. Recruitment, training, and reward systems are parts of the global approach to managing business.

Organizational routines are also a critical aspect of organizational capability because firm capabilities are embedded within their regular ongoing activities. This premise, popularized by the resource-based view of the firm, represents a significant shift from the industrial organization perspective of competitive advantage, which regards firm performance as a function of how it is positioned within its industry. Instead, this new perspective views firm performance as a function of how capable firms are at deploying their resources through ongoing routines. Routines are the source of a firm's differential and inimitable capabilities. For MNEs, overseas knowledge used through their routines is an important factor driving up global product development capabilities. With increasing globalization of markets, the capability of developing new products for multiple markets is of growing significance. MNEs using tacit overseas knowledge may gain greater global product development capabilities. Thus, an MNE's organizational capability can derive the regular activities through which it uniquely uses its knowledge resources. Tacit knowledge is difficult to codify; it consequently poses significant challenges in trying to transfer it across borders. These challenges make tacit overseas knowledge a unique resource that is difficult to imitate. Not all firms are able to transfer and use such knowledge. As a result, those MNEs that effectively use this resource are rewarded with greater benefits, such as worldwide product development and global coordination abilities.

Organizational learning has become increasingly important to international expansion. It concerns the capacity or processes within an organization that maintains or improves performance based on experience. In the learning process well-developed core competencies serve as launch points for new products and services. It is also imperative to support continuous improvement in the business's value-added chain. Moreover, firms should be able to renew or revitalize themselves fundamentally over time. As a dynamic, non-linear process, learning includes several stages, namely: knowledge acquisition (the development or creation of skills, insights, and relationships); knowledge sharing (the dissemination of what has been learned); and knowledge utilization (the integration of learning so it is broadly available and can be generalized to new situations). Kogut and Zander (1992) define MNEs as social communities that specialize in the creation and internal dissemination of knowledge. They arise out of their superior efficiency as an organizational vehicle that creates and transfers knowledge across borders. In these social communities, firms use their relational structures and shared coding schemes to enhance the transfer and communication of new skills and capabilities. Learning capabilities serve as efficient mechanisms for the creation and transformation of knowledge into economically rewarding products and services. Such capabilities constitute ownership advantages for the firm that help mitigate the liabilities of foreignness in international expansion. Further, the capacity to speed the internal transfer of a technological or production capability to new foreign markets is also of fundamental significance in a competitive environment.

Organizational learning is stimulated both by environmental change and internal factors in a complex, iterative manner. Organizational learning cannot be created or eradicated by varying external stimuli. Organizations affect learning processes and outcomes. Strategy plays a proactive role in stimulating the competitive accumulation of learning. MNEs need the ability to purposefully adopt structures and strategies that encourage learning. They can proactively seek to influence the environment in which they learn. As complex organizations, MNEs are characterized by a multiplicity of learning processes: each individual, group, and subunit within the network has its own knowledge base and learning capability. Therefore, learning is one of the major activities that needs coordination. Mechanisms used to achieve such coordination play a central role in shaping the organizational learning process and determining its outcome. Of these mechanisms, the structure of the MNE defines the way in which these processes interact and give rise to organizational learning. Although R&D is a major source of organizational learning, the processes and outcomes of learning can be facilitated drastically by other mechanisms, such as multimedia, information transfer, and training. Learning occurs throughout the activities of the firm.

Because corporate culture is the language that communicates a company's mission, the ability to transplant that culture from one country to another is critical to the success of an international business. No matter what the type of corporate culture, when business goes global the culture must be translated overseas. It mixes with the host country culture and changes. Those MNEs that are sensitive to local attitudes and customers are bound to be more successful. A firm's ability to transplant cultures across borders is reflected in clear mission and vision statements, supportive human resource management systems, appropriate compensation and recognition structure, and advanced communication networks. In an international setting attitudes, cognitive functioning, and beliefs are not randomly distributed in the population but tend to vary systematically with demographic variables, especially nationality. Thus, an expected consequence of increased cultural diversity in foreign companies overseas is the presence of different perspectives on problem solving, decision making, and creativity. Organizations wishing to maximize the benefits and minimize the drawbacks of cultural diversity in terms of group cohesiveness, interpersonal conflict, turnover, and coherent action on major organizational goals must create multicultural organizations.

Information technology simultaneously drives and facilitates global business. Worldwide networks of computers are inexorably transforming the nature of business even as firms seek to harness this technology to the task of managing that transformation. The winners in this global environment will be firms that can align worldwide information systems with integrated global business strategies. The synergy that develops from a close strategic linkage between information technology and business strategies will be critical to success in highly competitive global markets. The ability to create and utilize information technology to facilitate communications, reporting, and decision making within a globally integrated network will affect the competitive advantages of the firm in the global marketplace. Information technology can drive a firm toward globalization in a number of ways. Using computer and communications technologies, firms can extract information components from tangible products or substitute knowledge for materials and then instantly transport the electronically represented information or knowledge throughout the world. Value can be added or an information-based product can be used at the most economically advantageous location. The time delays, high costs, and lack of customer responsiveness associated with transportation, reproduction, and inventory can be reduced or even eliminated.

Financial Capabilities

The ability to execute strategy rapidly across the globe requires financial capability. Financial capability enables the organization to put into place its corporate mission. Today financial capabilities extend far beyond the traditional tasks of raising and managing funds. Financially capable MNEs tap global markets to get the best possible terms and seek out windows of opportunity and the right market conditions. Fund deployment involves the financial appraisal of strategic investment opportunities and the control and monitoring of working capital. Financial managers increasingly participate in solving corporate strategic issues. The globalization of competition in product and factor markets and the deregulation and integration of world financial markets are major forces shaping these changes. In such an environment financial managers can add value in addition to their basic role of evaluating and funding investment opportunities through the exploitation of pricing distortions in financial markets, reduction of taxes, and mitigation of risks. Reallocating financial capabilities among different parties can bring diversification benefits, create managerial incentives, and reduce costs of financial distress.

Investment assessment and capital budgeting ability are critical to international expansion. Without these abilities, MNEs would be unable to allocate financial resources to global projects in such a way as to get the highest returns. Projects in different countries face not only different business or commercial risks but also variable political risks. Financial managers need to be able to gauge the total risk of a foreign capital project and to develop appropriate risk-adjusted discount rates to be used in assessing the project. MNEs must develop investment estimates and the net cash flow generated by proposed foreign capital projects. They should also gauge the riskiness of these cash flows and summarize the cash flow and risk analysis information into a measure of desirability for the project, such as the net present value. As a consequence of an increase in the complexity of investment opportunities and the potential for management error in international expansion, a firm's ability to evaluate, analyze, and budget overseas investment opportunities becomes increasingly crucial.

Risk management ability is imperative to international expansion because global operations encounter various levels of exposure, uncertainty, and risk. Risk reduction in the form of hedging and risk sharing largely determines a firm's stability and pattern of growth. During the international expansion process, currency fluctuations can accentuate the volatility of earnings and cash flows. Such volatility can in turn distort management information systems and incentives, hinder access to capital markets, jeopardize the continuity of supplier and customer relationships, and even put the company into bankruptcy. For such reasons, MNEs overly exposed to exchange rates, interest rates, or commodity prices may benefit by dispersing these risks to other firms or investors that have smaller or perhaps even opposite exposures. Under global competition, exchange rate fluctuations affect not only the dollar value of the firm's foreign profits but also its overall position relative to its global competitors. Managing foreign exchange risks often calls for changes in operating variables, such as pricing, output, and sourcing. It may also involve strategic changes, such as shifting ownership of assets to other investors, relocating plants, and changing the internal organizational structure to improve the corporate-wide ability to respond to exchange rate shifts. Such strategic and tactical responses to exchange rate shifts will require far greater integration of finance into the once largely separate strategic and operating domains of MNEs. This implies that risk management and other financial capabilities bring financial perspectives to bear on business policies and strategic decisions, thereby enhancing the overall success of international expansion.

Hedging exposure has become increasingly complex because economic and operational exposures are more long-term than typical foreign exchange transactions. They arise from movements in real exchange rate (relative prices) as distinguished from nominal exchange rates. Moreover, they are not based on explicit commitments; thus, hedging these exposures may be subject to speculative rather than hedge accounting under Financial Accounting Standard Board No. 52. Short-dated forwards and options do not offset the effect of long-run cumulative exchange rate movements on operating profits. If a firm uses long-dated or forward options, then it will be exposed to differential movements in real and nominal exchange rates. A company should also develop an effective system for hedging foreign exchange exposure and reducing the possible risks from foreign exchange fluctuations. This system should be able to forecast exchange rates, project and track exposure, track hedging options and costs, and implement exposure management policies.

Although tax evasion is illegal, tax avoidance or reduction helps maximize net cash flows from geographically dispersed sources. This capability is essential to the prosperity of an MNE during international expansion. Relative to domestic firms, MNEs are generally in a better position to create financial synergies from transfer pricing. Although some of these synergies occur through transfer pricing of real inputs and outputs, the pricing of interaffiliate financial transactions also provides great opportunity and flexibility for reducing taxes. Facilities jointly used by multiple subsidiaries on a global scale can also help reduce corporate income taxes. Furthermore, an MNE may reduce taxes through structuring interaffiliate commercial and financial dealings as well as hedging the risks of individual subunits through external transactions so as to minimize the chance that any of its corporate components will experience losses on its tax account and, as a result, have to carry forward some of its tax shields. In sum, an environment of increasingly global competition puts MNEs under much greater pressure to match the lowest tax burden obtainable by any firm in the industry while increasing their flexibility in locating and coordinating activities. An MNE's financial ability in tax reduction will make the difference in its net income, cash flow, capital structure, and operational growth.

An MNE's financing and capital structure optimization capabilities are of significance to international expansion because they determine optimum composition of debt and equity that will minimize costs and risks. Such capabilities also affect the firm's liquidity, working capital structure, leverage, and cash positions, all of which influence a firm's financial position and structure. An MNE's capital structure optimization is much more complicated than that of a domestic firm because the former has to make its foreign subsidiaries' capital structure consistent with its parent company's overall capital structure with some modifications based on specific conditions in the markets and specific corporate financial strategies. To make the most of the advantages multinationality confers, financing strategy of the MNE should be global in scope. Sources for an MNE's financing include global equity markets, global debt markets, trade-related financing such as trade finance, project finance, and cross-border leases, local financial markets where a firm has subsidiaries, and the internal financial system of the MNE for unit-to-unit funds transfer. In general, the objective of a global financing strategy is to meet the funds needs of the various global units of the firm at the lowest possible cost, with due regard for the currency and political risk engendered by the financing strategy and with provisions for flexibility in meeting unanticipated financial needs without excessive delay or cost.

An MNE's ability to manage and mediate cash flows within a globally integrated network is a major source for improving its working capital management and financial synergy generation. Moving funds from one subunit to another within the MNE is by no means an easy task because there are many barriers hampering funds movement across borders. More importantly, such movements must be integrated with other financial and operational strategies. Funds move between the parent firm and subsidiaries along the following channels: initial capitalization from the parent may be in the form of capital investment in subsidiary equity or parent loans to the subsidiary; the subsidiary returns funds to the parent via repayment of loans, return of capital, payment of interest on loans, and payment of dividends; royalties, licensing fees, and management fees; leads and lags and movements arising from alteration in the transfer prices on inter-unit transactions; and inter-unit loans including direct loans, back-to-back loans, and parallel loans. Governmental restrictions and taxation considerations are two major complicating factors for MNEs in developing a system for global cash management. In this management process, firms should have a high ability to determine an appropriate level of dividend payment by subsidiaries. The most important factors include: the relative needs of the subsidiary and parent for funds; the exchange rate prospects of the local currency; the effect of the dividend on the firm's global tax bill; and short- and long-term attitudes of local authorities and legal restrictions on the level of dividend payments.

Overall, financial capabilities play an increasingly strategic role in the evaluation of corporate investment, whether in capital, technology, or product programs and in the enhancement of financial synergies and cash flow optimization, whether in the form of transfer pricing, lead and lag, taxation reduction, funds movement, or financing. The growing interaction between an MNE's corporate and financial strategies is perhaps most visible in the case of corporate takeovers, restructuring, and strategic alliance formations, which have been pervasive in recent years. Many MNEs are now using financial strategies as one of the major instruments balancing global integration and local responsiveness. Financial capabilities are important not merely to the realization of financial strategies but also to the implementation of global corporate strategies and international operational strategies.

TRANSFERABILITY OF CRITICAL CAPABILITIES

To ensure survival and growth in the global marketplace, MNEs need to be able to transfer successfully critical capabilities within their network of international operations. This is the process whereby the MNE draws on some or all of its distinctive competencies, assets, or capabilities from its home base or integrated network to give its operations in a foreign country a competitive advantage or fulfill a strategy derived from local operations. Transferability is the extent to which such a parent is equipped with or controls capabilities or competencies that can be transferred to a foreign subunit to result in competitive advantages or to contribute to business success in the target foreign setting (industry, segmented market, or host country). Although the transfer of critical capabilities can take place from one subunit to another within a network coordinated by the parent, the movement from parent to foreign subunit is of the most practical relevance because the substantial part of critical capabilities are usually based in parent companies and located in home countries.

Foreign companies must transfer those capabilities that are distinctive and competitive in the host market but not available to indigenous firms. This is imperative for firms trying to compensate for their liabilities of foreignness to compete against rivals in the local environment. Although foreign subunits could, in theory, rely only on local resources or develop capabilities as needed in a local setting, this is usually an unrealistic or inefficient strategy because indigenous firms are more effective and efficient in developing such capabilities. In other words, a foreign business can only gain an advantage if it is able to transfer some critical competencies that are not available to local players. In recent years, we have witnessed many examples demonstrating the importance of such transfer in propelling international expansion success. For instance, McDonald's tremendous overseas success has been built on the firm's ability to transfer rapidly to foreign entrepreneurs the capacity to operate its entire, complex business system. Similarly, Nissan, Toyota, and Honda have all pursued strategies in which major elements of vehicle development are performed by in-country design terms. For those firms that remain centralized, there is usually a heavy cross-fertilization of ideas resulting from temporary staff transfers as well as shared computer databases and telecommunications linkages.

The degree to which the same critical capability contributes to a firm's competitive advantage is generally not homogeneous across national markets. A particular organizational skill, for instance, may have a strong positive influence on the firm's efficiency and effectiveness in one country but not necessarily in another country. Some critical capabilities, especially technological and operational skills that affect market effectiveness, create economic value through interactions with corresponding markets. Such skills were initially designed based upon market conditions in the home country. As market conditions in other countries differ from those at the source country, the functioning of these skills will vary according to different market contexts. Furthermore, the extent of contextual change with respect to both industrial and macroeconomic environments varies from country to country. As many critical capabilities were initially designed under particular external, time-specific conditions, they will make variable contributions to businesses facing different environmental dynamics. The applicability of a capability in different countries is moderated by environmental change. The transferability of critical capabilities is also influenced by differences in sociocultural and political environments. Such environments constitute the institutional segment of the external environment, which is very difficult for companies to change or manipulate. In other words, firms essentially cannot shape such environments but must rather adapt to them with appropriate strategic responses. This adaptive necessity reduces the universality of critical capabilities in different contexts.

Heterogeneity takes place when a critical capability is irrelevant to a specific context or can be readily neutralized by local rivals. Thus, superior management in the home country may not be as superior in the target country. Products that are superior in the home market may not offer enough value to customers in the target country if the prices are too high or they are too sophisticated. The value of well-known brand names and trade marks can also be neutralized by piracy and imitation. Technological advantages can be undermined by weak intellectual or industrial property rights systems in the target country. Whether a critical capability retains its value in the target market therefore hinges on the fit between conditions in the target country and the nature of the capability.

To gain leverage of critical capabilities within or between markets is considerably complex. MNEs need to decide what should be transferred from the home base to subunits in target countries depending on what will give the firm a competitive edge. The conditions and contingencies of the target country, in conjunction with what is available from the source base, must both be considered. The MNE should also appraise which capabilities or resources will result in a distinctive edge in the competitive environment. Different target countries or settings have heterogenous market demands, industrial structures, governmental policies, and competitive threats from either existing rivals, new entrants, or substitutes. Firms facing these different contexts need different critical capabilities to outperform either local or other foreign competitors. An appropriate alignment between committed competencies and environmental characteristics is an important determinant of international expansion success.

Non-transferability occurs when critical capabilities are not mobile between the source country and the target country as a result of either external (as mentioned earlier) or internal (tacitness) barriers. In theory, codifiable knowledge approximates zero transfer costs; tacit knowledge (i.e., noncodifiable and organizationally embodied), however, is difficult and costly to transfer. First, tacit knowledge is usually acquired through individually or institutionally embedded experience. Second, tacit knowledge is complex, which makes it distinctive and hard to imitate. Third, the tacit knowledge resulting from organizational learning is collective, contingent upon specific contexts, and continuously evolving. Last, although the firm can dispatch expatriates as a substitute for capability transfer, this may not be economically feasible or operationally practical because of high costs and expatriate availability; furthermore, individuals may have difficulty transferring collective knowledge or processes to new environments. Such barriers explain why most international companies are more inclined to transfer abroad the exploitation of new technology than its creation. New products or the capacity to produce new products are transferred overseas, but not innovative abilities. What are transferred are the results of the innovation process, not the capability itself.

Transferability is thus heterogeneous among various capabilities. Technological capabilities are generally more transferable than organizational skills. Financial competencies are more transferable than operational capabilities. Capital or cash flow management skills may be more mobile than work force related capabilities. In general, a superior work force is a non-transferable advantage wherever the target country government imposes rigid controls on the movement of labor resources. Among strategic capabilities, superior market position or oligopolisitc market power represents a competitive edge that, however, is usually not directly or immediately transferable to another country. Possession or control of a superior distribution network in the home market is an advantage that cannot be shifted overseas. However, knowing how to establish and manage a distribution network is a critical capability that can be transferred to a foreign country. The existing relationships with customers or suppliers in the home country are not transferable to another country. The knowledge or expertise regarding how to build and maintain such superior relationships, however, can be applied to foreign markets. Although home country experience and reputation may not easily transferable abroad, a firm's international experience and reputation is transferable across borders.

A transfer of critical capabilities during international expansion necessitates reconfiguration of the bundle of capabilities in a foreign environment. Because some capabilities are directly transferable, but many others are not, MNEs need to reconfigure those capabilities that can be used to contribute more to their success abroad. In contrast, resources or capabilities that will not lead to a competitive edge in a specific foreign setting should not be transferred even though they may be transferable. Because foreign companies have to have more distinctive resources or capabilities than do local firms to overcome the inherent disadvantages of being foreign, MNEs must be proactive, innovative, and adaptive in contributing those critical resources or capabilities that can lead to a superior competitive advantage in the host market, as long as the protection and control of such resources are ensured.

Decisions on which critical capabilities to transfer are often associated with entry mode selection. Tacit knowledge may be non-transferable within the licensing mode but transferable to a wholly owned subsidiary, or it may be exchanged for some desired advantage through an international joint venture or strategic alliance. Exporting the product in which the advantage is embodied is a substitute for exporting the capacity to make the product (Hu, 1995). Because MNEs need to take into account both the potential contribution of capabilities and avoidance of their uncompensated leakage of such capabilities, entry mode selection can become a vehicle for both capability transfer and protection.

Building, diffusing, and transferring learning capabilities are all processes vital to the growth of MNEs. Learning capability is the capacity of international managers to generate and generalize ideas with impacts. This capacity constitutes a key part of the MNE's dynamic capabilities. Organizational learning capabilities are generally more transferable than rent-generating resources. Learning capabilities have a strong, enduring influence on the survival and growth of MNEs in foreign markets. Rent-earning resources cannot alone ensure the adaptability, innovativeness, and sustainability that are necessary for expansion success. Learning capabilities are a primary means of enhancing a firm's transferability of competitive advantages across borders.

MNEs need to build a commitment to learning capability. Firms should make learning a visible and central element of their strategic intentions. Investments in training and education are also needed. Some MNEs offer seminars in which senior managers regularly share their best practices and knowledge about foreign markets across functional, divisional, and geographical boundaries. Measuring, benchmarking, tracking, and rewarding learning systems may also increase the firm's commitment to learning. Next, firms should be able to generate innovative ideas useful in international expansion. Managers should generate ideas aimed at improving what has been and should be done. Managers can fulfill this purpose through competency acquisitions, experimentation, and spanning boundaries. MNEs can acquire competencies from either inside the company (e.g., human resource practice) or outside the company (e.g., strategic alliance). When learning through competency acquisition is coupled with a high capacity for change, MNEs generally have a high probability of succeeding in international expansion. With experimentation, managers are generally more innovative, proactive, and even risktaking. They react to market changes in different countries quickly. When businesses are undergoing a rapid pace of change this type of learning is necessary. Boundary spanning means generating ideas by going outside firm boundaries to learn what other companies do. Benchmarking best practices is commonplace. Many MNEs have gained ideas and experience from other foreign businesses that were early movers in the host country market.

The dominant managerial task of diffusing and generalizing learning capabilities involves creating an infrastructure that moves ideas, experiences, and cultural practices across boundaries and subunits within a globally integrated network. Sharing experiences and mindsets in training programs, efficient communications systems, and superior information flow are crucial. In addition, firms should establish a proper governance structure that facilitates the diffusion and transfer of learning and experience. Governance refers to a cluster of management actions that shape organizational structure, decision making, processes, and communications. To improve transferability of learning capabilities, it is often necessary to build a network organization that is fluid, flexible, and adaptive. In this regard, an MNE is an internally differentiated but globally integrated network community in which different subunits share learning capabilities in a stimulating atmosphere. Within this network the firm may establish several centers of excellence with job rotation in and out of the center to transfer know-how in major regional headquarters. Other managerial actions may include building more flexible, up-to-date information systems, encouraging external benchmaking and communications, and sharing information and successes.

Transferability of critical capabilities across borders certainly does not drive out the need for firms to create new knowledge and competencies in geographically dispersed settings. Increasingly, the creation of new organizational knowledge is becoming a managerial priority. New knowledge provides the basis for organizational renewal and sustainable competitive advantages. As a predominant mode of external learning or competency acquisition, learning from alliance partners has become extremely pervasive. The alliance experience and capabilities can trigger learning because they provide new stimuli that force changes in the mental maps of an organization. This external knowledge creation occurs in several stages. The first stage begins with the formation of the alliance and interactions among individuals from two or more firms. The second stage is the transfer of knowledge from the alliance to each of the partners. I refer to this as grafting: the process by which organizations increase their store of knowledge by internalizing knowledge not previously available within the organization. For this internalization to occur, companies must first engage in transferring skill-related knowledge from the alliance to the parents. These efforts create connections in which individuals can share their observations and experiences. The intensity of the parent firm's learning efforts reflects the degree to which the parent is actively trying to internalize the skills and capabilities of its partners. Further, the parent must ensure that the transferred knowledge is shared within the parent organization. The risk, particularly with tacit knowledge, is that knowledge transferred from an alliance to a parent will dissipate as it makes its way to the organizational level.

Human resource practices constitute a key method for internally enhancing international transferability of critical capabilities. Certain human resource practices have a high correlation with the ability to transfer critical capabilities successfully. Of these, global compensation systems, transferring managers globally, and global training systems have strongly favorable impacts on promoting transferability (Conn & Yip, 1997). In practice, MNEs have to find ways to manage the free flow of talent and necessary skills around the world with the objective of building a competence-based organization. The creation of internationalists is of utmost value to globally diverse businesses. Moreover, having a global company culture, as opposed to regional or local cultures, may also play a fundamental role in the transfer of critical capabilities. Global corporate culture does not conflict with the need for local responsiveness. Global culture instead shapes the paths and patterns of coordination and integration among geographically dispersed yet internally differentiated subunits. It creates a system of values shared by managers around the globe. This system has a positive impact on smoothing the global transfer of critical capabilities. Additionally, information technology is increasingly important for such transfer. Design and installation of an effective global information technology network is critical to the cross-border transfer of capabilities. Other communication mechanisms, such as written communications, memos, newsletters or magazines, release of information, and data transfer, may still be helpful in the transfer process.

REFERENCES

Barney, J. B. 1991. Firm resources and sustained competitive advantage. *Journal of Management*, 17(1): 99–120.

Bartlett, C. A. and S. Ghoshal. 1987. Managing across borders: New strategic requirements. *Sloan Management Review*, Summer: 7–17.

Buckley, P. J. and M. C. Casson. 1998. Models of the multinational enterprise. *Journal of International Business Studies*, 29(1): 21–44.

Collis, D. J. 1991. A resource-based analysis of global competition: The case of the bearings industry. *Strategic Management Journal*, 12: 49–68.

Conn, H. P. and G. S. Yip. 1997. Global transfer of critical capabilities. *Business Horizons*, 40(1): 22–32.

Dierickx, I. and K. Cool. 1989. Asset stock accumulation and competitive advantage. *Management Science*, 12: 1504–1511.

Hu, Y. S. 1995. The international transferability of the firm's advantages. *California Management Review*, 37(4): 73–88.

Kogut, B. and U. Zander. 1992. Knowledge of the firm, combinative capabilities, and the replication of technology. *Organization Science*, 3(2): 383–397.

Levitt, B. and J. G. March. 1988. Organizational learning. *Annual Review of Sociology*, 14: 319–340.

March, J. 1991. Exploration and exploitation in organizational learning. *Organization Science*, 2(1): 71–87.

Miner, A. S. and S. J. Mezias. 1996. Ugly duckling no more: Pasts and futures of organizational research. *Organization Science*, 7(1): 88–99.

Nelson, R. R. and S. G. Winter. 1982. *An evolutionary theory of economic change.* Cambridge, MA: Harvard University Press.

Tallman, S. 1992. A strategic management perspective on host country structure of multinational enterprises. *Journal of Management*, 18(3): 455–471.

Teece, D. 1982. Toward an economic theory of the multiproduct firm. *Journal of Economic Behavior and Organization*, 3: 39–63.

Wernerfelt, B. 1984. A resource-based view of the firm. *Strategic Management Journal*, 5: 171–180.

FURTHER READINGS

Birkinshaw, J., N. Hood, and S. Jonsson. 1998. Building firm-specific advantages in multinational corporations: The role of subsidiary initiative. *Strategic Management Journal*, 19: 221–241.

Dunning, J. 1995. *Multinational enterprises and the global economy.* Wokingham: Addison-Wesley.

Dunning, J. 1988. The eclectic paradigm of international production: A restatement. *Journal of International Business Studies*, 19(1): 1–32.

Fladmoe-Lindquist, K. and S. Tallman. 1997. Resource-based strategy and competitive advantage among multinationals. In H. V. Wortzel and L. H. Wortzel (Eds.), *Strategic management in a global economy*, 149–167. New York: John Wiley.

Loasby, B. J. 1998. The organization of capabilities. *Journal of Economic Behavior and Organization*, 35: 139–160.

Porter, M. E. 1990. *The competitive advantage of nations.* New York: The Free Press.

Tallman, S. 1991. Strategic management models and resource-based strategies among MNEs in a host market. *Strategic Management Journal*, 12: 69–82.

Teece, D., G. Pisano, and A. Shuen. 1990. Firm capabilities, resources, and the concept of strategy: Four paradigms of strategic management. CCC Working paper No. 90-8, University of California, Berkeley.

Zander, U. and B. Kogut. 1995. Knowledge and the speed of the transfer and imitation of organizational capabilities. *Organization Science*, 6(1): 76–92.

3

Evolutionary Perspective

International expansion is an ongoing, evolutionary process shaped by a multinational enterprise's (MNE) international experience, organizational capabilities, strategic objectives, and environmental dynamics. A firm's strategic behavior in this evolutionary process is generally mirrored in market commitment, resource contribution, investment size, product relatedness, and entry mode selection. This chapter first delineates several process models for international expansion with a primary focus on the Uppsala model. This is followed by a discussion of important factors associated with the evolutionary process, such as cultural distance, liability of foreignness, resource commitment, strategic orientation, and organizational capability. The third section focuses on the experience effect, in terms of both intensity and diversity, in internationalization. The fourth section illustrates the importance of environmental dynamics in affecting the evolutionary process.

INTERNATIONAL EXPANSION PROCESS MODELS

Three different models explain the dynamic process of international expansion, namely the product life cycle model, the innovation-adaptation inspired internationalization model, and the Uppsala (or Scandinavian) process model. In the product life cycle model (Vernon, 1966), four stages are distinguished: introduction, growth, maturity, and decline of products. A new product is first sold domestically, then internationally. This perspective provides an industrial organization economics-based look at the evolution of international markets and multinational firms. Vernon emphasized the importance of market development for changing the sources of competitive advantages in worldwide industry. Firms are forced to develop their market and production strategies and their strategic approaches to foreign countries both as markets and as locations for productive activity in order to remain competitive in an evolving industrial environment. Because of decreasing differences in product factor costs across borders and the increasing importance of strategic factors, however, this perspective has lost much of its validity in explaining the international expansion process for today's MNEs.

A second perspective builds on the behavioral theory of the firm, which holds that firms stay in the vicinity of their past practices and the routines that govern them. By analogy to the innovation-adaptation process, this perspective distinguishes a number of sequential stages of internationalization (Andersen, 1993). This perspective focuses on learning sequences in connection with innovation. The internationalization decision is considered an innovation. Classifying development stages takes precedence over explaining how MNEs move from one stage to another. The stages of international expansion are: nonexport firms, disinterested in gathering export-related information; nonexport firms, interested in gathering export-related information; export firms with export comprising less than 10 percent of output; and export firms with export comprising more than 10 percent of output. The higher stages represent more experience and market involvement than the lower stages. This perspective is mainly composed of nonobservable concepts and is restricted to small or medium sized manufacturing firms and their early export efforts.

The third perspective, which is most pertinent to this chapter, is the Uppsala model (Johanson & Vahlne, 1977; Welch & Luostarinen, 1988). Building upon the behavior theory of the firm, Johanson and Vahlne (1977) developed the international expansion process model. This theory sees international expansion as a process involving a series of incremental decisions during which firms develop international operations in small steps. The basic assumptions of the model are that lack of knowledge is an important obstacle to the development of international operations, but that the necessary knowledge can be acquired through experience with operations abroad. Accumulated knowledge about country-specific markets, practices, and environments helps firms increase local commitment, reduce operational uncertainty, and enhance economic efficiency (Davidson, 1980; Johanson & Vahlne, 1977; Welch & Luostarinen, 1988). The Uppsala process model is the most relevant to explanation of firm behavior during international expansion. The internationalization process evolves in an interplay between the development of knowledge about foreign markets and operations on one hand and an increasing commitment of resources to foreign markets on the other.

A distinction is made between state and change aspects of internationalization. The state aspects of internationalization are market commitment and market knowledge; the change aspects are current business activities and commitment decisions. Market knowledge and commitment are assumed to affect decisions regarding commitment of resources to foreign markets and the way current activities are performed. Market knowledge and commitment are, in turn, affected by current activities and commitment decisions. Thus, the process is seen as occurring in causal cycles.

Two kinds of knowledge are distinguished in the model: objective (which can be taught) and experiential (which can only be acquired through personal experience). A critical assumption is that market knowledge, including perceptions of market opportunities and problems, is acquired primarily through experience in current business activities in the market. Experiential market knowledge generates business opportunities and is consequently a driving force in the internationalization process. However, experiential knowledge is also assumed to be the primary way to reduce market uncertainty. Thus, in a specific country the firm can be expected to make stronger resource commitments incrementally as it gains experience from current activities in the market. This market experience is to a large extent country-specific; it can be generalized to other country markets only with difficulty.

The model suggests that additional market commitment will be made in small steps. There are three exceptions. First, when firms have large resources, the consequences of commitment are small. Thus, big firms or firms with surplus resources can be expected to take larger internationalization steps. Second, when market conditions are stable and homogeneous, relevant market knowledge can be gained in ways other than through experience. Third, when the firm has considerable experience from markets with similar conditions it may be possible to generalize this experience to a specific market.

A characteristic of the internationalization process model is that the firm is viewed as a loosely coupled system in which different actors in the firm have different interests and ideas concerning the development of the firm. In particular those who are engaged in a foreign market will see opportunities and problems in that market; they will also seek and promote solutions to those problems. Thus, the model expects that the internationalization process, once started, will tend to proceed regardless of whether strategic decisions continue to push the firm in that direction.

The internationalization process model explains two patterns of internationalization of the firm. One is that the firm's engagement in a specific country market develops according to an establishment chain. At the start, no regular export activities are performed in the market. Then, export starts to take place via independent representatives. Later, sales subsidiaries and eventually manufacturing facilities may be set up. This sequence of stages indicates an increasing commitment of resources to the market. It also indicates that business activities differ with regard to gaining market experience. The first stage gives practically no market experience. The second stage sees the firm as having an information channel to the market and receiving fairly regular but superficial information about market conditions. The subsequent business activities lead to more differentiated market experience, which even may include factor markets.

The second pattern is that firms enter new markets involving successively greater psychic distance. Psychic distance is defined as differences in language, culture, political systems, and so forth, which disturb the flow of information between the firm and the market. Thus firms start internationalization in those markets they can most easily understand, where it is easy to spot opportunities, and where perceived market uncertainty is low.

These patterns can be seen as operationalizations of the process model with activity stages and psychic distance as possible indicators. Other indicators may also be used. Market commitment can be indicated by the size of the investment in the market or the strength of links with the foreign markets, that is, the degree of vertical integration. Other patterns may be derived, such as involvement in joint ventures or acquisitions versus greenfield investments. Overall, the model has gained strong support in studies of a wide spectrum of countries and situations. Empirical research confirms that commitment and experience are important factors explaining international business behavior.

Indeed, country-specific knowledge about task and institutional environments is a critical driving force behind international expansion performance because this knowledge cannot be easily acquired in factor markets. This knowledge is thus considered an owner-specific advantage in MNE theory (Dunning, 1981, 1988; Hymer, 1976); it is a source of rent-generating intangible assets and monopolistic power. Previous studies have confirmed the positive correlation between ownership-specific assets and international expansion success (Kogut & Chang, 1991). In a similar vein, organizational learning theory maintains that time-related learning is imperative for the evolution of rent-generating capabilities that are created over time through complex interactions among resources (Levitt & March, 1988). Information flow into the organization is continuously primed by external message sources and time-keeping devices (Levinthal, 1991). Routinization of activities in an organization constitutes the most important form of storage of the organization's specific operational knowledge (Nelson & Winter, 1982). Therefore, organizational learning is incrementally accumulated over time through routine exercise, and organizational evolution is a continuous learning process spurred by the difference between expectation and experience.

Prahalad and Hamel (1990) propose that organizational learning can occur as a firm acquires new complementary competencies. This possibility does not directly emerge from the idea of resource utilization, but rather from knowledge accumulation over time. An organization's "liability of newness" will be reduced over time as it accumulates more external legitimacy, experience, and ties. Because of this external legitimacy, firms with different levels of time-based experience will have different performances. Zaheer (1995) argues that a foreign investor's intrinsic disadvantages derived from the "liability of foreignness" will be substantially diminished over time because its capabilities will improve through an incremental increase in organizational learning. The above view has been supported by Yu (1991) and Chang (1995).

Both the international expansion process model and organizational learning theory suggest that the acquisition of foreign country-specific knowledge and experience is highly time-related. This knowledge is typically accumulated through a process of learning by doing, which is a positive function of the length of a firm's presence in a host country (Davidson, 1980; Levitt & March, 1988). The development of knowledge about a foreign market is a sequential, evolutionary process (Chang, 1995; Welch & Luostarinen, 1988). According to organizational learning theory, learning, change, and development involve adaptive processes that progress over time (Levitt & March, 1988; March, 1991). Moreover, the institutionalization of learning takes place through organizational codes, procedures, and routines into which inferences about past successes and failures are embedded. This is a dynamic process in which internal changes also occur over time. When a firm operates internationally, autonomous learning becomes even more time-based because the firm confronts a variety of indigenous contingencies that vary greatly from those usually encountered in the home country.

According to Aliber (1970) and Hymer (1976), the costs of doing business abroad constitute a major determinant of international expansion performance. The existence of these costs has been empirically confirmed (e.g., Benito & Gripsrud, 1992; Zaheer, 1995). They can be progressively reduced over time as accumulated learning takes effect in a host country (Davidson, 1980; Johanson & Vahlne, 1977). Learning induces cost savings because of increased input efficiency, increased investment scale, and improved product and process innovation and standardization. On the revenue side, MNEs with a longer-term local presence are more likely to hold a superior position in selecting market segments, differentiating market and product offerings, accessing promotion channels, and building up organizational and product images.

FACTORS IN THE EVOLUTIONARY PROCESS

Culture Distance

One of the key notions of the international expansion process model is that cultural distance, as measured by differences in languages, values, and political systems, among other factors, influences the foreign entry process and subsequent firm performance (Johanson & Vahlne, 1977). In the international expansion process, MNEs learn about cultural barriers through time. As the distance between home country and foreign markets increases, the more difficult it becomes to collect and interpret incoming information properly. The firm's experiential knowledge derived from the domestic market is of limited value in markets located at a great psychic and cultural distance. This distance affects market selection as well as choice of entry mode in international expansion. Firms with little experience in foreign markets prefer those that are similar to their own domestic market and that are located at a short psychic distance. As firms accumulate experiential knowledge, the influence of this distance on the pattern and behavior of international investment decreases. Davidson (1980) has reported that firms in the initial stage of foreign expansion exhibit a strong preference for proximate and comparable cultures, but those in later stages show no such proclivity. Recently Barkema, Bell, and Pennings (1996) demonstrated that the presence of cultural barriers punctuates organizational learning and that cultural distance is a prominent factor affecting international expansion performance indicators such as longevity. It may also hinder the evolution and development of rent-generating capabilities in new domains (Chang, 1995). More recently, Barkema, Shenkar, Vermeulen, and Bell (1997) addressed the importance of an MNE's previous experience in foreign markets that are culturally analogous to the targeted host country in determining the net effect of organizational learning in the host country.

Liability of Foreignness

An MNE's costs of doing business abroad can be dissipated over time as the foreign firm gradually acquires market knowledge and as the local environment becomes accustomed to the presence of the foreign firm. As the tenure of foreign firms lengthens, they are likely to learn more about and become better integrated into their new environments. Some of the difficulties faced because of an initial lack of experience in that country diminish over time. Moreover, learning and legitimation play a part in the host country, as the local environment becomes more accepting of the foreign firm over time, provided the firm is making clear contributions to the host country. Both these factors contribute to a declining liability of foreignness over time. Chang (1995) finds that U.S. affiliates of Japanese firms first enter the U.S. market in their core business where they have the strongest competitive advantage over local firms. They diversify into noncore areas where they possess fewer advantages only after they have acquired some experience in the United States. This suggests that these U.S. affiliates acquire knowledge of the local market over time; the consequent decline in the liability of foreignness enables them to expand into product areas where they might otherwise be weaker from a competitive standpoint.

Resource Commitment

Organizational learning is inherently incremental (Cohen & Levinthal, 1990). When a firm expands abroad, learning is transmitted via institutionalized organizational practices, such as decision-making procedures and corporate policies, through which firms progressively acquire site-specific knowledge (Pennings, Barkema, & Douma 1994). This time-based knowledge enables them to reduce operational costs and uncertainty, enhance the effectiveness and efficiency of local operations, and boost their organizational and product images. Because the predominant motivation of most MNEs entering foreign markets is to attain long-term economic rents through business preemption and market expansion, the more site-specific experience a foreign subsidiary has accumulated, the more likely it is that it will increase its resource and market commitment to the local environment. This may be manifested in both the activity sequence and amount of resources committed to the target country. The firm may first try export, then establish a marketing subsidiary, and finally go into production. Meanwhile, as the firm learns more about the market, the amount of distinctive resources and its degree of local participation are expected to increase.

Site-specific knowledge can only be obtained through actual presence and operations in the market, not through objective information gleaned from market research. Davidson (1980) reported that less experienced firms often overstate risks and understate returns; consequently, they shy away from undertaking significant resource contributions and making stronger commitments to the local market. This in turn reduces the potential for the firm's growth, leading to low financial and market performances. With increasing experience, however, firms acquire more knowledge of the foreign market, perceive less uncertainty, and become more confident in their ability to correctly estimate risks and returns and manage foreign operations (Erramilli, 1991). As a result, they continuously reinvest distinctive resources and make more of a commitment to the local market over time. According to the resource-based theory, this commitment is crucial to a firm's achievement of superior efficiency, market power, and competitive position in a dynamic and complex environment (Prahalad & Hamel, 1990).

Strategic Orientation

The ingredients for success in internationalization include not only learning from global markets but also employing appropriate strategies (Mitchell, Shaver, & Yeung, 1992). The strategies of MNE subunits within diversified MNEs are substantially influenced by the roles they are intended to play in the corporate portfolio. A proactive and innovative subsidiary identifies and capitalizes on emerging market opportunities beyond the MNE network and maintains and bears the costs and risks inherent in maintaining extensive capacities for responding to market and contextual changes in the host country. A defensive, less innovative, and short-sighted subsidiary deliberately reduces the costs of innovation and adaptation by selecting a stable and narrowly defined product and market domain or by merely exploiting internalization benefits within the MNE network.

A foreign subsidiary's strategic orientation should evolve to align with the perceived complexity of the local environment and be reconfigured to alleviate this complexity. When a subsidiary possesses more of what the expansion process model calls experiential knowledge, it will expand foreign direct investment incrementally while committing more to that country. Familiarity with a market reduces the cost of serving it and enhances operational effectiveness in the market. A firm's introduction of a number of new products and its product and process innovation expenditures in the host market are generally positively correlated with its length of local presence. Dall and Tschoegl (1982) demonstrated that the longer the firm has been in a foreign market, the better it knows the market and the more willing and able it is to undertake new activities more aggressively there. As a result of increasing ability to reduce uncertainty in the local market because of the experience effect, the firm will progressively enhance its innovativeness and proactiveness over time. This orientation evolvement is critical for MNEs that wish to secure long-term market shares and growth in foreign markets. Because a proper configuration between strategic orientation and environment leads to high performance, increasing innovativeness and proactiveness as the firm's experience rises over time are expected to contribute to a superior operational outcome.

Organizational Capability

According to resource-based theory, a firm is viewed as a collection of productive resources. These resources are worth more than their individual market values because of specialized linkages between them within the firm. The dominant view in diversification research is that intangible resources, such as technology and marketing skills, encourage firms to diversify into new businesses or foreign markets. The value of such assets does not depreciate through being used in other markets; they therefore generate natural economies of scope. Because renting or licensing such resources through market transactions involves high costs, firms often utilize such resources through international expansion rather than by renting or selling them.

Organizational capabilities are firm-specific and created over time through complex interactions among resources. Organizational learning can occur as firms acquire new complementary competencies. This possibility does not directly emerge from the idea of resource utilization. In other words, organizational learning is an important feature in the evolution of rent-generating capabilities (Chang, 1995). As a consequence, the creation of a new line of business or geographic market can be represented as a sequential process in which initial exploration is followed by feedback on performance. This leads to a better fit between the venture's key success factors and the firm's capabilities. The outcome is either expansion or exit, depending upon whether the firm is successful in developing the capabilities necessary to build and maintain a competitive advantage in the new product or market domain (Chang, 1995). Thus, when a firm enters a new business or market, it starts with a small investment in an area more or less related to its core business. It then moves into another area that is less similar as the scale of investment grows over time. MNEs often start foreign operations in business areas in which they have the strongest competitive advantages (or least liabilities of foreignness), then move into those in which they are weaker.

EXPERIENCE IN THE EVOLUTIONARY PROCESS

Market-specific experiential knowledge is central to explaining the internationalization process. Multinational expansion is always challenging, calling for organizational learning to overcome the liability of foreignness. Experience is a prime source of learning in organizations (Barkema & Vermeulen, 1998). It leads to country-specific knowledge that helps firms overcome the liabilities of foreignness, which in turn improves the performance of foreign operations. As firms gain more country-specific knowledge over time, however, its favorable influence on performance gradually drops off as liabilities of foreignness diminish as a problem.

The Uppsala model assumes that firms have imperfect access to information, and international expansion is a process of increasing experiential knowledge. It postulates an unpredictable incremental interplay between market commitment and market knowledge development. Experiential knowledge not only yields a reduction of the risks involved in going abroad but also provides a vehicle for acquiring knowledge of internal and external resources and of opportunities for combining them.

Levitt and March (1988: 320) define organizational learning as organizations "encoding inferences from history into routines that guide behavior." Similarly, Huber (1991: 89) notes that "an organization learns if any of its units acquires knowledge that it recognizes as potentially useful to the organization." Although not the only source of learning, learning by doing is one of the most important sources of organizational learning. Because knowledge incorporates implicit and tacit dimensions along with those that are explicit and codifiable, organizations must "remember by doing" if they want to become well-versed in tacit knowledge (Nelson & Winter, 1982: 99). In other words, tacit knowledge is acquired through experience. Multinational expansion can be regarded as an option window permitting MNEs to gain more tacit knowledge about a host country (Kogut & Chang, 1991). An initial option involves a small amount of investment that can be used to explore emerging opportunities in a host country. Once enough experience is gained and the option calls for further investment, the MNE increases its commitment to exploit more opportunities. As a result, these options can be called learning options in that they serve as a means for MNEs to learn.

Similarly, the Uppsala model assumes that lack of knowledge is an obstacle to multinational expansion, but that it can be acquired through experience abroad. The development of such knowledge depends on the firm's "absorptive capacity," which is "largely a function of the firm's level of prior related knowledge" (Cohen & Levinthal, 1990: 128). Accumulated knowledge helps the firm overcome its initial concerns about foreign operations, while reducing operational uncertainties and enhancing performance.

Host country-specific knowledge is a driving force behind international expansion performance because such knowledge cannot be easily acquired. In other words, because of time compression diseconomies, MNEs that have spent time in a host country may acquire a significant competitive advantage compared to firms that are not in that country. Previous studies have found a positive correlation between ownership-specific assets and international expansion success (Kogut & Chang, 1991). In general, the longer MNEs operate in a foreign country, the more capability they tend to develop (Chang, 1995). As a result, the MNE's intrinsic disadvantages of foreignness can be substantially overcome (Erramilli, 1991; Hymer, 1976; Yu, 1991; Zaheer, 1995).

Chang (1995) observed that Japanese electronic firms entered their core businesses or those in which they had strongest competitive advantages over local firms first. The learning from early entry enabled them to launch further entry into areas in which they had the next strongest competitive advantages. Although firms can learn from other firms through the transfer or diffusion of experience, primary learning takes place within firms though learning by doing. Even learning from other firms is by no means an automatic process. It can be enhanced by membership in a corporate network. Firms associated with either horizontal or vertical business groups are more likely to initiate entry than independent firms.

There are two types of experience important for international business success: general international operations experience and country-specific experience. An MNE's knowledge about a country increases as its commitment to operations in that country and its sales there increase. This knowledge tends to encourage the firm to engage in further investment in that country. By contrast, general international operations experience, which is composed of both country-specific experience and experience gained from managing a network of operations in different countries, tends to lead a firm to conduct more international operations (Yu, 1991). An MNE with skillful country-specific or general international experience is still likely to be a formidable competitor even in the absence of other firm-specific advantages when it enters a target foreign market.

General international operations experience not only enhances an MNE's ability to expand internationally but also enables the firm to evaluate foreign opportunities more objectively. At the beginning of the internationalization process geocultural proximity may outweigh economic closeness, but at later stages, as firms eliminate geocultural biases from their decisions, decisions become increasingly rational. In other words, firms in the initial stage of foreign expansion exhibit a strong preference for markets that are culturally or economically similar to the home country, but as they gain international operations experience they base their investment decisions on more objective criteria. Experience gained in international operations drives firms toward increasing international involvement and expansion.

Prior experience in a host country, either at the industry or country level, is often correlated with the degree to which a firm undertakes further commitment and foreign direct investment there (Davidson, 1980). Familiarity with a specific host country reduces the costs of providing it service, which in turn increases the possibility that a foreign firm will further serve that market through direct investment. Davidson (1980) found that the presence of a subsidiary in the host country exerts a positive influence over the firm's foreign investment decisions. Country-specific experience has a positive impact on the number of new products developed for that market and the investment size committed to local participation.

Experience is associated with intensity of exposure to certain activities, which can be operationalized as time spent in a given host country. Such experience can induce cost savings through increased input efficiency, increased investment scale, and improved innovation and standardization. MNEs with a greater length of local presence are also likely to have a superior position in selecting market segments, differentiating market and product offerings, accessing promotion channels, and building up corporate and product image (Mitchell, Shaver, & Yeung, 1992). Moreover, a long-established presence in a dynamic foreign market often results in high credibility as perceived by customers, suppliers, competitors, and local governments; well-established marketing and distribution networks; familiarity with culture-specific business practice; and greater ability to reduce operational uncertainties and financial risks. Because many foreign markets have a stronger relationship-oriented culture, business operations can be enormously boosted by wide connections with business community and governmental authorities. In this environment, MNE subunits with a higher intensity of experience are likely to have a superior business network, which is an important factor driving performance.

Organizational learning theory suggests that the diversity of experience is also important (Levitt & March, 1988). Diversity of experience, which can be measured by the breadth of business activities in a host country, can permit the MNE to preempt new opportunities and boost competitive advantages (Chang, 1995). Diverse experiences may include carrying multiple products in a host country, having a marketing presence in more than one region of the country, and doing business with various groups of customers and buyers (Barkema & Vermeulen, 1998). Operating in diverse circumstances increases the variety of events and ideas to which a firm is exposed, leading to a more extensive knowledge base and stronger technological capabilities. Learning different ways of doing things promotes innovation and productivity, which in turn enhances performance. In contrast, firms that deal with relatively few products, markets, and customers have a narrower range of experience and narrower mental models because they confront a more limited range of challenges. This narrowness hurts performance if conditions change.

In addition, the relationship between host country experience and performance may be more complex than the linear association. The expansion process model argues that the organizational experience effect in relation to performance is particularly evident during the early stage of the internationalization process (Johanson & Vahlne, 1977) but becomes less obvious as an MNE subunit becomes more mature (Zaheer, 1995). In other words, in the early stage of internationalization, firms gain country-specific knowledge to overcome the liabilities of foreignness. As firms become more familiar with the local environment, however, the increasing function of experience in relation to performance is likely to diminish. Davidson (1980) and Li (1995) support this view by noting that as MNEs become more mature and gain experience in a given host country, market growth may peak and begin to decline, despite reduced operational uncertainty in that market.

EVOLUTION OF COOPERATION DURING INTERNATIONAL EXPANSION

Unlike sociological studies that emphasize trust and long-term relationships, alliances, ventures, or networks are viewed as a temporary strategies. In other words, stability and duration of collaboration cannot be considered a value per se. The breakup of an agreement can either be caused by failure or by the attainment of satisfactory results. Conversely, although continuity of cooperation may signal a successful and self-sustaining interaction, it can also indicate stagnation. Partners may be induced to maintain existing linkages because they do not wish to abandon irreversible investments or non-redeployable assets. Evolution of cooperation, therefore, is a complicated process in which the nature of assets, strategic motivations of firms, and institutionalized control mechanisms all play a large part in shaping its dynamics.

Learning is a key factor affecting the evolution of interfirm cooperation because it influences a partner's asset contribution, strategic motivation, and cooperation and control behavior. Knowledge accumulation though collaborative interaction heavily influences the decision to continue or discontinue interfirm agreements. Learning has two possibly conflicting effects on the stability of cooperation. On one hand, learning by cooperating is a fundamental source of instability. Cooperation will generally increase a firm's knowledge about the characteristics of its partners, the domain of collaboration, the environmental conditions and opportunities, and the management of interfirm agreements in general. Part of this knowledge can be redeployed outside the specific relationship that has generated it. Firms in a better position to gain access to and use such redeployable assets can increase their bargaining power within the network. This will possibly reduce the other party's incentives to invest in the agreement. The venture or alliance may then collapse because a party loses ground in the distribution of rents. Further, partners may use such assets competitively. This may occur though direct rivalry or through the formation of other alliances with conflicting outcomes. In these cases, the alliance may break up because firms fear their partners' opportunistic use of resources initially generated through cooperation.

On the other hand, learning by cooperation is also commitment intensive. Commitment is a precondition for learning. Firms tend to use commitment as a means to create more stable conditions for learning. Commitment will fix some relational parameters by reducing environmental variability. Evolutionary cooperation cannot be ensured by the mere imposition of preexisting standards, communications procedures, or conventions. It requires investments that may be even more costly and possibly irreversible than is the case with full integration because firms need to mediate with different cultures, competencies, and organizational structures. Therefore, the decision to continue or discontinue cooperation will depend on the balance between the allocation, use, and generation of redeployable information that guarantees flexibility and the allocation, use, and creation of specific assets that favor inertia. Strategic moves in the direction of more opportunistic use of general purpose assets, as well as the decision to generalize some of the specific outputs stemming from cooperation, will positively influence the stability of a given collaborative venture in time. Using non-specific, redeployable assets competitively against partners, however, immediately erodes trust and reduces the effectiveness of the collective routines governing the venture. When deciding how to utilize redeployable assets stemming from cooperation, firms need to evaluate the trade-off between the possible gains from opportunistic behavior and the possible losses it will suffer from the breakup of an existing alliance.

From the industry life cycle perspective, the propensity of firms to choose collaborative ventures and the characteristics of cooperative agreements depend upon the phase of the technological life cycle of the specific industry in which alliances are taking place. In particular, a propensity toward cooperation will be high in the introductory stage, where equity agreements may be used by MNEs to cope with market and technological uncertainty, lower mobility barriers and the risk of sunk costs, and obtain high adaptive efficiency. The propensity toward cooperation will reach its maximum value in the early development phase, owing largely to non-equity commercial and production agreements that allow firms to gain rapid access to specialized assets that are complementary and essential for their business success. During maturity non-equity collaborative ventures will be stimulated by the revitalization of technological trajectories, stabilization of market structure, and attempts by firms to exploit residual oligopolistic rents by transferring technology to peripheral areas of the world market. During the full development and decline phases, however, the number of agreements concluded may decrease drastically owing to a marked contraction of non-equity forms. In the full development stage, reduced opportunities to appropriate technology and growing competitive pressure stemming from the threat of new entrants will induce firms to internalize control over specialized complementary assets. Accordingly, internal growth and acquisitions will tend to replace cooperation with other firms. During the decline phase, characterized by the exhaustion of technological opportunities and contraction of the market, write-offs and divestment will prevail as vehicles for the rationalization of market structure.

Based on case studies of Ciba Geigy–Alza, AT&T–Olivetti, and GE–SNECMA, Doz (1996) found that successful partnerships were highly evolutionary and went through a sequence of interactive learning cycles, reevaluation, and readjustment. Failing ventures, conversely, were highly inertial, with little learning occurring, learning diverging between cognitive understanding and behavioral adjustment, or expectations being frustrated. Initial conditions (set in terms of task definition, partner's organizational routines, interface structures, and partner's expectations) may either lead to a stable imprinting of fixed processes that make international alliances highly inertial or to generative and evolutionary processes that make them highly adaptive.

According to Doz (1996), initial conditions facilitate or hamper partner learning along five dimensions: environment, task, process, skills, and goals. Learning, in turn, allows the partners to reevaluate their partnership on the basis of perceived efficiency, equity, and adaptability. Reevaluation then leads to readjustment to initial conditions and a new cycle of learning and reevaluation. Partners in more successful alliances engage in such a series of iterative and interactive learning cycles over time, typically characterized by greater trust and adaptive flexibility, as well as the willingness to make larger, increasingly specific, and irreversible commitments.

In contrast to these successful evolutionary and learning cycles, international ventures or alliances can fail in several ways. First, the configuration of initial conditions may block or at least delay learning, which can breed frustration and lead to unmet expectations. Second, initial conditions may allow cognitive learning but also make venture partners more aware of the difficulties of behavioral learning. Initial conditions that allow separate learning by partners but do not foster joint learning or even the sharing of insights between partners are likely to lead to more failure. Such discrepancies between cognitive and behavioral learning lead to a reevaluation, which lowers expectations and typically heightens suspicions between partners. Third, learning followed by a negative reevaluation can also lead to failure. The environment may change in a way that makes it less economically attractive to at least one of the partners. In such a case, one partner may become reluctant to make any irreversible commitment to the alliance, which in turn undermines some of the potential for making the alliance efficient.

It is important to appraise properly two patterns of interaction between behavioral and cognitive learning. When initial conditions allow cognitive learning but block behavioral learning and adaptation, efficiency quickly suffers as managers became increasingly aware of the difficulties facing their businesses and the little progress they are making in surmounting them. The initial conditions come to dominate business outcomes. When initial conditions allow both cognitive and behavioral learning to take place interactively, bringing trust, confidence, and greater candidness, the conditions progressively fade away as the relationship evolves to reflect learning. Early steps in the collaborative process may be usefully conceived as generative confidence-building steps, leading to constructive cycles of trust development and adaptation of initial conditions.

International managers should realize that alliances or ventures are not just a matter of implementing initial designs to accomplish set objectives, nor do they evolve independently from initial conditions. Initial conditions play a key role, but are either of a static type, blocking learning and adaptation, or of a generative type, fostering learning and adaptation. Early imprinting is not necessarily static and mutation is not random. Imprinting can lead ventures down an adaptive dynamic development path by providing the alliance partners with the capacity to learn how to learn, rather than locking them into a determined trajectory. Imprinting a generative process in which firms learn how to learn may lead to self-adjusting but structured evolutionary patterns occurring through a sequence of learning cycles that are neither emergent nor inertial: they are adaptive in content and responsive to new conditions, but the process is structured.

Strategic fit and operating fit are two main factors determining the evolution of cooperative relationships. In the context of strategic fit, the fundamental question to be answered is whether the prospective partners should cooperate. Strategic fit exists when the partners' interests in a specific area overlap and when each controls part of the resources needed to pursue shared goals. In other words, strategic fit gives both partners the opportunity and motivation to pursue joint interests by cooperating. Compatible interests and complementary resources are the fundamental basis for cooperative success. Operating fit, in contrast, addresses the ways and means in which the relationship can be implemented in a mutually beneficial way. In other words, it concerns whether the partners can make the venture work. To create and maintain operating fit, existing organizational incompatibilities must be counterbalanced. Otherwise, the inherent procedural, structural, and cultural differences between organizations at different development stages become insurmountable obstacles. If partners lack understanding of each other's operating requirements or if they are unwilling to make concessions and meet at a middle ground, misunderstandings will result. Lack of support for the relationship will give rise to frustration and disillusionment with the partnership (Niederkofler, 1991).

To build strategic and operating fit or mitigate strategic and operating misfit international managers can improve their behavior in three areas: the negotiation process, the boundary-spanning process, and cooperative flexibility. Negotiations should lay a sound foundation for a cooperative relationship by establishing a viable cooperative strategy on the basis of complementary resources and compatible interests. It should provide clear guidelines for implementation to give cooperation a head start and increase the likelihood of being able to keep the alliance running smoothly. This corroborates the initial conditions notion illustrated above.

Boundary spanning refers to all interorganizational activities between the firms. Careful interactions and cooperation in a climate of mutual trust are fundamental requirements for a beneficial relationship. Conscious boundary spanning must bridge existing organizational incompatibilities, promote the creation and maintenance of trust and goodwill, and deal with conflict. By limiting the actual amount of cooperation, a careful selection of appropriate boundary spanners, and stepping up involvement with the partner, the effects of organizational incompatibilities may be moderated. To achieve the purposes of cooperation, the relationship must be carefully structured through the selection of communication channels. Qualified boundary spanners must also have unwavering support from top management. A cooperative climate marked by the presence of goodwill and trust is helpful. As relationships are likely to be endowed with an initial stock of goodwill, specific effort should be invested at an early stage into building this endowment into a solid relationship. A high degree of communication between partners, open discussions of problems, and good personal understanding between the major players can help to reach this goal. The creation of trust and goodwill may require a firm to compromise some of its short-term interests, but it will be repaid in the longer run by a higher degree of tolerance and the partner's willingness to make valuable contributions.

Finally, partners are subject to the forces of change in their market positions, resources, and internal situations, which also affect their interests in the venture. Success in international cooperative ventures is closely tied to the ability to be flexible and adjust to these changes. The timely termination of a cooperative relationship may sometimes be necessary. The success of cooperative relationships ultimately depends on the ability to make adjustments as necessary, overcoming operating misfit with structural and procedural changes in the boundary-spanning process, and renegotiating and repositioning the partnership to reestablish a strategic fit. Both partners should be aware that dissolution of the relationship need not be a sign of failure. Management should not hesitate to dissolve those partnerships that have fulfilled their purpose or that are unlikely ever to do so. The right timing for the exit from a cooperative relationship, combined with efficient contractual exit clauses, is needed to conserve time, money, and reputation.

ENVIRONMENTAL DYNAMICS AND
EVOLUTIONARY PROCESS

Environmental dynamics in the international setting can shape the evolutionary process of international expansion. The population ecology perspective predicts a particular evolutionary dynamic and outcome. According to this perspective, firms have limited adaptability and the environment selects organizations with particular traits to survive. Industrial organization researchers assert that as concentration in an industry increases, large generalists (i.e., multi-product, multi-market firms) emerge, catering to the market center and creating conditions that enable specialists to survive at the periphery. Thus, a few generalists and many small, diverse specialists are expected to thrive under increasing industry concentration and to outperform firms in the middle, which face competitive pressure from both ends.

It is generally recognized that the organizational environment is a multidimensional construct including hostility (criticality and deterrence of environmental factors), dynamism (unpredictability and variability of environmental factors), and complexity (diversity and heterogeneity of environmental factors). In host country markets, these factors include not only economic ones, such as competitors, customers, and suppliers, but also institutional and sociocultural segments

Venturing into foreign markets, MNEs clearly need to pay attention to environmental forces. Given that the institutional, economic, and sociocultural environments in host countries could be dramatically different from those in home markets, one can hypothesize that environmental hostility, dynamism, and complexity can easily render prior learning gained in the home country ineffective in a new setting. In organization theory literature, the resource dependency perspective suggests that environmental hostility, dynamism, and complexity specifically affect the firm's ability to secure necessary resources, which in turn influences organizational performance. When operating in an environment that presents a threat to the growth of the firm and affects the firm's operations more fundamentally, a foreign company's experience in such an environment may become more valuable because this experience can improve the firm's strategic flexibility, operational adaptability, and risk reduction.

March (1991) argues that a dynamic environment allows the firm more opportunity for exploration and exploitation based on experiential knowledge. The contributions of more heterogeneous participation (i.e., diversity of experience) and longer presence (i.e., intensity of experience) to a foreign firm's performance may be greater in a dynamic foreign environment because the combination creates more financial or operational synergies. Experience dealing with dynamic environments increases the firm's ability to scan the external environment; analyze environmental changes; and seize emerging product, market, and technological opportunities. In a dynamic context, experience gained in such an environment is likely to contribute more to the growth and survival of the firm.

Complexity is a third critical dimension of the environment because it determines the diversity of environmental segments and the heterogeneity within each segment. When an environment is more complex the experience effects may become stronger or be sustained longer. An MNE's experience in a highly complex environment constitutes tacit knowledge that cannot be readily leared by followers or imitated by rivals. This tacit knowledge is a strategic asset needed for venture success in a complex setting. Such experience facilitates the strategy-environment configuration, improves resource deployment, and inflates the competitive edge of the firm. For firms encountering greater environmental complexity, the favorable impact of such experience secured from this environment on performance may be stronger.

The above reasoning suggests that the interactions between the experience factor and environmental variables are important for MNE success in the target market. This may compound the complexity of the nonlinear association between experience and expansion performance. The acquisition of culture-specific experience clearly represents a critical competitive edge for MNEs operating in a dynamic, complex environment. MNE managers need to pursue actively indigenous experience in operation and management through such channels as cooperative partners, local managers, early foreign entrants, and even local or foreign rivals. Moreover, culture-specific experience is often more important in the exploration stage than in the exploitation phase of overseas operation. This requires that MNE managers attach particular importance to experience in the early stage of foreign operation. Utmost attention must be paid to the proper configuration among strategy, experience, competence, and environment. To ensure survival and growth in a volatile but promising market, MNE managers should keep an eye on the dynamics of the local environment, especially in economic, institutional, and sociocultural segments. MNE managers should align investment strategies, business plans, and market orientations with the changing environment. This will help spur the favorable effect of experience on goal accomplishment.

REFERENCES

Aliber, R. A. 1970. A theory of foreign direct investment. In C. P. Kindleberger (Ed.), *The international corporation*. Cambridge, MA: MIT Press.

Andersen, O. 1993. On the internationalization process of firms: A critical analysis. *Journal of International Business Studies*, 24(2): 209–231.

Ball, C. A. and A. E. Tschoegl. 1982. The decision to establish a foreign bank branch or subsidiary: An application of binary classification procedures.

Journal of Financial and Quantitative Analysis, 17: 411–424.

Barkema, H. G. and F. Vermeulen. 1998. International expansion through start-up or acquisition: A learning perspective. *Academy of Management Journal*, 41: 7–26.

Barkema, H. G., J.H.J. Bell, and J. M. Pennings. 1996. Foreign entry, cultural barriers, and learning. *Strategic Management Journal*, 17: 151–166.

Barkema, H. G., O. Shenkar, F. Vermeulen, and J.H.J. Bell. 1997. Working abroad, working with others: How firms learn to operate international joint ventures. *Academy of Management Journal*, 40: 426–442.

Benito, G.R.G. and G. Gripsrud. 1992. The expansion of foreign direct investments: Discrete rational location choices or a cultural learning process? *Journal of International Business Studies*, 23: 461–476.

Chang, S. J. 1995. International expansion strategy of Japanese firms: Capability building through sequential entry. *Academy of Management Journal*, 38: 383–407.

Cohen, W. M. and D. A. Levinthal. 1990. Absorptive capacity: A new perspective on learning and innovation. *Administrative Science Quarterly*, 35: 128–152.

Davidson, W. 1980. The location of foreign direct investment activity: Country characteristics and experience effects. *Journal of International Business Studies*, 11: 9–22.

Doz, Y. L. 1996. The evolution of cooperation in strategic alliances: Initial conditions or learning processes? *Strategic Management Journal*, 17: 55–83.

Dunning, J. H. 1988. The eclectic paradigm of international production: A restatement and some possible extensions. *Journal of International Business Studies*, 19: 1–31.

Dunning, J. H. 1981. *International production and the multinational enterprise*. London: Allen & Unwin.

Erramilli, M. K. 1991. The experience factor in foreign market entry behavior of service firms. *Journal of International Business Studies*, 22: 479–502.

Huber, G. P. 1991. Organizational learning: The contributing processes and the literatures. *Organization Science*, 2(1): 88–115.

Hymer, S. H. 1976. *The international operations of national firms: A study of direct foreign investment*. Cambridge, MA: MIT Press.

Johanson, J. and J. Vahlne. 1977. The internationalization process of the firm: A model of knowledge development and increasing foreign market commitment. *Journal of International Business Studies*, 8: 23–32.

Kogut, B. and S. J. Chang. 1991. Technological capabilities and Japanese foreign direct investment in the United States. *Review of Economics and Statistics*, 73: 401–413.

Levinthal, D. A. 1991. Organizational adaptation and environmental selection-interrelated processes of change. *Organization Science*, 2: 140–145.

Levitt, B. and J. G. March. 1988. Organizational learning. *Annual Review of Sociology*, 14: 319–340.

Li, J. 1995. Foreign entry and survival: Effects of strategic choices on performance in international markets. *Strategic Management Journal*, 16: 333–352.

March, J. G. 1991. Exploration and exploitation in organizational learning. *Organization Science*, 2: 71–87.

Mitchell, W., J. M. Shaver, and B. Yeung. 1992. Getting there in a global industry: Impacts on performance of changing international presence. *Strategic*

Management Journal, 13: 419–432.

Nelson, R. R. and S. G. Winter. 1982. *An evolutionary theory of economic change.* Cambridge, MA: Harvard University Press.

Niederkofler, M. 1991. The evolution of strategic alliances: Opportunities for managerial influence. *Journal of Business Venturing*, 6: 237–257.

Pennings, J. M., H. G. Barkema, and S. W. Douma. 1994. Organizational learning and diversification. *Academy of Management Journal*, 37: 608–640.

Prahalad, C. K. and G. Hamel. 1990. The core competence of the corporation. *Harvard Business Review*, 68: 79–91.

Vernon, R. 1966. International investment and international trade in the product cycle. *Quarterly Journal of Economics*, 80: 190–207.

Welch, L. S. and R. Luostarinen. 1988. Internationalization: Evolution of a concept. *Journal of General Management*, 14(2): 34–55.

Yu, C. J. 1991. The experience effect and foreign direct investment. *Weltwirtschaftliches Archiv*, 126: 560–579.

Zaheer, S. 1995. Overcoming the liability of foreignness. *Academy of Management Journal*, 38: 341–363.

FURTHER READINGS

Baum, A. C. and J. V. Singh. 1994. *The evolutionary dynamics of organizations.* New York: Oxford University Press.

Bruderer, E. and J. V. Singh. 1996. Organizational evolution, learning, and selection: A genetic-algorithm-based model. *Academy of Management Journal*, 39; 1322–1349.

Butler, R. 1995. Time in organizations: Its experience, explanations and effects. *Organization Studies*, 16(6): 925–950.

Caves, R. 1971. International corporations: The industrial economics of foreign investment. *Economica*, 38: 1–27.

Day, G. S. and D. Montgomery. 1983. Diagnosing the experience curve. *Journal of Marketing*, 47(2): 44–59.

Doz, Y. L. and C. K. Prahalad. 1991. Managing DMNCs: A search for a new paradigm. *Strategic Management Journal*, 12: 145–164.

Jarillo, J. C. and J. I. Martinez. 1990. Different roles for subsidiaries: The case of multinational corporations in Spain. *Strategic Management Journal*, 11: 501–512.

Kogut, B. 1983. Foreign direct investment as a sequential process. In C. P. Kingleberger and D. Audretsch (Eds.), *The multinational corporation in the 1980s*, pp. 35–56. Cambridge, MA: MIT Press.

Levinthal, D. A. and J. G. March. 1993. The myopia of learning. *Strategic Management Journal*, 14: 95–112.

Luostarinen, R. 1980. *Internationalization of the firm.* Helsinki: Helsinki School of Economics.

Root, F. R. 1987. *Entry strategies for international markets.* Lexington, MA: Lexington Books.

Shaver, J. M., W. Mitchell, and B. Yeung. 1997. The effect of own-firm and other-firm experience on foreign direct investment survival in the United States, 1987–1992. *Strategic Management Journal*, 18: 811–824.

4

Global Integration Perspective

International expansion requires coordinating subsidiary activities across national boundaries. Given the increasing globalization of the competitive environment, the dual imperatives of global integration and local responsiveness are becoming more critical than ever before for the survival and growth of multinational enterprises (MNEs). This chapter elaborates the concepts and approaches of global integration of dispersed business activities across borders. It begins with an introduction to the importance of the issue, followed by key notions and perspectives on the global integration-local responsiveness relationship. The third section illustrates the strategic roles of subsidiaries and the relevant factors affecting these roles. The last section illuminates how to maintain global integration of geographically dispersed world businesses.

IMPORTANCE OF GLOBAL INTEGRATION

An MNE consists of a group of geographically dispersed, goal-disparate organizations that include its headquarters and different subsidiaries abroad. It is an interorganizational network embedded in an external context consisting of other organizations, such as customers, competitors, suppliers, and regulators, with which the different units of the MNE interact. Foreign subunits are subject to the laws of the country in which they are located as well as certain statutes of the nation in which the parent firm is domiciled. Foreign subunits must be differentiated enough to successfully confront cultures, markets, and business practices that contrast markedly with those of the home country, but this flexibility must be accommodated within a structure that will provide maximum contribution to corporate performance. Global integration is necessary.

The specialization of subunits that allows the organization to undertake complicated tasks requires an equally developed system of integration to bind them into an operational whole. In addition to the differentiation stemming from functional or geographic specialization, the organization is subject to divisiveness in the form of departmental interests, competing functional goals, and differential demands from the environment that lead subunits to pursue their own strategies. To overcome these centrifugal forces, the executives of MNEs must maintain a system of integration that maximizes the benefits from internalization while allowing various subunits the necessary flexibility to adapt to their particular environments.

Increasing globalization has captured the attention of practitioners searching for sustained competitive advantages in an ever-changing world. For managers the message seems clear: markets are fast becoming borderless; strategies that fail to recognize market integration are short-sighted and misguided. The central issue faced by international managers competing in a global environment is the strategic integration of international operations despite the pressure to be locally responsive and the consequent tendency toward fragmentation. Increasing economies of scale in many industries, improvements in transportation and communications, increasing homogenization of tastes and market structures between countries, and rapid technological developments have all contributed to the globalization of markets. In such contexts, MNEs can attain a sustainable competitive advantage by integrating the value chain activities performed in their subsidiaries around the world. Integrating these activities means raising the level of interdependence among subsidiaries by designing narrow product lines, concentrating production in a few plants, and using only the most efficient input sources.

Within many industries MNEs are no longer able to compete as a collection of independent subsidiaries. Competition has become based in part on the ability of the corporation to link its subsidiary activities across geographic locations. Although an MNE's headquarters has responsibility for activities that cross national boundaries, local markets vary substantially across host countries. This suggests that an asymmetrical treatment of its subsidiaries is necessary to coordinating worldwide businesses within a network. The transnational solution, where the roles and responsibilities of subsidiaries are varied to reflect explicitly differences in their external environments and internal capabilities, seems a better choice.

In being assigned differentiated roles, MNE subsidiaries are either a fundamental part of a global rationalization process or operate under a global mandate (Roth & Morrison, 1992). Global subsidiary rationalization occurs when the subsidiary specializes in a narrow set of value activities or the performance of the subsidiary's activities is dependent on other subsidiaries. The subsidiary is primarily an implementor of headquarters-developed strategy (Roth & Morrison, 1992). By contrast, with a global subsidiary mandate, the subsidiary works with headquarters to develop and implement strategy. The subsidiary is given worldwide responsibility for the complete set of value activities: managing research and development (R&D), production, marketing, and management activities for a global product (Roth & Morrison, 1992).

Global integration benefits from two forms of advantages: location-specific advantages and competitive advantages. Location-specific advantages are secured through exploiting differences in factor, capital, and product markets or governmental policies among countries. Competitive advantages are developed through international economies of scale and scope and organizational learning from various national markets. Operational flexibility serves as leverage for adjusting the degree of integration. Resource allocation and dispersal (both tangible and intangible) in turn serve to maintain flexibility in global business activities. Through directing resource flow, an MNE may shift its activities in response to changing tax structures, labor costs, exchange rates, governmental policies, competitor strategies, or other uncertainties. Thus, managing resource flow is necessary for achieving either location-specific or competitive advantages in global business.

Resource flow requires extensive coordination within an MNE network because it creates reciprocal interdependencies among subsidiaries. Such coordination is thought to require centralized decision-making responsibility and authority, particularly in the context of interdependency. Centralized control is necessary for making trade-off decisions between subsidiaries, but should be segmented by product line and distributed among different subsidiaries depending on particular capabilities and environmental contingencies. Examples of subsidiary mandates include such companies as Westinghouse Canada, which has the responsibility for gas turbines worldwide; Siemens' Japan which, in partnership with Asahi Medical, produces and markets compact magnetic resonance image machines for the world market; and Mack, a German subsidiary of Pfizer, U.S.A., which has worldwide responsibility for a variety of fine chemicals. These examples illustrate that implementing a global strategy does not imply that centralized control must reside at the headquarters for all organizational activities or product lines. Nevertheless, even when the subsidiary takes a dominant role in managing the resource flow associated with a particular product to pursue a global strategy, the subsidiary remains part of an interdependent network. The locus of control may shift but interdependency remains. Furthermore, although the subsidiary may be responsible for key strategic decisions, this does not imply total autonomy. The subsidiary remains interdependent with other subsidiaries and the parent corporation because it still acts within the overall parameters of a corporate strategy (Roth & Morrison, 1992).

GLOBAL INTEGRATION AND LOCAL RESPONSIVENESS

Several environmental changes in recent years have propelled the necessity to combine global integration with local responsiveness. First, the life cycle of most industries has shortened as technological development grows at a faster pace. At the same time, competition in the global marketplace has become fiercer. To survive and grow in such an environment, MNEs must maximize the benefits gained from both internalization (global integration) and internationalization (local responsiveness). Success often depends on the best coupling between the comparative advantages of host nations and the competitive advantages of firms.

Second, international joint ventures or global strategic alliances have become a predominant vehicle for international expansion. Unlike single-standing firms, joint ventures and alliances often confront the problems of opportunism and conflict during partnership. In attempting to obtain maximum compensation from the distinctive resources contributed to these ventures, MNEs have to maintain control over local operations and integrate such businesses with their networks. In the meantime, cooperation necessitates contribution, commitment, and compromise by all parties, which means that each party cannot hold too much centralized control over venture operations unless it has dominant ownership or strong bargaining power.

Last, many transitional or emerging economies provide both tremendous opportunities and uncertainty. These economies have recently become major hosts for foreign direct investment (FDI) from the Western world. Facing such situations, MNE headquarters need to delegate power to overseas managers to enable them to react and adapt quickly to changes in local environments, particularly the industrial, macroeconomic, and sociopolitical segments. Conversely, local operations in such economies need immense and varied support and resources from MNE headquarters. Without such contributions, foreign subsidiaries will be quite vulnerable to the uncertainty and risks resulting from complexity, dynamism, and unpredictability in the host environment.

Managing headquarters-subsidiary relationships involves balancing international integration and centralization against local responsiveness and subsidiary autonomy in the making of strategic decisions. Global integration needs usually stem from economic, technological, and competitive conditions. Integration usually involves the development of a network of subsidiaries in which R&D, manufacturing, and distribution tasks are centrally allocated and coordinated. In such a network each subsidiary may be responsible for developing or manufacturing some products and for sales of the complete product line. The part of the firm's product line that a subsidiary does not manufacture itself will be procured from other subsidiaries. Local responsiveness needs usually stem from diversity of market conditions and social and political environments found in various countries in which the firm operates. Responsiveness is necessary for responding to diverse consumer tastes, distribution channels, advertising media, and government regulations and constraints.

Prahalad and Doz (1987) offered one of the first conceptualizations for examining global strategy. Their framework, namely the global integration (I) and local responsiveness (R) paradigm, suggests that participants in global industries develop competitive postures across two dimensions. These two dimensions represent two salient imperatives that simultaneously confront a business competing internationally. The first one, global integration, refers to the coordination of activities across countries in an attempt to build efficient operations networks and take maximum advantage of similarities across locations. The second dimension, local responsiveness, concerns the attempt to respond to specific needs within a variety of host countries. MNEs can choose to emphasize one dimension over another or compete in both dimensions, resulting in three basic strategies: integrated, multifocal, or locally responsive. Firms that perceive a high level of pressure to integrate use a strategy of global integration. Globally integrated businesses link activities across nations in an attempt to minimize overall costs, avoid various taxes, or maximize income. Locally responsive businesses perceive pressures to respond strategically to local needs. Last, multifocal businesses perceive the need to respond simultaneously to pressures both for integration and responsiveness; they therefore employ multifocal strategies.

Recognizing that business managers often have varying perceptions of the environment, the I-R framework has been suggested as a way of capturing the pressures on a given business (Prahalad & Doz, 1987). Pressures to integrate globally derive from industrial and internalization forces that necessitate worldwide business resource deployment. Strategic decisions are made to maximize the collective organization so that activities are integrated across national boundaries. In contrast, local responsiveness pressures are industrial and national forces that necessitate context-sensitive strategic decisions. Management must respond predominantly to each local market or industry setting irrespective of the strategic needs of other business units within the network.

Pressures to integrate globally or respond locally variously affect the structure of different industries, the competitive positioning within industries, and even the configuration of organizations. The I-R framework may be used to define the pressures on each of these units of analysis to clarify the costs or benefits of responding to each pressure. The relative strength of global integration and local responsiveness pressures may be analyzed at the aggregate level of industries, at the level of individual businesses competing within industries, or even at a functional or task level within a business.

There are several different perspectives for explaining the I-R relationship, each with its own underlying logic and contingencies. Despite different foci, however, these perspectives are related and complementary. These perspectives include: the structural forces perspective, the environmental forces perspective, and the strategic flexibility perspective.

Structural Forces Perspective

The I-R relationship is affected by the nature and characteristics of an industry. The structural forces perspective on global strategy, which has its roots in industrial organization economics and contingency theory, assumes that pressures to integrate globally or respond locally vary along a broad spectrum with endpoints that can be labeled global and national (Morrison & Roth, 1992). According to this perspective, the importance of structural characteristics varies from industry to industry. In global industries, three broad factors have been cited as structural determinants: the potential for economies of scale in value-adding activities, differences in comparative advantages across countries, and standardized market demand across countries (Birkinshaw, Morrison, & Hulland, 1995). Although all industries share in these driving factors to various degrees, all three determinants function at a high level in global industries. In contrast, all three factors have little impact on national or multidomestic industries. Everything else being constant, global business strategies are encouraged in an industry dominated by factors that drive a global industry. A global strategy consists of globally integrated operations and the cross-subsidization of international market share battles. A business that adopts a global strategy maximizes its fit with structural imperatives.

Porter (1986) considers the essential structural characteristic of an industry to be the degree of interrelationship among competitive environments in different countries. If that interrelation is very high, he refers to it as a global industry. This contrasts with a multidomestic industry where what happens in one country has little effect on the rest. Yip (1995) further identified a series of specific structural determinants (called drivers) that drive an MNE's globalization and use of global strategy. These drivers can be grouped into four categories: market, cost, governmental, and competitive. Each driver of industrial globalization affects the use of five integration levers including market participation, product and service costs, location of activities, marketing, and competitive strategies. Of the four categories of drivers, market and cost drivers appear to be particularly relevant in explaining the trade-off between integration and responsiveness.

Strategic Flexibility Perspective

The strategic flexibility perspective is composed of two related, complementary views: operational flexibility and strategic options. Both views were elaborated systematically by Kogut (1985, 1990, 1994). The key notion in operational flexibility is that the balance of global integration and local responsiveness lies less in designing long-term strategic plans than in constructing flexibility that permits a firm to exploit future changes in the competition, government policies, and market dynamics. This flexibility is gained by decreasing the firm's dependence on assets already in place.

The central tenet of the strategic option view is that managers will alter their decisions when such changes are justified by emerging conditions in an uncertain and dynamic environment. If a decision made now has a chance of being altered later in response to new information, then the economic consequences of such changes should be properly accounted for when evaluating the current decision. For example, if the establishment of a joint venture with a local partner may lead to acquisition of the partner's stake in the future, the proper evaluation of the joint venture ex ante should take into account the economic impact of the possible acquisition. Essentially, operational flexibility and the strategic options notions share the same core of response to dynamism, an important issue in international expansion.

A Synthesis of Various Factors

Each of the three perspectives described places an emphasis on different sets of factors affecting the I-R balance. The structural forces perspective focuses on market and industrial characteristics, and the environmental forces perspective attaches greater value to the sociopolitical environment of the host country. The strategic flexibility perspective links both sets of contextual factors to the I-R balance and addresses the importance of flexibility in exploiting global opportunities derived from these two sets of factors.

I-R linkages are also affected by strategic objectives and internal capabilities (see Table 4.1). Specifically, pressures for global integration are stronger if an MNE aims to use extensive transfer pricing to gain more financial synergy; maximize the benefits of tax reduction or avoidance by manipulating prices in intrafirm transactions; increase the gross profit margin from globally coordinated operations and integrated value chain activities; minimize transaction, production, and operation costs through global integration; benefit from intrafirm financing, a superior capital structure, and external loans; attain operational and financial benefits from vertical integration of geographically dispersed activities; control the value chains in various foreign countries that are vital to corporate success; and mitigate operational uncertainty and financial risks that may arise from dispersed and scattered operations in various markets.

TABLE 4.1

Factors Contributing to Integration and Responsiveness

Global Integration	Local Responsiveness
Market and Industrial Characteristics	
Multinational customers	Diverse market structures
Global competitors	Peculiar industrial structure
High technology	Indigenous distribution channels
Scale and experience in manufacturing	Different market demands
Product standardization	Product differentiation
Low customer responsiveness	High customer responsiveness
Low competition	High competition
Sociopolitical Environment	
Stable environment	Volatile, complex, or hostile environment
Homogenous consumer behavior	Cumbersome regulations
Internationalized business atmosphere	Changing FDI policies
Efficient and supportive government	Unique business practices
Strategic Objectives	
Transfer pricing	Local market expansion
Tax or tariff avoidance	Presence in multiple markets
Transaction cost savings	Risk diversification
Profit margin increase	Factor endowment exploitation
Internalized financing	Transnational market power
Cost minimization	Opportunity preemption
Vertical integration	Learning from local firms
Value chain control	Host country experience
Risk reduction	
Internal Capabilities	
Information flow effectiveness	Uncertainty reduction
Coordination	International experience
Efficient organizational structure	Competencies needed in host markets
Global competitive edge	Local management
Efficient allocation of resources	Networking with local firms and government

In contrast, pressures for local responsiveness are stronger if an MNE attempts to pursue market share and competitive power in the host country, establish a presence in different foreign markets and seek transnational market power, diversify operational and financial risks by investing in foreign countries, explore the production factor advantages in specific host countries, preempt business potentials in a specific host market, enhance learning in a partnership with local firms, and improve host country experience by participating in the local environment.

The balance between global integration and local responsiveness is also associated with the internal capabilities of a focal MNE. For instance, MNEs have to assess whether they have the ability to maintain global integration if needed. In other words, firm capability balances the I-R linkage. Global integration is better ensured if an MNE is equipped with effective information flow systems, superior coordination and control skills and experience, an efficient organizational structure at the corporate and international levels, a high ability to allocate and use distinctive resources in geographically dispersed international markets, and a competitive edge in a global industry.

Local responsiveness is ensured if an MNE has superior risk reduction ability and the capacity to manage uncertainty; overall international experience and experience in the host country; competencies in local operations and bargaining power; managerial skills and the organizational expertise needed for local operations; and networking ability, both interpersonal and interorganizational, with the business community including suppliers, buyers, and competitors and with various governmental authorities.

Table 4.1 topically summarizes various factors affecting global integration and local responsiveness. It must be noted, however, that very seldom can a clear, exclusive choice be made between responsiveness and integration. Such choices are not of the either-or nature but rather involve difficult trade-offs in balancing the extent and form of integration and responsiveness. Some ambiguity is inevitable (Doz & Prahalad, 1984). The appropriate balance between the two keeps changing and needs to be reassessed from time to time.

THE STRATEGIC ROLE OF SUBSIDIARIES IN THE I-R BALANCE

Subsidiary strategies are a critical mechanism for dealing with the parent-subsidiary relationship. As the strategy-oriented approach is emerging in lieu of traditional control-centered approach, subsidiary strategies also play an increasingly important part in balancing integration and responsiveness. Table 4.2 synthesizes various classification schemes and their definitions concerning subsidiary strategies.

TABLE 4.2
A Synthesis of Multinational Enterprise Subsidiary Roles

Authors	Factors Affecting Strategy	Strategic Roles and Strategies
Jarillo & Martinez (1990)	i. Geographical location of value activities ii. Degree of integration with the network	*Autonomous:* a subsidiary with high degree of localization and low integration carries out most of its functions in the value chain independent of its parent. *Receptive:* a subsidiary with a low degree of localization and high level of integration carries out few activities within the local market. *Active:* a subsidiary with a high degree of both localization and integration has many activities locally, but they are carried out in close coordination with the rest of the firm.
Gupta & Govindarajan (1991)	Differences in knowledge flow patterns among subsidiaries	*Global innovator:* (high outflow and low inflow) serves as the fountainhead of knowledge for other units. *Integrated player:* (high outflow and high inflow) creates knowledge for other units but is not self-sufficient for its own needs. *Implementor:* (low outflow and high inflow) engages in little knowledge creation of its own and relies heavily on information from parent or other subsidiaries. *Local innovator:* (low outflow and low inflow) has all relevant knowledge and functions for local setting but too specific to be used elsewhere.

Bartlett & Ghoshal (1989)	i. Competence level of the subsidiary ii. Importance of local market	*Strategic leader*: a very competent subsidiary in an important market serves as a partner to headquarters in developing and implementing strategy. *Contributor*: a competent subsidiary in a relatively unimportant market contributes its expertise toward MNE projects. *Implementor*: a subsidiary with lower competence in a relatively unimportant market produces or markets some or all MNE products in its local market *Black hole*: a subsidiary with few capabilities in a very important market may serve as a listening post in that market until it obtains capabilities for managing itself out of this role.
Marcati (1989)	i. Dependence on headquarters for key capabilities ii. Degree of coordination required by headquarters	*Bridgehead*: subsidiary is dependent on MNE for know-how and guidance; it serves as an assembly operation in the local market. *Fragmented*: subsidiaries possess key know-how (except for R&D) and require little coordination; it replicates the parent firm in the local market. *Connected*: subsidiary is in an important market to make a contribution to integrated worldwide operations. *Loose*: an autonomous subsidiary is loosely coupled with the headquarters.
Poynter & White (1985)	i. Environment ii. Organizational slack iii. Values iv. Organizational relationships	*Miniature replica*: subsidiary serves as a pipeline to the host country by producing and marketing some of the parent's product line. *Marketing satellite*: subsidiary sells to local market products

TABLE 4.2, continued

Authors	Factors Affecting Strategy	Strategic Roles and Strategies
		designed and produced by the MNE.
		Rationalized manufacturer: subsidiary produces a designated set of components or products for an integrated, multi-country market.
		Product specialist: subsidiary develops products and markets a limited product line for a global market.
		Strategic independent: subsidiary is free to develop lines of business for either local or multicountry markets.
Hoffman (1994)	i. MNE strategy ii. Local environment iii. Subsidiary capability	*Partner, contributor, specialist, and satellite independent, interdependent, implementer, and isolate* (see detailed discussion)

In Jarillo and Martinez's (1990) scheme, the two basic dimensions underlying strategic choices are the geographic localization of activities (i.e., whether R&D, purchasing, manufacturing, marketing, etc. are performed in the same country), and the degree of integration of those activities with the same activities in other subsidiaries of the firm. These two dimensions are independent. A subsidiary that performs most activities of the value chain still has two very different options: it may either be highly autonomous from headquarters, selling most of its output in its local market; or very integrated with headquarters, exporting a large part of its production to the parent company or other subsidiaries, while importing from them many products or components. In light of these two dimensions, an *autonomous* strategy means that a subsidiary carries out most of the functions of the value chain in a manner that is relatively independent of its parent organization or other subsidiaries. It follows that in a *receptive* strategy, few of these functions are performed locally, and they are highly integrated with other business units. Last, in an *active* strategy, many activities are located locally, but they are carried out in close coordination with other subsidiaries, thus constituting an active node in a tightly knit network. The autonomous strategy is typical of subsidiaries in multinational firms competing in multidomestic industries. The receptive strategy is typical of subsidiaries in global firms competing in global industries. Finally, active strategies are used by subsidiaries in transnational firms with strong mandates from headquarters. Only those subsidiaries of a transnational firm that occupy important nodes in the network will follow such active strategies.

In Gupta and Govindarajan's (1991) scheme, the key factor underlying the design of control systems is knowledge flow patterns. Intracorporate knowledge flow is defined as the transfer of either expertise (e.g., skills and capabilities) or external market data of strategic value. The type of expertise transferred could refer to input processes (e.g., purchasing skills), throughput processes (e.g., product, process, and packaging designs), or output processes (e.g., marketing knowledge, distribution expertise). Any MNE subsidiaries can be arrayed along the two dimensions involving knowledge flow, that is, the extent to which the subsidiary receives knowledge inflow from the rest of the corporation and the extent to which the subsidiary provides knowledge outflow to the rest of the corporation. As a result, four generic subsidiary roles can be defined: global innovator (high outflow and low inflow), integrated player (high outflow and high inflow), implementor (low outflow and high inflow), and local innovator (low outflow and low inflow). In the global innovator role, the subsidiary serves as the fountainhead of knowledge for other units. The integrated player role is similar to the global innovator role because it also implies a responsibility for creating knowledge that can be utilized by other subsidiaries. However, an integrated player is not self-sufficient in fulfillment of its own knowledge needs. In the implementor role, the subsidiary engages in little knowledge creation of its own and relies heavily on knowledge inflows from either the parent or peer subsidiaries. Last, the local innovator role implies that the subsidiary has almost complete local responsibility for the creation of relevant know-how in all key functional areas. However, this knowledge is seen as too idiosyncratic to be of much competitive use outside of the country in which the local innovator is located. Traditional MNEs have consisted almost entirely of subsidiaries with local innovator roles.

In Bartlett and Ghoshal's (1989) scheme, the strategic importance of the local environment and competence of local organization are two key considerations in determining subsidiary roles. The strategic leader role can be played by a highly competent national subsidiary located in a strategically important market. In this role, the subsidiary serves as a partner of headquarters in developing and implementing strategy. Contributor subsidiaries refer to those operating in small or strategically unimportant markets but having distinctive capabilities. Implementor subsidiaries operate in less strategically important markets but have enough competence to maintain local operations. Their market potential is limited, as reflected by corporate resource commitment. The efficiency of an implementor is as important as the creativity of its strategic leaders or contributors, perhaps more so, for it is this group that provides the strategic leverage that affords MNEs their competitive advantage. The implementors produce opportunities to capture economies of scale and scope that are crucial to global strategies. Finally, black hole subsidiaries operate in important markets where they hardly make a dent, but their strong local presence is essential for maintaining an MNE's global position. Building a significant local presence in a national environment that is large, sophisticated, and competitive is extremely difficult, expensive, and time consuming. One common tack has been to create a sensory outpost in the black hole environment so as to exploit its learning potential, even if the local business potential is beyond its reach. Establishing strategic alliances represents a way of managing the subsidiary out of the black hole.

In Marcati's (1989) scheme, subsidiary strategies are identified in light of two combined dimensions, namely levels of coordination and extent of dependence from headquarters. A bridgehead is a headquarters-centered strategy in which the subsidiary deals mainly with assembly operations; it is dependent on its headquarters for products, know-how, and guidance and has only limited adaptation capabilities. It is unable to play any autonomous role. Fragmented means a strategy where the subsidiary is widely autonomous and only plays a financial or economic role within the firm. The connected strategy is a more integrated alternative in which the subsidiary is connected to the rest of the network and in a position to make a contribution to worldwide operations. Finally, loose subsidiaries are autonomous subunits loosely coupled with the headquarters. The parent-subsidiary relationship stands on financial and technological linkages; no real control takes place.

In Poynter and White's (1985) scheme, the underlying factors affecting a subsidiary's strategic roles include organizational slack, the local environment, the values of key implementors, and organizational relationships affecting both the development and execution of strategy. Of these, organizational slack is of particular importance in the dynamic world of the MNE and its subsidiaries. Organizational slack plays a major role in determining an organization's ability to deal with environmental variations or buffer itself against environmental influences. The amount of organizational slack is related to the firm's ability to generate innovative strategies. If slack is not carefully managed, however, the resulting subsidiary strategies can conflict with those of the MNE parent and with those that would best fit the competitive environment. In light of the above factors, a subsidiary can be defined as one of five types: miniature replica, marketing satellite, rationalized manufacturer, product specialist, or strategic independent. A miniature replica produces and markets some of the parent's product line in the host country. Some low volume products may be imported from the parent, but generally the business is a small-scale replica of the parent firm. A marketing satellite markets products manufactured centrally in the host market or trade region. Process and product development also occur centrally. These companies range from simple import firms to sophisticated marketers with extensive distribution, marketing, promotion, and customer support services. A rationalized manufacturer produces a designated set of component parts or products for a multinational or global market. Its product scope is limited. Marketing is usually performed by the MNE through marketing satellites. Generally, developmental activities are undertaken by the parent, but occasionally specific process improvements may be developed at the local plant. Major strategic decisions are made by the parent firm. A product specialist develops, produces, and markets a limited product line for global markets. Products, markets, or basic technologies are similar to the parent's, but exchanges are rare. The subsidiary is generally self-sufficient in terms of applied R&D, production, and marketing. The subsidiary has strategic control over its established products, but not over other major strategic shifts. Last, a strategic independent has the freedom and resources to develop lines of business for local, multinational, or global markets. It has unconstrained access to markets and the freedom to pursue new business opportunities. Administrative and financial relations are often the only links with the parent company. Of the above strategies, the miniature replica is most common for MNE subsidiaries. Marketing satellite and rationalized manufacturer strategies are usually found only

in highly integrated global MNEs. Although desired by host governments, the product specialist and strategic independent are uncommon.

Hoffman (1994) sought to integrate the above schemes. Subsidiary
strategies are determined not only by the host country environment but
also by parental strategies and subsidiary capabilities. These three dimensions help define various strategic situations a subsidiary is likely to confront. Although a parental strategy is defined at headquarters, subsidiary
capabilities and local environment are defined at the subsidiary level.

Parental strategy affects subsidiary strategy because it reflects the
strategic orientation at the corporate level of the parent-subsidiary relationship within MNEs. Strategies at the business level should be subordinated to strategy at the corporate level. The degree of integration of activities reflects the coordination needs of different MNE strategies. Global
strategies require higher levels of integration, compared to multidomestic
strategies. Global strategies are those in which the MNE markets standardized products and services to its international markets and takes
advantage of economies of scale (e.g., rationalized manufacturing) and
economic scope (e.g., worldwide brands). Using multidomestic strategies,
by contrast, MNEs adapt their products and services to the unique social,
economic, and technological characteristics of each local market. Each
subsidiary is fairly autonomous in its own market. Transnational strategies represent a mix of both approaches depending on the national or
regional market.

Subsidiaries abroad possess different internal resources or competencies, which may be available for use in the local market or transferred as
knowledge to the rest of the MNE network. A subsidiary having many
capabilities possesses the resources and skills required to be a full partic-
ipant in an MNE's strategy, whereas a subsidiary with few capabilities is
dependent on the parent or other subsidiaries for some of its resources
and skills.

Local environments may represent opportunities or threats in the formulation of subsidiary strategy. Subsidiary environments should be
viewed from the parental perspective because it is at this level that the
choice is made whether to operate a subsidiary in a particular national
environment. The local environment may be thence viewed as either
accommodating to MNE strategy or constrained. An accommodating
environment presents more opportunities than threats and has fewer
political or economic barriers. A constrained environment would present
more threats than opportunities.

By combining the three factors of parent strategy, subsidiary capability, and local environment, Hoffman (1994) presents eight strategic contexts for subsidiaries. Although eight generic subsidiary strategies are
depicted in his model, a given MNE needs to consider only four strategic
options for its subsidiaries based on the MNE strategy it is pursuing.

Thus, a subsidiary of an MNE pursuing a global strategy might pursue a partner, contributor, specialist, or satellite strategy depending on its particular situation. Alternatively, a subsidiary of an MNE pursuing a multidomestic strategy might pursue an independent, interdependent, implementor, or isolate strategy to exploit its particular context. Figure 4.1 exhibits the three-factor contingent perspective.

Setting strategic roles for subsidiaries is insufficient for managing subunits abroad. Corporate management faces two other important challenges in guiding the dispersion of responsibilities and tasks. These include building in differentiation, not only by designing diverse roles and distributing assignments but also by giving the managers responsibilities and power to do the same, and directing the process to ensure that various roles are coordinated and that the distributed responsibilities are controlled.

Once subsidiary roles are allocated, the head office has to empower managers to ensure that they will have an influence on the corporate decision-making process. This is not a trivial task, especially if strategic initiatives and decision-making powers have long been concentrated at headquarters. Often the most effective means of giving strategic access and influence to national units is to create entirely new channels and forums. This approach permits roles, responsibilities, and relationships to

FIGURE 4.1

A Three-Factor Contingency Model of Subsidiary Strategies

Parental Global Strategy

Subsidiary Resources		Partner	Contributor
	Many	Partner	Contributor
	Few	Specialist	Satellite
		Accommodating	Constrained

Local Environment

Parental Multidomestic Strategy

Subsidiary Resources		Independent	Interdependent
	Many	Independent	Interdependent
	Few	Implementor	Isolate
		Accommodating	Constrained

Local Environment

be defined and developed with far less constraint than would result from modifying existing communication patterns or shifting responsibility boundaries.

When the roles of foreign subunits are differentiated and responsibility is more dispersed, headquarters executives must be prepared to deemphasize their control over strategic content and develop the ability to manage the dispersed strategic process. In addition, the head office should adopt a flexible administrative stance that allows it to differentiate the way it manages each subsidiary and business within each unit.

Bartlett and Ghoshal (1989) have linked managerial approaches with different strategic roles of subsidiaries. In subunits with lead roles, the head office must ensure that developing business strategies fit the MNE's overall goals and priorities. Corporate management's major function is to support those with strategic leadership responsibility by giving them the resources and freedom needed for the innovative, entrepreneurial role they have been asked to play. Second, if the unit is placed in a contributory role, the head office should redirect local resources to programs outside the unit's control. In so doing, it must counter the natural hierarchy of loyalties that puts local interests above global ones. Head administrators must be careful not to discourage local managers so much that they stop contributing or leave in frustration. Third, if a unit is in an implementor role, the head office maintains tighter control. Such a unit represents an opportunity to capture the benefits of scale and learning. Therefore, the head office stresses economy and sales efficiency. Communication of strategies developed elsewhere and control of routine tasks can be carried out through systems that allow headquarters to manage these units efficiently. Finally, if a unit acts as a black hole, corporate management must develop its resources and capabilities to make it more responsive to the local environment. Managers of these units depend heavily on head offices for help and support, creating an urgent need for intensive training and transfer of skills and resources.

Formulating the Right Strategies

Multidomestic Strategy

A multidomestic strategy is one in which strategic and operating decisions are decentralized to the strategic business unit (SBU) in each country in order to tailor products to the local market. A multidomestic strategy focuses on competition within each country. It assumes that the markets differ and therefore are segmented by national boundaries. In other words, consumer needs and desires, industry conditions (e.g., number and type of competitors), political and legal structures, and social norms vary by country. Multidomestic strategies allow for the customization of products to meet the specific needs and preferences of local customers. Therefore, they should be able to maximize competitive response to the idiosyncratic requirements of each market. However, multidomestic strategies do not allow for the achievement of economies of scale and thus can be costly. As a result, firms employing a multidomestic strategy decentralize strategic and operating decisions to the strategic business units operating in each country. The multidomestic strategy has been more prominent among European multinational firms because of the varieties of cultures and markets found in Europe.

Global Strategy

A global strategy assumes more standardization of products across country markets. As a result, the competitive strategy is centrally controlled by the home office. The SBUs operating in each country are assumed to be interdependent, and the home office attempts to achieve integration among these businesses. Therefore, a global strategy is one in which standardized products are offered internationally and the competitive strategy is dictated by the home office. A global strategy emphasizes economies of scale and offers great opportunities for utilizing innovations developed at the home office or in country in other markets. However, a global strategy often lacks responsiveness to local markets and is difficult to manage because of the need to coordinate strategies and operating decisions across national borders. Achieving efficient operations with a global strategy requires the sharing of resources and coordination and cooperation across national boundaries. The Japanese have often pursued this centralized strategy with success.

Transnational Strategy

A transnational strategy is a corporate strategy that seeks to achieve both global efficiency and local responsiveness. Realizing the diverse goals of the transnational strategy is difficult because one goal requires close global coordination and the other requires local flexibility. Thus, flexible coordination is required to implement the transnational strategy. It requires building a shared vision and individual commitment through an integrated network. In reality, it is difficult to achieve a pure transnational strategy because of conflicting goals between headquarters and business units.

MAINTAINING GLOBAL INTEGRATION

Integration Processes: Control, Coordination, and Orientation

In large, complex MNEs, the balancing process can be institutionalized through the structuring of relationships between headquarters and

The integration of various subunits in foreign countries in a
[re]lies mainly on the manipulation of three processes of con-
[trol, coordina]tion, and orientation. Control is seen as the process that
[ensures a]dherence to a goal through the exercise of power or authority. Coordination is seen as more of an enabling process that provides the
appropriate linkage between different task units within the organization.
Coordination is associated with integrating activities dispersed across
subsidiaries.

Control is a more direct intervention into the operations of subsidiaries. It can be very specific and short term. It has a tendency to be
more costly because it requires direct forms of communication. For
instance, to agree upon a budget generally necessitates a great deal of
communication and expense. Coordination is distinguished not by direct
intervention but by situating the subsidiary in a network of responsibilities. The coordination pattern can be imposed, but the resulting
responsibilities are rooted in coordination. Coordination is generally
less costly because communications are minimal and routine. Compared
to control, coordination is less direct, less costly, and has a longer time
span.

MNE headquarters are often unable to use centralized decision-making processes to maintain global control for several reasons. First, the
diversity of countries in which the firm operates, the differences in the
extent of integration across functions, and the firm's evolving product
diversification make a centralized way of managing trade-offs between
responsiveness and integration impractical for large, complex MNEs. Second, maintaining the proper I-R balance is an ongoing process that
requires occasional reassessment. Last, there may be no single vantage
point within the firm from which to consider all its needs. The perceived
needs for responsiveness and integration are likely to come from different
parts of the organization in distant geographical locations. Closeness to
market conditions and the host country government and awareness of the
importance of success at the local level make subsidiary managers sensitive to needs for responsiveness. In contrast, perceiving needs for integration usually requires a multinational view of the business and its markets, technologies, and competitors. Such a view usually comes from
headquarters executives.

Coordination's contribution to integration has two dimensions:
breadth and diversity. Breadth of coordination refers to the number of
other units with which a subsidiary coordinates. The more extensive the
network of reciprocal obligations, the greater will be the burden of coordination and the more integrated the subsidiary. It will also have less
room for independent maneuvering. Similarly, if the subsidiary coordinates a number of different functions with the other units, it will be more
enmeshed in the network than if coordination were confined to a single

function. The breadth of coordination (the number of units in the coordination network) and the diversity of coordination (the number of functions coordinated) are both important aspects of the degree to which a
subsidiary is integrated into the MNE network.

The process of coordination requires mechanisms that can be divided
roughly into two groups: formal and informal or subtle. The formal
group contains five mechanisms including centralization, formalization,
planning, output control, and behavioral control. Centralization is the
extent to which the locus of decision making lies in the higher levels of
the chain of command. Formalization is the extent to which policies,
rules, job descriptions, and the like are written down in manuals and
other documents, generally leading to the establishment of standard routines. Planning refers to systems and processes like strategic planning,
budgeting, scheduling, and goal setting. Output and behavioral controls
are two independent forms of exercising control in organizations. Output
control is based on the evaluation of performance. In contrast, behavioral control is based on direct, personal surveillance of individual behavior.

The subtle group includes three kinds of managerial mechanisms,
namely lateral relations, informal communication, and organizational culture. Lateral relations cut across the vertical structure and include direct
contact between managers of different departments that share a problem,
task force, team, integrating role, and so forth. Informal communication
supplements formal communication by means of a network of informal,
personal contacts among managers across different units of the company:
corporate meetings, management trips, personal visits, transfers, and the
like. Informal communication differs from lateral relations in that it is not
structured around specific tasks, thus being even more indirect as a
means of coordination. Finally, organizational culture can be developed
through a process of socialization of individuals by communicating ways
of doing things, decision-making styles, and the objectives and values of
the company. Thus, a system of ideology is internalized by executives,
generating identification with and loyalty to the organization. This
process is performed by training corporate and subsidiary managers,
transferring them to different units, managing their career paths, and
evaluating and rewarding them appropriately.

Porter (1986) links network coordination with activity configuration.
Faced with an industrial structure, each firm has to devise a strategy
along two key dimensions: the configuration of activities in the firm's
value chain (i.e., where they are carried out), and the coordination of
those activities (i.e., how interdependent the different subsidiaries really
are). When international activities are geographically dispersed, high
coordination is needed if FDI is heavy. When international activities are
geographically concentrated and coordination of activities is high, it is

called a simple global strategy. When activities are geographically concentrated but coordination is low, it is then referred to as an export-based strategy.

Multinational corporations are increasingly using strategic orientation in lieu of conventional controls to monitor the operation of foreign subsidiaries. Strategic orientation is an efficient mid-range instrument linking global integration with local responsiveness. Compared to control and coordination, strategic orientation arrangement is least direct, least costly, and has the longest or most sustained effect. The global strategy literature asserts that the alignment of an overseas subsidiary with its environment is critical for international expansion because competition in the global marketplace occurs at the business unit level. There is a linkage between a firm's strategic profile and its external context, and this linkage has significant implications for international performance in an uncertain context.

When confronting a heterogeneous-to-home external environment and a complex interorganizational structure, an MNE subsidiary needs a pre-formulated strategic posture that governs and facilitates its role accomplishment. According to the neo-contingency framework, this necessity seems reinforced when a subsidiary operates in a complex and dynamic environment because its strategic choice determines its exposure to uncertain environmental components that impact firm performance.

The strategic context of MNE subsidiaries within a diversified MNE network is substantially influenced by the role and corresponding orientation the business is intended to play in the corporate portfolio. A foreign subsidiary can be a prospector, analyzer, or defender. A prospector subsidiary concentrates on scanning, identifying, and capitalizing on emerging market opportunities beyond the MNE network and maintains and bears the costs and risks inherent in maintaining extensive capabilities for responding to market and contextual changes in the host setting. In contrast, a defensive subsidiary is rigid, shortsighted, nonadaptive, and risk-averse. It deliberately reduces innovative and adaptive costs and risks by selecting a stable, narrowly defined product or market domain or by merely exploiting internalization benefits within an MNE network. As a hybrid orientation between proactiveness and defensiveness, the analysis strategy seeks both risk-adjusted efficiency and emerging market opportunities. A foreign business with this orientation defends existing product markets through efficiency-oriented strategies while cautiously penetrating new markets through intensified product or market innovation. From the ecological perspective, a subsidiary's orientation must be capable of accommodating both variability in its task and institutional environments and internal differentiation.

The impact of a host country's task and institutional environments on subsidiarys' decision-making characteristics and organizational behavior is fairly vigorous and direct. In the task environment, customers, suppliers, and competitors all shape competition in the industry and influence the input and output dimensions of local operation. In the institutional environment, regulatory, sociocultural, economic, technological, and international sectors all potentially affect the survival and growth of MNE subsidiaries in a given country. The above sectors represent a societal profile of a host country that has an ongoing influence on the operation and management of MNE subsidiaries.

The alignment of a subsidiary's strategic orientation to its uncertain host environment is of paramount importance for business performance. A good coupling between strategic orientation and the local environment can facilitate the exploitation of firm-specific competitive advantages and host country-specific comparative advantages. When managerial discretion is constrained in a complex, dynamic setting, the environment-strategy fit significantly affects financial and market performance. A foreign subsidiary's survival and expansion in a local economy depend on its ability to understand the environment and react in time to permit necessary organizational adjustments. From the neo-contingency perspective, a good fit between strategic orientation and environment conditions in a turbulent context can enable an MNE subsidiary to maximize economic rents from the interface between the societal effect and the organizational effect. A pre-arranged strategic orientation that is appropriate for both internal arrangements and external alignment can boost subsidiary incentives, reduce vulnerability to contextual changes, and spur the accomplishment of goals set for FDI.

Integration and Control Systems: Output, Bureaucratic, and Cultural

To maintain global integration, parental managers exercise different control systems as reflected by the influence they exert and the resources they commit to monitoring specific activities in foreign markets.

Put simply, output control concerns the measurement of outcomes. To apply output controls, an MNE estimates or sets appropriate targets or outcome indicators for its subunits abroad and then monitors their performance relative to these targets. Often the MNE's reward system is associated with performance, so that output control also provides an incentive structure for motivating overseas managers. In general, output controls require very little managerial direction and intervention, and hence are less likely to result in attempts to influence how individual activities are performed. Therefore, the relative amount of influence headquarters managers exert over how individual tasks are performed in the foreign market reflects a managerial control over monitoring outputs.

In contrast to output control, process control theoretically requires direct personal surveillance and high levels of management direction and intervention. To provide this, managers need to be involved in what and how activities are being carried out. Process control requires central managers to spend more time and effort monitoring foreign activities. Practically, such personal surveillance and direct intervention is neither appropriate nor realistic for global integration and control in large, complex multinational corporations. Instead, MNEs more often use bureaucratic and cultural control mechanisms to monitor and evaluate the performance of their subunits abroad.

Bureaucratic control is extensively employed by MNEs. It consists of a limited and explicit set of codified rules and regulations that delineate desired performance in terms of output or behavior. For individuals to become functional members of a bureaucratic organization, they must accept the legitimacy of organizational authority and its rules and regulations so that they can follow them. The authority and power exercised in this system is through control over resources. That is, it is of the remunerative type, and personal involvement is relatively limited.

A bureaucratic control system has several implications for the selection, training, and monitoring of organizational members. People must be found who have the required technical skills or are trainable, who will accept organizational authority, and who can learn to perform in accordance with the organization's rules and regulations. The selection and training process is relatively straightforward because rules and regulations are explicit and written down. In addition, new members must learn whatever technical competence is required of their position. Monitoring in a bureaucratic system involves comparing an individual's behavior and output to the standards set forth in the rules and applying the rewards or sanctions prescribed therein.

Organizational culture is often defined as a pattern of beliefs and expectations shared by the organization's members. It generates a system of symbols, language, ideology, rituals, images, and myths that shapes the behavior of individuals and groups in the organization. In a culturally controlled organization, there exists an inferred organizational code or game, which is an important guide to behavior in addition to explicit rules. This view of corporate culture as an adaptive and regulatory mechanism has been further identified in recent reviews of organizational theory literature.

A number of organizational practices facilitate the existence of a cultural control system. Most important are long-term employment guarantees, consensual decision making, and nonspecialized career paths. The consensual decision-making process forces interaction around organizational issues among organizational members. This interaction is one of the ways in which, through a process of repeated interactions over time, cultural values become systematized and shared. In addition, the fact that career paths in a culturally controlled organization are less than totally specialized means that people are rotated through the various functional areas of the organization, thus contributing to a greater organization-wide culture. A less than total commitment to a functional specialty on the part of organizational members reduces competition from outside professional groups for member loyalty, thus enhancing the potential strength of the corporate culture.

The use of a cultural control system has several implications for the selection, training, and monitoring of organizational members. Members of an organization with cultural control mechanisms must be integrated into the organizational culture to become functional members. Therefore, selection of members is of prime importance. In addition to having the requisite skills necessary for the job, a candidate for organizational membership must be sympathetic to the organizational culture and must be willing to learn and accept its norms, values, and behavioral prescriptions. Thus, the initial zone of indifference required of new members is fairly broad and specific.

Compared to bureaucratic controls, training and socialization in a cultural control system are also more important. An organizational member must not only learn a set of explicit, codified rules and regulations but must also learn to become a part of a subtle, complex control system that consists of a broad range of pivotal values. Training and socialization can be quite intense and extensive. The degree of socialization required is reduced if the broader societal culture approximates that of the organization.

Monitoring a pure cultural control system occurs through interpersonal interactions. All members of the culture are familiar with and share its expectations. Performance and compliance with the culture are observed during the course of interpersonal interactions. Feedback, often subtle, is given on a person-to-person basis. In addition, a culture is a very rich, broad guide to behavior; an individual and the people around him or her will always have an implicit sense of his or her performance in the context of that culture.

Integration Tools and Means

Delegating decision making to subsidiary managers abroad or product executives at headquarters without structuring its processes and rules will reduce the effectiveness and efficiency of international expansion. Tools that can be used to maintain global integration include data management and information systems, managerial mechanisms and human resource administration, conflict resolution methods, communication intensity, socialization practices, expatriate dispatching, entry mode selection and sharing arrangements, and global business structures.

Data management tools can be used to control the kinds of information gathered systematically by members of the organization; how such information is aggregated, analyzed, and given a meaning; how, in which form, and to whom it circulates; and how it is used in major decisions (Doz & Prahalad, 1984). Information systems have to have a dual focus. Accounting and strategic data must be aggregated both for analytical purposes and to support integration (a portfolio of countries within a business) and responsiveness (a portfolio of businesses within a country). Furthermore, the assumptions underlying how information is obtained, aggregated, structured, and presented must be understood and agreed upon, so that differences between cognitive maps reflect the actual ambiguity of choices, not fuzziness in the information. Information transparency also forces differences to be resolved on the basis of improved problem definition rather than smoothed over or decided on the basis of leadership skills, intellectual acumen, personal savvy, or hierarchical position. The flow of information can also be structured with sufficient asymmetry that individual managers will be encouraged to identify strongly either with responsive or integrative strategies while others will develop more balanced perspectives.

Management tools can be used to set norms and standards of behavior as well as personal objectives that are consistent with a desired strategic direction. Such tools work both directly (through their actual impact on managers) and indirectly (through the precedents they set and the meanings they assign to specific situations and choices). Selecting key managers, for instance, has both direct consequences on responsibility and power and indirect ones via signals sent to other members of the organization. Management tools also include more usual human resource management components, such as shaping careers, reward and punishment systems, and management development. Less formal tools can also help develop norms, standards, and personal objectives. Patterns of interaction between managers can be influenced by the nature of meetings, the way in which top managers spend their time and encourage or discourage dissent, the respect shown for analysis, and so on. Measurement systems can be used to orient managerial attention toward specific priorities, as can career paths and evaluation and reward criteria. Management tools, therefore, also ensure that relevant differentiated information will be brought to bear on decisions. Such tools help create an internal advocacy process that reflects the conflicting external needs for responsiveness and integration. Resource allocation procedures may also help ensure that checks and balances are introduced before resources are appropriated.

Several managerial mechanisms can be used integrally. Planning processes can catalyze the process of strategic convergence and consensus building among executives whose initial perceptions and priorities may differ widely. By imposing a framework creating multiple steps in making decisions, time horizons, and deadlines, these processes create some pressure and the necessary channels for convergence to take place. Specific conflict resolution tools can also be linked to the planning process. Management tools may create a climate where managers will be encouraged to interact and will be motivated to undertake successful lateral relationships. Rewards may be based more on participation and contribution than on individual results. Managerial development activities may emphasize a corporate-wide perspective and flexible attitudes. Career paths may create alternations between geographic and product-oriented responsibilities for individual managers so that they develop an empathy for both responsiveness and integration priorities.

The alignment of relative power with decision outcomes can also be performed through using multiple mechanisms. Observation shows that key managerial appointments, reward systems, apparent career tracks, and the interpretations these are given by other managers all play a central role in the allocation of power. Information and resource dependence are other well-known sources of power. The configuration of such tools as information systems and resource allocation procedures are also critical to the management of relative power.

Conflict resolution tools provide the needed channels for confronting perceived needs for integration and responsiveness. They provide the actual structure through which information is applied and behavior takes place. Beyond the more formal aspects (e.g., planning procedures), they structure how key processes actually work. Among such tools figure the creation of specialized coordinator roles, the clear assignment of responsibilities in the decision processes, and the provision of specific channels for preparing decisions, such as committees, task forces, study groups, and business teams.

Intensity of communication may be employed to balance I-R relations. The intensity of communication between a focal subsidiary and the rest of the corporation can be treated as a positive function of the frequency, informality, openness, and density of communications between the subsidiary, the other units, and the head office (Gupta & Govindarajan, 1991). Highly frequent inter-unit communications help facilitate the diffusion of innovations across multinational subsidiaries. More intense communication patterns create higher information-processing capacity; these patterns become especially desirable in contexts where such capacities are necessary. Openness in the parent-subsidiary relationship is even more beneficial in subunits that use differentiation strategies rather than harvest or cost-leadership business strategies. Effectiveness at adapting to environmental uncertainty requires unstructured decision-making processes involving highly open communication patterns. Overall, frequency, informality, openness, and density of communication between a focal subsidiary and the rest of the corporation should be higher for those subunits that play a greater part in global integration.

Corporate socialization of subsidiary managers can be applied as an effective tool for global integration. This is defined as the processes through which subsidiary managers' values and norms become aligned with those of the parent corporation. Socialization of managers can be a powerful mechanism for building identification with and commitment to the organization as a whole, as distinct from the immediate subunit in which the manager is operating. Some of the key processes through which such socialization occurs are job rotation across foreign subsidiaries and management development programs involving participants from several subunits. Global corporate socialization of a subsidiary's top management team should vary across subsidiary strategic roles. Using Gupta and Govindarajan's (1991) scheme, socialization should be high for integrated players, medium for global innovators and implementors, and low for local innovators.

Dispatching expatriates to foreign subsidiaries and manipulating the ratio of expatriates in the top management team of subsidiaries are also important for maintaining global integration. Host country nationals are generally more familiar with the local environment, develop stronger rapport with local managers, and have a stronger identification with and commitment to the local subsidiary than to the parent MNE. Cognitively, host country nationals are likely to have a more nearly comprehensive understanding of the local sociocultural, political, and economic environments. By contrast, expatriate managers are likely to have a more nearly comprehensive understanding of the MNE's overall global strategy. Motivationally, the local commitment of host country nationals results from the fact that, in most cases, their career progression outside of the local subsidiary and into the hierarchy of the parent corporation tends to be rare. Expatriate managers do not operate under such a constraint. Therefore, the ratio of expatriates as a percentage of the top management team should be higher for those subsidiaries that play a bigger role in the MNE's global integration.

Entry mode selection is a fundamental investment strategy that affects the MNE's ability to control local operations and integrate these businesses into its global network during subsequent operational stages. Other things being equal, the umbrella investment, wholly owned subsidiary, and dominant joint venture modes enable the MNE to maintain greater control and integration than minority joint venture or other cooperative arrangements in which the MNE is a minority owner. Among other entry modes, franchising and build-operate-transfer modes enable the MNE to control foreign operations more closely than in licensing and leasing. Therefore, MNEs should align their entry mode selection with their needs for organizational control and global integration. In joint ventures, the equity distribution between partners can make substantial differences in control and integration. Majority equity ownership helps the MNE not only protect its proprietary knowledge and control joint venture activities but also mitigate the partner firm's possible opportunism while strategically orienting the joint venture to comply with the MNE's global mission.

A company embarks on a global strategy when it starts to locate manufacturing and other value-creation activities in the lowest-cost global location to increase efficiency, quality, and innovation. In seeking to obtain gains from global learning, a company must cope with greater coordination and integration problems. It has to find a structure that can coordinate resource transfers between corporate headquarters and foreign divisions while providing the centralized control that a global strategy requires. The answer for many companies is a global product group structure.

In this structure, a product group headquarters (similar to an SBU headquarters) is created to coordinate the activities of the domestic and foreign divisions within the product group. Product group managers in the home country are responsible for organizing all aspects of value creation on a global basis. The product group structure allows managers to decide how best to pursue a global strategy. For example, they decide which value-creation activities, such as manufacturing or product design, should be performed in which country to increase efficiency. Increasingly, U.S. and Japanese companies are moving manufacturing to low-cost countries like China but establishing product design centers in Europe or the United States to take advantage of foreign skills and capabilities.

The main failing of the global product group structure is that although it allows a company to achieve superior efficiency and quality, it is weak when it comes to customer responsiveness because the focus is still on centralized control. Moreover, this structure makes it difficult for the different product groups to trade information and knowledge and thus obtain the benefits of cooperation. Sometimes the potential gains from sharing products, marketing, or R&D knowledge between product groups are very high, but because a company lacks a structure that can coordinate the group's activities, these gains cannot be achieved.

Recently more companies are adopting global matrix structures that let them simultaneously reduce costs by increasing efficiency and differentiate their activities through superior innovation and customer responsiveness. On the vertical axis, instead of functions are product groups that provide specialist services, such as R&D, product design, and marketing information to foreign divisions or SBUs. For example, they might be petroleum, plastics, drug, or fertilizer product groups. On the horizontal axis are the company's foreign divisions or SBUs, in the various countries or world regions in which they operate. Managers in the subsidiaries control foreign operations and report back to divisional personnel. They are also responsible, together with divisional personnel, for developing control and reward systems that promote the sharing of marketing or R&D information to achieve gains from synergies.

This structure both provides a great deal of local flexibility and gives divisional personnel at headquarters considerable access to information about local affairs. Additionally, the matrix form allows knowledge and experience to be transferred among geographic regions and divisions. Because it offers many opportunities for face-to-face contact between domestic and foreign managers, the matrix structure facilitates the transmission of company norms and values and hence the development of a global corporate culture. This is especially important for an international company, where lines of communication are longer and information is subject to distortion.

Intellectual Assets Control

As technological skills become increasingly critical in international expansion, proprietary knowledge protection constitutes an important part of global integration and control. In recent years the problems of counterfeiting, piracy, and security are growing around the world. Counterfeiting costs U.S. businesses about $300 billion a year. It takes the incentive away from innovators or entrepreneurs because anything they create could be compromised.

Copyright Protection

Copyright protection lasts substantially longer than patent protection. In the United States, the copyright term is the lifetime of the author plus 50 years. For an institutional creation, the protection lasts for 75 years from the date of publication or 100 years from creation, depending on when it is published. Copyright deals with expressions, not ideas. The idea for the layout of an accounting spreadsheet computer program, for example, is in all likelihood not copyrightable. Provisions in the copyright law limit the ability to claim copyright over a generally accepted or sole method of achieving an end. A spreadsheet would not be copyrightable because it is a basic accounting method. Moreover, copyright law only prohibits copying. In other words, if one's work is copyrightable and someone else develops the same thing independently, one does not have a claim against them. This makes copyrights susceptible to reverse engineering. Last, copyright laws include exceptions for methods of operation and procedures. This can be a problem for the software developer because, if taken literally, virtually any computer program can be defined as a method of operation.

Patent Protection

Patents have substantially shorter terms than copyrights. The term of a patent in the United States, for example, is 20 years from the date of the filing of the application. However, with that shorter life comes substantially stronger protection. For instance, even if a company independently develops an existing program it would be considered a patent infringement. However, a patent's protection is limited to the specific claims stated within the patent, making it possible to develop a competing program around those claims.

Trade Secret Protection

In theory, trade secrets, typically know-how, can last forever. Trade secret law extends to almost anything that a firm keeps confidential to give it a competitive advantage. For example, the courts in the United States have generally held that computer software programs can be protected as a trade secret even when the software is sold to the public. Trade secrets can be protected in several ways.

First, the design, development, manufacture, and service of a product manufactured by an alliance may be structured so as to wall off the most sensitive technologies and prevent their leakage to other participants. For example, in the alliance between GE and Snecma to build commercial aircraft engines, GE tried to reduce the risk of excess transfer by walling off certain sections of the production process. This modularization effectively cut off the transfer of what GE felt was key competitive technology, while permitting Snecma access to final assembly. Similarly, in the alliance between Boeing and the Japanese to build the 767, Boeing walled off research, design, and marketing functions, considered more central to Boeing's competitive position, while allowing the Japanese to share in production technology. Boeing also walled off technologies not required for 767 production.

Second, contractual safeguards can be written into an alliance agreement. For example, TRW has three strategic alliances with large Japanese auto component suppliers to produce seat belts, engine valves, and steering gears for sale to Japanese-owned auto assembly plants in the United States. TRW has clauses in each of its alliance contracts that bar the Japanese companies from competing by introducing component parts. These protect TRW against the possibility that the Japanese companies are entering into the alliances to gain access to TRW's home market and become its competitor.

Third, both parties to an alliance can agree in advance to exchange skills and technologies that each wants from the other, thereby ensuring a chance for equitable gain. Cross-licensing agreements are one way of achieving this goal. For example, in the alliance between Motorola and Toshiba, Motorola has licensed some of its microprocessor technology to Toshiba, and in return Toshiba has licensed some of its memory chip technology to Motorola.

Fourth, the risk of opportunism by an alliance partner can be decreased if the company extracts in advance a significant credible commitment from its partner. This makes it less likely that the alliance would end with the company giving away too much and receiving too little. The long-term alliance between Xerox and Fuji to build photocopiers to supply the Asian market illustrates such a commitment. Xerox insisted that Fuji invest in a 50/50 joint venture to serve Japan and East Asia. This venture consisted of such a significant investment in people, equipment, and facilities that Fuji was from the outset committed to making the alliance work in order to earn a return on that investment.

Appropriate Control Mechanisms for Transferring Knowledge

The transfer of knowledge within a joint venture requires control mechanisms suited to the characteristics of the particular type of knowledge each partner seeks. Control categories range from highly formal to highly informal (Martinez & Jarillo, 1989). The range of controls within a given category can be extensive as well as specific to a given organization. In general, the more predictable, regular, and explicit the information to be transferred, the more formal and structural the relevant controls are likely to be. In contrast, the more uncertain, ambiguous, and organizationally embedded the information, the more informal the controls will be.

There are many other ways of controlling intellectual assets. Legal contractual arrangements are most appropriate when the information to be transferred is precise. They allow for clearly specified outcomes and sanctions. Structural grouping and departmentalization are relevant when information needs to be aggregated into a coherent body and routed in predictable ways for learning to occur. Here as well, performance outcomes for the group are clearly specified. Formal authority relationships have a similar function yet differ from the preceding two controls in their ability to handle greater ambiguity of information and less certain outcomes. When an overall guiding framework is necessary for transferring pertinent information, standardized procedures and rules (including codes of conduct, written policies, and job descriptions) will be employed. In this case, outcomes are ensured through a preestablished pattern by which information is processed. Although there is little need to continually revisit this information, its alteration is not difficult. Planning and budgeting mechanisms also provide a guiding framework but allow for much greater flexibility in the treatment of relevant information. Supervision and performance evaluation are important for facilitating learning that requires significant monitoring, guidance, and feedback. The sharing of information here takes place in a directed fashion, yet there is still less standardization of the manner in which these processes are utilized.

Terms and task forces are appropriate when the learning process requires the pooling of multiple or diverse sources of information for creative problem solving. Such mechanisms are suitable for handling more embedded, subtle information. The emphasis here is more on processes, yet outcome expectations still govern the behavior of parties involved. When the learning process is even less amenable to the imposition of a structure, meetings and organized personal contacts may be used. These approaches are more informal than the preceding ones in that their duration is much more limited and idiosyncratic and information flows and outcomes cannot be completely specified. Transfer of managers and lateral movements within the organization involve even more nonsystematic learning, allowing the sharing of information or capabilities not otherwise possible across divisions. Finally, when the learning process requires challenging and modifying current assumptions and theories-in-use so that congruence in norms, values, and beliefs can be achieved, the last two categories of control are appropriate. Both rituals, traditions, and ceremonies and networking and other socialization processes substantially affect the process by which learning occurs rather than its outcome. Of these two categories of controls, the first is somewhat more organized and amenable to manipulation than the second. The second set pertains to the broader organizational climate that allows or encourages certain learning behavior outside of organized or articulated rituals and ceremonies while discouraging other such behavior

REFERENCES

Bartlett, C. A. and S. Ghoshal. 1989. *Managing across borders*. Boston, MA: Harvard Business School Press.

Birkinshaw, J., A. Morrison, and J. Hulland. 1995. Structural and competitive determinants of a global integration strategy. *Strategic Management Journal*, 16: 637–655.

Doz, Y. and C. K. Prahalad. 1984. Patterns of strategic control within multinational corporations. *Journal of International Business Studies*, Fall: 55–72.

Gupta, A. K. and V. Govindarajan. 1991. Knowledge flows and the structure of control within multinational corporations. *Academy of Management Review*, 16(4): 768–792.

Hoffman, R. C. 1994. Generic strategies for subsidiaries in multinational corporations. *Journal of Managerial Issues*, 6: 69–87.

Jarillo, J. C. and J. I. Martinez. 1990. Different roles for subsidiaries: The case of multinational corporations in Spain. *Strategic Management Journal*, 11(7): 501–512.

Kogut, B. 1985. Designing global strategies: Profiting from operational flexibility. *Sloan Management Review*, Fall: 27–38.

Kogut, B. 1994. Options thinking and platform investments: Investing in opportunity. *California Management Review*, Winter: 52–71.

Kogut, B. 1990. Joint ventures and the option to expand and acquire. *Management Science*, 37(1): 19–33.

Marcati, A. 1989. Configuration and coordination: The role of U.S. subsidiaries in the international network of Italian multinationals. *Management International Review*, 29(3): 35–50.

Martinez, J. I. and J. C. Jarillo. 1989. The evolution of research on coordination mechanisms in multinational corporations. *Journal of International Business Studies*, 20(3): 489–514.

Morrison, A. D. and K. Roth. 1992. A taxonomy of business-level strategies in global industries. *Strategic Management Journal*, 13(6): 399–417.

Porter, M. E. 1986. Competition in global industries: A conceptual framework. In M. E. Porter (Ed.), *Competition in global industries*, pp. 15–60. Boston, MA: Harvard Business School Press.

Poynter, T. A. and R. E. White. 1985. The strategies of foreign subsidiaries: Responses to organizational slack. *International Studies of Management and Organization*, 14(4): 91–106.

Prahalad, C. K. and Y. Doz. 1987. *The multinational mission: Balancing local demands and global vision*. New York: Free Press.

Roth, K. and A. J. Morrison. 1992. Implementing global strategy: Characteristics of global subsidiary mandates. *Journal of International Business Studies*, 23(4): 715–736.

Yip, G. S. 1995. *Total global strategy*. Englewood Cliffs, NJ: Prentice Hall.

FURTHER READINGS

Baliga, B. R. and A. M. Jaeger. 1984. Multinational corporations: Control systems and delegation issues. *Journal of International Business Studies*, Fall: 25–40.

Cray, D. 1984. Control and coordination in multinational corporations. *Journal of International Business Studies*, Fall: 85–98.

Doz, Y. and C. K. Prahalad. 1991. Managing MNCs: A search for a new paradigm. *Strategic Management Journal*, 12: 145–164.

Doz, Y. and C. K. Prahalad. 1981. Headquarters influence and strategic control in multinational companies. *Sloan Management Review*, 22(4): 15–29.

Gencturk, E. F. and P. S. Aulakh. 1995. The use of process and output controls in foreign markets. *Journal of International Business Studies*, 26(4): 755–786.

Golden, B. R. 1992. SBU strategy and performance: The moderating effects of the corporate-SBU relationship. *Strategic Management Journal*, 13: 145–158.

Guisinger, S. 1985. *Investment incentives and performance requirements*. New York: Praeger.

Gupta, A. K. 1987. SBU strategies, corporate-SBU relations, and SBU effectiveness in strategy implementation. *Academy of Management Journal*, 30(3): 477–500.

Johnson, J. H., Jr. 1995. An empirical analysis of the integration-responsiveness framework: U.S. construction equipment industry firms in global competition. *Journal of International Business Studies*, 26(3): 621–635.

Kobrin, S. J. 1991. An empirical analysis of the determinants of global integration. *Strategic Management Journal*, 12(Summer): 17–32.

Kogut, B. 1985a. Designing global strategies: Comparative and competitive value-added chains. *Sloan Management Review*, Summer: 15–27.

Nadler, D. A. and M. L. Tushmean. 1987. *Strategic organization design*. Glenview, IL: Scott, Foresman.

Roth, K. and A. J. Morrison. 1991. An empirical analysis of the integration-responsiveness framework in global industries. *Journal of International Business Studies*, 21(4): 541–564.

Roth, K., D. Schweiger, and A. J. Morrison. 1991. Global strategy implementation at the business unit level: Operational capabilities and administrative mechanisms. *Journal of International Business Studies*, 22(3): 369–402.

II

ENTRY STRATEGIES

5

Location Selection

Location selection for foreign direct investment (FDI) projects is critical because it affects both the efficiency and effectiveness of investment. Cultural distance, business atmosphere, government policies, foreign business treatment, stage of economic development, and degree of openness, among other factors, vary substantially across different countries and even different regions within a country. This chapter aims to shed some light on how multinational enterprises (MNEs) should opt for an ideal foreign country (national selection) and an appropriate region within a target country (sub-national selection). This chapter first introduces the conceptual background on location selection in international expansion. This is followed by a concrete description and reiteration of an array of locational determinants, which are grouped into cost-tax factors, demand factors, strategic factors, macroeconomic factors, and sociopolitical factors. The last section provides international managers with an integrated framework for selecting country and region.

CONCEPTUAL BACKGROUND

Locational advantages are fundamental to trade theory and every model of international economic activity. Vernon's locational theory (1966) treated trade and FDI as part of the same process of exploiting foreign markets and from this standpoint examined the international locations of corporations. In his theory Vernon suggests that location selection is a dyadic integration of product life cycle and locational characteristics.

For new products, locational factors, such as market demand, communication and external economies, and flexibility of production, are critical to market formation and development. For standardized products, the costs of various production factors become more important to market extension and penetration. According to Vernon, FDI projects for new products should be located in developed countries whereas standardized products should be located in developing nations.

International trade theory forms the underpinnings of the eclectic paradigm's explanation of locational advantages, or the where of economic activity. Advantages are postulated as specific to a geographical region, typically a country, and central to the nature of economic activity in that region. Location specific advantages may be natural or created resource endowments and include such things as economic systems, factor prices and endowments (labor, raw materials), and investment incentives (Dunning, 1988). The eclectic paradigm (Dunning, 1980, 1988, 1993) highlights the role locational factors play both as FDI pull factors (i.e., from the country of destination) and push factors (i.e., from the country of origin) when MNEs decide to expand beyond their national borders.

The economic perspective of MNE theory predicts that a company investing in production facilities will choose the location that minimizes total costs, given demand in local markets. Labor cost differentials, transportation costs, the existence of tariff and non-tariff barriers, as well as government policies (e.g., taxes affecting the investment climate) are generally held to be important determinants of location choice. Aliber (1970) also takes into account the size of foreign markets and the costs of doing business abroad. Hirsch (1976) includes the costs of controlling foreign operations. Such costs are likely to be less in familiar markets, that is, markets that are culturally similar to the home country or markets with which the company has previous experience.

In the international economic model, location selection is determined by the target country's comparative advantages or factor proportions (the Heckscher-Ohlin-Vanek hypothesis). This view sees FDI as an international transfer of certain specific and mobile factors of production to locations where the local costs of immobile production factors (natural resources, labor, human capital, machinery, and plants) are most advantageous. Profit maximizing firms choosing to exploit these specific advantages must select a cost minimizing location. Where the final product is perfectly traded, one would expect the location of FDI to be related to factor endowments and comparative advantages.

However, the existence of non-tradable goods and impediments to trade introduces other elements into the location decision. These barriers will cause the actual location of FDI to diverge from that which factor costs alone would suggest. Thus, a modified view of the international economic model is that FDI arises when trade in goods according to

Heckscher-Ohlin-Vanek principles is impeded or prevented. This impediment produces a difference in relative factor prices, which induces a flow
of capital to the economy with a higher relative return on capital. This
perspective corroborates the wisdom of the FDI-MNE theory that market
structural imperfections across borders provide an incentive for MNEs to
locate production in local markets (Caves, 1982). Under these circumstances, MNEs can maximize profits by internalizing markets for relevant
intermediates and utilizing their monopolistic advantages (Dunning,
1980).

According to the macroeconomic model, trade balances and exchange
rates are quite responsive to changes in the relative attractiveness of locating production facilities or storing other taxable forms of wealth in different countries. Authorities can influence exchange rates in the very short
run by changing monetary conditions. In addition, there are at least three
channels through which fiscal policy changes may be transmitted to
exchange rates. One channel involves changes in the short-term composition of the demand for and suppliers of different goods as purchasing
power is shifted between public and private sectors when revenue-neu-
tral tax reforms change the incentives faced by consumers and producers.
A second transmission channel involves changes in the mid-term pattern
of private spending, often referred to as the crowding-out or crowding-in
effects, which are generally associated with changes in the market-clearing levels of interest rates. Third, taxation changes often provide incentives for changes in the location of physical capital and other taxable
forms of wealth. In general, factors that affect the desired levels of FDI in
different countries, other things being equal, create ex ante imbalances
between savings and investment, with consequent pressures on exchange
rates and other market-clearing prices.

Economic geography theorists state that firms in the same industry
may be drawn to the same location because proximity generates positive
externalities or agglomeration effects (Head, Ries, & Swenson, 1995). In
other words, industry-level agglomeration benefits play an important
role in location decisions. Under this view, host country government
inducements can have a lasting influence on the geographical pattern of
manufacturing. Local expansion of a sector sows the seeds for further
expansion by increasing the supply of the factors that made the location
attractive in the first place, rather than simply bidding up the price on a
given stock. Japanese MNEs generally do not simply mimic the geographical pattern of U.S. establishments in an industry. Instead, initial
investments by Japanese firms spur subsequent investors in the same
industry to select the same states. At the sub-national level, inter-state differences in endowments of natural resources, labor, and infrastructure are
therefore not the sole factors explaining location decision.

Theoretical attempts to formalize agglomeration effects have focused on three mechanisms that yield positive feedback loops: inter-firm technological spillover, specialized labor, and intermediate inputs. First, useful technical information seems to flow between entrepreneurs, designers, and engineers in a variety of industries. A large part of the spillovers between foreign businesses may include the flow of location-specific, experience-based knowledge. Physical proximity may enhance knowledge flow by making casual communications less costly. Typical examples of this include the high-technology cluster in Silicon Valley and the high-fashion cluster in Milan. Second, a localized industry creates a pool for workers with specialized skills. It attracts workers because an increased number of firms reduces the likelihood that a worker will suffer a long bout of unemployment. This reduced risk will ultimately benefit the firms as well by increasing the supply of specialized labor and reducing the risk embodied in wages. In addition, workers in a given location will be more inclined to invest in industry-specific human capital if they feel confident of their ability to appropriate benefits. Last, the combination of economies of scale and moderate transportation costs will encourage the users and suppliers of intermediate inputs to cluster near each other. Such agglomerations reduce total transportation costs and generate large enough levels of demand to warrant the effort of producing highly specialized components. This attracts assemblers, which in turn encourages new arrivals and additional specialization.

Two opposing hypotheses about the essential character of MNEs have been offered to explain their decision making with respect to choosing locations for international production. The market scanning hypothesis holds that MNEs use superior knowledge to locate manufacturing activities in countries that are most advantageous from the standpoint of market opportunities and cost considerations. The other hypothesis views MNEs as market creators. MNEs are regarded as sheltered from competition and consequently so powerful and profitable that their strategies for dealing with taxes and other host government impositions tend to subordinate the economic factors (especially cost considerations) that ordinarily affect location choice. Resolving these apparent oppositions is best done empirically and within specific context. It is certain, however, that making a location decision in a host country is the result of the interaction of two sets of factors: external characteristics (e.g., country environment and market context) and internal characteristics (e.g., strategic goals and organizational competence).

Similarly, although the advantages or disadvantages of particular locations are treated separately from the ownership advantages of a particular MNE in the eclectic paradigm, the decision on where to situate a mine, factory, or office is neither independent of asset ownership nor the route by which their ownership rights are transacted. MNEs will engage in foreign production whenever they perceive it is in their best interests to combine spatially transferable intermediate products produced in the home country with at least some immobile factor endowments or inter-mediate products in another country (Dunning, 1980). The choice of loca-tion may be prompted by spatial market failure; historically the imposi-tion of trade barriers has led to a lot of foreign manufacturing investment by MNEs. At the same time a reduction in transport costs and the forma-tion of customs unions or regional trading blocs have prompted greater regional specialization of production.

According to Dunning (1988), there are two different kinds of market imperfections that may influence locational decisions. Structural market distortions arising from some kinds of government intervention may either encourage or discourage FDI. However, even without such distor-tions MNE activity will still occur wherever gains are likely to result from the common governance of activities in different locations. Such advan-tages include enhanced arbitrage and leverage opportunities, the reduc-tion of exchange risks, better coordination of financial decision making, protection afforded by a hedged marketing or multiple sourcing strategy, and gains through transfer price manipulation, leads and lags in pay-ments, and so on. The ability to sustain such ownership advantages strengthens the competitive position of MNEs vis-à-vis uni-national firms.

Location choice in international expansion may also be affected by the market orientation of an FDI project. Woodward and Rolfe (1993) argue that export-oriented FDI projects differ from local market-pursuing pro-jects in terms of critical factors underlying location selection because the market is external to the country of location for export projects. Clearly, production for an external export market can be located with little or no regard for domestic demand. In fact, many countries prohibit or limit the amount of production export-oriented investors can sell in the domestic market. Market-related variables, such as GNP growth and national income growth, have emerged as the dominant factors attracting local market-oriented FDI, whereas labor costs, infrastructure quality, import duties, and foreign exchange restrictions have a stronger influence on choosing location for export-oriented FDI. Political stability and govern-mental intervention may also have more of an impact on local market pro-jects than on those aimed at export.

Firm experience, both international and host-country specific, further influences project location. Initially culturally close markets are evaluated as likely locations, but as companies acquire more experience from oper-ating in foreign markets, more distant markets may be regarded as good potentials. As a result, a stepwise pattern of international location evolves for some MNEs. Firms in the initial stage of foreign expansion are expect-ed to exhibit a strong preference for near and similar cultures. Davidson

(1980) concluded that the presence of an existing subsidiary in a foreign market increases the firm's propensity to make subsequent investments in that market. Those in advanced stages of foreign operations will, therefore, exhibit little if any preference for near and similar cultures. The seminal work on the internationalization process by Johanson and Vahlne (1977) also holds that MNEs are assumed to enter foreign markets successfully at an increasing cultural distance from the home country, as measured by differences in language, values, political systems, and so on. Thus, firms are predicted to take steps by starting their internationalization in those markets they can most easily understand, then entering more distant markets only at later stages.

Mariotti and Piscitello (1995) suggest that foreign investors suffer from a condition of asymmetry in information costs incurred in forecasting or assessing locational determinants. They further classified these costs into location-specific observation costs, market and event observation costs, and communication, monitoring and control costs. Some kinds of information, especially regarding the cost and availability of traditional location factors (manpower, raw materials, market areas, and transport costs) can be acquired at nearly zero cost because extensive statistical data are available. However, high-cost information is needed to reduce uncertainty concerning the quality of available location factors, customer behavior in the local market, culture-specific business practices, institutional framework, and so on. The locational behavior of MNEs differs from that of local firms because of these higher information costs. The spatial distribution of inward FDI is governed by information costs. In a hostile and volatile environment, the importance of information costs in affecting location choice may even overwhelm that of production and transport costs. These latter costs have a greater influence on indigenous firms choosing locations for their plants. Information costs cause MNEs to prefer specific countries or regions within a country. This partially explains why MNEs tend to concentrate in more sociopolitically stable regions in a dynamic, complex country, even when these regions do not offer preferential treatments to FDIs.

Many governments at both the national and sub-national levels compete vigorously to attract FDI (i.e., location tournaments). From the perspective of the host country, many government planners believe that locational advantages, once gained, will be self-perpetuating. Arthur (1986) sheds some light on this issue by recalling the fundamental distinction between ergodic and non-ergodic systems. An ergodic system returns to its initial state when initial conditions are replicated. A non-ergodic system, by contrast, can exhibit strikingly different and irreversible responses to small changes in initial conditions. For location theorists, non-ergodicity resides in agglomerative economies; increasing benefits come from colocation by various economic units. A specific example is provided by regional groupings of specialized service suppliers. More suppliers (each providing a different service) create finer divisions of labor in intermediate input markets, thereby lowering unit costs for final producers. A firm's early decision to invest in a region can promote the creation of such specialized services, reinforcing the area's attractiveness for other MNEs. Arthur (1986) demonstrates that this factor can translate a minor regional advantage into a major concentration of industrial activity. Agglomerative economies can imply big rewards for the winner of a location tournament. The contrasting ergodic view, however, suggests that location patterns are essentially preordained by geographical endowments, relative prices, and transport costs. In an ergodic world, once the winner of a location tournament halts its subsidies, industrial location patterns will revert to a predetermined state.

LOCATIONAL DETERMINANTS

Previous Studies

The locational advantage is thought to be manifest in the financial performance of the subsidiary. In empirical examinations of locational advantages, factors, and decisions, the foreign investor is viewed as a profit maximizer in which a particular region (be it country, state, province, or rural or urban area) is selected if the region provides lower costs or higher revenues relative to other choices. Dunning (1993: 81) lists the following location-specific variables: spatial distribution of natural and created resource endowments and markets; input prices, quality, and productivity (e.g., labor, energy, materials, components, semifinished products); international transport and communication costs; investment incentives and disincentives; artificial barriers (e.g. import controls) to trade in goods and services; societal and infrastructure provisions (commercial, legal, educational, transport, and communications); cross-country ideological, language, cultural, business, or political differences; economies resulting from centralization of research and development (R&D), production, and marketing; and economic systems and governmental strategies (the institutional framework for resource allocation). The factors already examined in the literature include taxes and promotional incentives offered by national or local governments, the quality of local infrastructure, the quality and availability of local labor, local market characteristics, and agglomeration effects (Coughlin, Terza, & Arromdee, 1991; Culem, 1988; Friedman, Gerlowski, & Silberman, 1992; Hennart & Park, 1994; Yamawaki, Thiran, & Barbarito, 1996). Empirical work modeling the effects of these determinants has had much to say about why particular nations and regions within nations are chosen as sites for FDI.

At the national level, various determinants have been found to affect the distribution of FDI among countries. For instance, market size, market growth, and tariff barriers appeared to be important locational determinants of FDI within the European Economic Community (Culem, 1988). Similarly, large internal markets and high propensities to trade were positively associated with the location of FDI. At the sub-national level, market access factors and financial incentives are important determinants of FDI distribution in the United Kingdom (Hill & Munday, 1992). Several studies on the location of FDI in the United States concur that market size is a strongly positive determinant of FDI flow, but factors like the unemployment rate, productivity, and transportation were identified as positive or non-significant. Higher wage rates and unionization were often found to deter FDI. The presence of existing activity in the subsidiary's industrial sector is also important.

Agglomeration economies or positive externalities occur when firms locate nearby. These externalities are generated from such things as technology spillovers generated by casual or intended contact between engineers, designers, or managers working in the same field. Agglomeration economies are an increasing function of the number of firms in a region. The density of previous entrants in a region is also positively correlated with the propensity for new entrants to locate there.

Loree and Guisinger (1995) separate the locational determinants of FDI into policy and non-policy variables. As tariff barriers and prohibitions against inflows of FDI decline, differences in taxation, incentives, and performance requirements among host countries have a greater influence on the allocation of private investment worldwide. Although non-policy variables are generally exogenous, policy contingencies are subject to high manipulation by host country governments. Three major policy contingencies include: performance requirements, such as export ratios, import limits, input localization, and equity ceilings put on joint ventures; investment incentives, such as tax concessions, tariff concessions, subsidies, and others including financing, R&D support, and land rent; and effective tax rates on corporate income. Non-policy variables in their study include political stability, market characteristics, cultural distance, infrastructure, and wage levels. They observed significant effects of investment incentives (positive), performance requirements (negative), and tax rates (negative) on the location of U.S. FDI. Non-policy variables including political stability, cultural distance, gross domestic product per capita, and infrastructure are also found to strongly affect location choice.

Previous approaches building upon economic theories emphasize factors such as transport costs, exchange rates, taxes, labor rates, and other cost-based variables. Such a quantitative emphasis, however, underestimates the importance of strategic or qualitative factors that are more likely to provide long-term advantages under conditions of high competition.

For example, location dictates the level of knowledge embedded in the workforce. It can affect the ability of firms to implement skill-based process technologies, or it can limit the effectiveness of quality programs. Another disadvantage of strictly cost-based analyses is that they tend to focus on factor cost advantages, which are often transitory. Government regulations, tax systems, and exchange rates can quickly change. Strategies based on such parameters may be rendered obsolete by the very factors that first created these advantages. When formulating a location selection strategy in international expansion, MNEs should, therefore, attach high importance to the strategic or qualitative factors required to support expansion strategies. These strategic factors may include, but are not limited to, labor skills, resource munificence, infrastructure access, industry entry barriers, the threat of competition, supporting industry conditions, efficiency and assistance from local governments, distribution channels, culture-specific business practices, intellectual property rights protection, local consumer behavior, and environmental uncertainty. Only after establishing a set of desirable location options should companies refine choices using cost-based algorithms.

The importance of these strategic factors stem from both macro- and micro-level conditions. At the macroeconomic level, we have witnessed several trends. First, the development of large, sophisticated overseas markets dictates the necessity of a global presence for leading manufacturers. Many countries once regarded as less developed or developing now constitute large markets for leading edge, quality products (e.g., China, Southeast Asia). The United States no longer possesses the world's largest, most sophisticated market. The collective income of Europe now surpasses that of North America. Japanese consumers have the highest per capita income of any large industrialized nation. Firms cannot compete in these global markets by simply pushing mature products overseas or focusing only on cost minimization. Locating production in such large, sophisticated foreign markets facilitates customer responsiveness and product differentiation and helps capture spillover benefits from the local industry base.

Second, increasing non-tariff barriers are forcing firms to localize production resources. By placing restrictions on local content, sales volume, or market share, non-tariff barriers interfere with a firm's ability to serve a market through an export-based strategy. In Europe and some emerging economies there has been an increase in restrictive rules of origin and local content requirements, forcing firms to localize more parts of their manufacturing value chain and shift toward FDI. This promotes a decentralized manufacturing strategy. For MNEs that have established facilities within a region or target country, these policies expand the scope of local activities. More components are bought from local suppliers or other local strategic business units, or the MNE increases its local value additions within its manufacturing process.

Third, regionalization of trading economies increases the benefits of decentralized manufacturing structures. The European community constitutes one focus of regional trade; it encompasses 12 member nations and has special arrangements with most European states. The United States, Canada, and Mexico, through the North American Free Trade Agreement, are also linking their economies. The Pacific Basin, centered principally in China and Japan, but including the newly industrialized countries and Association of South-East Asian Nations, although technically not a free trade area, has become the fastest growing trade region in the world. Finally, no fewer than four free trade blocs have been created or proposed in Latin America. The evolution of a world trade system based on regional blocs creates incentives for firms to locate their FDI sites directly in the target market to pursue market growth there. Firms using cost-minimization strategies via export face more administrative, regulatory, and financial hurdles and, more importantly, more difficulty in gaining a competitive edge in the global marketplace.

Last, fluctuating exchange rates and other risks are forcing MNEs to be more flexible in terms of capacity and location and to view their global networks coherently. Exposure to risk becomes critical as MNEs develop global networks with multiple facilities serving many markets. If an MNE sells in a particular market, not producing in that market exposes it to the risk of currency depreciation, thus lowering revenues. From a financial and operational point of view, increased flexibility reduces risk and can even reduce average cost. From a production viewpoint, such flexibility can be gained by having a number of plants serving demand, with the ability to vary plant loadings according to exchange rate trends. In general, MNEs need to examine the complexities and uncertainties of multiple markets, sources, and production stages through sophisticated modeling approaches and location arrangements that consider the entire supply chain. The recent financial crisis in Asia has made many MNEs approach sourcing, production, and marketing more flexibly by adjusting locations.

At the micro-business level, the emergence of manufacturing technologies and methodologies, such as flexible manufacturing systems, just-in-time manufacturing, and total quality management, have reduced scale, increased the importance of worker education and skill, and placed demands on local infrastructures. A flexible manufacturing system integrates computer-controlled tools and material handling systems with centralized monitoring and scheduling functions. It offers significant advantages when demand for differentiated products is high. In the United States and Japan, the number of installed flexible manufacturing systems appears to be doubling every two years.

Such dynamics have to do with the emerging features of market demand and competition in the international setting. Product life cycles are increasingly shorter, and customers are tending to prefer customized rather than generic products. Therefore, firms have to produce greater product variety within shorter lead times. The benefits of flexible manufacturing systems can be obtained only through a dramatic change in the nature of the workforce. In considering a location selection for these systems or other highly automated manufacturing facilities, the company must consider the local engineering labor pool and the quality of direct labor. Employees must be highly flexible and multiskilled. Evidence corroborates this notion. Many MNEs save more on costs by shifting location from less developed countries to newly industrialized nations than they save on labor costs in less developed countries. Newly industrialized countries, therefore, seem more competitive than less developed countries even though they have higher factor costs.

Emerging manufacturing and technological changes increase an MNE's dependence on local suppliers, resource munificence, and support services. A reliable institutional infrastructure is, therefore, critical. Although MNEs might be able to create such a network by themselves, as some Japanese automobile giants did in the United States, most MNEs possess neither the scale nor the leverage to establish their own supplier network wherever they choose to locate. It is generally better to opt for a production location where the infrastructure and support environment already exist. These considerations have influenced Motorola's location selection in the cellular telephone industry. Its prior decision to take advantage of cost-based factors through locating in Puerto Rico proved unsuccessful. To serve the European market better, Motorola chose to produce cellular phones in Scotland. By locating in Easter Inch, the Silicon Glen of Scotland, Motorola was supported by vendor proximity, resource availability, and a well-educated labor pool.

Finally, the necessity for localized learning increases the need to be close to all major foreign markets. Host country-specific knowledge is a driving force behind international expansion performance because such knowledge cannot be easily acquired. In other words, because of time compression diseconomies, MNEs that have spent time in a host country may acquire a significant competitive advantage compared to firms that are not experienced in that country. Within the eclectic paradigm, such knowledge and experience is considered an ownership-specific, intangible asset that can generate economic rents. In general, the longer MNEs operate in a foreign country, the more capability they tend to develop. As a result, the MNE's intrinsic disadvantages of foreignness can be substantially overcome.

In sum, macroeconomic trends suggest that MNEs should locate their manufacturing presence in each region where there is significant demand.

Micro-business trends indicate a need for highly skilled labor and developed communications, transportation, and institutional infrastructures (e.g., suppliers, buyers, distributors, and governments). These trends have inflated the effects of strategic factors on location selection during international expansion, although cost-related factors are also important.

Factor Synthesis

Locational determinants can be categorized into the following groups: cost and tax factors, demand factors, strategic factors, macroeconomic factors, and sociopolitical factors. Overall, these factors are important considerations underlying both the selection of a country and a region within the country, although a few factors may have different influences depending on the location level being considered.

Cost and Tax Factors

Transportation Costs. The investor's home country is often the source of product components and the market for finished products. Because of this two-way flow of goods, transportation costs can be a concern. High transportation costs result in an increase in delivered cost. Everything else being constant, this encourages foreign production rather than export. This negative relationship between transportation costs and FDI propensity holds if the firm's products are sold to customers in the target market.

Wage Rate. Labor costs constitute a substantial proportion of total production costs. Foreign production is more likely to occur when production costs are lower abroad than at home. Labor costs sway investment location decisions, particularly for firms within labor-intensive industries. It is apparent that the decision by many MNEs to locate assembly plants in developing countries is heavily influenced by prevailing wages. Wage cost advantages are the primary reason MNEs integrate low labor cost nations into their global production strategy. Wage costs may decrease in importance, however, as new production systems reduce the amount of direct labor in product costs. Capital has become proportionately more important. Capital costs are essentially the same the world over. Increasing the capital intensity of the production process decreases its sensitivity to site location. Companies continuing to focus on direct labor cost savings may find transitory advantages, but eventually, as has happened in Korea, cost pressures will wipe out such advantages. Given these factors, locating facilities closer to final markets, with less emphasis on labor cost, is a natural progression.

Availability, Suitability, and Costs of Land. Availability of suitable plant sites, the cost of land, space for expansion, and local government policy on renting or purchasing land have been recognized by managers as critical factors in the early stages of project development and late stages of project operation. In some cases, this factor may overwhelm other location factors as it influences other costs, such as transportation and construction.

Construction Costs. This type of cost accounts for a substantial part of capital investment. Different sites vary in the cost of construction materials, labor, land, equipment rental, and quality of construction.

Costs of Raw Materials and Resources. MNEs are increasingly heightening the percentage of local suppliers in total production. This change is conducive to reducing foreign exchange risks from devalued currencies and improving relationships with local governments and indigenous firms. Under these circumstances, the costs of local materials and resources needed in production will affect the firm's gross profit margin.

Financing Costs. The cost and availability of capital is a major concern for MNEs because local financing provides much of the capital needed for mass production and operations. Financing by local institutions also helps the MNE mitigate possible financial risks arising from fluctuations in foreign exchange rates and uncertain foreign exchange policies in the host country.

Information Costs. Economic theorists argue that the conduct and hierarchical structures of MNEs are the result of rational responses by economic agents to the existence of information costs. An MNE's decision-making processes regarding its locations abroad are considerably affected by the market and event uncertainty characterizing target countries. Because the antidote to uncertainty is the acquisition of correct information, the costs incurred in searching, scanning, and acquiring necessary information become fundamental in overcoming the liabilities of foreignness.

Tax Rates. Both statutory and effective tax rates influence a firm's profitability. The statutory rate determines the general level of the tax burden shouldered by firms. The effective tax rate on corporate income, which is the statutory corporate rate adjusted for all other taxes and subsidies affecting an MNE's taxable income, determines the company's net return from its revenues and turnover. Depending on the extent of these other subsidies and taxes, the statutory corporate tax rate may differ substantially from the effective corporate tax rate, because the latter is adjusted to include incentives, such as investment tax credits and accelerated depreciation. Economic theory suggests that MNEs allocate capital internationally to maximize the marginal risk-adjusted after-tax return, where after-tax refers to the marginal effective tax.

Tax Holidays. Preferential tax rates are widely offered by countries or regions focused on attracting FDI. They affect the financial returns gained from local operations. Although evidence is inconclusive as to whether tax incentives influence the allocation of multinational investments, it is certain that preferential tax treatment is at least one credible factor in choosing a location, especially for those firms placing a high value on gaining profit through international expansion.

Profit Repatriation. Repatriation restrictions have a negative impact on the net income or dividends remitted to foreign headquarters. Restrictions usually include levying a remittance tax on the cash repatriated to a home country. In some developing countries, investors must obtain approval from the central bank or foreign exchange administration to repatriate dividends. It can, therefore, become a deterrent to FDI.

Demand Factors

Market Size, Potential, and Growth. At the national level, the size and growth rate of markets imply market opportunities and potentials for MNEs to explore. In general, previous studies find a positive correlation between these market demand variables and FDI inflow. At the subnational level, per capita consumption and the growth rate of consumption in the respective regions (province, city, and so forth) may be better constructs for measuring market potential and growth. The growth of income per capita is also an appropriate supplementary measure of market growth within a target region.

Presence of Customers. MNEs may find it desirable to locate their manufacturing sites in the area where they have long-standing customers. The closer operations are to major buyers, the higher the cost efficiency and marketing effectiveness, *ceteris paribus*. As competition in the host market from both local rivals and other foreign businesses appears to be increasingly fierce in recent years, customer responsiveness has become key to an MNE's competitive position in a local market. Locating the site close to major consumers is deemed to promote customer service.

Industrial Linkages. The nature and quality of complementary industries, external economies, and special services (consulting, auditing, insurance, and so forth) have become more important recently as MNE operations interact more actively with various sectors in host country economies. These include suppliers, distributors, and competitors within a specific industry as well as major players in other supporting or related industries. Industrial linkages with these businesses affect the firm's ability to pursue value creation and addition in its value chain.

Local Competition. The intensity of competition in a host country or specific region is of utmost importance because it directly impacts a firm's market position and gross profit margin from local sales. In general, MNEs should locate in places where competition is relatively low unless they have sufficient competencies to ensure their competitive edge in the market.

Market Opportunities and Threats. Market demand does not necessarily indicate market opportunities if high market competition, governmental intervention, or low purchasing power are in place. To identify the degree of market opportunities and threats, firms need to assess all related forces in addition to market demand. In high potential markets, international expansion is expected to provide greater long-term profitability to an MNE through the opportunity to achieve economies of scale and lower marginal production costs. Even if scale economies are not significant, an MNE may still select this location because it provides the firm with the opportunity to establish a long-term market presence and competitive power.

Consumer Behavior. Host country consumers often have consumption behaviors different from home country consumers. Even within the same target country, consumers in different regions may have different utility functions. Thus, a location choice has to align with an analysis of consumer behavior in the area. In particular, an MNE should assess whether it is worthwhile, and, if so, whether the firm has an ability to differentiate products or services to country- or region-specific consumer preferences.

Strategic Factors

Investment Infrastructure. A superior infrastructure may increase FDI in a country or region. Major infrastructure variables include transportation (highways, ports, airports, and railroads), telecommunications, and utilities. As the infrastructure in many countries is not yet well developed, MNEs often face daunting difficulties. Attaining access to needed infrastructure from the local government is important to production and market development if the MNE is to locate in such areas. Nevertheless, investors will probably differ in the importance they attach to infrastructure depending on the special requirements of their industries.

Manufacturing Concentration. One of the major determinants of location selection is the strength of existing manufacturing activities. The mutual cost savings that result from manufacturers locating in close proximity is a major feature of industrial location theory. A country or region with a strong concentration of manufacturing activity in certain industries or products is more likely to have an adequate labor pool and supply network supporting production, operation, and management. Just-in-time systems require a supplier base that is capable, reliable, and physically close (around two hours or 100 miles away). Such requirements dictate that existing industrialized regions will increasingly attract the investment of global manufacturing firms. Deploying manufacturing resources in larger, more sophisticated regions will allow leverage of existing suppliers' capabilities. This will aid entry strategies that rely on significant outsourcing during initial production while higher value-added capabilities are developed.

Labor Productivity. The availability of qualified workers is an FDI attraction factor, although its relevance is strongly industry-specific. As a result of increasing technological permeation and process innovation, international production requires high worker productivity and superior labor skills. High productivity nourishes production efficiency and spurs value creation across various nodes in the value chain. The labor requirements of new systems and techniques are driving the need for a better educated direct-labor workforce. Just-in-time and total quality management systems place greater importance on the flexibility of workers and their ability to operate under growing autonomy. The increasing sophistication of product and process technologies has also increased skill requirements.

Skilled Human Resource Availability. Although labor productivity determines process innovation, managerial and technical expertise influence both managerial and product innovation. Because these innovations directly affect production differentiation, they become primary forces in gaining competitive advantages in the market.

International Concerns. These include the availability of international seaports and import-export facilities and proximity to home country or other export markets. This is a strategic factor because most FDI projects have operational linkages with home and other international markets. According to the strategic option notion, these linkages promote strategic flexibility during international expansion, which in turn contributes to the survival and growth of foreign operations.

Logistic Synergies. These include proximity to other plants and companies in the same industry. Being near other plants owned by the same MNE influences the creation of operational synergies, which in turn have an impact on cost savings and adaptability to market changes.

Input Logistics. Typical input logistics include proximity to suppliers and sources of raw materials and inputs. This factor is one of the major determinants of input efficiency, which is one of the four building blocks of competitive advantage (the other three are quality, innovation, and customer responsiveness). Because MNEs have a tendency to rely more on local input sources, this type of logistics should be among the critical considerations in the mind of international managers.

Market Logistics. On the revenue side, market logistics are mainly composed of proximity to major buyers and end consumers. This factor can have a substantial influence on the effectiveness and efficiency of customer responsiveness. When the firm pursues market penetration and product specialization strategies, the firm's profitability will be strongly associated with market logistics.

Investment Incentives. Although these are country- and time-specific, an array of investment incentives that attract FDI include: state and local tax breaks and reductions on corporate income, export profits, capital expenditures, sales, exports, license fees, turnover, and the like; state and local financial assistance, such as preferential terms of financing, wage subsidies, investment grants or loans at below market interest rates, and foreign exchange concessions; tariff concessions including exemption from or reduction of duties on imports, additional duties on imports of competing goods, or rebates of duties on imported inputs; business assistance, such as employee training, R&D support, land grants or sales concessions, site improvements, and site selection assistance; and other incentives, such as infrastructure development and access, legal services, and business consultation. These incentives may have a positive effect on the MNE's after-tax return on investment.

Performance Requirements. Performance requirements set minimum percentages of production to be exported, maximum total imports, minimum amounts of local inputs, minimum amounts of local labor, or limited proportions of equity that the parent may hold in an affiliate. Everything else being constant, these requirements will have a negative effect on luring FDI but may be necessary for rationalizing structural imperfections in an industry or developing a national economy.

Local Business Practices. Culture-specific business practices often constitute a key form of knowledge that MNEs must learn. In fact, the prominent logic behind formation of international cooperative ventures with developing country enterprises is to gain such country-specific knowledge. Superior technological and organizational skills cannot guarantee the success of international operations unless the firm is able to integrate country-specific knowledge with its firm-specific knowledge. The ability to integrate these two types of knowledge often determines the survival and growth of MNEs in foreign markets.

Macroeconomic Factors

Per Capita Gross National Product. Many economic and social indicators are correlated with the level of GNP per capita. Of these, market size, infrastructure quality, consumption level, and economic development stage are positively associated with the level of per capita GNP. Thus, those FDI projects that are more reliant on the infrastructure and economic development level or are targeting the local market should be located in a country or region where the level of GNP per capita is high, *ceteris paribus.*

Inflation Rate. Monetary stability has a favorable effect on the inflow of FDI because an MNE's assets and liabilities are less exposed to economic risks and foreign exchange risks. Higher inflation rates lead to greater political and real foreign exchange premium, which in turn creates a volatile financial environment for international operations. Moreover, high inflation rates often drive up production costs through increased materials prices, loan interest, and even labor wages. In a competitive environment, a rise in selling prices generally cannot compensate for the increase in costs of goods sold and other expenses.

Unemployment. According to macroeconomic theories, unemployment rates are positively linked with incoming FDI. When unemployment rates are high, MNEs are easily able to hire labor at relatively low costs. MNEs are also in a better position to ask for governmental support in this situation. If unemployment is mostly caused by deflation, MNEs, particularly those in technology- or capital-intensive industries, will benefit from cheaper production factors, preferential treatment, and easier access to scarce resources.

Foreign Exchange System. A host country can influence its FDI stock by changing its foreign exchange system. This system can contain numerous policies that affect MNE operations. Examples include devaluation, dual track rates, foreign exchange balances, foreign exchange expenditures or remittances, interest rates on foreign currencies, and supervision and administration of foreign exchange markets. The impact of this system on firm operations, however, differs from company to company depending upon each firm's products, source strategy, market orientation, risk-taking attitude, risk reduction ability, capital structure, financing sources, and so on. For example, a devaluation in the local currency may enable the MNE to benefit by offsetting wage rate increases, exporting products, converting foreign currencies to local currency, and contributing foreign-made equipment and machinery to local operations. A devaluation, however, could also make the MNE suffer when importing materials and other inputs, repatriating profits to its headquarters, translating losses from consolidation of the financial statement at the current rate (for both monetary and non-monetary assets, according to Financial Accounting Standard Board No. 52), and the like.

Tariff and Non-tariff Barriers. Academics often suggest that FDI is a substitute for export in that it can bypass tariff and non-tariff barriers. This is not precisely correct. Most FDI projects still need to import materials from and export products to foreign countries. MNEs confront most non-tariff barriers within a host country even when they focus on the local market (e.g., peculiar commercial practice). Therefore, a strategic response to overcoming these barriers is not simply substituting FDI for export but realistically selecting the right location where these hurdles are low.

Unionization. Unionization is an important dimension of the political economy of both developed and developing countries. Research on manufacturing locations within the developed world has uncovered a clear anti-union orientation. High unionization is often a strong repellent to inward FDI and MNE operations in the local economy. High unionization may cause conflict in labor-management relations that may in turn increase costs and instability.

Availability of Special Economic Zones. One of the major ways many countries, especially in the developing world, attempt to attract FDI is through the establishment of special zones, such as free trade zones, special economic zones, economic and technological development zones, high-tech development zones, open economic regions, bonded areas, and so on. In general, these zones provide preferential treatment in terms of taxation, import duties, land use, infrastructure access, and governmental assistance to MNEs. However, many of these zones are regulated regarding eligibility for preferential treatment. For instance, MNEs located in Chinese economic and technological development zones must export 75 percent of output or bring in advanced technologies as verified by governmental authorities.

Sociopolitical Factors

Political Instability. This factor reflects uncertainty over the continuation of present political and social conditions and government policies that are critical to the survival and profitability of a firm's operations in a country. Changes in government policies may cause problems related to repatriation of earnings, or, in extreme cases, expropriation of assets. The restrictive policies of a host country's government are likely to impede inward FDI. Political uncertainty often outweighs other contextual factors. MNEs and even local companies have very little power to change or stabilize such uncertainty. Although international lobbying on foreign country policies has become pervasive, the magnitude of politically induced environmental uncertainty still overwhelms transaction-related risks affecting MNE operations. In contrast, political stability reduces investor uncertainty and therefore may increase the level of FDI that flows to that country. Unless an MNE has the ability to alleviate unpredictable variabilities, the firm should opt for a location where the political environment is reasonably stable.

Cultural Barriers. Another dimension of the uncertainty is related to differences in culture between the home and host countries. This factor determines a firm's receptivity and adaptability to the social context of a host country. As a general definition, culture may be viewed as the set of attitudes and values that are common to a group of people. Because foreign investment requires an interface at many levels, including the state, local competitors, and at least some element of the foreign work force, FDI levels may be higher between home and host countries where similarity eases the cultural dimension of business relations. Apart from these, language barriers are also an important consideration underlying location selection. Although every foreign business can recruit local people, communications with headquarters as well as between employees within the company are crucial to business success.

Industrial Policies. A host government's industrial policies affect project selection, industry selection, entry mode selection, and investment commitment. MNEs need to make sure that the policies of the target industry in a host country are reasonably favorable or at least not a hindrance. Industrial policies have a more direct impact on an MNE's operations and strategic options than do the macroeconomic policies of the host government. In many countries, industrial policies are used to control new entrants (both foreign and local firms), net profit margins, degree of competition, structural concentration, and state or social benefits.

Foreign Direct Investment Policies. The array of FDI laws, rules, and regulations should be a predominant concern for MNEs when they make a location decision. MNEs should assess these policies and the possibility that they will change during the term of the MNEs' operations. Firms need to appraise both the benefits and costs of current policies. Firms normally have two choices involving location strategy in response to FDI policies. One is realistically to pick a location where FDI policies are favorable and stable. The other is to pioneer in a market where policies may be unstable or even deterrent. In the former case, as followers or later entrants, MNEs benefit from the more favorable, stable environment but suffer from fewer opportunities and greater competition. In the latter case, as first movers, MNEs take advantage of preemptive potential and competitive position but encounter more operational risks and environmental uncertainty. Thus, location selection should be appropriately integrated with other important strategic decisions, such as entry timing.

Government Efficiency and Corruption. International managers often perceive the soft infrastructure (e.g., regulatory environment and government efficiency) as having a greater and more enduring impact on firm operations than the hard infrastructure (e.g., transportation and communication). Efficient governments are more responsive to an MNE's requests or complaints, provide shorter times for obtaining project approval or other ratifications, and give superior assistance and support in various matters. The biggest headache for MNEs investing in many developing countries is the low efficiency and high bureaucracy of many of their governments. Corrupted governments further hinder MNE operations. Although each firm may have different capabilities for cultivating and maintaining relationships with government authorities, no business in the world would wish to deal with a corrupt host government. Governmental corruption implies not only low efficiency and awful red tape, but also the high costs of bribery in setting up governmental linkages to get project approval, infrastructure access, and acquisition of scarce resources.

Attitudes to Foreign Business. Social and governmental attitudes toward foreign businesses often have visible or invisible influences on MNE operations and management. If the society and government of the host country are fairly friendly to foreign business, MNEs will benefit from the congenial environment. This attitude has an enduring effect on both firm operations and the commitment of employees to the foreign firm.

Community Characteristics. Site selection must include considerations of aspects of community environment such as size of the community, educational facilities, housing facilities, police and fire protection, climate, suitability for expatriates and their families, facilities for children, social environment for spouses, hotel accommodations, crime level, and so on. This environment is highly relevant as it affects costs, quality, and security of living for foreign expatriates and their families. Many of them often attach more importance to community environment than to their salary level. From the firm's perspective, selecting an appropriate community may also be more crucial than wage costs because the selection fundamentally influences the future of expatriates willing to commit to the MNE's local operations. In general, the longer they are willing to work in the local context, the more benefit the firm will receive. The country-specific experience its employees accumulate is of paramount value to the firm.

Pollution Control. Environmental protection laws and regulations in the target location (country or region) influence the choice and cost of investments. Before making a location decision, an MNE should appraise these laws and regulations, assess whether the firm is able to comply with them, and evaluate if it is financially efficient to invest in pollution control.

Table 5.1 summarizes the major factors behind location selection.

ANALYTICAL FRAMEWORK

An Integrated Model

The above section presented various locational determinants that must be assessed and analyzed in the course of choosing a location. These determinants constitute the core in the framework of a location decision-making process. Aside from this core, MNEs also need to take into account some other factors that are important to making the right selection of sites abroad. These factors must be incorporated into the framework because they determine the particular profile that differentiates one firm's choice of location from another firm's. The firm-specific factors affecting locational choice include strategic objectives, market orientation, organizational competencies, and global integration requirements (see Figure 5.1).

TABLE 5.1
Locational Determinants

Micro-Context	Macro-Context
Cost/Tax Factors	*Macroeconomic Factors*
Transportation costs	Per capita GNP
Wage rate	Inflation rate
Availability, suitability, and costs of land	Unemployment
Construction costs	Foreign exchange system
Costs of raw materials and resources	Tariff and non-tariff barriers
Financing costs	Unionization
Information costs	Availability of special economic
Statutory and effective tax rates	zones
Tax holidays	
Profit repatriation restrictions	
Demand Factors	*Sociopolitical Factors*
Market size, potential, and growth	Political instability
Presence of customers	Cultural barriers
Industrial linkages	Industrial policies
Local competition	FDI policies
Market opportunities and threats	Government efficiency and
Consumer behavior	corruption
	Attitudes to foreign business
	Community characteristics
	Pollution control
Strategic Factors	
Investment infrastructure	
Manufacturing concentration	
Labor productivity	
Skilled human resource availability	
International concerns	
Synergy logistics	
Input logistics	
Market logistics	
Investment incentives	
Performance requirements	
Local business practices	

Location and Objectives

MNEs have diverse strategic objectives underlying international expansion. Each MNE may have idiosyncratic purposes compared with those of other companies. As one part of investment strategy, location selection should be subordinate to realizing the firm's strategic goals in expanding internationally. Specifically, different goals will place different weights on the importance of various locational determinants.

If an MNE aims to pursue market growth and competitive position in the host country, demand factors and strategic factors appear to be its

FIGURE 5.1

An Integrated Model of Location Selection in International Expansion

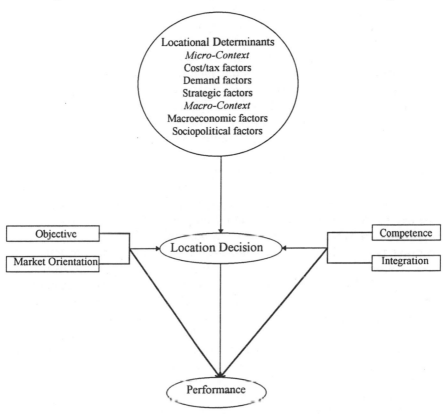

most critical considerations. As these aims generally concern long-term investments and operations, macroeconomic factors and sociopolitical factors also have a moderate impact on location selection. In general, MNEs seeking market growth should opt for locations that offer more market potential, preemptive opportunities in product development, market expansion, technological leadership, superior hard and soft infrastructures, supportive industrial linkages and value chain networks, and a munificent supply of production factors, particularly skillful workers.

If an MNE seeks short- or mid-term profitability, it should attach more value to cost and taxation factors. Infrastructure conditions and investment incentives may also be influential. The costs of production factors and operational expenses will determine the gross profit margin, and the rate of income tax will affect the level of net return. Remittance taxes or profit repatriation restrictions have a big impact on the level of dividends that the parent firm finally receives. Some MNEs with this objective select locations where they can take advantage of the preferential cost or tax treatments offered by local governments.

If an MNE strives to diversify risks or operate in a stable environment, sociopolitical factors become most fundamental to the decision. As some macroeconomic factors, such as exchange rate and inflation rate, are related to contextual variability, they should also be included in the analytical framework. These macro contextual factors usually overwhelm uncertainty derived from other sources. In other words, they are largely outside the sphere of control by foreign firms. Therefore, the proper approach to mitigating these environmental risks is to select a country or region that is relatively more stable and predictable, less complex and hostile.

If an MNE intends to secure innovation, learning, and adaptation from international expansion, strategic factors seem to outweigh other groups of factors in affecting locational choice. Nevertheless, industrial linkages, competition intensity, cultural distance, and attitudes toward foreign businesses may also influence the accomplishment of this goal. On the one hand, an MNE goes abroad to make more profits by exploiting its technology, brand name, or management capabilities in different countries around the world. On the other hand, the diversity of environments in which an MNE operates exposes an MNE to multiple stimuli, allows it to develop diverse capabilities, and provides it with a broader learning opportunity than is available to a purely domestic firm. The enhanced organizational learning that results from the diversity internalized by the MNE may be a key explanation of its ongoing success, and its initial stock of knowledge may well be the strength that allows it to create such organizational diversity in the first place. The mere existence of diversity, however, does not enhance learning. To exploit this potential, an MNE should create mechanisms and systems for such learning to take place. Location selection then constitutes one of these means to optimize diversity in foreign markets.

Location and Market Orientation

Market orientation is mainly concerned with whether an MNE primarily targets a host country market, export market (home or other foreign markets), or both. Although many MNEs attempt to improve their market power and firm growth in both developed and developing countries, export assembly platforms undertaken by MNEs also increasingly figure in international production strategies, particularly in labor-intensive industries in developing countries. This investment generally reflects an underlying trend toward global sourcing in intermediate production. Where it is possible to divide manufacturing tasks into highly routine operations, firms seek low cost sites for intermediate phases of the production process. No doubt low wages encourage firms to disperse operations away from developed market economies. Investment incentive programs and duty-free component imports in free trade zones may further induce manufacturers in the developed world to move operations to developing economies.

In recent years, more and more MNEs have used a dual emphasis orientation by selling to both the local and foreign markets. Foreign subsidiaries with a dual emphasis orientation are market driven in searching for both risk-adjusted efficiency and emerging business opportunities. They scan and interpret the environment and make appropriate decisions concerning both internal arrangements and external alignment. Many important activities of these subsidiaries are located in the host country; they are carried out in close coordination with the rest of the MNE, thereby constituting an active node in a tightly knit network. The dual emphasis orientation is deemed more flexible in gaining economic efficiency from the interplay of firm-specific competitive advantages and country-specific comparative advantages. Because of this operational and market orientation flexibility, the dual emphasis orientation can reduce an MNE's dependence on local settings, diminish its vulnerability to governmental interference, and increase its bargaining power with the host government. Further, the dual emphasis orientation is superior at achieving internalization benefits. In sum, the dual emphasis orientation increases market orientation flexibility, which in turn spurs managerial discretion in responding profitably to new business potentials in the global market.

Naturally, different market orientations vary in their relationship with locational determinants. Local market-oriented projects are highly sensitive to demand and strategic factors in the local environment because these factors determine the degree of market potential and growth opportunities that the MNE can exploit. Some macroeconomic factors, such as inflation rates and unionization, are also relevant because they affect the stability and economic exposure of firm operations to the local environment. Certain sociopolitical variables including cultural distance, government efficiency or corruption, and political stability are likely to have a stronger effect on the local market orientation than on an export orientation. The latter, by contrast, relies more on various cost and tax factors. Plants producing for an export market can be located with little regard for domestic demand. Export-oriented projects pursue cost minimization by locating a production platform in the host country where production factors are cheap. Therefore, cost and tax factors, together with some strategic factors, such as investment incentives, input logistics, labor productivity, and infrastructure, are prominent micro-contextual determinants underlying this location strategy. Some macroeconomic factors, such as exchange rates, availability of special trade zones, and tariff and non-tariff barriers, may also impact export growth. Last, the dual emphasis orientation may be influenced by all five group factors. In other words, the dual emphasis orientation necessitates the most comprehensive scheme in the appraisal of locational determinants. Nevertheless, this orientation may put the firm in the best position to take advantage of favorable locational factors while reducing or alleviating the unfavorable impact of other locational determinants. This indicates one of the major advantages of the dual emphasis orientation.

Location and Competence

Normally, the market for intangible assets, such as proprietary knowledge, is often imperfect. MNEs that invest in these intangibles have a propensity to invest abroad. Knowledge is often difficult to codify into patents and patent rights are costly to enforce, so protection against infringement tends to be uneven. Therefore, firms with proprietary knowledge often find it necessary to exploit it abroad through internalized manufacturing.

Distinctive competencies are often mirrored in four areas: technological, operational, organizational, and financial. Superior competencies enable the MNE to maximize the benefits of favorable locational determinants or reduce their vulnerability to contextual uncertainties. Among these competencies, technological skills should be deployed in locations where market demand is high, preemptive opportunities exist, and industrial linkages and a skillful labor force have been developed. In addition, these locations must have a well-developed intellectual property rights system. MNEs will capitalize on advanced technology or tacit knowledge more proactively in the host market when their intellectual property rights are protected.

Operational expertise is imperative for MNEs wishing to take full advantage of the potential of a local market. Managerial innovation, marketing and promotional skills, and networking capabilities with suppliers, distributors, competitors, and government agencies are some of the key indicators of operational strength. To benefit fully from these strengths, an MNE should identify a location where the interplay between firm-specific operational skills and location-specific business opportunities could create the highest possible financial and operational synergies.

Organizational skills are often tacit and sustainable. They should be allocated in such a way that the firm earns maximum benefit from these skills. A target location should present favorable strategic factors, such as labor productivity, a good infrastructure, input logistics, and qualified human resources. An MNE's experience both internationally and in the host country is also a key element of organizational superiority. An MNE with more experience is more likely to commit more and invest more in the host country (experience intensity). The knowledge gained in producing one product in a specific country can be transferred to another product (experience diversity). This experience is usually positively associated with industrial linkages, product image, organizational reputation, marketing effectiveness, consumer loyalty, and governmental relationship. Everything else being constant, MNEs with superior experience can take the plunge into a location perceived as challenging but promising. This location strategy will bring the company preemptive opportunities. It may be safer for unexperienced MNEs to use a wait and see strategy so they can take advantage of a more stable environment later on and lessons learned from early movers.

Last, financial strengths are important for reducing vulnerability to unfavorable production input conditions, especially capital costs. Unlike local businesses, MNEs in the host country often have difficulty attaining bank loans or other credit. High interest rates or harsh financing terms are often imposed by indigenous providers. In general, an MNE equipped with weak financial resources should locate its FDI projects in a country or region where it can be financed under favorable conditions. Although MNEs are able to acquire financing from international financial markets, financing in the local currency at host country institutions is often imperative for reducing financial exposure.

Location and Integration

International expansion generally attempts to pursue two types of advantages: location-specific advantages (comparative advantages) and competitive advantages. Location-specific advantage arises from factor cost differences between countries. Consequently, an MNE may locate certain labor-intensive processes in countries that are relatively well endowed with abundant labor or locate an R&D facility in an area where a high level of research activity is occurring or abundant technological capabilities exist. This type of advantage is primarily achieved through locational presence. In contrast, competitive advantages are firm-specific competencies. Competitive advantages are generally considered to be developed through international economies of scale, economies of scope, and organizational learning.

One of the key tasks faced by international managers concerns linking or integrating the MNE's functional activities across locations. This is because the geographic specification or configuration of functional activities establishes the MNE's capacity to exploit location-specific advantages. Linking activities across locations is fundamental to capturing international scale, scope, and learning economies. Such economies imply that resource flows must exist throughout a multinational network. In Porter's framework (1986), the configuration and coordination dimensions are posited as determining alternative international strategy types within global industries. Specifically, configuration ranges from dispersed (the entire set of the firm's functional activities are replicated within each country) to concentrated (activities in the value chain are desegregated). Coordination ranges from low, where each functional activity at different sites is performed independently, to high, where functional activities are tightly linked or integrated across locations. Alternative strategic approaches are thought to be based on the combinations of emphasis within these two continua.

The alignment of location selection to global integration is of paramount importance for business performance. A good coupling between these two can facilitate the exploitation of firm-specific competitive advantages and the exploration of host country-specific comparative advantages. From the neo-contingency perspective, a good fit in a dynamic context can enable an MNE to maximize economic rents from an interface between the societal effect and organizational effect (Mueller, 1994). Prearranged strategic orientations that are appropriate both to internal arrangements and external alignment can boost subsidiary incentives, reduce vulnerability to contextual changes, and spur the accomplishment of the role set for FDI.

Location and Performance

Transaction cost theorists view production site specificities as fundamental to foreign investment choice and its economic outcome. The interaction between location-specific factors and the investor's competence is now widely recognized as a source of competitive advantages in host country and international markets. Firms located in different areas face different external conditions. Those located in more favorable locations may enjoy preferential treatment, a more congenial business atmosphere, and a better infrastructure. These differences are expected to affect the financial and market performances of international investments and have strong risk and efficiency implications for MNEs.

Not surprisingly, neither the stage of economic development nor levels of consumption are even across different countries and regions. For example, the open coastal cities and open economic regions in China have historically been more developed economically and contain better infrastructures (transportation, communication, production and business service, and so forth) than other areas. Moreover, the open areas have been provided with greater autonomy and authority for conducting their economic affairs. In addition, the open areas generally provide more Western style business facilities and a cultural atmosphere facilitating international business activities. Further, MNEs located in open areas benefit from many privileges in terms of income tax and other fees. For instance, the income tax on MNEs established in Chinese open coastal cities is levied at the reduced rate of 24 percent; ventures located in non-open areas are taxed at 33 percent. MNEs in open areas are also exempt from paying the industrial and commercial consolidation tax for imported production equipment, business facilities, building materials, and vehicles; raw materials, spare parts, components or packing materials imported for producing export products; and export products. In this particular case, it is likely that MNEs in open areas will outperform those in other areas in terms of both profitability and stability, other things being equal.

Different sets of locational determinants may have heterogenous influences on performance indicators. First, favorable cost and tax factors will have a positive effect on an MNE's financial returns. These factors reduce direct production costs, overhead, and indirect expenses. Second, favorable demand factors contribute to an MNE's sales growth. Given a constant asset level, demand factors also lead to high asset turnover. Third, strategic factors have a positive effect on economic efficiency. Favorable strategic factors provide a cost-effective, growth-driven environment in which an MNE can operate effectively. Fourth, macroeconomic factor conditions influence the pace and path of firm growth. A favorable macroeconomic environment helps an MNE grow and flourish. Finally, sociopolitical factors have an impact on operational riskiness and performance stability. A favorable sociopolitical environment stabilizes the possible variability encountered during transactions and operations in an indigenous setting.

The integrated model is, in principle, applicable to both national and regional selection. Both the micro- and macro-contexts are important. Nevertheless, once the target country has been identified, MNEs may attach more importance to the verification and appraisal of the possible impact of micro-context attributes including cost and tax factors, demand factors, and strategic factors on regional or site selection within the country. In the selection of a region within a country, macroeconomic and sociopolitical factors mainly involve relevant policies stipulated by a regional government or surrounding conditions.

REFERENCES

Aliber R. Z. 1970. A theory of direct foreign investment. In C. P. Kindleberger (Ed.), *The international corporation*, pp. 8–22. Cambridge, MA: MIT Press.

Arthur, B. 1986. Industry location patterns and the importance of history, Paper No. 84. Stanford, CA: Stanford University, Center for Economic Policy Research.

Caves, R. E. 1982. *Multinational enterprise and economic analysis*. London: MacMillan.

Coughlin, C. C., J. B. Terza, and V. Arromdee. 1991. State characteristics and the location of foreign direct investment within the United States. *The Review of Economics and Statistics*, 73(4): 675–683.

Culem, C. G. 1988. The locational determinants of foreign direct investments among industrial countries. *European Economic Review*, 32(4): 885–894.

Davidson, W. H. 1980. The location of foreign direct investment activity: Country characteristics and experience effects. *Journal of International Business Studies*, 11(2): 9–22.

Dunning, J. H. 1993. *Multinational enterprises and the global economy*. Reading, MA: Addison-Wesley.

Dunning, J. H. 1988. *Explaining international production*. London: Unwin Hyman.

Dunning, J. H. 1980. Towards an eclectic theory of international production: Some empirical tests. *Journal of International Business Studies*, 11(1): 9–31.

Friedman, J., D. A. Gerlowski, and J. Silberman. 1992. What attracts foreign multinational corporations: Evidence from branch plant location in the United States. *Journal of Regional Science*, 32(4): 403–418.

Head, K., J. Ries, and D. Swenson. 1995. Agglomeration benefits and location choice: Evidence from Japanese manufacturing investments in the United States. *Journal of International Economics*, 38: 223–247.

Hennart, J. F. and Y. R. Park. 1994. Location, governance, and strategic determinants of Japanese manufacturing investment in the United States. *Strategic Management Journal*, 15(6): 419–436.

Hill, S. and M. Munday. 1992. The UK regional distribution of foreign direct investment: Analysis and determinants. *Regional Studies*, 26(6): 535–544.

Hirsch, S. 1976. An international trade and investment theory of the firm. *Oxford Economic Papers*, 28: 258–270.

Johanson, J. and J. E. Vahlne. 1977. The internationalization process of the firm: A model of knowledge development and increasing foreign market commitment. *Journal of International Business Studies*, 8: 23–32.

Loree, D. W. and S. E. Guisinger. 1995. Policy and non-policy determinants of U.S. foreign equity investment. *Journal of International Business Studies*, 26(2): 281–299.

Mariotti, S. and L. Piscitello. 1995. Information costs and location of FDIs within the host country: Empirical evidence from Italy. *Journal of International Business Studies*, Fourth Quarter: 815–841.

Mueller, F. 1994. Societal effect, organizational effect and globalization. *Organization Studies*, 15(3): 407–428.

Porter, M. E. 1986. *Competition in global industries*. Boston, MA: Harvard Business School Press.

Vernon, R. 1966. International investment and international trade in the product cycle. *Quarterly Journal of Economics*, May: 377–392.

Woodward, D. and R. Rolfe. 1993. The location of export-oriented foreign direct investment in the Caribbean Basin. *Journal of International Business Studies*, First Quarter: 121–144.

Yamawaki, H., J. M. Thiran, and L. Barbarito. 1996. Regional and country determinants of location decisions: Japanese multinationals in European manufacturing. Paper presented at Academy of International Business Annual Meeting, October, Banff, Canada.

FURTHER READINGS

Agarwal, S. and S. Ramaswami. 1992. Choice of foreign market entry mode: Impact of ownership, location and internalization factors. *Journal of International Business Studies*, First Quarter: 1–27.

MacCormack, A. D., L. J. Newman, and D. B. Rosenfield. 1997. The new dynamics of global manufacturing site location. In H. V. Wortzel and L. H. Wortzel

(Eds.), *Strategic management in a global economy*, pp. 354–367. New York: John Wiley & Sons.

Roth, K. 1992. International configuration and coordination archetypes for medium-sized firms in global industries. *Journal of International Business Studies,* Third Quarter: 533–549.

Terpstra, V. and C. M. Yu. 1988. Determinants of foreign investment of U.S. advertising agencies. *Journal of International Business Studies,* 19: 33–46.

6

Entry Mode Selection

Emerging world economy dynamics and global competition patterns are now encouraging the use of more diverse and creative entry modes by international investors. This chapter first presents the theoretical underpinnings of entry mode selection in international expansion. The ownership-location-internalization (OLI) paradigm, transaction cost theory, bargaining power theory, organizational capability theory, evolutionary perspective on internationalization, and managerial model are introduced as the leading theories on entry mode selection. Section two illustrates various entry modes available at present to multinational enterprises (MNEs). These entry modes include trade-related (export, subcontracts, leases, and countertrade), representative or branch offices, licensing, franchising, build-operate-transfers, cooperative joint ventures, equity joint ventures, wholly owned subsidiaries, and umbrella investment companies. Overall, risk, return, control, integration, commitment, and strategic flexibility increase along with this sequence of entry modes. The merits and limitations of each entry mode are discussed. The last section describes four groups of factors affecting choice of entry mode at the country, industry, firm, and project levels. In general, entry mode selection is determined by both firm characteristics (firm and project levels) and situational contingencies (country and industry levels).

CONCEPTUAL BACKGROUND

An MNE seeking to enter a foreign market must make an important strategic decision concerning which entry mode to use. Normative decision theory suggests that the choice of foreign market entry mode should be based on trade-offs between risks and returns. Each entry mode has implications for the level of control the firm will enjoy over its foreign operations, the amount of investment required, and the degree of risk the firm faces in venturing into the foreign market. It is generally acknowledged that as a firm moves from licensing or franchising to joint ventures to wholly owned subsidiaries, control, investment, and risk all increase accordingly (Agarwal & Ramaswami, 1992; Anderson & Gatignon, 1986; Erramilli, 1991).

Different entry modes provide different levels of control over operational and strategic decision making in foreign operations. In the case of licensing, control over operations and strategy is granted to the licensee in exchange for a lump sum payment, a per-unit royalty fee, and a commitment to abide by the terms set out in a licensing contract. At the other end, ultimate control over wholly owned subsidiaries resides at the MNE's corporate office. In a joint venture, level of control is dependent upon the ownership split and bargaining power; it falls somewhere between the case of licensing and wholly owned subsidiaries.

Different entry modes also require different levels of resource commitment (Hill, Hwang, & Kim, 1990). In licensing, for example, the licensee bears most of the costs of opening and serving the foreign market. Thus, the level of resource commitment required from the MNE is low. In the case of wholly owned subsidiaries, the MNE has to bear all of the costs of opening and serving the foreign market; its level of resource commitment is correspondingly high. Resource commitment can constitute an impediment to the strategic flexibility of international operations. When resource commitments are extensive, the international company cannot exit from a foreign market without incurring substantial sunk costs. Therefore, strategic flexibility is greatest in the case of licensing and lowest for wholly owned subsidiaries.

An MNE is expected to choose the entry mode that offers the highest risk-adjusted return on investment. A firm's choices are also determined by behavioral factors, such as resource availability and need for control. In recent years, Dunning's OLI paradigm, transaction cost theory, bargaining power theory, organizational capability theory, the evolutionary perspective on internationalization, and the managerial model of entry mode selection have emerged as the leading theories for explaining choices of entry mode during international expansion by MNEs.

Ownership-Location-Internalization Advantages and Entry Mode

Dunning (1980, 1988) proposed a comprehensive framework, namely, the eclectic or OLI paradigm, which stipulated that the choice of entry mode during international expansion is influenced by three types of determinants (i.e., OLI advantages): ownership advantages of a firm, location advantages of a market, and internalization advantages of integrating transactions within the firm. First, MNEs must possess superior assets and skills that can earn economic rents high enough to counter the higher cost of servicing these markets. Firm competence is needed for competing against local firms, absorbing the costs of scanning for information, enforcing patents and contracts, and achieving economies of scale. Once an MNE's technological, operational, organizational, and financial competencies are strong enough, it may opt for a high risk mode of entry that has greater potential for high return.

Second, MNEs interested in serving foreign markets are expected to use selective strategies and favor entry into more attractive markets. In countries offering high market potential, investment modes are expected to provide greater long-term profitability to a firm, compared to noninvestment modes, such as export. Host country factors, particularly market opportunities, contextual uncertainties, and governmental policies, often have a fundamental impact on the entry mode selection. Once a mode is chosen, the interactions between these factors and the mode will be largely exogenous, meaning that it will not be economically feasible to switch entry modes once an MNE has already entered the target market.

Last, low control modes are generally considered superior for certain transactions because they allow a firm to benefit from the scale economies of the marketplace without encountering the bureaucratic disadvantages that accompany integration (Williamson, 1985). Low control modes, however, have higher costs compared to modes providing better integration of firm assets and skills if managers fail to predict future contingencies correctly and if the market is unable to provide competitive alternatives. Entry mode selection, therefore, must be determined by the requirements of global integration and internalization. When high integration is required, high control entry modes are preferred. By contrast, low control modes may be more appropriate for MNEs that do not desire integration with the target host country.

Transaction Costs and Entry Mode

Transaction cost theory suggests that the governance structure an MNE chooses for a venture is driven by a desire to minimize transaction costs (Williamson, 1985). Transaction costs are associated with transacting business with other parties in the market, including the costs of drafting and negotiating contracts and monitoring the behavior of those who enter into the contracts. If transaction costs are low, a rational firm will prefer market governance on its transactions. However, if the costs of adaptation, performance monitoring, and safeguarding against the opportunistic behavior of other parties are too high, the firm will prefer an internal governance structure (e.g., a wholly owned subsidiary).

Transaction cost theory assumes that in a perfectly competitive market, market specialists will perform efficiently and, thus, keep transaction costs low. By allowing specialists to perform some of its functions, an MNE can avoid some of the disabling forces associated with building intrafirm bureaucracies. Therefore, the MNE is better off using a market governance structure for its transactions. In practice, however, the market is often imperfect. There are some instances in which bounded rationality and opportunism can lead to increased transaction costs, making an internal governance structure more attractive. Bounded rationality refers to the belief that managers by nature have limits on their ability to process information and have to make decisions with limited or imperfect information, and opportunism suggests that some parties to an agreement may choose to act out of self-interest and shirk their contractual responsibilities (Williamson, 1985).

Bounded rationality and opportunism are likely to increase transaction costs under uncertain conditions in which transaction-specific assets are present and transaction frequency is high. Bounded rationality makes the firm vulnerable to environmental and behavioral uncertainty and makes it difficult for the firm to specify all future contingencies and anticipate all necessary adaptations. Opportunism becomes especially problematic in a transaction that involves transaction-specific assets, such as proprietary technology or knowledge. When transaction-specific assets are present, the risks accompanying their possession are increased, concerns about opportunism are heightened, and the costs of safeguarding those assets from other parties may rise.

According to transaction cost theory, low control entry modes (i.e., market governance structures, such as licensing and franchising) are likely to be selected if transaction costs are low. If transaction costs are high, MNEs may opt for high control modes (i.e., intrafirm governance structures, such as dominant joint and wholly owned ventures). Specifically, a high control entry mode may be chosen if uncertainty of demand for an MNE's products or services in a foreign market is high; foreign market attractiveness is high; cultural distance between an MNE's home country and host country is high; specificity of the assets that an MNE contributes to the foreign venture is high; or the need for local contributions, such as indigenous capital, technology, and skilled manpower is low.

Bargaining Power and Entry Mode

Bargaining power theory argues that the specific mode chosen by an MNE depends on the relative bargaining power of the firm and that of the foreign government. Bargaining power refers to the bargainer's ability to set discussion parameters, win compromises from the other party, and skew the outcome of the negotiation toward the desired ownership alternative. Access to foreign markets is controlled by political actors at home and abroad, so the initial market entry decision must take into account political imperative (Gomes-Casseres, 1990). MNEs often have to negotiate with a variety of governmental actors to accomplish all or some of their objectives (Boddewyn & Brewer, 1994). Thus, the bargaining power of both political and corporate actors is a salient consideration.

A major source of a host government's power is its ability to control market access and hand out or withdraw investment incentives. An MNE's bargaining power stems from the ownership advantages it possesses. Therefore, bargaining power theory assumes that MNEs typically negotiate with foreign governments for high control modes of entry because these are the most desirable arrangements in terms of sustained ability to dominate the market and protect proprietary technology. In contrast, host governments often prefer investing firms to use a low control mode to enter their countries because such modes help transfer technology and know-how to local firms and allow local firms to share in the profits coming from the success of a foreign direct investment (FDI) project.

The stakes bargainers have in a negotiation, along with the availability of alternatives, influence bargaining power. A stake is the level of dependence a bargainer has on the negotiation relationship and its outcome. As stakes increase, bargaining power decreases. Moreover, having alternatives determines the extent to which parties can choose among different arrangements for attaining the same goals. Whichever party has more alternatives is more powerful because it can exercise its best alternative to negotiate the agreement. Consequently, stakes and availability of alternatives are sources of context-based bargaining power (Yan & Gray, 1994).

These are often influenced by such factors as industry structure, competition, market conditions, and the firm and the foreign government's dependence on each other. To be more specific, a high control entry mode is likely to be selected by an MNE when the degree to which the host government perceives a compelling need to attract FDI is high, the extent to which the MNE perceives itself as having a critical need to enter a foreign market is low, level of investment competition in the host country is low, host government restrictions on FDI are few, the MNE's need for local resources and contributions is low, the level of the MNE's resource commitment is low, and the level of risk (political and economic) is high.

Organizational Capability and Entry Mode

Another line of argument addressing entry mode decision focuses more closely on a firm's capabilities. To cope with the pressures of intense global competition and increasingly complex and rapid technological development, MNEs are now extending all over the globe for a multitude of purposes and through a multitude of forms. Of these forms, there has been a phenomenal increase recently in interfirm collaborations, both within and across borders. The major reason is that in today's environment, characterized by intense global competition and technological dynamism, MNEs feel inadequately equipped to remain competitive through reliance on their own capabilities and, therefore, perceive a stronger need to complement and reinforce their knowledge through collaboration (Madhok, 1997). Collaborations are formed for the purpose of developing firm capabilities. Thus, collaborative modes should not be regarded simply as cost-efficient alternatives to markets or wholly owned subsidiaries but rather as alternatives to other modes of knowledge acquisition.

The organizational capability perspective rests on the notions of bounded rationality, incrementalism, and the primacy of organizational routines in determining firm behavior. It regards the firm essentially as a bundle of relatively static, transferable resources that are then transformed into firm capabilities through dynamic, interactive, firm-specific processes where individual and organizational skills are inextricably woven together (Teece, Pisano, & Shuen, 1990). Capability thus encompasses resources and infuses them with sustainable value. Its accumulation is a dynamic process in which the information management attributes of the firm, that is, the firm's ability to acquire, evaluate, assimilate, integrate, diffuse, deploy, and exploit knowledge, are crucial. This process is dependent on the relatedness of new flows of knowledge to the existing stock of knowledge, it is largely idiosyncratic for each firm.

The nature and pattern of organizational capability and experience are critical to understanding the international activities of MNEs. Organizational capability is a source of competitive advantage as well as a constraint. Issues related to capability accumulation and deployment are of strategic significance (Madhok, 1997). In the context of foreign market entry, compatibility between the requirements of the operational context and the existing knowledge base is a primary factor in the firm's strategic evaluation of a particular mode. The cost of developing and deploying requisite capabilities in-house is critical because the choice of entry mode is influenced by the costs of replicating knowledge within the firm relative to its market transactions.

In general, high control and internalized entry modes provide competitive advantages. They would be preferable in domains where the firm has a strong knowledge base and possesses the necessary routines because incremental costs are marginal. This increases the efficiency of resource utilization and the effectiveness of its transfer in-house. Where the firm lacks the requisite capabilities, it may be too daunting to operate in a new context within an acceptable time or cost limit. A more effective, less costly alternative might be to supplement the firm's resources by grafting on new knowledge from other firms' experiences.

Entry mode decisions should be made with consideration for the deployment and development of an MNE's capabilities. Where knowledge resources are the primary concern, interfirm collaborations will involve restructuring the information boundaries of the firm and managing knowledge flow. FDI made through a wholly owned subsidiary results in the perpetuation of the firm's routines. Licensing, in contrast, does not involve adequate interaction for significant exposure to new information to occur. MNEs find joint ventures attractive to enhance the capabilities of their core businesses. The development of all necessary know-how in-house is viewed as too slow a process, and licensing is an inadequate way to gain more subtle aspects of know-how. Joint ventures provide the structural mechanisms for more intimate interactions that allow deeper exchanges of knowledge.

Evolutionary Process and Entry Mode

Rooted in the behavioral theory, the evolutionary perspective on the internationalization process attaches significant importance to behavioral factors as driving forces. Any given step is seen as an integral part of the overall process (Johanson & Vahlne, 1977). The most consistent pattern is evolutionary rather than revolutionary. That is, the movement from low commitment to high commitment modes occurs gradually over time, although some firms may leapfrog over some steps or speed up the whole process. Generally, however, international expansion behavior, especially of small or inexperienced firms, follows the learning curve of accumulating competence, knowledge, and confidence.

According to this perspective, an MNE's initial foreign involvement usually takes place in markets that are culturally and geographically proximate. The internationalization process is one of increasing commitment to foreign markets (Chang, 1995). Firms move sequentially from no international involvement to export, to overseas sales subsidiaries and, ultimately, to overseas production. Increasing levels of involvement in foreign markets relate to a firm's accumulation of experiential and local knowledge. Typically, joint ventures with local firms represent bridges between no equity involvement and equity involvement in a host country.

The firm may also acquire a domestic incumbent in order to gain the knowledge of a local firm. Acquisition can serve as a means of overcoming location-specific disadvantages. An acquisition of a domestic incumbent represents the purchase of stock in location-specific resources and capabilities that are bundled with the other resources of a local firm. Although an acquisition provides an MNE with an immediate stock of capabilities, it also comes with high costs that may outweigh expected benefits. Information asymmetry, organizational restructuring, and strategic integration all bring high costs. This has led to the view that acquisitions may be less efficient than greenfield investments.

Relevant knowledge and experience are acquired preeminently through actual presence and activities in a foreign market. Without appropriate experience and knowledge, there tends to be a stronger sense of risk and uncertainty among decision makers, which is likely to constrain the entry mode decision. Perceived risk exposure can be altered with the appropriate choice of entry mode. For example, high risks might be counterbalanced by the use of a low commitment mode, such as international licensing. Control concerns could also influence choice of entry mode because they are associated with risk, knowledge, and experience factors. Without knowledge and experience in a foreign market, it is difficult to achieve effective control of foreign operations. The firm tends to be less prepared to operate in ways that require stronger involvement and control and ends up depending more on locals for knowledge and networks. Deeper experience can shift the balance and allow deeper commitment.

Many companies perceive higher levels of risk and uncertainty as they gain information and knowledge during internationalization. Decision makers with an entrepreneurial orientation and a strong focus on international market opportunities may have only a limited initial awareness of the practical problems of foreign market penetration. Such ignorance can also result from the fortuitous, unplanned way in which many firms start foreign operations. As companies gain experience and seek external information and advice, they may become more conscious and concerned about the problems and risks of international involvement. In general, the tendency is to become more cautious in subsequent foreign moves. In some cases this will lead to reversals of foreign market involvement or even total withdrawal.

Managerial Considerations and Entry Mode

Entry mode selection is the result of managerial decision processes, influenced by expectations of economic performance as well as the dynamics of internal and external organizational demands (Tallman & Shenkar, 1994). In the process of choosing an entry mode, economic and noneconomic factors are assessed and given priorities by managers in investing firms who have limited information processing capabilities and a tendency toward making only satisfactory choices. At any given time, members are aware of only some of the organization's interdependencies in an external bargaining relationship and act only on those of which they are aware, precluding purely rational responses. Decisions are made by humans, not merely driven by the invisible forces of technology, transaction economics, or resource dependence.

Managers have variable degrees of access to relevant information by virtue of their divisional, functional, and interpersonal affiliations, as well as variable perceptions of the benefits and costs that they may accrue personally. Entry strategies are the result of managerial attempts to reduce uncertainty and improve performance in host markets. Constrained by the firm's idiosyncratic resources and its worldwide strategy, these managers are also subject to a variety of subjective concerns related to their inherently bounded rationality. In such circumstances, the economic rationality of cost minimization and profit maximization can provide feedback during an ongoing decision process.

Entry mode decision may be also an internal bargaining game (Tallman & Shenkar, 1994). Managerial limitations result in coalition building and a negotiated internal organizational environment. Organizational issues, both inside and outside the firm, become political power concerns when managers are active participants in strategic and organizational processes. The negotiated aspect of internal decision making also reflects the difficulty of finding an optimal outcome in an uncertain environment. Decision makers in some companies may have to use their authority to overcome resistance to proposed entry strategies from other managers who fear high risks, low profits, huge start-up costs, or creation of new competitors.

The corporate culture may also have a certain impact on the choice of entry mode. Corporate culture can be used to control behavior. A strong corporate culture can serve to lower transaction costs as subsidiaries become more similar to their parent firm. Some corporate cultures are more amenable to joint ventures or alliances. Others favor wholly owned subsidiaries or international acquisitions. Firms will opt for the entry mode that is most congenial with their corporate culture or would seem to incur the least adaptation costs.

Organizational strengths in overcoming cultural barriers across nations may also influence entry mode. Perceived cultural distance is positively related to the level of risk and uncertainty in the environment facing an MNE. Companies from the same home country operating in the same host country will perceive different levels of cultural difference given the variable levels of experience and knowledge among individual firms. Some companies may opt to go it alone by capitalizing on their considerable host country experience. Other companies may prefer a joint venture where they can take advantage of interpartner learning. Foreign experience and cultural adaptability are therefore an important managerial factor underlying entry mode decisions.

ENTRY MODE CHOICES

Entry modes for international expansion fall into two categories: trade-related or investment-related. International trade businesses include conventional import and export, subcontracts (i.e., processing imported materials or foreign samples and assembling imported parts and components), international leases, and countertrade (i.e., barter, counterpurchase, offset, switch trading, compensation trade, or buybacks). FDI entry modes include representative or branch offices, international licensing, international franchising, build-operate-transfers (BOTs), contractual joint ventures, equity joint ventures, wholly owned subsidiaries, and umbrella investment companies. Along the investment sequence from representative office through to umbrella company, the levels of both risk and control increase. Greenfield investments and acquisitions are not entry modes; rather, they represent two major forms of capital investment or presence establishments. Although this chapter focuses on investment-related entry modes, trade-related entry modes are briefly introduced.

Trade-Related Entry Modes

Export

It is natural for most MNEs to get their start in international expansion through export businesses in which the firm maintains its production facilities at home and sells its products abroad. Export offers the advantage of not requiring a very substantial presence in foreign countries. Its major disadvantages are high transportation costs; the difficulty of dealing at a distance with problems, such as government regulations, cultural differences, and currency exchange; and the inability to explore higher possible profits stemming from different market structures and factor endowments between countries.

Subcontracts

Subcontracting, also known as flexible trading, has been extensively used by MNEs that only intend to exploit cheap labor costs in a host country. Thus, this mode has been mostly used by MNEs in labor-intensive industries. Subcontractors are generally processing and assembling businesses. Foreign firms provide local manufacturers with raw materials or semi finished products for producing final goods to be directly distributed internationally. Nike, for example, is still using subcontracting as its primary mode in China. The company provides raw materials and technology, maintains proprietary rights over materials and products, controls production processes and product quality, and pays processing fees to local factories.

International Lease

In this mode, the foreign party retains ownership and, therefore, equity and equipment risks throughout the period of a lease. The major advantages of this mode for MNEs include quick access to the target market, efficient use of superfluous or outmoded machinery and equipment, and accumulated experience within a host country. From the local firm's perspective, this mode helps reduce the cost of using foreign machinery and equipment, mitigates operational and investment risks, and increases its knowledge and experience with new products and operations.

Countertrade

Countertrade has evolved into a diverse set of activities that can be categorized as five distinct types of trading arrangements: barter, counterpurchase, offset, switch trading, and compensation or buyback. Barter is the direct exchange of goods or services between two parties without a cash transaction. Barter trade occurs either between governments, between firms from two different countries, or between one country's government and another country's firm. Firms using barter may run the risk of having to accept goods that may be difficult to market or earn a satisfactory profit margin from. A counterpurchase is a reciprocal buying agreement. It takes place when a firm agrees to purchase a certain amount of materials back from a country to which a sale has been made. For example, a British company sells construction equipment to a Chinese firm. The Chinese firm pays the British firm in pounds; in exchange, the British company agrees to spend some of its proceeds on silk garments produced by the Chinese company. An offset is similar to a counterpurchase in that one party agrees to purchase goods and services with a specified percentage of its proceeds from an original sale. The difference is that this party can fulfill its obligation with any firm in the country to which the sale has been made. From an exporter's perspective, this is more attractive than a straight counterpurchase agreement because it gives the exporter greater flexibility in choosing which goods to buy. Switch trading refers to the use of a third-party trading house in a countertrade agreement. Typically, when a firm enters into a counterpurchase or offset agreement with a country it often ends up with counterpurchase credits that can be used to purchase goods from that country. Switch trading occurs when a third-party trading house buys the firm's counterpurchase credits and sells them to another firm that can make better use of them. Last, compensation or buyback occurs when a firm builds a plant in a country or provides local partners with inputs for manufacturing products to be sold either in the domestic or international markets, and agrees to take a certain percentage of the output produced by the local firm as partial payment for the contract.

Investment Mode 1: Representative or Branch Offices

Although technically not considered an FDI, a representative office is a quick and relatively simple way to become acquainted with a target market. It is used by many foreign companies new to a host country. This helps foreign companies test the waters before taking the plunge of forming a subsidiary.

Representative offices allow firms to establish contacts with key industrial ministries and build their reputations in host countries. By law, representative offices are prohibited from engaging in direct, profit-making business activities. They are allowed to undertake non-commercial activities including business communications, product promotion, market research, contract administration, and negotiations on behalf of their head offices. Equally important, they can also act as liaisons to potential trading partners as well as various commercial and government offices in the host country; they lay the foundation for further investment by promoting the foreign company's name and reputation. Corporate giants like Bechtel and Apple Computer had representative offices in China for at least ten years before building legal-person status subsidiaries.

The most apparent advantages the representative office has over other entry modes are its simplicity and flexibility. Unlike an equity joint venture or wholly owned subsidiary, a representative office gives a foreign company a formal presence in the host country without the complications of an unfamiliar local partner or hefty financial commitment. A representative office, unlike other investment vehicles, has no minimum registered capital requirements. Many foreign businesses find the establishment of representative offices, although not necessarily cheap, an excellent way of becoming familiar with the target country's business environment before making a major commitment.

One flexible feature of representative offices is lack of restriction on the line of business in which the company can engage. Other entry modes, by contrast, can only participate in sectors and industries designated by governmental authorities. For example, the Chinese government discourages foreign participation in media communications except for representative offices. In countries that restrict MNE operations to certain industries, such as insurance, banking, or trading, MNEs have found that the establishment of representative offices offers them a platform from which to try to convince local government officials to open other sectors to foreign activity.

As the representative office operates independently, it can proceed with liaison, market research, and consulting activities in whatever fashion it sees fit. Closing a representative office is also relatively easy compared to terminating a joint venture. It is also fairly easy for representative offices to hire talented local college graduates or managers who see employment at the office as a way to gain exposure to the world of international business or a job at the head office in the future. Such benefits make the representative office an ideal means for exploring further investment in the foreign market, establishing a presence in other regions of the country, or arranging future investment projects.

Nevertheless, this entry mode has several disadvantages. Although establishing a representative office is comparatively easy, a host of regulatory and start-up costs can make them quite expensive to maintain. In addition to high labor costs paid to local employees, representative offices must usually pay high rents because they tend to be located in major cities where office spaces are in chronic short supply. For instance, of the total 24,402 representative offices operating in China as of 1994, 3,802 were located in Beijing, 3,294 in Shanghai, and 6,918 in Guangzhou. Far fewer have been established in interior locations. Moreover, a representative office cannot issue invoices or receive payment directly for services to local customers. It may also have to pay duties on all imported office equipment. The imposed tariffs on computers, photocopiers, fax machines, video and audio equipment, air conditioners, and other office items can be as high as 100 percent. Despite these problems, the merits of this entry mode make it an invaluable way to sample the fruits of economic dynamism and growth in a target host country.

Similar, but not the same as, representative offices are branch offices, which can undertake business transactions in a host country. Company law in many developed and developing countries allows foreign companies to open branches that engage in production and operating activities. A foreign subsidiary can also open a branch office in another region of the host country to expand its operations there. In recent years, many transnational banks and law firms have established branch offices overseas. Branch offices may offer a relatively simple means for establishing or expanding a presence in a target country, but the fact that they do not have legal-person status means that the foreign parent company is liable if civil charges are brought against the branch. To shield the parent company from unlimited damage claims, foreign companies interested in establishing branch offices may designate an offshore subsidiary as the parent.

Investment Mode 2: International Licensing

Two forms of contractual arrangements often used during international expansion are franchises and licenses. Both involve a contract between parties in different countries, but franchise contracts cover more aspects of the operation and are typically of a longer duration than licensing. A licensor in one country makes limited rights or resources available to the licensee in a foreign country. The rights or resources may include patents, trademarks, technology, managerial skills, and so on. These allow the licensee to produce and market a product similar to the one the licensor has already been producing in its home country without requiring the licensor actually to create a new operation abroad. For instance, licensees in China and other countries have contracts to produce and sell toys and clothing bearing pictures of Mickey Mouse and other Disney characters.

In general, an MNE may use international licensing to: obtain extra income from technical know-how and services, spread around the costs of company research and development programs, or maximize returns on research findings and accumulated know-how; retain established markets that have been closed or threatened by trade restrictions, reach new markets not accessible by export from existing facilities, or expand foreign markets quickly with minimum effort or risk; augment limited domestic capacity and management resources for serving foreign markets, provide overseas sources of supply and services to important domestic customers, or develop market outlets for raw materials or components made by the domestic company; build goodwill and acceptance for the company's other products or services, develop sources of raw materials or components for the company's other operations, or pave the way for future investment; or discourage possible infringement, impairment, or loss of company patents or trademarks, or acquire reciprocal benefits from foreign know-how, research, and technical services.

An international licensing agreement may include the delivery by the licensor to the licensee of one or more of the following: a patent or patented product or process; a trademark or trade name; manufacturing techniques and other proprietary rights generally referred to as company or industrial know-how; components, materials, or equipment essential to a manufacturing process; technical advice and service; marketing advice and assistance; and capital or managerial personnel. Licensing is a relatively flexible working arrangement that can be tailored to the needs of both the licensor and the licensee. It is not unusual for licensing agreements to be negotiated between a parent company and its wholly owned subsidiaries or branches. A company may also have licensing agreements with its foreign joint venture partners.

Licensing is a popular method for profiting from a foreign market without committing sizable funds. Because the foreign producer is typically 100 percent locally owned, political risk is minimized. Licensing provides a foothold in a foreign market without a large capital investment. It can be less risky than starting a manufacturing operation. This mode is highly attractive to firms that are new to international business. Most countries require that patents and trademarks be used within a certain number of years of being granted or registered; licensing is a viable option for protecting the company's patents and trademarks. In addition, there is less foreign exchange exposure and risk involved in licensing arrangements. The licensor may find it to be the best way to tap a foreign market if the market potential in the country is too small to support a manufacturing plant. Licensing is a good method of securing business in foreign countries that have nationalized industries, such as radio, television, telephone, transportation, oil, steel, and public utilities.

Income from licenses, however, is lower than from other FDI entry modes, although the return on the marginal investment can be higher. Loss of quality control can be another major disadvantage of this entry mode. The experience of many firms indicates that it is difficult for the licensor to maintain satisfactory control over the licensee's manufacturing and marketing operations. This can result in damage to a licensor's trademark and reputation. Moreover, a foreign licensee can also become a competitor to the licensor. If the original licensing agreement does not stipulate the region within which the licensee may market the licensed product, the licensee may insist on marketing the product in third country markets in competition with the licensor. Further, a local licensee may benefit from improvements in its technology, which it then uses to enter the MNE's home market.

It is critical for an MNE to consider how its licensing program fits into its overall long-range strategic objectives and policies. If a company can establish its own manufacturing and sales facilities, it should do so because it is to its advantage to reap maximum benefits from global markets for its products. Possible repercussions on domestic, export, and other foreign operations and prospective return in terms of resources and risks involved must be carefully determined prior to signing any license agreement with a foreign firm. If a company does decide to enter into a licensing agreement, then it should consider the following factors that will largely influence its success:

choice of a reliable, competent, and compatible licensee;

inherent value of the licensed patents, trademarks, or know-how;

thorough advance research and understanding of the market;

mutual confidence and respect for each other's interests and objectives;

participation in ownership or management;

close personal contact and public relations efforts with licensees;

the prestige and favorable reputation of the licensor and its product;

margin of technical and research lead maintained by the licensor;

provision of merchandising and sales assistance to licensees;

organized supervision and service provided licensees by a special licensing staff;

scale of activity and amount of effort and attention devoted to the license business;

correct timing and pacing of licensing activity;

detailed listing of contractual obligations and interfirm relationship;

effective coordination with other parts of the foreign business program; and

legal regulations on licensing imposed by the host government.

For example, Chinese law tends to encourage the conversion of a licensing contract into an installment sale plan by forbidding restrictions on the licensee's continued use of the know-how, trademark, or technology received from the foreign firm after expiration of the license contract. The Chinese government also mandates that license contracts shall not exceed ten years.

Investment Mode 3: International Franchising

Compared to licensing, a franchise usually includes a broader package of rights and resources. Production equipment, managerial systems, operating procedures, access to advertising and promotional materials, loans, and financing may all be part of a franchise. In addition, franchising tends to involve longer-term commitments than licensing. The franchisee operates the business under the franchisor's proprietary rights and is contractually obligated to adhere to the procedures and methods of operation prescribed in the business system. The franchisor generally maintains the right to control the quality of products and services so that the franchisee cannot harm the company's image. In exchange for the franchise, the franchisor receives a royalty payment that amounts to some percentage of the franchisee's revenues. Sometimes the franchisor mandates that the franchisee must buy equipment or key ingredients used in the product. For example, Burger King and McDonald's require the franchisee to buy the company's cooking equipment, burger patties, and other products that bear the company name. In general, licensing is pursued primarily by manufacturing firms, and franchising is used mainly by service companies.

The merits and limitations of international franchising are similar to those of licensing. The main advantages include little political risk, low costs, and fast and easy avenues for using assets, such as a trademark or brand name. For example, McDonald's has been able to build a global presence quickly and at a relatively low cost and risk by using franchises. Nevertheless, the franchisee may spoil the franchisor's image by not upholding its standards. Even if the franchisor is able to terminate the agreement, some franchisees still stay in business by slightly altering the franchisor's brand name or trademark.

It is important for foreign franchisors to familiarize themselves with the legal framework for international franchising in the host country. In addition, foreign companies should confirm the identity, legal status, and authority of potential local recipients. The simplest verification is a review of their business license and, if possible, articles of association.

Investment Mode 4: Build-Operate-Transfer

BOTs are a newly emerging mode of entry into many developing countries. A BOT is essentially a turnkey investment in which a foreign investor assumes responsibility for the design and construction of an entire operation, and, upon completion of the project, hands over its total management to local personnel whom it has trained. In return for completing the project, the investor receives periodic payments. BOT is especially useful in the power generation sector and for other large-scale, long-term infrastructure projects, such as airports, dams, expressways, chemical plants, and steel mills. For instance, negotiations for one of the first BOT power projects were recently completed in China. According to officials in Southeastern Guangxi, the final contract for the Laibin B power plant will soon be signed with Electricité de France, Britain's National Power International, and Barclays Bank. Recently, China's State Planning Committee has ratified ten more BOT projects calling for foreign operations.

BOT is a guaranteed fee method of cooperation by which an investor identifies a project in a host country, assumes sole responsibility for investing in the construction and operation of the project, and, after recovering investment and obtaining compensation, returns the project to the local organization in the host country. It is popular in developing countries short on capital and technology. For example, the first BOT project, implemented in China on a trial basis, was the Beijing-Tongxian Expressway. It was built by Beijing civil construction departments and a U.S. company. Construction started in September 1994, with 20 months as the projected time for completion. The approved term of this BOT is 20 years, after which the expressway will be returned to China.

Partly because of difficulties in working out financing and equity arrangements, the BOT approach is often used in combination with other entry modes. Foreign businesses may set up BOT project firms by means of either equity or cooperative joint ventures with local partners or wholly foreign owned ventures. Because of their ability to provide foreign investors with returns in excess of their proportional contributions to the venture's total registered capital, contractual joint ventures have been the vehicles of choice for BOT infrastructure projects.

Investment Mode 5: Contractual Joint Ventures

The contractual joint venture (also known as a non-equity cooperative joint venture or arrangement) is an investment vehicle in which profits and other responsibilities are assigned to each party according to a contract. These do not necessarily accord with each partner's percentage of the total investment. Each party cooperates as a separate legal entity and bears its own liabilities. The two firms entering into a contractual joint venture also have the option of forming a limited liability entity with legal person status, similar to that of an equity joint venture.

In recent years many cooperative programs between firms involve joint activities without the creation of a new corporate entity. Instead, carefully defined rules govern the allocation of tasks, costs, and revenues. Joint exploration, research partnership, and coproduction are typical forms of cooperative joint ventures (others may include joint marketing, long-term supply agreements, or technological training and assistance).

Joint exploration projects (e.g., offshore oil exploration consortia) are a special type of contractual joint venture. Under these arrangements, the exploration costs are borne by the foreign partner, with development costs later shared by a local entity. Although such explorations allow the foreign firm to manage specific projects, this type of FDI does not necessarily result in the establishment of new limited liability enterprises. By comparison, the costs of a research partnership or consortium may be allocated by an agreed upon formula, but the revenue of each partner depends on what each company independently does with the technology created. In coproduction agreements, such as the Boeing 767 project involving Boeing and Japan Aircraft Development Corporation (itself a consortium of Mitsubishi, Kawasaki, and Fuji), each partner is responsible for manufacturing a particular part of the product. Each partner's costs are therefore a function of its own efficiency in producing that part. However, revenue is a function of successful sales, as of the 767 by the dominant partner Boeing.

Major features of contractual joint ventures include liability, capital requirements, import tax exemptions, and strategic flexibility.

Liability

A contractual joint venture is allowed to adopt a non-legal person status. The liability of investors in a venture with non-legal person status is unlimited, but the liability of investors in a joint venture with legal person status is limited to the amounts they have invested. Legal person status is automatic for equity joint ventures. Contractual joint ventures may elect either status. Contractual joint venture investors may be able to use the unlimited liability option in the tax structure for their venture.

Capital Requirements

In many developing countries, foreign investors in contractual joint ventures with legal person status are required to contribute a certain percentage of the venture's total registered capital (e.g., 25 percent in China). This requirement does not apply to contractual joint ventures that adopt non-legal person status. In practice, this percentage was generally assumed to be the minimum amount that a foreign investor could contribute to a contractual joint venture with non-legal person status.

Import Tax Exemptions

Like equity joint ventures, contractual joint ventures are generally exempt from paying transfer taxes and duties on imported equipment used as part of the foreign partner's investment in the enterprise, provided the equipment is required for the operation of the joint venture and is valued at no more than the total investment amount specified in the contract.

Strategic Flexibility

There are no limits on the duration of the contract or prohibitions for withdrawal of registered capital during the contracted term. Contractual joint ventures have great freedom to structure their assets, organize their production processes, and manage their operations. This flexibility can be highly attractive for a foreign investor interested in property development, resource exploration, or other production projects in which the foreign party incurs substantial initial development costs. A partner can build into the contract an accelerated return on its share of investment to allow it to recoup its equity share by the end of the term. Further, contractual joint ventures can be developed quickly to take advantage of short-term business opportunities, then dissolved when their tasks are completed.

Contractual joint ventures differ from equity joint ventures in several ways. First, profit distributions among parties to a contractual joint venture need not be in strict proportion to their registered capital contributions. The foreign party may, for example, recover its investment earlier than the local partner upon meeting certain conditions, including reversion of all fixed assets to the local partner. In contrast, the parties to an equity joint venture can distribute profits only in strict proportion to their total registered capital. Moreover, a contractual joint venture may distribute profits both in cash and in venture output, while an equity joint venture is restricted to making cash distributions. Second, as noted above, the contractual joint venture's ability to adopt non-legal person status also distinguishes it from an equity joint venture. Besides affecting the liability of the joint venture partner, non-legal person status may allow foreign contractual joint venture partners to contribute less than the usually required percentage of registered capital. Foreign partners in an equity joint venture must contribute a minimum percentage of registered capital.

Because of their ability to provide foreign investors with returns in excess of their proportional contributions to the venture's total registered capital, contractual joint ventures have been the vehicles of choice for BOT infrastructure projects. The contractual joint venture option is expected to continue to be useful in BOT projects and, as a result of new regulations, will become a more popular option for other types of ventures as well, especially those in which foreign investors seek a preferential return.

Table 6.1 lists some examples of various forms of contractual or cooperative joint ventures in the automotive industry.

Investment Mode 6: Equity Joint Ventures

The most common foreign entry for MNEs has been through equity joint ventures. An international equity joint venture involves equity ownership and control by an international company of a venture shared with local partner(s) in a host country. To set up an equity joint venture, each partner contributes cash, facilities, equipment, materials, intellectual property rights, labor, or land-use rights. According to joint venture laws in most countries, a foreign investor's share must be over a certain percentage of the total equity (e.g., 25 percent in China). Generally, there is no upward limit in deregulated industries in most countries, whether developed or developing. However, in governmentally controlled or institutionally restricted sectors, foreign investors are often confined with respect to equity arrangements.

Equity joint ventures need not involve production. A company may establish one that is involved in the distribution of the company's products or in marketing services, such as advertising, accounting, engineering, or legal or management consulting. As an alternative to either full integration or a simple market exchange, the equity joint venture facilitates interfirm learning and transfer of intangible assets while mitigating incentives for opportunism by creating interdependence between transacting parties. If the benefits derived from joint efforts, minus its transaction costs, are greater than the sum of benefits obtained from exploiting firm-specific advantages separately, an equity joint venture creates synergies that enhance economic rents to its partners. These synergies can be the result of risk reduction, economies of scale and scope, production rationalization, convergence of technologies, and improved local acceptance.

Equity joint ventures are, however, notoriously hard to sustain even in relatively stable environments, such as the United States and Europe. Developing countries are even more difficult investment environments because they are more uncertain and complex, their cultures and

TABLE 6.1
Forms of Contractual (Cooperative) Joint Ventures in the Automotive Industry

Company	Equity Venture	Supplies/Buys Components	Marketing/ Distribution Arrangement	Technology Arrangement	Manufacturing/ Assembly Arrangement
General Motors (USA) (includes Opel, Vauxhall, Holden's, Saturn	Chrysler Daewoo Ford FSO Isuzu Nissan Saab Suzuki Toyota Volvo	Fiat Fuji Heavy Honda Isuzu Mitsubishi Nissan Renault Rover Saab Suzuki Toyota VAZ	CAC Isuzu Renault Saab Toyota	Chrysler Ford Honda Isuzu Suzuki Toyota	Bertone CAC Daewoo Isuzu Suzuki
Ford (USA) (includes Jaguar)	Fiat GM Mazda Nissan Toyota Volkswagen Volvo	AZLK Fiat Fuji Heavy Mazda Nissan Renault Volkswagen	Fiat Kia Mazda Suzuki	Chrysler GM Kia Mazda Nissan	BMW Kia Mazda Nissan Rover Suzuki

158

Chrysler (USA)	Beijing Auto De Tomaso GM Mitsubishi Steyr-Daimler-Puch	Beijing Auto Mitsubishi Rover Steyr-Daimler-Puch	Honda VAZ	Beijing Auto Ford GM Mitsubishi Steyr-Daimler-Puch	Mitsubishi Peugeot Steyr-Daimler-Puch
Toyota (Japan)	Daihatsu Ford GM Nissan Renault	Daihatsu GM	Daihatsu GM Volkswagen	Daihatsu GM Nissan Volkswagen	CNAIC Daihatsu Volkswagen
Honda (Japan)	Mitsubishi Rover	Daewoo GM Mitsubishi Rover	Chrysler Daewoo Rover	Daewoo GM Rover	Daewoo Isuzu Mercedes-Benz Mitsubishi Peugeot

Source: Adapted from Yoshino, M.Y. and Rangan, U. S. 1995. *Strategic alliance.* Boston, Mass.: Harvard Business School Press, pp. 10–15.

traditions are profoundly different from those in the West, and their social, governmental, and economic systems are particularly complex. Joint venture negotiations can be lengthy and complicated. Often negotiation continues even after the signing of the contract. Therefore, a foreign company should choose effective negotiators, prepare for time-consuming meetings, and develop a sophisticated strategy before starting negotiations. An equity joint venture abroad could be a new start investment, which involves building the venture from the ground up, or it may involve a merger with a local firm.

Previous studies have suggested that the following factors influence the choice of an equity joint venture.

Technological characteristics: MNEs that have a product whose value is based upon unique production processes, trademarks, brand names, or know-how are hesitant to establish equity joint ventures because of the danger that their production processes and core technologies may be leaked to third parties.

Integration requirements: When an MNE uses a global strategy to integrate subsidiaries in different countries, particularly with vertical integration (i.e., production-assembly-distribution systems), MNEs are likely to oppose equity joint ventures because ventures with local partners decrease their flexibility and increase the control required to integrate the different subsidiaries into the network.

Interpartner learning: MNEs seek joint ventures or alliances when they need complementary knowledge or expertise that can best be provided by a local firm. The knowledge sought by an MNE may include technological skills, process know-how, research and development expertise, country-specific knowledge, unique marketing skills, distribution channels, and interorganizational or interpersonal relationships.

Investment Mode 7: Wholly Owned Subsidiaries

The wholly owned subsidiary form offers foreign investors increased flexibility and control. It allows international managers to expand as quickly as they want and where they want without the burden of an uncooperative partner. Wholly owned subsidiaries also allow foreign investors to set up and protect their own processes and procedures, which leads to more careful strategic and operational oversight. Moreover, they can be established more quickly than equity joint ventures.

Nevertheless, the establishment of a large, wholly owned project abroad, such as the Mercedes-Benz plant in Alabama, can be a complex, costly, lengthy process. An MNE must choose between the importance of protecting its core technology and controlling its manufacturing and marketing processes on the one hand, and the costs of establishing a new operation on the other. Many MNEs choose this alternative only after expanding into markets through other modes that have helped them accumulate host country experience. This particular mode may be more attractive or appropriate, *ceteris paribus*, either in high-technology industries where protecting a technological competence is critical to gaining a competitive advantage in global markets or in geographical markets where the local operations have to be highly integrated with other global businesses within the network.

Wholly owned subsidiaries have traditionally been viewed by many host country governments, particularly those of developing economies, as offering little in the way of technology transfer or other benefits to local economies. Recently, this entry mode has gradually become more attractive to them. When domestic credit is tight, this mode provides host countries with a means of attracting foreign investment. Nevertheless, the governmental support for this mode often trails far behind that of joint ventures in many countries.

To establish a wholly owned subsidiary, an MNE can either set up a new operation in a country (i.e., greenfield investment) or it can acquire an established local firm and use that firm to promote its products in the country's market (acquisition). International acquisition of a local firm or another foreign company with local ventures is the quickest way to expand one's investment in the target country. An acquisition is particularly useful for entering sectors formerly restricted to state-owned enterprises. Moreover, cash flow may be generated in a shorter time than in the case of greenfield investment, because the acquired firm, by definition, does not have to be built from scratch. Furthermore, acquisition deals may be more attractive than greenfield investment because acquisitions offer immediate access to resources, such as land, distribution channels, and skilled labor, even when acquired firms have been losing money.

Foreign investors generally target those enterprises with strong market niches in sectors with potential for growth. A foreign company acquiring a local firm should be familiar with two types of limited companies: those that issue privately held shares and those that issue publicly traded shares. Which form the company takes depends upon the percentage of shares held by its founders, who must be legal persons. To set up a private limited company, the firm issues shares that it or its sponsor buys back to maintain full ownership. In contrast, in publicly traded limited companies the founding companies may purchase only a certain percentage of the venture's shares and the rest is sold to the public.

Investors buying a stake in a local company must first evaluate various risks. Gaining government approval for the transfer of ownership and clearance of property titles is often a difficult hurdle. Foreign investors should be careful to obtain accurate information, particularly concerning existing liabilities, when buying into an indigenous entity. Analysis of investment risks should also take into consideration the locality, including the local bureaucracy, transportation links, and other infrastructure issues, because regional rivalries and an aged and inadequate infrastructure often hamper the efficient movement of goods, information, services, and labor throughout many developing countries.

Some notes of caution should be stated. First, wholly owned subsidiaries must handle various industrial linkages with local firms. Many foreign investors need to rely on indigenous agents to make liaisons on their behalf and help procure land, materials, and services. Second, wholly owned foreign subsidiaries may not be allowed to invest and operate in certain industries that are vital to the host country economy. Third, because wholly owned subsidiaries operate without the control of local partners, investment approval authorities often hold them to higher standards of pollution control, technological level, capital contribution, foreign exchange administration, and the like. Last, wholly owned subsidiaries are more vulnerable to criticism relating to cultural and economic sovereignty. Naturally, local people do not want foreign companies taking advantage of their country. Managers in wholly owned subsidiaries should recognize and address this concern. One way is to localize production, that is, to buy as many parts and components as possible from local suppliers. Another way is to hire local managers. Motorola (China), for example, only employs Chinese managers, very few of whom hold U.S. passports. Foreign companies can also be active in socially responsible projects by financing schools, sports events, the arts, public safety, or other community service projects.

Investment Mode 8: Umbrella Companies

Many foreign companies are now seeking greater flexibility of operations in a target market. A growing number of firms are interested in establishing fully integrated companies that can combine sales, procurement, subsidiary investment, manufacturing, and maintenance service for a broad range of products within a host country. Foreign investors interested in the concept particularly include those seeking to unite various existing investments in a foreign country under a parent company. The growing complexity of operations of many MNEs in a single, major foreign market (e.g., China) and the need to coordinate more closely numerous joint ventures or wholly owned subsidiaries have led several firms to set up holding companies in recent years. The umbrella enterprise, also known as an investment company or holding company, is able to unite existing investments under one umbrella to combine sales, procurement, manufacturing, and maintenance. It can help improve the cash flow and capital structure of various investments by acting as a clearinghouse for intra-group financing. It can also smooth the establishment of new investments. Like all legally independent subsidiaries, an umbrella enterprise has legal person status in a host country.

The umbrella model is especially useful for companies that are multi-divisional, where each division enters and runs differently while the holding company coordinates them. This also suits the way the company is run worldwide. Individual businesses are preferred so as to avoid building up reserves that would limit the volume of cash that can be cycled globally. With a holding company in a host country, profits can be more easily transferred among different strategic business units (SBUs) and taken out of the country.

A foreign investor may consider establishing an umbrella enterprise to achieve some or all of the following objectives:

investment in subsidiary projects;

manufacturing products;

facilitating cash flow (in developed countries) or foreign exchange balance (in developing countries) for all local activities;

centralized purchase of production materials for subsidiary projects;

provision of product maintenance services and technical support;

training of subsidiary project personnel and end users of products;

coordination and consolidation of project management (Without an umbrella company, each subunit has a separate company structure; an umbrella enterprise can centralize management and streamline the subsidiaries as operating units.);

marketing subsidiary products (Usually, each manufacturing SBU has to set up its own sales capabilities; an umbrella enterprise can achieve greater efficiency by establishing one marketing entity.); and

conversion of representative offices into umbrella or subsidiary branch offices, thus removing many operating restrictions, such as the need to hire personnel through labor service companies.

An umbrella company may provide a range of services to its subsidiaries including:

assisting personnel recruitment;

providing technical training, market development, and consulting assistance;

assisting borrowing, including providing guaranties;

acting as an agent for subsidiaries in the procurement of machinery and equipment, including office equipment, and raw materials, components, and spare parts necessary for production;

acting as an agent for SBUs in the sale of products and providing after-sales service;

balancing cash flow or foreign exchange among SBUs; and

providing financial support to subsidiaries.

The establishment of an umbrella company has to comply with certain conditions set by the host country government. In China, for example, Chinese partners in prospective joint investment (umbrella) companies must have a minimum total asset value of ¥100 million. Foreign applicants for wholly owned or joint investment companies must meet one of two sets of criteria. In one set, the foreign company must have had a minimum total asset value of $400 million in the year prior to its application, have established one or more subunits in which it has contributed at least $10 million in registered capital, and have obtained approvals for three additional SBU project proposals. Applicants meeting this first set of conditions have the option of establishing an investment company in the name of a wholly owned subsidiary rather than in their own names, which may offer some comfort to foreign investors who want to insulate corporate headquarters from direct exposure to liabilities in China. The second set of conditions stipulates that the foreign investor must have established a minimum of 10 subunits in China and engaged in manufacturing or infrastructure construction to which it has contributed at least $30 million in registered capital. Presently, the investment company itself must have a registered capital of at least $30 million.

An umbrella company and its various subunits are each treated by Chinese tax authorities as separate entities; consolidation of revenue and expenditures for tax purposes is not allowed. Subsidiary profits that are remitted to the umbrella enterprise as dividends will not be taxed, however. An umbrella enterprise with no manufacturing of its own will be taxed at 33 percent with no tax holidays. Like all other subunits, an umbrella enterprise must balance its foreign exchange.

Combining Options

Selecting between an equity joint venture and a wholly owned subsidiary is not necessarily an either-or decision. Sometimes a local partner does have a strong distribution network or operates in a restricted sector that is attractive to a foreign investor. In such situations, foreign companies can, for instance, surround their wholly owned subsidiary production operation with equity joint ventures that market and sell their products in the host market. Motorola does exactly that. Since 1993 Motorola has been laying the groundwork for the biggest U.S. manufacturing venture in China. Its commitment of more than $300 million to China focuses on pagers, simple integrated circuits, cellular phones, and, eventually, automotive electronics. The production site in the Tianjin Economic Development Zone is a wholly owned subsidiary, but marketing and sales of products will be done through various equity joint ventures with local partners.

Another approach is to start an equity joint venture and a wholly owned subsidiary in sequence. A foreign investor can get initial entry as part of an equity joint venture for a fixed period stipulated in the duration clause of the contract. At the end of the stipulated term, it can take over the assets from the local partner and continue to run the operation as a wholly owned subsidiary. This is an attractive alternative if the added value of the local partner is significant but limited to the early stages of the venture. Some equity joint ventures have included this option in the termination clause of the joint venture contract.

It is also possible to structure a wholly owned subsidiary under the legal umbrella of an equity joint venture. In other words, the project would be an equity joint venture as a legal entity but would be run and operated as a wholly owned subsidiary. Many foreign partners that have increased their equity stakes in existing ventures are going in that direction. In some cases, they turn their local partner into a silent partner with a minority stake.

FACTORS AFFECTING ENTRY MODE SELECTION

MNEs can structure their entry into a target market in many different ways. Some will be more suitable than others depending upon a variety of contingencies. Inevitably, there are trade-offs in choosing one entry mode over another. Once a foreign investor decides to pursue an FDI project, its choice of entry mode will depend on a wide range of factors. Broadly, these contingencies can be classified into country, industry, firm, and project factors. Foreign firms should make sure they know all possible options for the entry into a target country before determining the best one. The impact of each of these categories on entry mode decision is elaborated below. Figure 6.1 schematically shows an integrated framework for entry mode selection.

Country-Specific Factors

Several exogenous host country-specific factors have an impact on choice of entry mode. First, government FDI policies may directly or indirectly influence entry mode selection. The laws in some countries mandate that foreign firms must choose joint ventures, as opposed to wholly owned subsidiaries, as an entry mode. This policy holds particularly true in pillar industries or those vital to the economic development of the host country. In some countries MNEs with different entry modes are treated differently in terms of taxation, infrastructure access, local financing, and resource or material procurement by the local government. For instance, joint ventures enjoy preferential corporate income tax rates in many

FIGURE 6.1
Entry Mode Selection in International Expansion: An Integrated Model

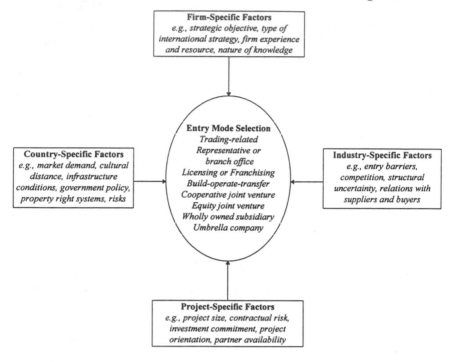

developing countries. This idiosyncracy influences entry mode selection because it has implications for expected risk-adjusted profitability.

Second, the conditions of the infrastructure and support industries will affect the extent to which an MNE plans to commit distinctive resources to local operations and the degree to which it perceives operational uncertainty and contextual unpredictability. These in turn influence the entry mode option. In practice, MNEs often have to make a trade-off between two different control mechanisms. On one hand, the wholly owned subsidiary option can enable the MNE to maintain better control over its internal operations than the joint venture mode, thus reducing its vulnerability to contextual volatility. On the other hand, a wholly owned subsidiary is at a disadvantage relative to a joint venture in counteracting environmental risks in a complex, hostile, or uncertain setting. This is largely because of the lack of a local partner who would otherwise help mitigate these contextual difficulties. To appropriately select an entry mode, an MNE needs to gauge whether internally induced uncertainties outweigh externally induced variabilities or vice versa.

Third, property right systems and other legal frameworks in a host country appear to be increasingly important to entry mode selection. This is because technological competencies or tacit knowledge are emerging as prominent determinants of an MNE's sustained competitive edge in the global marketplace. Without sufficient legal protection, an MNE's property rights and tacit knowledge, such as trademarks, brand names, know-how, patents, copyrights, and the like, will be exposed to possible infringement and piracy by local firms. In such circumstances, the MNE may have to use a high control entry mode, such as a wholly owned subsidiary or dominant equity joint venture.

Fourth, host country risk as perceived by an MNE may affect its resource commitment, strategic flexibility, and expected return-risk trade-off, which in turn affect the selection of entry mode. The managers of MNEs have to deal with a variety of host country risks including general political risks (e.g., instability of political system), ownership and control risks (e.g., price control, local content requirements), and transfer risks (e.g., currency inconvertibility, remittance control). When these risks are high the MNE is advised to limit its exposure by reducing its resource commitment and increasing its ability to exit from the market quickly without taking a substantial loss should the environment worsen. This suggests that, other things being equal, licensing and joint ventures will be favored over wholly owned subsidiaries when country risk is high. Joint ventures with local partners experience a relatively low rate of expropriation compared to wholly owned subsidiaries. This is because joint ventures have local equity partners who may have some influence on host government policy, along with a vested interest in speaking out against expropriation.

Fifth, cultural distance between home and host countries influences foreign entry decision and process. Over time, MNEs learn how to overcome cultural barriers and move from low risk entry modes (e.g., representative or branch offices, licensing, and franchising) to high risk modes (e.g., dominant equity joint ventures, wholly owned subsidiaries, and umbrella companies) and move from culturally proximate countries to more distant countries. The perceived distance between the home and host country in terms of culture, economic systems, and business practices also determines location familiarity; the shorter perceived distance, the greater the location familiarity. Perceived distance is a function of both basic psychic distance and the firm's prior experience in that culture. The greater the perceived distance between home and host countries, the more likely it is that MNEs will favor licensing or a joint venture over a wholly owned subsidiary. Not being comfortable with the culture, economic system, and business practices of a host country makes executives shy away from direct investment. Faced with the uncertainty that arises from the unknown, an MNE may be unwilling to commit substantial resources to a foreign operation because such a commitment would substantially reduce the MNE's ability to exit without cost if the host market should prove unattractive.

Last, demand conditions in a host country affect expected net return and firm growth during international expansion. This affects resource commitment, strategic orientation, and entry mode decision. When future host country demand for an MNE's product is unknown, an MNE may be unwilling to invest substantial resources in that country. Extensive resource commitments may limit the firm's ability to reduce excess capacity or exit from the host country without incurring substantial sunk costs if demand should fail to reach a significant level. As has been argued elsewhere, uncertainty as to future demand conditions is likely to be greatest in either embryonic or declining industries. Thus, MNEs may favor low resource commitment modes of entry (e.g., licensing) when a host market is in its embryonic or declining stage. When demand conditions become more stable and predictable, as tends to happen in mature markets, the MNE is better able to identify the optimal capacity necessary to serve a foreign market. However, this does not imply that the MNE will have a preference for a particular entry mode. Indeed, the MNE is likely to be indifferent. Factors other than demand conditions will determine the MNE's choice of entry mode when the host market is mature.

Industry-Specific Factors

Various industry-specific factors, such as entry barriers, industrial policies set by the host government, structural uncertainty, degree of competition from both local and other foreign firms, and relationships with suppliers and distributors, are important considerations underlying entry mode selection. First, the nature and degree of competition from either local or other foreign businesses in a target market may have a direct impact on whether an MNE chooses an arm's length approach to its contract or sets up an internal organization to undertake business transactions. Licensing can be viewed as an arm's length contractual relationship; setting up a wholly owned subsidiary, in contrast, involves an extension of the MNE's organizational boundaries and a commensurate reduction in the firm's strategic flexibility. When competition is volatile, any reduction in strategic flexibility is not economically advisable. A volatile market is one where rapidly changing technological, macroeconomic, social, demographic, and regulatory factors produce a situation of intense competition, be that on the basis of price, marketing expenditures, or investments. Such conditions require quick responses from the MNE. Insofar as resource commitments limit an MNE's ability to adapt to changing market circumstances without incurring substantial sunk costs, an MNE theoretically favors entry modes involving low resource commitments when competitive pressures in the host market are intense.

Second, entry barriers into a target industry in the host country constitute a significant impediment to entry mode selection. When such barriers are high, MNEs have very little freedom to choose among entry
modes. MNEs often have no choice but to accept host government-instituted modes of entry into certain industries. Broadly, these barriers result
from either industry- or government-induced factors. Of the former set,
possible factors include a large minimum scale, high capital requirements, high exit costs, superfluous production capacity, predatory selling
prices, supply and distribution monopolies, and superlative customer
loyalty. Among the latter set, possible factors include policies, such as
control over entry, local partner, location, timing, and equity along with
financing policies, tax law, scarce resource procurement, infrastructure
access priorities, and so on.

Third, structural uncertainty, complexity, and hostility may lead
MNEs to use high control or low commitment entry modes, such as representative offices, licensing, franchising, loosely structured cooperative
joint ventures with little resource commitment, or minority equity joint
ventures. The impact of an industry's structural dynamics on MNE operations is normally enduring and fundamental. It is necessary for MNEs to
make sure that the chosen entry mode will minimize such an impact on
firm operations or that the firm has a sufficient ability to mitigate against
dynamics if opting for a high risk entry mode. This suggests that MNEs
should consider various factors at different levels simultaneously in the
process of making an entry mode decision.

Fourth, availability and favorability of supply and distribution in the
industry will determine the rationalization of value chain linkages needed for an MNE's local operations and the vertical integration of other
units within the MNE network. Although this impact is firm-specific,
depending upon the firm's objectives, competencies, and strategies, relationships with local suppliers and local distributors are influential on the
firm's product quality, on-time delivery, customer responsiveness, and
competitive power, which in turn affect profitability, sales growth, liquidity, and asset efficiency. When an MNE relies more on local resource
procurement or emphasizes the local market, it is more vulnerable to
industrial linkages with suppliers and distributors. Entry modes involving partners turn out to be the superior choice when the MNE needs but
lacks industrial linkages in the host country.

Last, its relationship with buyers may affect an MNE's growth potential, resource commitment, and strategic orientation. These in turn affect
the entry mode selection. When an MNE has strong, diverse linkages with
various buyers, customers, and end users established through previous
export-import (direct or indirect) businesses, it is advisable for the firm to
employ a high resource-committed mode, such as a dominant joint venture, wholly owned subsidiary, or umbrella company. In contrast, a firm

may use a low resource-commitment mode, such as a representative office, licensing, franchising, or minority or split joint venture, to enter the host market. Because it takes time to build and develop relationships with various buyers, entry mode selection is an evolutionary process that relies heavily on linkages with local buyers.

Firm-Specific Factors

Entry mode selection is contingent on several firm-specific traits as well. First, a firm's resource munificence in internationalization will influence the firm's ability to explore market potentials and earn a competitive edge in the global marketplace. It affects entry mode decision because it impacts resource commitment, control mechanisms, partner selection, and knowledge transfer. A firm without these resources but wishing to share in the risks associated with having them is often compelled to enter the market through a joint venture where its resource commitment will be minimized. Firms having less knowledge about a foreign market tend to reduce their strategic risk by entering these markets though licensing agreements or joint ventures rather than wholly owned modes. Some firms use acquisition to procure a new set of resources, but firms using the new venture mode (i.e., greenfield) rely on their previously developed resources. A firm will use the joint venture mode to rectify a resource deficiency only if it is willing to risk providing access to such resources and can find a willing and suitable partner having appropriate resources to share. The critical factor is finding partners predisposed to provide such access to resources. This predisposition must be based on interfirm trust and a perception that sharing resources will not negatively impact the firm. An MNE will tend to favor an acquisition mode if it cannot find a suitable partner to provide access to required resources or if it is not itself willing to provide access to internal resources because it fears the risk of their exposure.

Second, the nature of strategic assets or knowledge may affect an MNE's competitive and control capabilities. If it has tacit strategic assets or distinctive knowledge, a wholly owned subsidiary mode increases the firm's ability to use that knowledge. Thus, tacitness is positively related with degree of control. In general, the risk of knowledge exposure is perceived by management to be lower when the exposed resources are peripheral or if the core competencies are difficult to imitate or transfer. A firm unnecessarily exposing its critical resources may accidentally provide its partner firm with a competitive advantage in the future. Therefore, the perceived nature and type of resources being exposed is important to the entry mode selection process.

It is imperative to distinguish between technological and managerial know-how. If a company's competitive advantage derives from its control over proprietary technological know-how, licensing and joint venture arrangements are not advisable because of the risk of losing control of that technology. A wholly owned subsidiary might be a better choice. Licensing or joint ventures can be used only if the arrangements are structured to reduce the risk of the technology being expropriated by licensees or joint venture partners. Companies can arrange to prevent leakage of their most sensitive technologies by only allowing their partners access to limited production processes. Contractual safeguards can also be written into a joint venture contract. Cross-licensing agreements between parties can also protect a foreign investor's technological know-how if both parties agree in advance to exchange skills and technology. Comparatively, the risk of losing control over management skills is not that great. This is one of the reasons that many service MNEs favor a combination of franchising and subsidiaries that control its franchises.

Third, the type of international strategy (i.e., multidomestic, transnational, or global) is expected to affect entry mode selection. A multidomestic strategy is based upon the belief that national markets differ widely with regard to consumer tastes and preferences, competitive conditions, operating conditions, and political, legal, and social structures. Maximizing value in such circumstances requires that MNEs assign key operating and strategic responsibilities to national subsidiaries. Each subsidiary will have its own marketing functions and autonomous manufacturing facilities, their products will vary between nations according to the tastes and preferences of different consumers, and their competitive strategies will vary to reflect different competitive conditions. A relatively low degree of control is usually required for firms pursuing a multidomestic strategy. Thus, multidomestic forms favor licensing or joint ventures as the mode of entry, because these are low cost modes (i.e., they entail fewer resource commitments).

In many industries, however, modern telecommunications and transport technologies have created a convergence of tastes and preferences among consumers from different nations. The result is the emergence of enormous global markets for standardized products, to which MNEs respond with a global strategy. A global strategy involves configuring the firm's value chain in such a way that value added at each stage is maximized. Thus, a national subsidiary may specialize in manufacturing only part of the product line or certain components of an end product, while exchanging parts and products with other subsidiaries in the MNE's global system. Achieving coordination within the context of an interdependent global manufacturing system necessarily requires a high degree of control over the operations of different national affiliates. These operations have to be prepared to accept centrally determined decisions as to what they should produce, how much they should produce, and how their output should be priced for transfer between operations. Licensees or venture partners are hardly likely to accept such a subservient role. Therefore, MNEs pursuing a global strategy may favor high control entry modes, such as wholly owned subsidiaries and umbrella companies.

Fourth, a firm's strategic goals for international expansion are one of the foremost determinants underlying entry mode selection. It is widely realized that foreign venture success is a function of how the firm enters the target market. When an MNE attempts to pursue local market expansion, high commitment choices, such as cooperative or equity joint ventures, wholly owned subsidiaries, and umbrella companies, are better because they enable the firm to have a deeper, more diverse involvement with the indigenous market, bringing more opportunities to accumulate culture-specific experience. If an MNE aims only to exploit factor endowment advantages, low commitment entry modes, such as subcontracting, compensation trade, coproduction, cooperative arrangement, and minority equity joint venture, may be superior to other options because risks and costs are low. If an MNE aims at overall corporate efficiency maximization, tight coordination is necessary for the effective execution of its strategies. This tight coordination may be difficult to accomplish in coalitions or through licensing. Such agreements link a foreign entrant to independent firms with different strategic motivations and a potential for conflict. Therefore, high control entry modes are a better choice when tight coordination within an MNE network is necessary. Specifically, by manufacturing in a location where factor conditions are optimal, then exporting products to the rest of the world, a foreign company may realize substantial location economies along with a positive experience curve. This arrangement also gives the company the tight control over marketing that is required for coordinating a globally dispersed value chain. It can also engage in transfer pricing to avoid various taxes or tariffs. Thus, foreign companies pursuing global strategies may prefer to establish wholly owned subsidiaries.

Last, international or host country experience reduces the uncertainty associated with assessing the true economic worth of entry into a foreign market. It follows, therefore, that MNEs with little or no experience with international business or multinational operations will try to limit their risk exposure. Such firms prefer low control and low resource commitment entry modes, such as export, subcontracting, international leasing or franchising, or countertrade. In contrast, MNEs with significant multinational experience prefer high control and high resource commitment entry modes, such as cooperative or equity joint ventures, wholly owned subsidiaries, and umbrella investment companies. In addition, firms can be expected to pursue a wholly owned entry mode relative to a joint venture as they gain experience in the local environment. A foreign company that is unfamiliar with the host country environment may want to engage a dependable distributor to sell its goods. Those firms that want to minimize capital and resource investments at the initial stage may find contract manufacturing suitable. Some may want to test the market first and establish a relationship with their current and potential customers by setting up a representative office.

Project-Specific Factors

In the course of entry mode selection, MNEs also need to consider some attributes of the FDI project itself. These attributes are associated with resource commitment, strategic orientation, and transaction costs, which affect the choice of entry modes in international expansion. First, project size influences the extent of control sought by an MNE. Firms may shy away from wholly owned entry mode in favor of joint venture when the project is big. Transaction cost theorists suggest that investors deal more cautiously with transactions that involve greater investment commitment. A large investment implies higher start-up, switching, and exit costs, thus involving higher financial and operational risks. To reduce such transaction costs, firms become more circumspect when considering entry mode. Moreover, a firm's commitment is positively related to its expected stakes, that is, the perceived importance of possible gains or losses associated with the investment commitment. When stakes are high, firms are likely to enter the foreign market more cautiously. Therefore, risk and cost-sharing entry modes are favored.

Second, project orientation (i.e., export oriented, technologically advanced, local market oriented, import substitution, or infrastructure oriented) influences an MNE's resource dispersal and strategic orientation and, therefore, influences firm behavior in terms of governance structure and entry mode. For example, other things being equal, MNEs investing in import-substitution projects may be inclined to establish partnerships with local government agencies or state-owned enterprises holding monopoly positions because this type of FDI project is markedly vulnerable to host government control and hindrance. If a project is local market oriented, the MNE may choose cooperative or equity joint venture mode because the local partner can provide distinctive supply and distribution channels, governmental networks, and culture-specific business knowledge and experience. If a project is technologically advanced, the firm may opt for a wholly owned subsidiary mode to protect its know-how or a joint venture mode if it needs complementary technologies or knowledge from a partner firm. Last, when a project is infrastructure oriented, the MNE may apply the BOT mode if it plans only on having a short-term run or a majority joint venture mode if it has a long-term strategic plan and is willing to take risks.

Third, contractual risks and costs associated with a particular FDI project may affect an MNE's commitment, contribution, and control.

Licensing may avoid the resource commitment associated with opening a foreign market. However, if an MNE grants a license to a foreign enterprise to use firm-specific know-how to manufacture or market a product, it runs the risk of the licensee, or an employee of the licensee, disseminating that know-how or using it for purposes other than those originally intended. Similar arguments can be made with respect to joint venture partners. In a complex and uncertain world populated by economic actors of bounded rationality and opportunistic tendencies the costs of negotiating, monitoring, and enforcing contracts are non-trivial. There is always the possibility of unanticipated contingencies giving rise to opportunistic actions against which the MNE has no defense. According to transaction cost logic, by establishing a wholly owned subsidiary an MNE can reduce dissemination risk and therefore economize on the transaction costs of licenses or ventures. If the reduction in transaction costs exceeds the bureaucratic costs of establishing and running an internal market to transfer know-how, establishing a wholly owned subsidiary makes the most sense.

Last, the availability of proper local partners for a particular project may affect an MNE's entry ability and choice. An MNE's ability to establish a joint venture or any other form of unintegrated entry mode depends upon the availability of capable, trustworthy partners. In the absence of acceptable local partners, the MNE may be forced to start a wholly owned subsidiary. When an MNE has a variety of choices in partner selection, it will have much greater freedom in choosing among entry modes ranging from trade-related and BOT modes to cooperative and equity joint ventures. The availability of acceptable local partners boosts the effectiveness of entry mode selection.

In sum, the selection of entry modes in international expansion depends upon the following four groups of factors: host country-specific factors including government FDI policies, conditions of infrastructure and support industries, property right systems and other legal frameworks, host country risk, cultural distance, and demand conditions; industry-specific factors, such as the nature and degree of competition, entry barriers, structural uncertainty, complexity, and hostility; firm-specific factors, such as resource munificence, the nature of strategic assets or knowledge, type of international strategy, strategic goals, and international or host country experience; and project-specific factors including project size, project orientation, contractual risks and costs, and availability of proper local partners.

The above integrated framework may serve as a useful tool for selecting an appropriate entry mode that fits both external forces (at the country and industrial levels) and internal competencies (at the firm and project levels). Among a wide range of entry mode choices, it is up to international managers of each firm to opt for the one most appropriate to the firm's capabilities, goals, and risk propensity. It is important that each entry mode decision be considered in light of contextual facets, such as market demand, governmental policy, country risk, entry barriers, and industrial competition. This may allow the MNE to effect a strategy that derives the maximum possible benefit from the different markets in which it invests and operates.

Figure 6.2 summarizes the implications of various entry modes in terms of risk, return, control, integration, commitment, and flexibility. Individual firms should combine this general framework with specific firm characteristics and situational contingencies. These dimensions serve as base points for MNE managers considering various entry modes. Overall, risk, return, control, integration, commitment, and flexibility all increase step by step through the mode sequence of trade-related modes; representative or branch offices; licensing, franchising, or BOT; cooperative joint ventures; equity joint ventures; wholly owned subsidiaries; and umbrella investment companies.

FIGURE 6.2
Critical Implications of Various Entry Modes

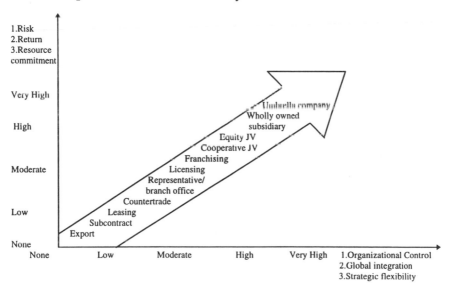

REFERENCES

Agarwal, S. and S. N. Ramaswami. 1992. Choice of foreign market entry mode: Impact of ownership, location, and internalization factors. *Journal of International Business Studies*, 23(1): 1–27.

Anderson, E. and H. Gatignon. 1986. Modes of foreign entry: A transaction cost analysis and propositions. *Journal of International Business Studies*, 17(Fall): 1–26.

Boddewyn, J. and T. L. Brewer. 1994. International business political behavior: New theoretical directions. *Academy of Management Review*, 19(1): 119–143.

Chang, S. J. 1995. International expansion strategy of Japanese firms: Capability building through sequential entry. *Academy of Management Journal*, 38: 383–407.

Dunning, J. H. 1988. The eclectic paradigm of international production: A restatement and some possible extensions. *Journal of International Business Studies*, 19 (Spring): 1–31.

Dunning, J. H. 1980. Toward an eclectic theory of international production: Some empirical tests. *Journal of International Business Studies*, 11(First Quarter): 9–31.

Erramilli, M. K. 1991. The experience factor in foreign market entry behavior of service firms. *Journal of International Business Studies*, 22(Fall): 479–501.

Gomes-Casseres, B. 1990. Firm ownership presences and host government restrictions: An integrated approach. *Journal of International Business Studies*, 21(1): 1–21.

Hill, C.W.L., P. Hwang, and W. C. Kim. 1990. An eclectic theory of the choice of international entry mode. *Strategic Management Journal*, 11: 117–128.

Johanson, J. and J. E. Vahlne. 1977. The internationalization process of the firm: A model of knowledge development and increasing foreign market commitments. *Journal of International Business Studies*, 8(1): 23–32.

Madhok, A. 1997. Cost, value and foreign market entry mode: The transaction and the firm. *Strategic Management Journal*, 18: 39–61.

Tallman, S. B. and O. Shenkar. 1994. A managerial decision model of international cooperative venture formation. *Journal of International Business Studies*, 25(1): 91–114.

Teece, D. J., G. Pisano, and A. Shuen. 1990. Firm capabilities, resources and the concept of strategy, Working Paper No. 90-8. Berkeley: University of California, Center for Research in Management.

Williamson, O. E. 1985. *The economic institutions of capitalism*. New York: The Free Press.

Yan, A. and B. Gray. 1994. Bargaining power, management control, and performance in United States–China joint ventures: A comparative case study. *Academy of Management Journal*, 37(6): 1478–1517.

Yoshino, M.Y. and Rangan, U. S. 1995. *Strategic alliance*. Boston, Mass.: Harvard Business School Press,

FURTHER READINGS

Contractor, F. J. 1984. Choosing between direct investment and licensing: Theoretical considerations and empirical tests. *Journal of International Business*

Studies, 15: 166–188.

Davidson, W. H. and D. G. McFetridge. 1985. Key characteristics in the choice of international technology transfer mode. *Journal of International Business Studies,* 16(2): 5–21.

Hennart, J. 1989. Can the "new forms of investment" substitute for the "old forms?": A transaction costs perspective. *Journal of International Business Studies,* 20(2): 211–234.

Kim, W. C. and P. Hwang. 1992. Global strategy and multinationals' entry mode choice. *Journal of International Business Studies,* 23(1): 29–53.

Kumar, V. and V. Subramian. 1997. A contingency framework for the entry mode decision. *Journal of World Business,* 32(1): 53–72.

Kwon, Y. and L. Konopa. 1993. Impact of host country market characteristics on the choice of foreign market entry mode. *International Marketing Review,* 10(2): 60–76.

Osborn, R. N. and C. C. Baughn. 1990. Forms of interorganizational governance for multinational alliances. *Academy of Management Journal,* 33(3): 503–519.

Root, F. R. 1994. *Entry strategies for international markets.* Washington, DC: Lexington Books.

Shane, S. 1994. The effect of national culture on the choice between licensing and foreign direct investment. *Strategic Management Journal,* 15: 627–642.

7

Timing of Entry

Timing of international expansion plays a critical role in shaping transnational firm behavior and represents an important source of competitive advantage in international settings. It is associated with the height of entry barriers, evolving industry and market structures in the host country, and degree of access to indigenous resources. In today's increasingly integrated global marketplace where demand level, consumption sophistication, factor costs, input characteristics, and rivalry intensity are all changing drastically, the decision of when to embark on international expansion is critical for transnational operations. This chapter illuminates the theoretical background of entry timing, reiterates the advantages and disadvantages of early movers compared to late entrants, provides a framework for timing strategy formulation, presents some empirical evidence, and highlights managerial implications for international executives.

THEORETICAL BACKGROUND

The population ecology model suggests that a firm can achieve a competitive edge through either the r-strategy or k-strategy (Hannan & Freeman, 1977). In the ecological model, the growth process is modelled formally as $dn/dt = rn*(k-n)/k$. In this equation, the rate of change in a population of size n is a function of some natural rate of increase r and the upper limit or carrying capacity k. The r term is most important in the early stage of population development (when n is small). Conversely, when the population becomes large, the k term becomes more important.

An investor using the r-strategy enters a new product market at an early stage when the population of competitors is few in number. In contrast, a firm using the k-strategy joins later when the population members are more numerous. Thus, the development of a new population of businesses may be viewed as a series of waves, with additional businesses appearing with each successive wave. When a new product market emerges that is substantially different from existing ones, its early development is usually characterized by high uncertainty and radical change. Once initial market uncertainties are reduced by the first entrant, late entrants increasingly pursue strategies that are efficiency-oriented to cope with intensifying competition and reduced uncertainty (Lambkin, 1988). The population ecology model suggests that r-strategists have the best chance of success in market expansion at the expense of risk (Luo, 1998).

In contrast, late entrants pursuing k-strategies are likely to enjoy a high level of efficiency in their concentrated segments but face more institutional barriers (Hannan & Freeman, 1977). Wherever environmental resources are unequally distributed between niches in the environment and environmental conditions are changing over time, the population ecology model suggests that firms entering with each successive wave need to have different resources, capabilities, and strategies if they are to carve out sustainable competitive positions (Hannan & Freeman, 1977). In essence, the ecological framework corroborates the microeconomic model of firm behavior regarding investment timing. According to the microeconomic model, early entrants may gain advantages from early association with the product category and accumulated experience, but assume the risks of technological obsolescence and proprietary technology diffusing to competitors, along with the burden of educating a changing market (Anderson & Engers, 1994).

A few attempts to analyze the optimal timing of foreign direct investment (FDI) have been made by Aliber (1970) and Buckley and Casson (1981). These researchers used the neoclassical model in which the criterion for optimal timing included minimizing costs or maximizing the net present value by switching from licensing or export to FDI. FDI will occur when switching at time t from one mode (e.g., export) to another mode (FDI) generates lower recurrent variable costs and a non-recoverable setup cost. Specifically, in Buckley and Casson's model, investment is ideally timed to maximize the net present value (NPV) when switching at time t from mode i (e.g., export) to a mode j (FDI) with lower recurrent variable costs $C_j(t) < C_i(t)$ and a non-recoverable setup cost $f_{ij}(t)$, that is: $NPV(t) = C_i^*(t) - C_j^*(t) - f_{ij}^*(t)$ where $C_i^*(t) = \int_t^\infty c_i^*(T)dT$, $C_j^*(t) = \int_t^\infty c_j^*(T)dT$, $f_{ij}^*(t) = f_{ij}(t) \exp[-\int_0^t r(T)dT]$. Two necessary conditions for a maximum of NPV are: $c_i^*(t) - c_j^*(t) = -df_{ij}^*/dt$ and $C_i^*(t) - C_j^*(t) > f_{ij}^*(t)$. It would be better, however, if the model incorporated the income effect into the formulas because national differences, particularly industry and market structure heterogeneity, are likely to result in a superior net income stream for investors. In this case the decision can be modeled as $Max[NPV(t)] = Max\{[I_j^*(t) - C_j^*(t)] - [I_i^*(t) - C_i^*(t)] - f_{ij}^*(t)\}$. In Aliber's model, the costs of doing business abroad and the rate of capitalization on the currency of denomination are also incorporated.

Building upon extant theory, Rivoli and Salorio (1996) argue that when environmental uncertainty is high or information is exogenous, timing of entry into a foreign market does not depend merely on cost minimization. The presence of uncertainty may increase the value of a wait and see attitude. Moreover, international expansion decisions are not always based upon the costs of a shift from licensing or export to FDI; instead, they are often undertaken to accomplish various strategic goals.

Early movers into a foreign market are expected to have considerable preemptive opportunities and benefit from market, product, and technological leadership. Luo (1998) contends that having an appropriate level of technology, a dominant design, or the presence of complementary assets determines a firm's ability to preempt opportunities in a dynamic market. As a result, a firm that has failed to dominate its home market may be able to pioneer in a promising foreign market, especially in those industries that are in an embryonic or growing stage. It would be a mistake, however, to assume that all foreign markets can provide opportunities for every foreign entrant at any time. According to the garbage can theory, investment opportunities are like garbage cans in that they each have streams of choices, problems, and solutions and participants with limited time, resources, and energy flowing through them (Luo, 1997). Even in some emerging economies, the windows of opportunity during a given period are often manipulated by central governments that control the number of firms, especially in abnormally profitable industries. Success often goes to those investors who reach first into the can and quickly grab a combination of opportunities, resources, and solutions to make a successful deal. Mascarenhas (1992) finds that first entrants in international markets maintain higher market performance at the corporate level. This evidence corroborates Porter's assertion (1986) that the ultimate leaders in the world market are often first movers.

Early movers, however, assume substantial costs from the liability of foreignness. According to multinational enterprise (MNE) theory, such a liability not only stems from the usual costs of doing business overseas but also from the dramatic variations in institutional structure, organizational form, and managerial psyche among different countries. These add to the scale and scope of uncertainty and risks of failure. The host country government and local businesses are often in a position to influence the rules of the business game in their favor, creating further transaction hazards for early investors from abroad. Local decision makers often resent dominant foreign control over indigenous enterprises. In contrast, late movers can wait and learn while first movers make mistakes; educate local governments, partners, and consumers; and lobby for more accommodating legal and institutional frameworks for FDI (Luo, 1998). In other words, late entrants benefit from early investors' endeavors in two key areas: learning and environment stabilization. Late movers are hence in a better position to leapfrog initial market hurdles and obstacles.

The competitive market entry of a foreign investor in relation to its performance is influenced by the entry position of local firms. Mitchell, Shaver, and Yeung (1993) have demonstrated that early foreign investors are more likely to enter niches where there are few threats from local rivals to their core product. In new product market niches, local firms are more likely to be early followers or late entrants because they are wedded to historical ways of doing business and unlikely to be proactive, given the risks of disruption to their existing organizations or cannibalization of existing products. Moreover, local firms in foreign markets are likely to be unable fully to exploit market possibilities and exhaust business potentials in existing and emerging product markets because of insufficient technological or operational skills. Organizational inertia stemming from a long presence in the market may compound the indolence of these firms in reacting to market opportunities. Moreover, distinctive competence in product differentiation often enables an MNE to create a new segmented product market in which it can pioneer. Thus, early FDI entrants may have first mover advantages not only in locally existing industries but also in those markets they have developed.

EARLY MOVER ADVANTAGES AND DISADVANTAGES

A first mover opportunity may arise when a firm develops a unique product or process to fit a market opportunity that has gone unperceived by other firms. Alternatively, a firm may be the first to act upon an opportunity perceived by many others. Despite the importance of initiative, the availability of first mover opportunities sometimes depends purely on luck.

Aside from noticing an opportunity, the decision on when to invest is broadly based upon the potential entrant's assessment of entry barriers erected by the host government and existing firms relative to the factors promoting entry. Potential entrants weigh the expected benefits and costs of entry; entry occurs when the former outweigh the latter.

Early Mover Advantages

When entering the market a pioneering firm generally has advantages over a late mover. The pioneering firm is able to invest strategically in facilities, distribution channels, product positioning, patentable technology, natural resources, and human and organizational know-how. If imitation of its product is expected to be expensive or involve a long time lag, a preemptive investment can be transformed into significant long-run benefits for the first mover firm. Furthermore, the cost of acquiring resources will be lower in the early period because of lack of competition. Moreover, market pioneers may benefit from the advantages of holding technical leadership, seizing scarce resources, and creating buyer switching costs. Finally, early movers have the right to preempt marketing and distribution channels, while gaining information and brand recognition. In brief, pioneering investors tend to outperform following firms in acquiring market power. Empirically, accumulating evidence based on advanced market economies demonstrates that successful market pioneers hold higher market shares than late entrants. In general, the order of entry has much to do with market share variance.

Transnational investors are likely to have more preemptive investment opportunities in foreign markets than in their home markets. This is largely because of the different market and industry structures between home and host economies. By investing in an emerging market, a later mover in the home country could become an early entrant in the host country. It could enjoy more favorable business opportunities in sectors that are in early stages of the industry life cycle in the local environment or in industries in which it has distinctive competitive advantages and is encouraged by the host governments to invest. In many foreign markets, the window of opportunity for long-term profitable business exists only during a specific time and in a specific region or industry and is available only to a limited number of foreign investment projects. For example, to pursue economic reform and political stability, the State Council's Planning Commission of China required local authorities and industrial ministries to set a ceiling on the number of foreign-funded projects involved in modernizing the economy in each region or sector. Under such conditions, early investors not only enjoy superior market expansion, but also have more options in selecting industries, locations, and market orientations (e.g., import substitution, local market oriented, and so forth). In addition, early movers are often given priority access to natural resources, scarce materials, distribution channels, promotional arrangements, and infrastructure. Moreover, early investors have a superior opportunity to select better local firms for equity or contractual joint ventures or for supply-purchase business relations. Finally, early movers are in a better position to formulate strategies for dealing with competition from local firms, particularly state enterprises. They can place their strength in businesses, industries, and markets where competition from local firms is weak or where they have better technological and organizational competencies.

Early Mover Disadvantages

Early movers are confronted with more operational risks and uncertainty. Causes of operational risks can be either contextual or transactional, the former stemming from environmental uncertainty and the latter from business activity variations in the indigenous setting. In other words, the former represents country- or industry-specific risks, and the latter represents firm- or business-specific ones. Contextual uncertainty may be lowered as the local governments become more familiar with how to deal with foreign businesses. However, political and social uncertainties often widen the variations in contextual conditions, particularly for those foreign companies that are new to the local environment. Dramatic changes in foreign industrial and market structures can also bring about significant variations in the investment environment. In general, early comers will face higher contextual risks and uncertainty. When late movers come, the host country environment is usually more stable.

Earlier movers from foreign companies are usually relatively unfamiliar with the local environment. Many of them, therefore, select the joint venture mode for FDI entry. In the joint venture business, however, the objectives of local partners usually diverge from those of their foreign partner. The pursuit of self-interest rather than common goals, as well as lack of autonomy among local partners, can result in significant uncertainty for joint venture operations. These uncertainties and risks are often beyond the control of foreign investors. They cannot, therefore, be internalized through the global integration of transnational business as they would in wholly owned subsidiaries. Because late investors can usually choose to establish wholly owned subunits, their risks are less substantial than those faced by early movers. In sum, the earlier the foreign investment, the greater the operational risks that will be faced.

According to Aliber (1970), one of the most important issues in FDI decision making in the international context is the cost of doing business abroad. This cost can be reduced by the learning curve effect, according to early FDI and MNE literature. Whenever there is uncertainty, the learning effect is more obvious. The effect is even more emphasized in transitional economies where the rules of the game are different from those in market economies. Therefore, a first mover in a foreign market will pay higher learning costs than a later comer. Scholars in the business field recognize that later transnational investors can gain learning experience from the earlier investors.

In addition to the costs of doing business, early movers have to pay higher switching and start-up costs. Later movers, in contrast, can piggyback on early investment if imitation is easy, thereby gaining profit without having to pay as much as innovators. As a result, late movers are likely to outperform early investors in terms of profitability in the beginning stages of FDI. Figure 7.1 presents an organizing framework incorporating both the economic merits and costs of FDI timing.

FIGURE 7.1
Timing of Foreign Direct Investment — Risk-Return Model

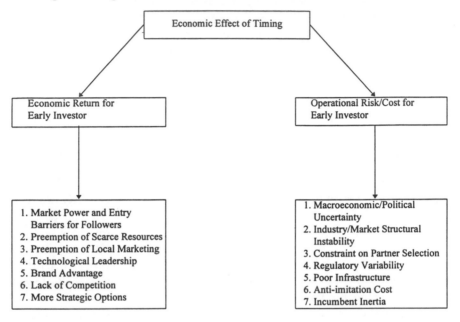

TIMING STRATEGY FORMULATION

Based on the above discussion, early timing of FDI has the following advantages: market advantages, such as gaining a new market, new segmentation, or new distribution channel, while creating buyer switching costs and avoiding strong competition; product advantages, such as positioning a new product, material supplies, and brand loyalty; technological advantages, such as introducing new patents and seizing technological leadership over local firms and other foreign businesses; and resource access advantages, such as to facilities, information, partner selection, scarce materials, human and natural resources, and other investment infrastructure. The disadvantages of early FDI timing can be summarized as the following: risks from high contextual and operational uncertainties; costs from searching, switching, start-up, and doing business abroad; and imitation by late investors free riding on early entrants who have invested in product and process innovation and learned how to deal with local governments, customers, suppliers, competitors, and other stakeholders in the value chain. Obviously, the advantages of early investors are the disadvantages of late movers, and vice versa. The combination of these advantages and disadvantages has an impact on market growth, risk reduction, asset efficiency, and accounting returns among foreign ventures.

As mentioned earlier, a potential FDI stakeholder enters the market only if expected benefits outweigh potential costs. Entry decisions must be based on rigorous cost-benefit analysis, having a realistic strategy, and prudent timing. Entry timing is only one of many issues one has to consider in formulating FDI strategy. Other factors include: the transnational investor's technological, production, marketing, capital, and organizational resources and capabilities; the host country environment in terms of technology, customer needs, industry structure, market demand, and FDI and industrial policies; and potential competition from the same or different foreign countries and the host country. A timing strategy formulation framework is presented in Figure 7.2.

A transnational investor's distinctive resources determine its competence in the FDI market, its ability to reduce risks, and its ability to seize preemptive investment opportunities. A pioneer entrant must wait for a feasible opportunity for investment, the appearance of which depends on the investor's foresight, skills, resources, and good fortune, as well as the competitive situation. The resource-based theory suggests that when environmental uncertainty is high, the necessity for distinctive competence in a firm's pursuit of sustained economic rents is reinforced. In a dynamic foreign market, distinctive technology, product and process innovations, capital, international distribution and promotion, and organizational and managerial skills are prerequisites for survival and expansion. The investor's ability to allocate and utilize these resources is another necessary condition for maximizing the benefits of entering an FDI market.

The market expansion, operational risk, and economic efficiency effects of FDI timing at the business unit level largely depend on the particular characteristics of the investment environment in the host country. The technological level, customer needs, market demand, industry structure, and government policies are all likely to affect the interrelationship between FDI timing and the venture's profitability and stability. Moreover, first mover opportunities are often generated by environmental changes in the host country. The transformation of national economies, market structures, and government policies are often so uncertain in emerging economies that this factor must be given the highest priority while making decisions about FDI timing.

The option of being a first mover is not entirely under the firm's control. Preemptive investment opportunities may be perceived by local rivals as well as foreign competitors. The responses and actions of its competitors need to be carefully examined. The transnational investor

FIGURE 7.2
Timing of Foreign Direct Investment — Strategy Formulation Model

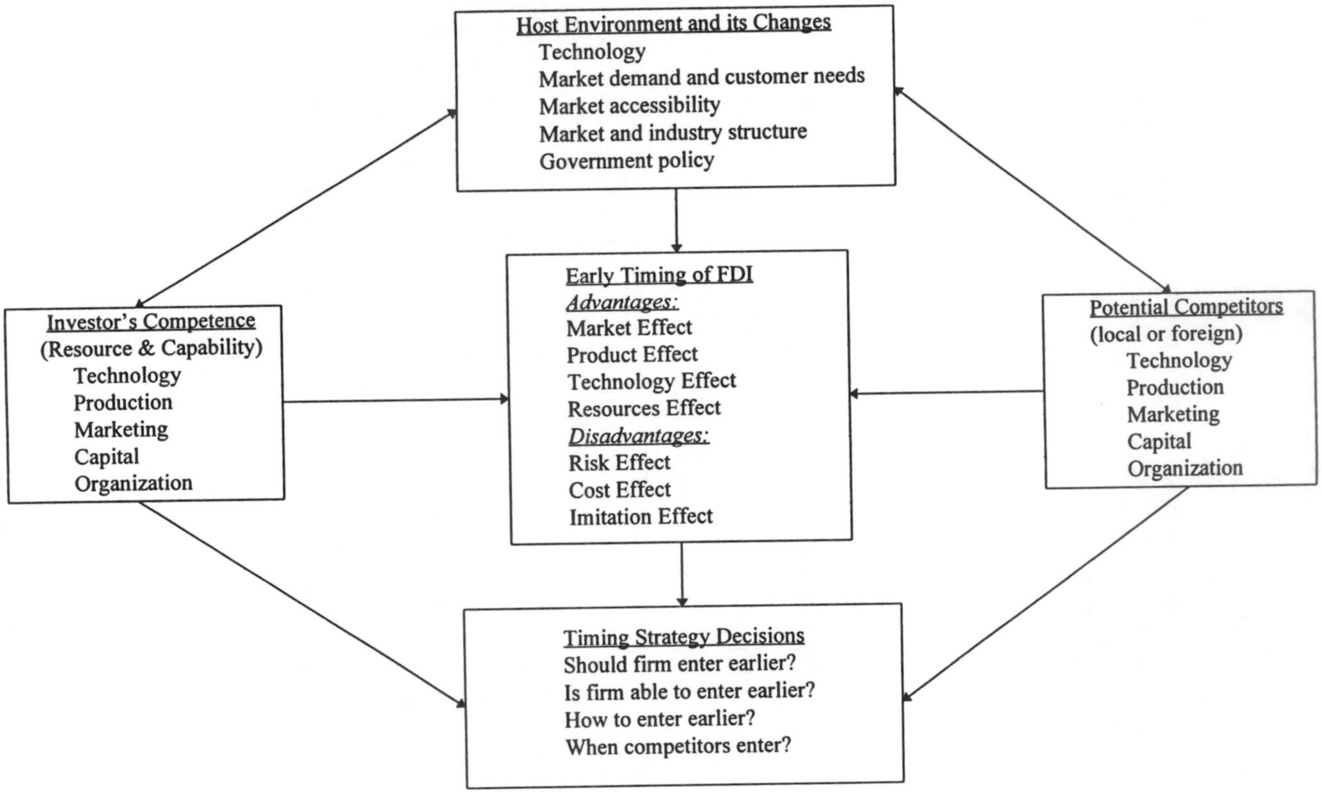

Potential Competitors
(local or foreign)
Technology
Production
Marketing
Capital
Organization

Host Environment and its Changes
Technology
Market demand and customer needs
Market accessibility
Market and industry structure
Government policy

Early Timing of FDI
Advantages:
Market Effect
Product Effect
Technology Effect
Resources Effect
Disadvantages:
Risk Effect
Cost Effect
Imitation Effect

Timing Strategy Decisions
Should firm enter earlier?
Is firm able to enter earlier?
How to enter earlier?
When competitors enter?

Investor's Competence
(Resource & Capability)
Technology
Production
Marketing
Capital
Organization

must study the strengths and weaknesses of potential rivals in areas such as technology, production, marketing, capital, and organization.

When an opportunity presents itself, the investor must decide whether it should enter the foreign territory as a first mover or early entrant, and then whether it has the capacity to build a sustainable advantage from its entry timing. If the answers are yes, the firm must then decide how to enter the host market and best to exploit the opportunity. Many issues need to be analyzed, including entry mode (joint venture versus wholly owned), sharing arrangements, selection of project location (open versus closed areas), and so on. These factors will either facilitate or inhibit the form and strength of the relationship between timing strategy and foreign venture performance because they influence the venture's vulnerability to the external context and ability to control the venture. Once a pioneering strategy is chosen, the investor must react faster than its rivals, contribute proactively to its own pioneering opportunities, and take measures to keep its first mover advantages. If the investor chooses not to be an early mover, or if a rival has preempted this position, then the investor must decide whether, how, and when to follow.

SOME EVIDENCE FROM AN EMERGING MARKET

National Survey

A national survey ranking foreign-invested firms in China supports some of our conclusions. As Table 7.1 shows, the top 30 foreign-invested manufacturing firms, measured by revenues, are very early movers that established their operations before 1984. This list includes some of the best known joint ventures in China, such as Shanghai Volkswagen, Beijing Jeep, and Fujian Hitachi. All these entrants have become leaders in their respective industries in China. In the automotive industry, Shanghai Volkswagen and Beijing Jeep occupy top spots; in the electronics industry, Shenzhen Gangjia, Huaqiang Sanyo, Shunde Huabao, Beijing Matsushita, and Fujian Hitachi are primary leaders within the top 20 list; and, similarly, in the electrical machinery industry, Jiangsu Chunlan Refrigerators, Shanghai Mitsubishi Elevator, and China Tianjin Otis Elevator are among the top three industry leaders.

It is worth noting that automotive joint ventures (Shanghai Volkswagen and Beijing Jeep) are currently the two largest foreign-invested firms in China. These high profile foreign investors, Volkswagen and AMC/Chrysler, have deliberately and successfully used first mover strategies in acquiring and sustaining advantages in China's emerging market. From the start, each publicly acknowledged the difficulties and risks in China; their entry decision was motivated by the long-run prospects instead of short-term profits. During the course of operations,

TABLE 7.1
Top 30 Foreign-Invested Manufacturing Firms in China in 1993

Rank and Company	FDI Origin	Industry	Sales (million yuan)
1 Shanghai Volkswagen AG	Germany	Automotive	10,529
2 Beijing Jeep Corp.	United States	Automotive	3,275
3 Shanghai Bell Telephone	Belgium	Telecom equipment	2,826
4 Guangzhou Peugeot Motors	France	Automotive	2,536
5 Chongqing Qingling Motor	Japan	Automotive	2,290
6 Shenzhen Gangjia Electronics	Hong Kong	Electronics	2,203
7 Nanhai Oils and Fats Industry	Malaysia	Food processing	2,000
8 Fujian Yongen Group	Unknown	Unknown	1,867
9 Huaqiang Sanyo	Japan	Electronics	1,865
10 Shunde Huabao Electric	Hong Kong	Electronics	1,776
11 Shenzhen Zhonghua Bicycle	Hong Kong	Automotive	1,755
12 First Auto Works Volkswagen	Germany	Automotive	1,655
13 Shanghai Phoenix Bicycles	Unknown	Automotive	1,554
14 Beijing Light Automobile	Hong Kong	Automotive	1,513

15	Beijing Matsushita TV	Japan	Electronics	1,504
16	Fujian Hitachi TV	Japan	Electronics	1,441
17	Guangdong Jianlibao Group	Macao	Food processing	1,397
18	Shanghai Ciba-Geigy	Switzerland	Pharmaceutical	1,397
19	Shenyang Jinbei Minibus	Hong Kong	Automotive	1,377
20	Jiangsu Chunlan Refrigerators	Unknown	Electrical machinery	1,352
21	Shanghai Mitsubishi Elevator	Japan	Electrical machinery	1,329
22	Shanghai Ek Chor Motorcycle	Thailand	Automotive	1,296
23	Wuyang-Honda Motors	Japan	Automotive	1,292
25	Huafei Color Kinescope Systems	Netherlands	Electronics	1,148
26	Beijing Int'l Switching System	Germany	Telecom equipment	1,103
27	China Tianjin Otis Elevator	United States	Electrical machinery	1,084
28	China-Schindler Elevator	Switzerland	Electrical machinery	1,070
29	Shenzhen Saige Hitachi	Japan	Electronics	1,067
30	Shanghai Yongxin Color TV	Hong Kong	Electronics	1,064

Source: "Top-500 Foreign-Affiliated Industrial Enterprise in China in FY 1993," *Guoji Shangbao* (International Commercial News), October 28, 1994. According to *Renmin Ribao* (People's Daily), February 20, 1996, the top 30 foreign-invested manufacturing firms were all established before 1984.

both companies have run into various difficulties, ranging from problems with product quality to foreign exchange shortages. At one point, Beijing Jeep was close to bankruptcy but was bailed out by the Chinese government. While these early movers gained experience and a hands-on education in China, their global competitors watched, unable or unwilling to enter. As the Chinese economy came of age in the mid-1990s, numerous late movers decided to join the competition. A new wave of FDI came from players such as General Motors and Mercedes-Benz. As of the end of 1995, however, these late movers had yet to produce a single car in China, while Volkswagen and Chrysler respectively sold about 400,000 and 60,000 cars each year. It seems clear that early entrants have built up enviable market share positions in China through years of sustained effort. This advantage may be particularly strong for Volkswagen, which currently has two successful joint ventures and occupies 60 percent of the Chinese automobile market.

This evidence strengthens our theme that FDI timing is significant. Overall, the lessons from FDI in China seem to indicate that, despite facing operational risks, early movers are able to build strong market shares with which late movers will have difficulty competing.

Timing Effect During the Early Period

To determine whether early movers and late entrants differ significantly in economic returns and operational risks during the early period of operations, a univariate analysis of the data obtained from Jiangsu Provincial Commission of Foreign Economic Relations and Trade was employed whereby the difference in group means for each dimension of performance was tested using the t-test statistics. This analysis included 7 early foreign entrants (established in 1980 and 1981) and 24 late foreign movers (established in 1989 and 1990) in light industries in the province. Economic returns comprised returns on investment, sales growth, and asset turnover. All these indicators referred to the foreign ventures' first three years of performance after formation. Operational risks were measured with a geometric average of standard deviations of the above three economic indicators. The test results are revealed in Table 7.2.

As shown in Table 7.2, early entrants are significantly superior to late entrants in terms of sales growth. Although the context of an emerging economy is dynamic, complex, and uncertain, the promising market provides early entrants with many preemptive investment opportunities and commercial potentials upon which they can capitalize. As a result of deliberate investments through contributing competencies, early investors achieve greater market power in the host market than late investors. It is also found that early foreign entrants faced far more operational risks

TABLE 7.2
Timing Effect During the Early Period: Univariate *t* Test

Variable	Early Entrants	Late Entrants	*t*-statistics
Return on Investment	8.20	13.10	1.906*
Sales Growth	26.78	15.28	−4.274†
Asset Turnover	4.93	3.29	−3.312†
Risk	87.66	53.34	−6.228†

*5% significance level
†1% significance level

than late movers in the start-up phase of expansion into China. In other words, the superiority of early investor market growth accrues at the expense of high operational risks in the indigenous setting.

This test also observes that late investors have a higher performance in terms of return on investment over the first three years. The *t*-test shows, however, that early entrants outperform late movers with regard to asset turnover. High asset turnover combined with low return on investment suggests that early movers entering a frontier territory, such as China, make low capital contributions during the initial period of operations. This complies with the transaction cost perspective, which argues that when environmental uncertainty is high, the firm should make minimum commitments because of high switching, start-up, and anti-imitation costs.

Timing Effect During the Late Period

A second test involved a nationwide mail survey of foreign-invested firms in manufacturing industries. High-level executives, such as general and deputy general managers, were surveyed in 1996. We sent 500 questionnaires to a random sample of foreign-invested firms that had been operating in China for at least eight years (i.e., established by 1988). Because of limited data, we defined the late period as $t \geq 8$ years, where t refers to the length of operations. We received 96 questionnaires in usable form, representing a 19.2 percent response rate.

FDI timing is measured as the difference in time between a foreign-invested firm's operation commencement date and January 1979. In other words, we use the watershed date of January 1979, when China officially opened its door to FDI, as the base for appraising the timing of foreign investment. The lower the difference between the commencement date (month and year) and January 1979, the earlier the timing of FDI. The larger this measure, the later the entry.

Firm performance was defined as a multidimensional construct, including not only financial measures, such as profitability and asset efficiency, but also strategic criteria, such as risk reduction and competitive position in the target market. As a result, firm performance was measured by: after-tax returns on sales (ROS), after-tax returns on equity (ROE), sales growth (SALE), asset turnover (ASTN), competitive position (CMPO), and level of operational risk (RISK). Each respondent was asked to indicate the firm's current performance on a five-point scale in comparison with its major competitors in the local industry. Firm size, industry growth, equity distribution, and research and development intensity were controlled for.

A multiple regression analysis (see Table 7.3) shows that the later the FDI entry, the worse the performance, as evidenced by the significant and negative signs in all six models. By implication, the earlier the entry, the better the FDI performance during the late period. Specifically, earlier entry is superior with respect to return on sales, return on equity, and sales growth. According to the same analysis, earlier entry also outperforms later investment in asset turnover, competitive position, and risk reduction. This evidence demonstrates that entering earlier into a transitional economy such as China's gains more profitability, market expansion, asset efficiency, competitive position, and risk reduction over time.

In summary, the second test finds noticeable first mover advantages for early investors in a transitional economy such as China over time. Specifically, this test finds that early investors have superior performance in profitability, sales growth, asset turnover, competitive position, and uncertainty reduction relative to late entrants in the late operation period. Taken together, the results from the above tests provide a clear answer to the question of whether there are noticeable first mover advantages in emerging markets. Drawing on two separate samples of foreign-invested firms operating in different time periods in China, we have found the existence of significant first mover advantages. In contrast, we have also found that first movers face substantially higher operational risks and lower profitability during the initial phase of operations.

MANAGERIAL IMPLICATIONS

Opportunities

As the year 2000 approaches, markets are increasingly opening throughout the world. In Eastern and Western Europe, the post-Soviet republics, Greater China (Hong Kong, Taiwan, Macao, and the Peoples Republic of China) and Asia, and North America trade and investment walls are beginning to crumble in the face of political unrest and technological innovation. In anticipation of these changes, a do-or-die atmosphere

TABLE 7.3
Timing Effect During the Late Period: Multiple Regression Analysis

Variables	ROS	ROE	SALE	ASTN	CMPO	RISK
Independent variable						
Timing	−0.41[a]	−0.43[a]	−0.26[b]	−0.34[a]	−0.24[b]	−0.28[b]
Control variables						
Industry	0.22[b]	0.27[a]	0.31[a]	0.27[a]	0.35[a]	0.20[c]
Size	0.01	−0.08	0.05	−0.05	0.03	−0.20[c]
Equity	0.10	0.02	0.11	0.09	0.12	0.13
R&D	0.41[a]	0.34[a]	0.41[a]	0.43[a]	0.47[a]	−0.17
Model F	21.25	21.60	15.04	20.76	20.66	7.12
$p <$	0.001	0.001	0.001	0.001	0.001	0.001
R^2	0.54	0.55	0.46	0.53	0.53	0.36
Adjusted R^2	0.51	0.52	0.42	0.51	0.51	0.32
DF (model)	5	5	5	5	5	5

Note: The entries in the table are the standardized ß$_s$.
[a]$p < 0.001$
[b]$p < 0.01$
[c]$p < 0.05$

is forcing many European, Japanese, and U.S. companies to make critical decisions on whether, when, and how to expand into uncharted territories. Although Western companies have experienced deregulation over the past two decades, this has largely been a domestic event with few traumatic consequences. The competitive dynamics, risk factors, and socio-institutional environments that unfold when taking the plunge into a foreign market are markedly different from those revealed when artificial constraints are lifted domestically and new entrants rush in. The actions required for survival in the early years of a foreign market's opening are not the same as those that bring success in the second phase of open market domestic competition.

Today opportunities for early mover advantages come from the following sources. First, some previously regulated industries may be deregulated by governments in industrialized countries. This deregulation creates first mover opportunities for MNEs originating from other countries. For instance, the certificate of need program stipulated by the Health Planning Act in the United States has been used by existing firms to limit the entry of potential competitors from both home and foreign countries. This program is now being pressured to deregulate. Second, some centrally planned economies or developing countries may open up to the outside world (e.g., North Korea and Cuba). The pent-up market demand of industries long stifled by governmental control and closed-door policies can provide early foreign movers with tremendous opportunities for sales and profitability despite high outcome uncertainty. Third, governmentally controlled industries in manufacturing and service sectors (particularly in the latter) may be opened to FDI in transitional economies (e.g., airplane manufacturing and insurance services in China). As these industries are normally characterized by a shortage of supply, opening them offers enormous potential to foreign investors who react quickly and enter early. Last, in some economically or politically diverse emerging economies, such as Russia, China, and Vietnam, there are many geographical regions (e.g., inland provinces) still closed to the outside world. Once these regions are opened, foreign pioneers are expected to enjoy immense market opportunities.

Implications for First Movers

The lessons from the above tests and other studies based on industrialized economies suggest that the potential investor should articulate its strategic objectives before making an entry timing decision. Foreign markets are not easy to enter. Even advanced market economies can present harsh, unfamiliar environments. If the objectives of FDI entry are to diversify the global business portfolio, reduce the operational risks, or gain immediate profit, then becoming a first mover in a high risk foreign economy is not advisable.

However, if the objectives are to build a strong market share and develop local markets over the long run, then early FDI entry may be advisable. In fact, pioneers in a foreign market often erect high barriers to later entrants. As a result, late entrants may have a hard time catching up. For example, in the automobile industry in China, late entrants have found that the domestic market has already been carved up by early movers, such as Volkswagen and Chrysler.

Despite the sacrifice of higher operational uncertainties during the early phase of investment, first movers appear better off over time from superior market positions, localized organizational learning, better relationship with governmental authorities and business community, and established organizational reputation and product image. Foreign investors entering some emerging markets indeed need some patience to achieve their strategic goals in expanding and exploring such markets.

Implications for Late Entrants

The above evidence indicates that late movers have better early stage performance in accounting returns and risk reduction than first movers do. This advantage may derive from organizational learning from early movers; a more stable regulatory environment in the host country; and improved investment infrastructure. This implies that late investment is an appropriate strategic choice for those investors who pursue short-term profitability or risk aversion in transitional economies. If, however, market expansion and asset efficiency are sought, late entry is disadvantageous.

Over the long run, late entry is less advantageous than early investment in both market and financial arenas. Test two observed that late entrants have lower operations performance than early movers when comparing late stage outcomes. Late foreign entrants compete not only with early foreign investors but also with local firms. The later the entry into a foreign market, the more competition is encountered.

Being left behind by early entrants can become a real and urgent risk. If a target foreign market is indeed of strategic importance, companies must act quickly to draw on the lessons learned by pioneering or more aggressive players in the market. Late movers should be aware that most pioneers will purposefully and aggressively preempt, if possible, entry by late entrants in order to build and hold their dominant share in the market.

Overall Considerations

Although the FDI timing is an important decision, it is not the sole determinant of FDI entry choice. Premature entry can easily backfire. FDI entry decisions must be made in conjunction with other strategic considerations, such as global positioning, organizational learning, and the MNE's own advantages. In the context of transitional economies, the impact of government policy on FDI decision making is also significant. For example, despite the adoption of free market principles, the Russian government has mainly encouraged early movers and threatened late movers. In a meeting with U.S. executives in 1990, Mikhail Gorbachev remarked: "Those companies who are with us now have good prospects of participating in our great country . . . whereas those who wait will remain observers for years to come — *we will see to it*" (*Economist*, June 8: 63–64). Foreign investors have to consider seriously governmental commitments to help first movers and prevent late entrants when making FDI timing decisions.

A pioneer investor that aims to maintain its position over the long term should exploit first mover advantages (e.g., market expansion and asset efficiency) while mitigating the disadvantages (e.g., risk and cost effects). Some tactics may include: preempting potential opportunities through obtaining patents or copyrights or filling positioning gaps on the marketing side in the host territory; minimizing technological leakage to rivals in the local settings by retaining employees, limiting access, or developing organizational capabilities; and avoiding excessive inertia by tracking indigenous customer needs, being willing to cannibalize, and maintaining operational flexibility.

For late movers in search of market expansion in a foreign country, some strategies are: entering through a market niche in which they have distinctive advantages and which avoids direct confrontation with a strong pioneer; purchasing or acquiring a pioneer firm, local or foreign, if it is capital-constrained, lacks resources, and has not yet achieved its market potential. Recently some emerging economies have allowed transnational investors to acquire indigenous state-owned enterprises, many of which are local pioneer firms but lack capital, technology, or organizational resources; and learning from early entrants of FDI how to reduce contextual risks and operational uncertainty and enhance the cross margin rate in dealing with local governments, supplies, customers, and other stakeholders in the value chain.

In the course of formulating FDI timing strategy, both early and late entrants should attach the utmost importance to integrating timing with other investment strategies, such as entry mode and location selection. In the joint venture entry mode, a good local partner can spur an early mover's market expansion and enhance its market power against rivals because of operational synergy between a local partner's existing market power and a foreign partner's technological and organizational competencies. Moreover, when early investors tread uncharted waters, local partners can greatly assist in reducing contextual or transactional risks using country-specific knowledge. In a similar fashion, locating in open areas in emerging economies fosters risk reduction for early investors. Indeed, open areas provide international firms with a better business atmosphere and a superior investment infrastructure that are conducive to operational stability and risk reduction.

Emerging Markets

As China, Eastern Europe, and the post-Soviet republics undertake political and economic transitions toward more market-based systems, foreign investors have been increasingly interested in these countries. Transitional economies, taken together, represent the world's largest emerging markets. They have become the new battleground for FDI. MNEs must secure their positions in these markets if they want to remain competitive in the next millennium.

Having been isolated from the rest of the world for several decades, transitional economies are characterized by a great deal of potential opportunity and markets, on one hand, and a tremendous amount of uncertainty and difficulty on the other hand. Although political, economic, and social uncertainty affect both foreign and domestic firms, certain events have caused particular anxiety among foreign businesses. These include, for example, the evacuation of most expatriate personnel to Hong Kong in the aftermath of the Tiananmen Square Incident in China in 1989 and the panic surrounding the violent coup in Russia in 1991 and 1993. These devastating but rare events aside, small-scale environmental changes, such as sudden changes in tax codes and regulations, are numerous.

Although the outcomes of such carrot and stick policies in Russia and Eastern Europe are not yet clear because of a relatively short period of FDI absorption, in China a large number of early movers have been rewarded handsomely in their collaborations with the government. Perhaps the foremost example is Volkswagen, which currently operates the largest foreign-invested firm in China (Shanghai Volkswagen) as well as a number of other joint ventures. Because the Chinese government regards automobiles as one of the pillar industries earmarked for strong support, Volkswagen has been identified as a key player in the market. In contrast, late movers, such as General Motors, Ford, and Mercedes-Benz, have had a hard time gaining government approval for their FDI projects.

Rapid economic expansion combined with pent-up demand often leads to an inability of local producers to exploit market opportunities fully and exhaust business potentials. Foreign investors thus have more opportunities abroad than in home markets. In China, for example, gross domestic product has grown tenfold in the past 15 years; it will continue to expand to almost $6 trillion, almost ten times its size in 1994, over the next 25 years. Foreign-funded enterprises are already accounting for 15 percent and 35 percent of China's total GNP and exports, respectively. The heterogeneity of industry and market structures between transitional economies and advanced market economies also increases the likelihood that foreign firms will achieve higher performance than when operating domestically. Moreover, distinctive technological and organizational skills often enable foreign companies to create new segments in which they can pioneer their products.

In such an environment, foreign investors have to confront the question of whether they will be better as early entrants despite all the start-up difficulties, or if they should wait and see until the pioneers get bloodied and then enter with the expectation of greater performance. Each of these two investment strategies has merits as well as costs, leading to vigorous but inconclusive debates, such as the one on the Russian investment dilemma.

In recent years China's remarkable economic progress has led transnational investors, particularly early movers, to revise radically their view of the opportunities and redouble their efforts to capitalize on its potential. As senior managers of many early movers originating from North American, European, and Asian MNEs come to believe that the forces working to open China's economy are irreversible, they are hastening to expand the scale, scope, and structure of their activities in the country.

These early investors are there for the long haul. They have already figured out how to make and sustain profits while locking out late-moving competitors. Indeed China is, and will long remain, a difficult and uncertain operating environment for transnational investors. The long-term economic opportunities China offers are, however, so remarkable that senior managers will find it prudent to continue paying attention to the experiences of those companies most active there.

Most early movers began with one or two small ventures as a way of putting an opportunistic toe in the water. Successful pioneering ventures took frustrations in stride, viewing them as an unavoidable part of the learning process in a complex and unfamiliar environment. These early entrants are now making explicit, strategic decisions to move beyond the experimental stage. Experimentation is no longer the goal; the new objective is to build and hold a dominant share of the foreign market, while blocking entry by other MNEs.

As transitional economies continue to move toward more market-based systems, many foreign investors have come to realize the irreversible forces working to open up these economies. As a result, both early and late entrants are hastening to expand the scale, scope, and structure of their FDI activities in these countries. Following the experience in China, it is predicted that a similar transformation of first generation FDI movers will occur in Eastern Europe and the post-Soviet republics. Therefore, it is critical to draw on the lessons from China. To summarize, there are both advantages and disadvantages to early FDI entry during the initial phase of operations. Early entrants, which face initial high risks and low profits, should compete for future, rather than immediate profits. Finally, first movers can expect significant advantages over the long run.

REFERENCES

Aliber, R. Z. 1970. A theory of foreign direct investment. In C. P. Kindleberger (Ed.), *The international cooperation*, pp. 5–22. Cambridge, MA: MIT Press.

Anderson, S. P. and M. Engers. 1994. Strategic investment and timing of entry. *International Economic Review*, 35: 833–853.

Buckley, P. J. and M. Casson. 1981. The optimal timing of a foreign direct investment. *The Economic Journal*, 91: 75–87.

Hannan, M. T. and J. Freeman. 1977. The population ecology of organizations. *American Journal of Sociology*, 82: 929–964.

Lambkin, M. 1988. Order of entry and performance in new markets. *Strategic Management Journal*, 9: 127–140.

Luo, Y. 1998. Timing of investment and international expansion performance in China. *Journal of International Business Studies*, 29: 391–408.

Luo, Y. 1997. Pioneering in China: Risks and benefits. *Long Range Planning*, 30(5): 768–776.

Mascarenhas, B. 1992. Order of entry and performance in international markets. *Strategic Management Journal*, 13: 499–510.

Mitchell, W., J. M. Shaver, and B. Yeung. 1993. Performance following changes of international presence in domestic and transition industries. *Journal of International Business Studies*, 24: 647–669.

Porter, M. E. 1986. Competition in global industries: A conceptual framework. In M. E. Porter (Ed.), *Competition in global industries*, pp. 15–60. Boston, MA: Harvard Business School Press.

Rivoli, P. and E. Salorio. 1996. Foreign direct investment and investment under uncertainty. *Journal of International Business Studies*, 27: 335–358.

FURTHER READINGS

Conner, K. R. 1988. Strategies for product cannibalism. *Strategic Management Journal*, 9: 9–26.

Green, D., D. Baclay, and A. Ryans. 1995. Entry strategy and long-term performance: Conceptualization and empirical examination. *Journal of Marketing*, 59: 1–16.

Kerin, R. A., P. R. Varadarajan, and R. A. Peterson. 1992. First-mover advantages: A synthesis, conceptual framework and research propositions. *Journal of Marketing*, 56: 33–52.

Kvint, V. 1994. Don't give up on Russia. *Harvard Business Review*, 72(2): 62–74.

Lieberman, M. B. and D. B. Montgomery. 1988. First-mover advantages. *Strategic Management Journal*, 9: 41–58.

Lilien, G. L. and E. Yoon. 1990. The timing of competitive market entry: An exploratory study of new industrial markets. *Management Science*, 38: 568–585.

Luo, Y. and M. Peng. 1998. First mover advantages in investing in transitional economies. *Thunderbird International Business Review*, 40(2): 141–163.

McCarthy, D., S. Puffer, and P. Simmonds. 1993. Riding the Russian roller coaster: U.S. firms' recent experience and future plans in the former USSR. *California Management Review*, 36(1): 99–115.

Mitchell, W. 1989. Whether and when? Probability and timing of incumbents' entry into emerging industrial subfields. *Administrative Science Quarterly*, 34: 208–230.

Nehrt, C. 1996. Timing and intensity effects of environmental investments. *Strategic Management Journal*, 17: 535–547.

Robinson, W. T. 1988. Sources of market pioneer advantages: The case of industrial goods industries. *Journal of Marketing Research*, September: 47–67.

Sharmar, A. 1995. Entry strategies of U.S. firms to the Newly Independent States, Baltic States, and Eastern European countries. *California Management Review*, 37(3): 90–109.

Tan, B. and I. Vertinsky. Foreign direct investment by Japanese electronics firms in the United States and Canada: Modelling the timing of entry. *Journal of International Business Studies*, 27(4): 655–682.

Teplensky, J.D., J. R. Kimberly, A. L. Hillman, and J. S. Schwartz. 1993. Scope, timing and strategic adjustment in emerging markets: Manufacturer strategies and the case of MRI. *Strategic Management Journal*, 14: 505–527.

Ursacki, T. and I. Vertinsky. 1992. Choice of entry timing and scale by foreign banks in Japan and Korea. *Journal of Banking and Finance*, 16: 405–421.

8

Industry Selection

As industry structure is partially exogenous, industry selection will have a strong impact on international expansion performance. It determines the industrial environment and market demand that a firm faces abroad, which in turn affects its profitability, stability, sales growth, and competitive position in the host country. This chapter elaborates on the importance of industry selection in international expansion and presents the structural imperfection argument on how a host country industry influences a multinational enterprise's (MNE's) foreign operations. The following section provides analytical approaches to selecting an industry.

INDUSTRY AND INTERNATIONAL EXPANSION

In recent years both the intensity and frequency of foreign direct investment (FDI) have greatly magnified. According to industrial organization theory, strategic choices and outcomes are significantly determined by industrial conditions, which drive globalization (Yip, 1994). These conditions, which vary in strength from industry to industry (Porter, 1986), include globally common customer needs (Yip, 1994); cost determinants, such as economies of scale or technological and advertising intensity (Porter, 1986); international trade agreements that affect government policy (Willmore, 1994); and conditions, such as cross-border subsidization, that drive up competition (Teece, 1985). Global strategy must be formed in light of these factors if a firm is to gain benefits, such as cost reduction, improved product quality, enhanced customer loyalty, or an increased competitive edge.

Yip (1994) provides more detail on four categories of industrial conditions that drive globalization. First, market globalization is driven by market- and customer-based conditions that favor the use of a global strategy as indicated by a global commonality in customer needs and tastes, the importance of global customers and channels, and the transferability of marketing approaches worldwide (e.g., reaction of local customers to foreign marketing, the effect of being exposed to new products while overseas). Second, cost globalization is enhanced by cost-based conditions that favor the use of a global strategy as indicated by global economies of scale, a steep experience curve, sourcing efficiencies, favorable logistics, differences in country costs (including exchange rates), and high product development costs. Third, government globalization is driven by the imposition of policies that favor the use of a global strategy, including tariff and non-tariff barriers, compatible technical standards, and common marketing regulations. Last, global competition is affected by conditions that require the use of a global strategy, especially the extent to which competitors make use of such strategies.

The above scheme applies ideally to a global or borderless world, not necessarily to an international or imperfect business world. In a truly borderless world, MNEs can and should adopt global strategies that maximize integration and minimize differences among countries. A global strategy is defined as a coordinated or integrated approach to operating globally, particularly in contrast to multidomestic or multi-local strategies. On the global integration versus local responsiveness grid, MNEs should tilt heavily toward integration. Other things being equal, this scheme is expected to hold true when MNEs expand into territories within harmonious, borderless regions, such as North American Free Trade Agreement countries or the big European market, where entry barriers and costs are low and consumers tend to share homogenous utility functions. This complies with Linder's (1961) model of international economics in that MNEs often dominate in neighboring countries that have similar demand sophistication. A good example illustrating this scheme is the dominance of Chinese investments (Hong Kong, Taiwan, and Singapore) in the People's Republic of China. For sociocultural reasons, there are marked similarities in demand conditions and consumer utility functions between mainland China and other members of the Chinese community. MNEs from this community make direct investments in the mainland by contributing unique competencies. They provide technology appropriate to local environmental conditions, such as factor costs, input characteristics, demand level, and consumption sophistication.

The conventional wisdom of FDI theory remains valid in explaining the logic and behavior of MNEs undertaking international expansion.

There are three major reasons to expand. First, differences in industry and market structure still exist between countries, with the largest variations between developed and developing economies. As a result of increasing regionalization, barriers to production factor flows have been fundamentally reduced, thus facilitating intra-regional trade and investment. Trade barriers, however, remain evident in production input and output flows in different regions. More importantly, market imperfection is still present in many countries, especially in developing economies. This implies that MNEs can benefit more from international expansion than domestic operations because of heterogenous market demands. As most developing countries and some industrialized nations are undergoing a transformation in their industrial structure, imperfections on the supply side are becoming even greater. The deregulation of certain sectors in advanced economies and the opening of some industries in emerging markets create the potential for abnormal profitability for MNEs expanding internationally.

Second, the intensity of competition and the life cycle of the industry are often idiosyncratic in different countries. Although some industries, such as the television, semiconductor, copy machine, and watch industries, are truly global in that rivals compete worldwide, there are certainly a large number of other industries characterized by less vigorous competition and different life cycle stages in different countries. Because competition is increasingly recognized as a predominant driving force underlying international expansion, firms in a harsh, competitive, domestic sector may expand overseas to regions where competition is low, the industry is growing or embryonic, or a competitive position would be more readily attained and sustained. Today, most service industries and numerous manufacturing sectors (e.g., consumer packaged goods, caustic chemicals) provide tremendous opportunity to MNEs pursuing economic rents by competing at different magnitudes or in various life cycle phases.

Last, but not least, production factor advantages in foreign markets attract international expansion. Although the competitive advantage gained solely on the basis of factor advantages, such as cheap labor, may be unstable in a world of technological change and rapid substitution, factor advantages in the host country are still critical to the long-term profitability of international expansion. When international competition is fierce, a firm's business level advantages are generally dependent upon such factors, whether its products are labor-, capital-, or technology-intensive.

STRUCTURAL IMPERFECTION ARGUMENT

A major challenge today for multinational corporations is how to become competent and attain sustained superior performance in the global marketplace. One paradigm that explains superior firm performance is the industrial structure view. This model maintains that particular industries are more attractive to the degree that they contain structural impediments to competition, thus allow participating firms to sustain competitive advantages once their positions in the industry are obtained (Porter, 1991; Teece, Pisano, & Shuen, 1991).

There are two related and overlapping types of market imperfections in FDI and MNE theories. One emphasizes industrial structure as a source of market power (Hymer, 1976); the other focuses on transaction costs as barriers to international trade and licensing (Dunning, 1979). The former is more relevant in explaining how industrial characteristics drive internationalization, whereas the latter explains economic rationales for internalization. The industry structure imperfection perspective in FDI theories argues that MNEs can achieve higher performance than firms operating domestically because they benefit from the industry structural variance between the host and home countries. In industrial organization economics, a widely accepted conceptual framework holds that structural conditions determine the behavior and subsequent performance of a firm (Scherer & Ross, 1990). When the industrial structure of a host country is imperfect and entry barriers are low, FDI will flow in as a direct response (Hymer, 1976). Structure imperfection in a foreign market constitutes a dominant factor that not only makes FDI preferable to trade or licensing (Contractor & Lorange, 1988) but also determines the relative attractiveness of one host country over other countries (Dunning, 1979). Firms in oligopolistic industries enjoy the advantages of economies of scale and other characteristics that give them market power. This power allows them to overcome the disadvantages of being foreign and compete with local rivals. Early researchers have reported the existence of a systematic linkage between MNE performance and structural variables in the advanced market economy context (Caves & Mehra, 1986; Kogut & Singh, 1988; Mitchell, Shaver, & Yeung, 1993).

A widely accepted conceptual framework in industrial organization holds that structural conditions determine the behavior and subsequent performance of a firm. In an economy unfettered by structural imperfection of output, profit rates across industries should fall to some equilibrium rate reflecting the risk-adjusted marginal efficiency of capital. In the presence of structural imperfections, however, inter-industry variations in profitability abound because entry barriers prevent new competition and expanded output (Scherer & Ross, 1990). In a similar vein, the industry structure paradigm maintains that competitive advantages and inter-firm differences in efficiency cannot persist over a long period unless structural imperfections are present (Porter, 1986; Teece, Pisano, & Shuen, 1991). Porter (1991) also notes these strong industry effects on the selection of business level strategies. A large body of research on corporate business portfolios concurs in pointing out the importance of industry structure variables in explaining performance (Bettis & Mahajan, 1985; Montgomery, 1985).

Direct investment tends to involve market conduct that extends the recognition of mutual market dependence — the essence of oligopoly — beyond national boundaries (Teece, 1985). Likewise, it tends to broadly equalize the rate of return on capital (equity) throughout a given industry in all the countries where production actually takes place. This common profit rate, however, may exceed a normal or competitive one because a persistent oligopoly, nationwide or worldwide, is marked by barriers to the entry of new firms and, perforce, to the inflow of capital (Caves, 1971; Teece, 1985).

Today, the structural imperfection argument seems to be more useful in explaining an MNE's expansion into emerging economies than into other industrialized nations. This is simply because the degree of industry structural imperfection in emerging markets or transitional economies is immensely greater than in advanced market economies. Theoretically, the greater the structural imperfections, the more potentials to be explored and exploited.

Despite great improvements in recent years, industry structure in most emerging economies remains one of the bottlenecks hampering economic development. Luo (1999) identified several characteristics of industry structure in these economies. First, there are great differences in after-tax profitability across industries, resulting primarily from long-rooted industry structure imperfections and cumbersome consolidation tax systems. Second, there are also fundamental differences in sales growth across industries, caused mainly by governmental policies that allow only some industries to be decentralized and privatized. Third, one major structural headache is that central governments in these economies have to control state firm assets while allowing other firms to be acquired by or merge with domestic or foreign companies. Industries with higher asset intensity are subject to greater government interference. In other words, inter-industry variations in asset intensity can lead to variable treatment. Fourth, growth of the number of firms in an industry is extremely idiosyncratic across industries. Controlling the number of new firms established in an industry is a predominant means by which governments monitor structural development. This entry barrier leads to heterogeneity of competition vigor in different industries. Finally, industry structure is highly uncertain, arising mainly from the transformative nature of the national economy and the experimental nature of an array of new industrial policies.

Theoretically, international competition and expansion reduce structural imperfections in the host country. In practice, however, this effect differs according to industry and country. The structure of some industries may be more exogenous than that of others, as reflected in higher entry barriers, more governmental regulations, greater asset intensity, and the like. Structural imperfections are also more exogenous than in advanced market economies. Such imperfections partially result from a paradox wherein governments aim to alleviate structural distortions by injecting more competition and assimilating more foreign capital yet simultaneously impose policies that present new obstacles to the mitigation of imperfection. Some policies may increase rather than reduce structure distortions when a government attaches high value to social stability, infant sector protection, and pillar industry subsidies.

For example, the Chinese government has determined which industrial sectors are appropriate for FDI in complying with plans for national economic growth and social development. FDI guidance is usually maintained through laws and regulations relevant to specific sectors, periodic updates of the *Orientation Directory of Industries for FDI*, and implementation of policy by government departments in charge of FDI projects.

In most emerging economies FDI is sought for building infrastructure, renovation of basic industries, and funding technology-intensive industries. Governments usually seek FDI for: new agricultural technologies, comprehensive agricultural development, energy, communications, and raw materials industries needed for development; advanced technologies urgently needed in the economy or new equipment or materials that can improve product performance, conserve energy and raw materials, upgrade the technological level of businesses, or result in manufacturing import-substitution products that meet market needs; projects generating more foreign exchange revenues by satisfying international market demand, improving product quality, opening new markets, and increasing product export volume; and new technologies or equipment that comprehensively utilize or recycle resources or reduce environmental pollution.

Industries that are often restricted from utilizing FDI include: sectors in which the country has already developed or introduced advanced technologies and where production is already satisfying domestic needs, sectors in which the country is implementing a trial introduction of foreign investment or businesses are monopolized by the state, and exploration or mining of rare natural resources. In China, for example, the projects that cannot obtain FDI are classified as Restricted Category A (wristwatch chips or assembly, refrigeration boxes, cans, aluminum materials, photocopiers, one-time syringes, cassette recorders, ordinary antibiotics, luxury office buildings) or Category B (offshore or inland fishing, table salt, cigarettes, cotton or woolen textiles, chemical fibers, film, sedan cars, air conditioners, color television sets, video recorders, arterial railways, aviation and water transportation, foreign trade, luxury hotels, banks, insurance, publishing, and printing).

Governments may take various measures to constrain FDI in some industries. For example, the length of operations of FDI projects often must be specified in joint venture contracts, and certain project proposals may have to be approved by government authorities. Even projects falling within restricted categories, however, may be treated as though free from restrictions after approval, so long as their export value is over a certain percentage of total production.

Governments may also provide preferential treatment to boost FDI in industries they wish to encourage. Regardless of where it is located, projects exceeding specified minimum amounts (e.g., $30 million in China) may be entitled to enjoy the same preferential taxation treatment applied to those taking place in economic and technological development zones. Furthermore, FDI projects that build and operate energy or communications infrastructure facilities (coal, electric power, local railway, highway, or harbor) and involve a large investment and a long projected time for returns on investment may be allowed to expand their business scope. FDI projects introducing advanced technologies urgently needed by the nation or new equipment or materials to manufacture import substitution products, and which can balance their own foreign exchange, may be freed from exporting requirements. Priority may also be given to FDI projects requesting export quotas when their products involve such quotas.

MODELS FOR CHOOSING THE RIGHT INDUSTRY

Five Forces Model

Although Porter's five forces model was designed for domestic settings, it can be applied to industry selection in a foreign context with certain revisions. Selecting the right industry overseas largely determines an MNE's profitability and competitive position in the host country market. The intensity of industrial competition and profit potential is a function of five competitive forces, whether in a domestic or host market: threat of new entrants, suppliers, buyers, product substitutes, and intensity of rivalry among competitors. A foreign company should analyze each of these five forces, identify possible opportunities or threats generated by each, and then select an industry in the target country that best fits its organizational competencies and strategic goals.

In recent years global industrial boundaries have become blurred. As a result, competition is no longer viewed as limited to direct business rivals. Instead, it as seen as coming from all the means by which customers seek value. In this regard, the five forces model sheds light on selecting a foreign industry in which a firm can achieve a sustainable edge over competitors. Porter argues that the stronger each of these forces, the more limited becomes the ability of established companies to raise prices and earn greater profits. A strong competitive force is regarded as a threat because it depresses financial returns. A weak competitive force is viewed as an opportunity, for it allows a firm to earn more profits. Firms that constitute competitive forces include not only local companies but also other foreign investors or marketers that may influence each of the five forces.

It is also important to recognize the industrial evolution and dynamism of each force. When operating in a foreign market, an MNE often confronts greater operational uncertainty and risks derived from the industrial or macro-national environment that may be quite dissimilar to that of the home country. The strength and sources of the each of the five forces can change through time. For instance, suppliers could become competitors (by integrating forward), as could buyers (by integrating backward). In such circumstances, the task facing international managers is to choose the industry that will allow them to seize opportunities while overcoming threats from these forces.

Industry Life Cycle Model

In selecting a target industry overseas, an MNE should also identify the stage of the industry's life cycle. Although the five forces model addresses relevant competitive forces, it focuses more on the supply side of an industry and cannot be applied to a dynamic framework. The industry life cycle model offers insight into the demand side of an industry, revealing a more evolutionary perspective on industrial development. Combining the industry life cycle model with an analysis of the five forces is strongly advisable when selecting a foreign industry.

Over time, most industries pass through a series of phases, from growth through maturity and eventually into decline. The strength and nature of each of the five forces typically changes as an industry evolves. This is particularly evident when analyzing existing and potential competition. The changes in these forces give rise to different opportunities and threats at each stage of an industry's evolution. International managers must be able to identify the current stage of a candidate industry and anticipate how long the industry will remain at that stage before moving to the next phase.

The industry life cycle is used by international managers to assess whether the company is able to take advantage of opportunities and counter emerging threats in light of its strategic goals. In general, the life cycle has a greater impact on those MNEs pursuing long-term market power and a competitive position in a host country market than those seeking short-term profits or using a host country as a manufacturing platform for worldwide export.

Five industrial environments can be identified, each linked to a distinct stage of an industry's life cycle: embryonic, growth, shakeout, mature, and declining. An embryonic industry is one that is just beginning to develop (for example, personal computers in 1980). Growth is slow because of such factors as consumer unfamiliarity with the industry's product, high prices caused by the inability of companies to reap any significant economies of scale, and less developed distribution channels. MNEs investing at this stage are generally recognized as first movers or early entrants who face many trade-offs between preemptive opportunities and financial or operational risks. An MNE, therefore, needs to assess whether the company should and can capitalize on such opportunities while countering emerging threats if opting for this industry in a host country.

Once market demand for the product begins to take off, a growth industry develops. First time demand expands rapidly as many new consumers enter the market. In the internationalization process, investing in a growing industry in a target country is generally an ideal choice. A growing stage can be readily identified by evaluating growth of an industry's sales, profitability, output, and capital investments. This information is usually available from statistical yearbooks or other periodicals.

The length of the growth stage differs from industry to industry because it depends on such factors as entry barriers, capital requirements, economies of scale, technological requirements, risk and cost factors, and the openness of the industry to new local and foreign entrants. MNEs often encounter daunting challenges when taking the plunge into a foreign growth industry because host governments are likely to impose more entry or operational barriers on their fastest growing sectors. This is done to protect domestic firms or control the speed and pattern of foreign investment.

During the shakeout stage, market demand approaches saturation. Foreign companies may consider entering a shakeout industry if they aim to exploit short-term profitability or establish a presence in the market for exploring product, market, or technological niches in the host country. This stage can be identified by looking at changes in the growth pattern over time. In general, if entry barriers are low to both local and foreign firms, the shakeout stage cannot last very long. It is critical for foreign companies to find a market niche or new opportunities from product differentiation when they plunge into a shakeout industry overseas.

An industry enters the mature stage as the shakeout stage ends. Although investing in a mature industry in a foreign market is generally inadvisable, some MNEs choose to enter if their objective is simply to shift home manufacturing sites to a target foreign country where production factors cost much less. In other words, when an MNE's foreign operations are not designed to explore the economic benefits of pent-up demand, the impact of an industry's life cycle stage is minimal. In fact, MNEs with this orientation may be able to acquire more benefits from a mature industry by taking advantage of greater bargaining power with suppliers.

An industry enters the decline stage when growth becomes negative for various reasons including demographical changes, technological substitution, and international competition. Although there is no economic logic for local market-oriented MNEs to enter a declining industry in a host country, MNEs focused on minimizing costs may still benefit from starting production at a host site as a platform for export or vertical integration. Medium and small MNEs may use such sites for export to neighboring countries, its home country market, or other countries. As a result of increasing regionalization and gradual removal of trade barriers worldwide, this strategy will enable medium and small international firms to maximize benefits from their competencies in international distribution, strategic flexibility, and entrepreneurial orientation. Indeed, many Asian MNEs have been successfully operating in neighboring countries using this strategy.

In sum, it is generally advisable for MNEs to select a growing industry when expanding into a target country. This is particularly true for MNEs seeking a long-term market share and competitive position in the local industry. Today most Western MNEs have this orientation when investing in emerging foreign markets. An embryonic industry appears to be an appropriate choice if an MNE wants to pursue first mover advantages in a foreign market. In highly competitive industries, the early mover position is imperative if an MNE wants to become a market leader in the global marketplace.

It is critical for MNEs to know the industry life cycle stages in both home and foreign industries. A mature industry at home may be embryonic or growing stage in a foreign country. MNEs pursuing market power should be able to preempt first mover opportunities not only in a home industry but also in embryonic industries in foreign markets. Firms that aim at cost minimization, transnational distribution, local market niche, or vertical integration within a global network may consider entering mature or declining industries where they can still benefit from cheaper production factors or comparative advantages in the host country. The market orientation (local market versus export market), strategic goals (profit versus market share), distinctive competencies, rival behavior, and host country government policies are all important factors in making a life cycle analysis before selecting an industry.

Structural Attributes Model

The nature of an industry is a multidimensional construct containing several different traits, such as sales growth and profitability growth. Within an industry, each attribute may have a different influence on firm operations. For instance, a growing industry may show sales growth but not necessarily profitability growth because of the heavy burden of classified or accumulated corporate income taxes in the host country. The important task of international managers, therefore, is to select a foreign industry whose structural characteristics best match the firm's strategic goals for expansion. In other words, different structural attributes within the same industry may have varying features. Further, each individual attribute may have a different effect on the various aspects of international expansion success. Some of the key attributes are detailed below.

Profitability

Inter-industry variance in profitability has been an enduring characteristic of many economies in the world. In developing countries, the breadth and depth of the removal of government-induced asymmetries in an industry during economic reform depend largely upon that industry's profit level. In high profit industries, although competitive entry from both domestic and foreign firms can gradually erode supra-normal profits on invested capital, continued government hinderance of the structural adjustment process results in appreciable barriers to entry and enables established firms to keep their market power and competitive position for some time. Additionally, when operating in high profit industries, foreign companies are likely to confront more government constraints on materials supplies and product distribution, latent competition pressure, and market fluctuations. These risks can be even greater when MNEs invest in emerging economies, because the objective of economic reform is normally to orient the industry structure toward more equilibrium and market force determination.

Sales Growth

Industry sales growth is a key component of market attractiveness for both local firms and foreign businesses. Growth serves as an indicator of disequilibrium, a condition favorably associated with entry, and as an indicator of industrial evolution. Porter (1986) argues that rapid industry growth ensures strong financial performance for incumbents even though new entrants take some market share. In general, when a particular industry is deregulated or freed from government control over market supply, rapid initial development ensues. This take-off is reflected in a surge in industry sales growth. In such circumstances, many new firms enter the industry unless start-up costs or other non-government instituted entry barriers are extremely high. Further, when the local market for a particular industry appears to grow dramatically, it is reasonable to expect that foreign companies will pursue local market expansion rather than export growth.

Asset Intensity

Asset intensity is a plausible indicator of capital requirements, a proxy for entry barriers, and a determinant of economies of scale. The imperfect capital market argument in industrial organization studies contends that firms in an industry that requires a large initial capital investment can obtain monopolistic profits in the long run because few truly qualified competitors can enter the industry and exit barriers created by substantial resource commitments may not be fully recoverable (Scherer & Ross, 1990). High asset intensity hence discourages entry of new firms into the industry. As a result, foreign businesses already operating in industries with high asset intensity are likely to have high profits. Additionally, such industries usually require foreign investors to commit a great deal of investment capital or other distinctive resources. According to resource-based theory, the strategic objectives of firms are determined by their core competencies or resources. By contributing their distinctive resources to local capital- or technology-intensive industries, MNEs manifest their long-term commitment to indigenous production and host market expansion.

Growth in Number of Firms

In examining the degree of competition in an industry in market economies, the most widely used measure is the leading firm concentration ratio (CR) (for example, CR4 for the United States, CR5 for the United Kingdom, and CR3 for Germany). However, the degree of inequality of firm shares in an industry does not necessarily reflect the vigor of competition. Government intervention and the identity of publically owned lead firms also have an influence. Although the CR indicates the existing pattern of competition intensity, growth in the number of firms in an industry reflects ex post patterns of competition that are expected to take place sooner or later, depending upon the average length of time needed for a firm to reach full operation after entry in an industry. Therefore, this growth measure can be used as an important proxy for assessing the degree of competition in an industry. When a new industry emerges or the government deregulates or opens up an industry with pent-up demand, the number of firms, whether local or foreign, in this industry is expected to grow drastically as long as entry barriers are not enormously high. Over time, however, the increase in the number of firms in the industry is likely to boost competition, decrease disparities in profitability between industries, and slow down the average growth rate of local sales for individual firms. Whenever a host country industry appears to be highly competitive as a result of a continuous increase in the number of firms in the industry, MNEs may consider shifting their focus from local market development to production factor exploitation or production rationalization through a globally integrated network.

Structural Uncertainty

Strictly speaking, uncertainty means unpredictable variability, whereas dynamism comprises both predictable and unpredictable elements. Both dynamism and uncertainty in an industry carry opportunities and challenges. Uncertainty may arise because of market force fluctuations or changes in industrial policies in the host country. Structural uncertainty often mirrors high fluctuations in prices, sales, and material supplies. Under these circumstances, foreign companies are expected to confront more operational risks. If they intend to avoid these risks, they should reduce their reliance on local settings. In an effort to do this, foreign investors can decrease the portion of local sourcing and marketing while increasing exports. Many Asian MNEs investing in neighboring countries used this strategy to adapt and respond to the financial chaos that recently occurred in Asia. Generally, MNEs interested in entering an industry characterized by structural uncertainty should consider whether their ability to offset risks is sufficient to enable them to realize their international expansion goals.

Structural Complexity

Structural complexity refers to the diversity and heterogeneity of environmental factors (for example, competitors, customers, and suppliers). Structural diversity means with how many different factors and issues a firm must deal. Structural heterogeneity refers to how different each factor is from the others. High complexity in an industry reinforces the difficulty of using standardization and cost efficiency strategies. It also increases an MNE's operational uncertainties and production instabilities. As a strategic response to structural complexity, strategic and operational flexibility is imperative. A more focused strategy with respect to the scope of both products and markets appears to be the proper solution in this environment for firms with little host country-specific experience or having a short period of presence in the market. When a foreign firm has gained more diverse experience in dealing with competitors, customers, and suppliers and has thus reduced the liabilities of foreignness, the firm may consider extending its line of business in an attempt to explore more opportunities. In deciding product portfolios for investment in a complex foreign industry, the use of related diversification, particularly a firm's core competency, seems a better choice than the use of an unrelated strategy. Nevertheless, the firm's length of operations, the diversity of its host country experience, and the contribution of its local partner (if in a joint venture) may moderate this relationship.

Structural Deterrence

Structural deterrence concerns resource availability from a specific industry and supporting industries. A foreign industry that an MNE plans to enter may not be complex or uncertain but may still be hostile. In this situation, the foreign business has constraints in implementing its business and operational level strategies, deploying and utilizing internal resources contributed to local operations, and participating in indigenous markets. Resource munificence, instead, helps firms achieve operational and financial synergies from the interactions between internal resources (competitive advantages) and external resources (comparative advantages). The reliance on external resources in the host country comes from either the firm's strategic intent and needs or the host government's required localization of product components. In general, structural resources include: natural resources, raw materials, parts, and components; investment infrastructure, such as power supplies, telecommunications, and transportation; product factors, such as land, capital, labor, information, technology, and management; and governmental treatment, assistance, and efficiency. MNEs need to ensure that all of these resources are available in the industry within which they will operate as well as in related or supporting industries.

In sum, it is important for MNEs to analyze an industry's structural attributes and assess whether the dynamics of these attributes fit their strategic goals and capabilities. MNEs should configure their market and strategic orientations with the structural attributes of the foreign industry. Market orientation choices include local, export, and dual market foci. In principle, an MNE's orientation should be structured such that it cannot only achieve its goals but also keep a certain degree of flexibility in responding to market changes in the host country and beyond.

Integrated Framework

Each of the three models discussed (five forces, life cycle, and structural attributes) is a useful instrument for analyzing and selecting an industry in a foreign country. The five forces model is useful for analyzing a firm's competitive environment, the industry life cycle perspective reveals market demand, and the structural attributes model provides guidelines for identifying structural traits. Because each model focuses on a different arena of industrial environment analysis and is complementary to the others, firms should use all three perspectives within an integrated framework to assess specific overseas industries. For example, all models are relevant to Motorola's decision to enter the Chinese telecommunications industry. The five forces model shows that the degree of existing and potential rivalry from both local and foreign firms was low, as was the threat of substitutes. Buyer and supplier bargaining power in the early years after entry was also relatively weak. The life cycle stage of the industry was embryonic in the early 1980s, and Motorola knew that the pent-up demand for its products could create tremendous market opportunities. Finally, although uncertainty was expected to be high, the industry's sales growth and profitability growth were also high. Moreover, the high asset intensity of the industry could decrease the threat of new entrants and increase the company's bargaining power with the local government. By allocating most of its FDI projects on the east coast of China and in major municipalities, such as Tianjin and Shanghai, Motorola could largely mitigate the risk of structural deterrence.

As Figure 8.1 shows, each of the three analytical models is influenced by two types of governmental policies, one relating to industrial regulations, the other to FDI. In fact, most national governments have utilized these two sets of policies to manipulate and oversee FDI inflow. Some typical industrial policies include: classification of industries as prohibited, restricted, permitted, or encouraged. Each category is treated differently in terms of taxation, financing, land rent, infrastructure access, and the like; ratification of projects in certain industries. In general, these industries are state monopolized or controlled; and giving preferential treatment to those MNEs that bring in more advanced technologies, managerial skills, foreign exchanges via export, or substitute imported products. Discriminatory treatment is often designed by a government to rationalize its industrial structure, alleviate resource or price distortions across industries, create foreign exchange earnings, and modernize pillar industries.

Some typical FDI policies include: (i) entry mode control, that is, MNEs are allowed to enter into certain industries only through certain entry modes (for example, joint ventures, coproductions, technology transfers via international licensing or franchising, or build-operate-transfer). Generally, the host country government requires at least one state-owned local enterprise to participate in the venture or collaboration; (ii) equity control, that is, foreign investors are restricted from holding a certain percentage of equity in the joint venture. For instance, MNEs entering Chinese auto assembly industries can maintain 49 percent of equity in the venture; (iii) location control, that is, the host government requires MNEs to locate projects in certain geographical regions. This requirement is expected to help boost regional economies by launching heavy investments in certain industries planned by the central or federal government. Projects in different locations are also taxed differently. Even within the same city, ventures in different locations can be subject to different treatment. For example, the Chinese Economic and Technological Development Zones provide more tax breaks than non-zones within the same city or county; (iv) duration control, that is, each FDI project should specify its

FIGURE 8.1
An Integrated Framework of Industry Selection

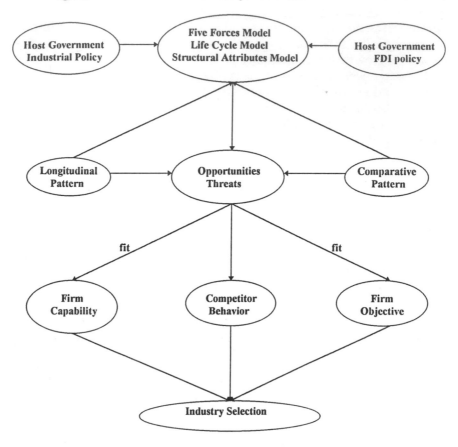

term (number of years) in its joint venture contract. Although this term can be renewed, such renewal is not automatic but usually subject to a new round of approval by relevant governmental authorities; (v) partner control, that is, certain big projects must include local firms assigned by the government. These firms may or may not have previous cooperation history with the foreign investors; (vi) timing control, that is, the host government may stop or freeze the approval of certain FDI projects for certain periods. This often occurs when the government and its agencies have over-approved a number of projects until they surpass the actual need for economic development. Major FDI policies may also be changed for a variety of economic and political reasons; (vii) project orientation control, that is, each project must be identified in its application and confirmed by the government as belonging to one orientation category:

export, technologically-advanced, infrastructure, import-substitution, or local market. Each of these orientations is offered different treatment and support by the government. In general, the first three enjoy preferential treatment, including lower income tax and tariff rates, refunds of value-added taxes, lower financing costs, better infrastructure access, government support, and cheaper land rent; and (viii) size control, that is, projects with different investment sizes have to be ratified by different levels of the government. The greater the size, the higher the rank of the authority in charge. When a project plans to increase its investment size, it usually has to be approved by the same authority that previously ratified the project. In general, most developed countries provide foreign investors with national treatment, meaning that foreign companies enjoy the same treatment as local enterprises. Thus, only some of the above industrial and FDI policies have been used in these countries. However, these policies are representative of most developing countries.

It is crucial for MNEs to analyze the industry and its opportunities and threats both longitudinally and comparatively. The competitive environment (competitors, customers, and suppliers), life cycle, and structural attributes of the industry in the host country are generally different from at home. In other words, MNEs are often unfamiliar with these segments in a foreign context unless they have operated there for enough time. As most foreign industries that MNEs plan to enter are dynamic, MNEs need to scan, analyze, and interpret the competitive environment, life cycle, and structural attributes based on longitudinal information as a prerequisite for analyzing emerging markets where unusual fluctuations frequently occur. In addition, MNEs need to compare the target country's competitive environment, life cycle, and structural attributes with those of home and other foreign countries. In recent years there is an increasing tendency for industrial changes in one country to partially correlate with those in others as the result of technological advancement, international competition, capital flow, and reduction of entry barriers. Therefore, a firm should use the home or third country as a benchmark for assessing opportunities and threats in a target foreign industry.

The next step is to evaluate whether or not the firm has the ability to seize these opportunities and counter these threats. This match often determines the eventual success of international expansion in a dynamic and complex market. In practice, this match requires the firm to identify correctly what resources and competencies are distinctive and mostly needed in host country operations and then properly deploy these resources to local subunits. For instance, technologies that a Western MNE plans to contribute to its local operations in developing countries may not have to be advanced. It may be more appropriate if the MNE commits lower level technology that local firms or partners are able to absorb and assimilate. Misallocation of distinctive resources will waste not only internal resources but also external opportunities.

Another imperative match lies between the firm's objectives and the emergence of opportunities and threats in the foreign market. Every foreign market has opportunities that MNEs can explore or exploit. However, it is not realistic for an MNE to plunge into every market because its distinctive resources and competitive edge are limited. Therefore, in international competition, an MNE's industry selection in a foreign country has to link with its strategic goals. These goals include not only its objectives in operating in a foreign country (for example, local market share, risk reduction, financial returns) but also its aim at overall global expansion. For example, if an MNE seeks horizontal FDI (that is, FDI in the same industry abroad as a firm operates in at home) or forward vertical FDI (that is, FDI in an industry abroad that sells the output of a firm's domestic production processes), the firm should opt for a fast growing, low risk, and less competitive industry in the host country. By contrast, if an MNE seeks backward vertical FDI (that is, FDI into an industry abroad that provides inputs for a firm's domestic or other foreign subunits' production), the firm should attach more value to comparative advantages of the host country in production factors, because it is less vulnerable to local market demand and competition. In principle, this decision should be made in such a way that the company can optimize goal fulfillment while using limited resources.

When promising opportunities emerge in a foreign market, other MNEs are expected to move in as well. If a firm enters a promising industry overseas, it will face competition from local businesses and other foreign rivals. Thus, before making a final decision on industry selection, an MNE should watch the corresponding behavior of its major rivals. This means that the firm has to ask itself at least three questions before moving ahead: whether the firm should go if the rival goes, or vice versa; when the firm should go (that is, early versus late mover); and how to enter the target industry (that is, entry mode selection).

In sum, the selection of a foreign industry is a system project in which the firm should analyze the competitive environment, industry life cycle, and structural attributes; identify opportunities and threats longitudinally and comparatively; and assess the possible impact of industrial and FDI policies by the host country government on the planned entry and subsequent operations. Moreover, the industry selection decision should be appropriately coupled with the firm's strategic objectives, organizational capabilities, and competitor behavior. International managers need to ensure that the firm has the ability to enter the target industry successfully, explore efficiently market opportunities and overcome threats, and compete against major rivals in the industry. If these are probable, then the firm's goals will most likely be accomplished.

REFERENCES

Bettis, A. R. and V. Mahajan. 1985. Risk/return performance of diversified firms. *Management Science*, 31: 785–799.

Caves, R. E. 1971. International corporation: The industrial economies of foreign investment. *Economica*, 38: 1–27.

Caves, R. E. and K. Mehra. 1986. Entry of foreign multinationals into US manufacturing industries. In M. E. Porter (Ed.), *Competition in global industries*, pp. 89–112. Boston, MA: Harvard Business School Press.

Contractor, F. J. and P. Lorange. 1988. The strategy and economic basis for cooperative venture. In F. J. Contractor and P. Lorange (Eds.), *Cooperative strategies in international business*, pp. 1–22. Lexington, Mass.: Lexington Books.

Dunning, J. H. 1979. Explaining changing patterns of international production: In defense of the eclectic theory. *Oxford Bulletin of Economics and Statistics*, 41: 269–296.

Hymer, S. H. 1976. *The international operations of national firms: A study of direct foreign investment*. Cambridge, MA: MIT Press.

Kogut, B. and H. Singh. 1988. Entering US by joint venture: Competitive rivalry and industry structure. In F. J. Contractor and P. Lorange (Eds.), *Cooperative strategies in international business*, pp. 67–89. Lexington, MA: Lexington Books.

Linder, S. B. 1961. *An essay on trade and transformation*, New York: John Wiley & Sons.

Luo, Y. 1999. Structure-performance relationships in the transitional economy context: An empirical study of the multinational alliances in the P. R. China. *Journal of Business Research*, forthcoming.

Mitchell, W., J. M. Shaver, and B. Yeung. 1993. Performance following changes of international presence in domestic and transition industries. *Journal of International Business Studies*, 24: 647–669.

Montgomery, C. A. 1985. Product market diversification and market power. *Academy of Management Journal*, 25: 789–798.

Porter, M. E. 1991. Towards a dynamic theory of strategy. *Strategic Management Journal*, 12: 95–117.

Porter, M. E. 1986. *Competition in global industries*. Boston, MA: Harvard Business School Press.

Porter, M. E. 1980. *Competitive advantage*. New York: Free Press.

Scherer, F. M. and D. Ross. 1990. *Industrial market structure and economic performance*, 3rd ed. Boston, MA: Houghton Mifflin.

Teece, D. J. 1985. Multinational enterprises, internal governance, and industrial organization. *American Economic Review, Papers and Proceedings*, 75: 233–238.

Teece, D. J., G. Pisano, and A. Shuen. 1991. Dynamic capabilities and strategic management. Working paper. Berkeley: University of California.

Willmore, L. 1994. Determinants of industrial structure: A Brazilian case study. In J. H. Dunning (Ed.), *Transnational corporations: Market structure and industrial performance*, pp. 96–129. New York: United Nations Library on Transnational Corporations.

Yip, G. S. 1994. Industry drivers of global strategy and organization. *The International Executive*, 36(5): 529–556.

FURTHER READINGS

Bain, J. S. 1959. *Industrial organization*. New York: Wiley.

Brewer, T. L. 1993. Government policies, market imperfections, and foreign direct investment. *Journal of International Business Studies*, 24: 101–120.

Conner, K. R. 1991. A historical comparison of resource-based theory and five schools of thought within industrial organization economics: Do we have a new theory of the firm? *Journal of Management*, 17: 121–154.

Katrak, H. 1991. Market rivalry, government policies and multinational enterprise in developing countries. In P. J. Buckley and J. Clegg (Eds.), *Multinational enterprises in less developed countries*, pp. 92–110. London: MacMillian.

Luo, Y. 1997. Industry attractiveness, firm competence, and international investment performance in a transitional economy. *Bulletin of Economic Research*, 49(3): 1–10.

Luo, Y. 1995. Business strategy, market structure, and performance of international joint ventures: The case of joint ventures in China. *Management International Review*, 35(3): 241–264.

Luo, Y. and J. Tan. 1997. How much does industry structure impact foreign direct investment in China. *International Business Review*, 6(4): 337–359.

Newfarmer, R. and L. Marsh. 1992. Industry structure, market power and profitability. Industrial Series Paper No. 63. Washington, D.C.: World Bank.

Rumelt, R. P. 1991. How much does industry matter? *Strategic Management Journal*, 12: 167–185.

III

COOPERATIVE STRATEGIES

9

Partner Selection

The success of international cooperative ventures (ICVs) largely depends on appropriate selection of local partners. This chapter illuminates various partner selection criteria that are important to the survival and growth of ICVs. Broadly, this study reiterates three categories of criteria: strategic, organizational, and financial. A partner with superior strategic traits but lacking strong organizational and financial characteristics may result in an unstable joint venture. The possession of desirable organizational attributes without corresponding strategic and financial competence may leave the joint venture unprofitable. A partner with superior financial strengths without strategic and organizational competencies can lead to an unsustainable venture. The implications for world business managers are highlighted.

CONCEPTUAL BACKGROUND

In an attempt to accomplish sustained competitive advantages in global marketplaces, multinational corporations (MNCs) have in recent years turned increasingly to the use of ICVs. However, the inter-cultural and inter-organizational nature of ICVs results in many challenges and enormous complexity and dynamism in managing this cross-border, hybrid form of organization. One popular argument is that inter-partner comparative or configurational features, variously termed as strategic symmetries (Harrigan, 1985), interfirm diversity (Parkhe, 1991), or complementary resources and skills (Geringer, 1991), create an inter-partner fit that is expected to generate a synergistic effect on ICV performance (Luo, 1997).

Local partner selection is critical to the success of ICVs in foreign markets. They can make it possible to invest in restricted industries and help MNCs gain access to marketing and distribution channels in a host country while meeting government requirements for local ownership. In addition, having recourse to an ICV as a means of reducing political risks or achieving political advantages is a logical choice for many MNCs operating in strategic sectors. Moreover, local partners can assist foreign partners in obtaining insightful information and country-specific knowledge concerning governmental policies, local business practices, operational conditions, and the like. Furthermore, the ICV form helps MNCs gain access to, or secure at a low cost, locally scarce production factors, such as labor, capital, or land.

According to the strategic behavior model, the decision to form an ICV assumes that the added costs of interfirm coordination reflect the managerial perception that one or more partners would enhance the venture's competitive position (Contractor & Lorange, 1988; Kogut, 1988). The more the technological and organizational skills contribute to an ICV, the more likely their possessor will be selected as a venture partner (Luo, 1998). In typical manufacturing ICVs, the major contributions of foreign investors are technology and know-how, capital resources, business expertise, management capabilities, international market knowledge, and distribution channels (Beamish, 1987). The local partner, in turn, contributes market knowledge, distribution channels, market power, government contacts, and industrial experience pertinent to the domestic context (Zeira & Shenkar, 1990). A successful ICV creates operational and financial synergies derived from asset complementarity or indivisibility in terms of strategic, organizational, and financial fits that produce a premium exceeding the partner's pooled resources (Buckley & Casson, 1988; Contractor & Lorange, 1988; Hamel, Doz, & Prahalad, 1989).

Partner selection determines an ICV's mix of skills, knowledge, and resources, its operating policies and procedures, and its vulnerability to indigenous conditions, structures, and institutional changes (Geringer, 1991). This selection is even more important when an ICV involves the firm's core markets or technologies (Harrigan, 1988). When expanding into a dynamic, complex, or hostile environment, the importance of local partner selection to ICV success is further magnified, because the right partner can spur its adaptability, strategy-environment configuration, and uncertainty reduction (Luo, 1997).

In general, the mix of skills and resources in ICVs is composed of three important elements: strategic fit, organizational fit, and financial fit. From a process perspective, these three types of fit may constitute the midrange variables between local partner attributes and ICV performance (see Figure 9.1). Strategic fit may be defined as the degree to which an ICV's partners augment or complement one another's strategies and capabilities in light of industry, market, product, customer, capital, or technology-related issues. This, in turn, involves a configuration comprising the inter-partner arrangements, external environment, and joint venture effectiveness. Each of these three elements is constrained, quasi-deterministic, and multidimensional. Thus, the successful configuration of these elements requires not only an appropriate alignment of an ICV's organizational capabilities to the external industry or market and its strategic goals but also a proper match between one partner's competitive advantages with the other's distinctive operational competencies. The operational competencies, mirrored in operation-related attributes, such as market share, industrial experience, and relationship with the local government, constitute a necessary condition and a primary source for the venture's success in exploring market opportunities and exploiting product potentials in the host environment.

In contrast to strategic fit, organizational fit may be defined as the match between each partner's administrative practices, control mechanisms, cultural practices, and personnel characteristics and may directly affect the efficiency and effectiveness of inter-partner cooperation. It may be useful to conceive of strategic fit (or its source of variance: operation-related partner attributes) as a necessary, but not sufficient, condition for ICV success and organizational fit. Thus, one cannot merely address strategic fit or operation-related attributes without understanding that the organizational integration between partners may also be a prerequisite of synergy creation. According to the learning model of ICV theory, this organizational integration influences the ease with which two partners can be assimilated after the formation of an ICV. Although organizational fit between partners can be assessed along a number of dimensions (e.g., administrative, control, cultural, and personnel), the major areas often mentioned as being particularly important from the perspective of inter-partner integration and collaboration lie in past cooperation between partners, a local partner's foreign experience, and its organizational size or structure. A local partner's experience in foreign business and international cooperation is important in maintaining a pleasant and harmonious atmosphere in the day-to-day management and administration of an ICV. Moreover, since a local partner's international experience only reflects its static strength or weakness, its actual contribution to the ICV also depends upon its commitment to the venture. As a result, the local partner's organizational size, a proxy for this commitment, is likely to have a positive impact on the ICV's market and financial performance.

Financial fit concerns the degree of match in cash flow position and capital structure between partners. Reducing uncertainty in operational cash flow is usually one of the major reasons behind ICV formation. The

FIGURE 9.1
Six-Cs Scheme for Partner Selection

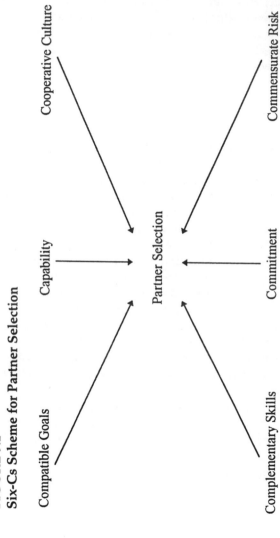

reduction of default risk depends on the correlation of the pre-venture cash flows of the two partners. A larger firm, as a result of an alliance, will have better access to capital markets and lower financing costs. This cost advantage implies a reduction in the firm's risk from the lender's viewpoint, which can be achieved by corporate diversification or a conglomerate merger. Tax savings on interest payments or transfer pricing are additional benefits from financial fit. In an international context, these gains from international expansion are even greater given the partial segmentation of national economies and segments. The additional gain results from a lower systematic risk premium in world capital markets than in the domestic market, which is caused by the less-than-perfect correlation of national capital market returns.

From a systems theory perspective, it is impossible to understand fully the operations of ICVs without considering the attributes and contributions of the participating firms. Benefits from a partner's contributions might occur throughout the entire range of an ICV's value chain. Management may hierarchically rank those activities, however, focusing its attention on a few key activities that affect the overall operations most decisively. Moreover, the criteria for partner selection are considerably context-specific. This suggests that the relative importance of partner selection criteria should be determined on a contingency basis by variables associated with the strategic context of the ICV. Therefore, transnational investors need to scrutinize those partner attributes that are pivotal in helping them realize their strategic goals.

THE SIX Cs

It is assumed that firms establish ICVs only when the perceived additional benefits of exercising the ICV option outweigh its expected additional costs. These additional benefits will accrue only through the retention of a partner who can provide the six Cs: compatibility of goals, complementarity of skills, commensuration of risks, cooperative culture, commitment, and organizational capability. If the six Cs are present, the partners have a good chance of successfully working together. Figure 9.1 schematically illustrates the six Cs affecting ICV operations and performance.

Compatible Goals

A firm must be willing to give as much as it gets. Executives rank compatibility as one of the most important ingredients for a successful ICV. No matter how elegant the strategic business concept behind a cooperative deal or how capable the participants, the partners have to be able to work together. Otherwise, there is a slim likelihood that the venture will stand the test of time and cope with changing market and environmental conditions.

ICVs in which one party is out to take as much as possible without giving anything in return are bound to fail. As in any relationship, both sides of an ICV should complement each other. Similarly, an ICV is more likely to fail if it does not advance both firms' strategic goals. Goal assessment is particularly important when a firm is searching for a partner. Each company should evaluate the objectives of the partner and identify whether or not they are compatible with its own.

The situation that holds the most promise for compatibility is one in which strategic goals converge while competitive goals diverge. For example, Dupont and Philips have a strategic alliance in which both manufacture compact discs yet respect each other's market boundaries. Unfortunately, not all ICV goals are as compatible. Large companies sometimes send a string of employees to smaller partners for the sole purpose of gaining knowledge. To avoid the pitfall of ambiguous or different goals, participants should make sure they synchronize to begin with, then review what has been accomplished in terms of their original goals at least every three to six months. The success of a consortium between Boeing and three Japanese heavy industry companies to design and build the 767 and future Boeing aircraft is partially attributable to goal compatibility. Boeing sought foreign partners to ease its financial burden and operational risks, and the Japanese tried to expand their role in the aerospace industry. The Japanese are now increasing their participation in the industry significantly, providing an ever-increasing portion of production parts and assembly. Boeing has reduced the risks of development by adding a large potential customer and by lowering the financial commitment required for production.

Many MNCs compare ICVs to marriages in that compatibility and the ability to resolve problems and differences are key ingredients of a prosperous relationship. Compatibility does not mean there is no friction; rather, it means that because the partners respect and appreciate each other, they will be able to manage their differences.

Virtually all ICV partners cite the value and importance of compatibility in corporate partnerships. Japanese companies especially emphasize the particular importance of compatibility and evolutionary development.

Complementary Skills

One of the major themes in ICV literature has been that the possession of complementary assets and skills is one of the major reasons for ICV formation and success. In essence, an ICV is a special mechanism for pooling complementary assets. Embedded in the complementary skills approach is the assumption that a firm will seek skills it perceives as lacking but considers vital for the fulfillment of its strategic objectives. From the learning perspective, firms are aggregates of complex organizational routines that cannot be efficiently transferred in the marketplace and cannot be specified in a licensing agreement. Ideally, knowledge is transmitted in a replication of the organization itself.

When knowledge is proprietary, non-transferable, or prohibitively expensive to develop independently, a firm will turn to an ICV as a possible solution. Some kinds of knowledge, however, are more tacit. Tacit or embedded knowledge limits transferability via contractual channels because it requires a replication of the organization. The more tacit and embedded the technology, the more desirable it is to pool complementary information to exploit it more effectively. From among the three realms of technology, marketing, and management, it seems that management, with its emphasis on social, interpersonal skills, is the least amenable to transfer as a packaged, transacted commodity. Management skills are often learned through intensive interpersonal contact, requiring attitudinal, cognitive, and behavioral change.

What exactly constitutes complementarity remains vague in the literature. Harrigan (1985) takes a broad view, applying complementarity to missions, resources, and managerial capabilities. These complementary skills can create a strategic fit in which the bargaining power of the venture's sponsors is evenly matched. Arrangements involving complementary assets include vertical quasi-integration, in which each partner contributes one or more distinct elements in the production and distribution chains, as well as horizontal linkages among partners with strengths in different geographical areas, product lines, and so forth.

The case for complementary skills seems to be particularly strong when the partners represent developing and developed economies, respectively. In such ventures, the typical contributions of developed countries' MNCs comprise manufacturing technology, product know-how, patents, business expertise, technical training, and management capabilities. A United Nations (1989) report summarizes complementary local contributions as follows: "The national partner in a manufacturing joint venture commonly contributes some combination of capital, management, knowledge of the environment of the country and the market, contacts with the government, financial institutions, local suppliers and labor unions, and marketing capabilities" (United Nations, 1989: 59).

Beamish (1987) categorized partner needs in ventures involving developing and developed country partners into five groups: readily capitalized items, human resources, market access, government and political access, and knowledge needs. In his study, foreign managers of successful ventures rated local knowledge (e.g., politics, culture) and the availability of general managers as the most important and consistent contributions from local partners and as key ingredients for long-term success. This ranking by foreign managers is virtually identical to the one identified by the United Nations (1989) report.

Commensurate Risk

A commensurate level of risk is needed to hold the ICV together. If nothing is at risk, there is less of an incentive to stay together. This risk can be financial, operational, or both. Risk sharing is becoming increasingly necessary as certain industries change faster than individual firms can keep up. In situations where technology is rapidly developing, a firm could expose itself to major failure unless it spreads the risk across a consortium. Nevertheless, if a firm only enters into an ICV to reduce risks on its initial investment, the ICV may become simply a tool to be used and then discarded.

The fact that successful ventures must share risks also means that equal risks must be maintained. If one firm learns substantially more than the other firm, risks will no longer be in balance and the venture will quickly dissolve, leaving one firm with a substantial disadvantage in the marketplace. By keeping the levels of risk commensurate with each party, an ICV tends to be more stable and have a more cooperative culture.

In an effort to evaluate the commensurate level of risk, MNCs should examine manufacturing, marketing, and financial risks. Analyzing manufacturing risks requires asking what your strategies are for obtaining products, components, and so on. If you are co-producing, are both partners' facilities up to the task? Do you have the same attitudes and skills in quality management? If the ICV is to be a separate joint venture company, what are your respective compensation programs, hiring strategies, and so on? How do labor relations compare? Are the partners union or nonunion? Are relations smooth or strike prone? How does management view its employees? Marketing questions include: What do analyses of market share and sales growth of the potential partner reveal? How close are your customer service policies and philosophies? What image does a potential partner project in different regional markets? What are the market perceptions of a potential partner's products? How do the products rank in quality, image, and pricing? Finally, judge financial risk based on: How do you and your prospective partner compare regarding financial strength, risk orientation, dividend policies, reinvestment, debt-equity ratios, currency management, and so on? Based on analyses of sales and profitability trends, how well could a potential partner weather unforeseen financial pressures? Who are the key shareholders for the partner? Are the partners publicly held, privately held, or state owned?

Cooperative Culture

Every company has its own unique corporate culture. Companies need to ascertain how well they can manage their differences. Management needs to weigh the pros and cons of cultural differences and how they will impact the ICV. Cooperative cultural and management styles influence mutual trust, which in turn affects venture success. Symmetry must exist at the top level of management. Peer relationships between the top executives of the joint venture partners should be established. These relationships are especially important in ICVs that are dissimilar in size.

Normally, maintaining cooperation can become difficult when partners come from different countries. Americans tend to be individualistic. They are not, generally, group-oriented. Unlike Europeans, their business culture is not as responsive in its approach to ICVs involving firms from other countries. This individualistic attitude is in sharp contrast to that of the Japanese, for example, whose entire cultural direction is oriented toward participation within the group context. Such differences can be complementary, however. The mix of Toyota's team approach and General Motors' corporate style contributed significantly to doubling productivity at New United Motor Manufacturing Company, an ICV between the two companies.

A great danger that exists when cooperative culture is maintained is that one firm may inadvertently relinquish its unique core technology, expertise, or knowledge to the other firm. For example, U.S. companies are generally not as skillful at learning from their venture partners as the Japanese, for example. Many foreign firms view ICVs as an easy way of gaining access to U.S. markets and learning U.S. technologies at the expense of U.S. firms. Not only do many foreign companies seek optimal benefit from their venture partners in the United States but also the culture they originate from (especially Japanese culture) is better equipped to accomplish this task.

A company needs to take a close look at compatibility in organizational and management practices with a potential partner. For instance, it should ask: Are both companies centralized or decentralized? If not, are both managements flexible and committed enough to overcome potential conflict? Do prospective partners use line or matrix organizations, international departments, or global product groups? How compatible are customer service policies and philosophies?

The chemistry between corporate cultures or, more importantly, between both senior managers and the executives who will be in charge of the venture can make or break an ICV. The search for the right chemistry is not limited to any single regional or national group of executives. Managers from Asia, Latin America, and Europe share the judgment of one U.S. executive, who stated during an interview, "First and foremost companies are people. They are not business or financial machines. Consequently, the strength and success of a venture rest on the interactions of its people." Thus, when meeting with a potential partner, many executives admit to asking themselves, "Are they our kind of people?" Clearly, however, there is no hard and fast rule for determining whether there is any compatibility between a given set of partners. In fact, each alliance is different. The chemistry can be based on factors totally unrelated to the core business of the venture. For instance, in one Italian-U.S. venture, one executive attributed much of the venture's success to the compatibility factor and a close friendship between the chairmen of the two companies. According to the executive, at the root of these close bonds was the fact that the U.S. chairman was of Italian origin. When the U.S. MNC first sought a European partner, the chairman zeroed in on the Italian company because of his desire to maintain strong ties with the country of his ancestors. As a result of the connection, the chairman has taken an active role in the venture, and an amiable and trusting atmosphere between the partners has developed, contributing tremendously to its success.

Perhaps one of the most important soft factors to seek is mutual trust. According to William Glavin, mutual trust was strongly advocated by former Xerox presidents Peter McCullough and Joe Wilson. As Glavin explains,

Outside of the US, every Xerox entity commenced as a joint venture; whether you look at Rank Xerox or Fuji Xerox or any other operation within Europe, Asia or Latin America. When I started with Xerox in 1970, I worked primarily with Rank Xerox and Fuji Xerox. At the time, McCullough explained to me, "Bill, you have to trust them in all endeavors. If you lose trust, the alliance crumbles." Initially, I wondered how the success of a joint venture could weigh so heavily on simple trust. Yet, through the years, it proved accurate. Mutual trust at senior management levels has carried Xerox's ventures through some turbulent times. (The Conference Board, 1995)

In fact, most complaints and problems in ICVs hatch from jealousies or misunderstandings. If the partners trust each other, they can rise above pettiness and iron out their problems.

Perhaps the greatest testimonial for the importance of trust in a partnership occurred as a result of the relationship between Westinghouse and Mitsubishi. These two companies have been linked through a variety of cooperative ties for more than 70 years. Yet difficult market conditions and new competitive pressures forced the breakup of one of their 50-50 joint ventures. As Jon Elmendorf, former president of Westinghouse Energy Systems in Japan and current director for Westinghouse's environmental compliance operations, explains,

The collapse of the circuit-breaker venture was a true test of the relationship. There was a great deal of unhappiness and frustration. But the long-standing trust and commitment between the partners enabled us to deal with the immediate problems and focus on the future. In fact, the breakup of the circuit-breaker venture potentially could have destroyed the entire alliance. Yet this mutual trust and respect prevented any ill will or resentment from boiling over and ruining our other collaborative activities in nuclear energy and gas and steam turbines. (The Conference Board, 1995)

Commitment

Partner commitment determines its contribution to venture operations and management. Finding a partner with an equal sense of commitment to the ICV is the keystone to success. It is also crucial to the realization of the other five Cs. Even if partners appear capable and compatible, the chances of the venture weathering changing market conditions are slim unless they are both willing to invest time, energy, and resources in the alliance. Without this commitment, a partner's resources, complementary or not, cannot help the venture realize its strategic objectives. Without commitment, compatible goals and commensurate risks remain uncultivated. A partner's commitment also affects ongoing trust building and maintenance. Commitment counters opportunism and fosters cooperation.

Often ICVs face unexpected environmental changes and market dynamics. In this situation, commitment serves as a stabilizing device offsetting contextual uncertainties. Commitment is, therefore, even more critical in a volatile environment or over a longer term. Inter-partner conflict is more or less inevitable as ICVs evolve. If commitment from both partners is reasonably high, such conflicts may not seriously impair the profitability and stability of the ICV. If it is low, however, these conflicts will become a primary source of instability and even termination of the venture.

A proposed ICV should be central to both partners' mainstream activities or growth strategies. Dangers arise if these conditions are not met. First, the company will probably not be willing to devote the time and resources necessary to making the venture succeed. Second, the partner could easily withdraw from the ICV, leaving the other company in the dust.

Capability

Organizational capabilities are important partner attributes affecting the profitability and stability of the ICV. These capabilities are prerequisite for complementary skills that the firms can contribute. Without distinctive competencies, it is impossible to realize complementarity of resources even though two firms have compatible and complementary goals. Resource complementarity affects collaborative synergies only within a specific time period; it is not alone sufficient to support ongoing joint venture development. Organizational capability, in contrast, provides an essential supply base for the resources needed in the cyclical development of long-term partnerships. Broadly, these resources and capabilities are of four elements: technological, organizational, operational, and financial. Because technological and operational competencies affect strategic traits of the firm, these elements can be further classified into strategic, organizational, and financial attributes, which will be detailed in the next section.

Before seriously approaching any prospective ally, the capabilities of the targeted candidates should be subjected to a rigorous test. Many ICV practitioners recommend establishing a team of experts to undertake a feasibility study on each candidate. The team's composition and the delineation of its investigation will, of course, depend on the nature and scope of the venture. In general, however, it should be a multi-functional team that includes operating managers plus functional experts from finance, legal, taxation, and so on.

All companies try to present themselves in the best possible light. A potential partner may describe itself as possessing exciting technology, marvelous managers and sales staff, penetrating distribution networks, and so on. Investigations may reveal that what the company says about itself is not the same as what the balance sheet and independent analysts say. The team must, therefore, be prepared to undertake a tough, critical examination of a potential partner. A former ICI executive said companies should not make the mistake of letting apparent compatibility interfere with a thorough analysis of capabilities and resources.

PARTNER ATTRIBUTES: THREEFOLD CLASSIFICATION SCHEME

During the process of ICV formation, foreign parent firms must identify appropriate criteria for local partner selection as well as the relative importance of each criterion. These diverge depending on firm, setting, and time. Broadly, the criteria can be classified into three categories related to: tasks or operations, partnership or cooperation, and cash flow or capital structure. Operation-related criteria are associated with the strategic attributes of partners including marketing competence, technological skills, relationship building, market position, industrial experience, strategic orientation, and corporate image. Cooperation-related criteria often mirror organizational attributes, such as organizational leadership, previous collaboration, ownership type, learning ability, foreign experience, and human resource skills. Cash flow-related criteria are generally represented by financial attributes, such as profitability, liquidity, leverage, and asset management. A partner's strategic traits influence the operational skills and resources needed for the joint venture's competitive success, organizational traits affect the efficiency and effectiveness of inter-firm cooperation, and financial traits impact the optimization of capital structure and cash flow.

Strategic, organizational, and financial attributes are all crucial to ICV performance. A partner with superior strategic traits but lacking strong organizational and financial characteristics results in an unstable joint venture. The possession of desirable organizational attributes without corresponding strategic and financial competence leaves the joint venture unprofitable. A partner with superior financial strengths without strategic and organizational competencies can lead to an unsustainable venture. From a process perspective, the linkage between partner selection and ICV success lies in inter-partner fit (Hamel, 1991; Yan & Gray, 1994). Strategic attributes affect strategic fit between partners, organizational traits are likely to influence organizational fit, and financial attributes impact financial fit. Figure 9.2 summarizes these relationships.

The threefold classification scheme in Figure 9.2 may be of interest to both business theory and practice. The literature on partner selection has paid little attention to systematic categorization of partner attributes. Such a classification is imperative because each group affects a different kind of fit, thus influencing different dimensions of ICV performance. Moreover, most previous studies in the area have not yet incorporated financial attributes into the framework. Such attributes are important because cash flow positions, financial strategies, and capital structures of partner firms impact the degree of both financial and operational synergies derived from venture activities. Further, some strategic and organizational attributes, such as strategic orientation, relationship building, learning ability, organizational leadership, and rank remain under-researched in the study of partner selection. We aim to integrate all relevant attributes that may influence ICV success in this scheme. International managers may find this scheme useful for clarifying the strengths and weaknesses of potential partners and determining whether partner attributes fit their own strategic, organizational, and financial needs.

Strategic Attributes

It is important to note that different strategic, organizational, and financial traits may have a heterogeneous effect on different aspects of ICV performance. MNCs need to discern not only important partner selection criteria in general but also which ones are crucial to their specific strategic goals. We sought to address the performance implications of each attribute as specifically as possible throughout this chapter. Specific performance effects include profitability, market growth, cost minimization, stability, risk reduction, export growth, and the like. The term "ICV

FIGURE 9.2
Partner Attributes and Joint Venture Success:
Threefold Classification Scheme

success" is here defined as the accomplishment of a parent firm's strategic goals through participation in the venture.

Marketing Competence

The costs of establishing distribution channels or business networks in a host country market by foreign businesses are likely to outweigh potential benefits. Establishing a network can be such a long process that foreign companies may be unable to seize market opportunities or align with contextual changes in a timely fashion. A local partner's marketing competencies (distribution channels, promotional skills, knowledge about local business practices, and relationships with major buyers, wholesalers, and relevant governmental authorities) are, therefore, fundamentally important to foreign companies seeking market position and power in a host country. A partnership with a local firm with superior marketing competence enables a foreign company to establish quickly its market position, organizational image, and product reputation in the host country. This also helps the foreign company increase profitability, reduce uncertainty, and boost its competitive edge. A foreign company's technological strengths and a local partner's marketing competence create operational synergies that are mutually beneficial to both parties.

Technological Skills

Although the importance of a partner's technological skills may vary across different industries, these skills are a basic qualification for MNCs interested in international expansion. The level of a partner's product and process innovation affects the production and efficiency of operations. When competition is high a firm's competitive edge in the market is largely determined by its ability to develop and innovate. Process and managerial innovation have a strong influence on the firm's pursuit of value creation and product competitiveness. An MNC collaborating with a partner possessing these skills will be better able to promote its product innovativeness as demanded by local consumers. Moreover, absorptive capabilities also necessitate technological skills. These capabilities are fundamental to the venture and the local partner itself because they directly determine how much one party can learn from the other party. For example, Kubota, Japan's largest producer of farm equipment, previously never made anything more complex than a tractor. Today the company is shipping supercomputers worldwide. This resulted from setting up an ICV with some of the sharpest startups in Silicon Valley. The design, chips, and software were all from U.S. partners. Kubota used its superb assembly know-how to combine the parts into high quality products.

Relationship Building

Foreign companies can gain an edge over their competitors in the host country if they have a network with the business community (e.g., suppliers, buyers, distributors, and banks) and government authorities (e.g., political governments, industrial administration departments, foreign exchange administration bureaus, foreign trade and economics commissions, commercial administration bureaus, and taxation departments). Although a foreign company can establish and maintain its own networks in the host country, the more efficient and effective way is certainly to utilize a local partner's existing business or personal connections. This is because network cultivation in a foreign market is a complicated social investment that can be costly, unstable, and unreliable if the relationship is constructed inappropriately or with the wrong people.

A local partner's network constitutes strategic assets for all ICVs regardless of their strategic goals or orientations. Such networks help foreign companies obtain scarce production factors, facilitate value chain contributions, promote relationships with various governmental institutions, and increase the effectiveness of market penetration. Recently, various studies have found that the utilization of local business or personal connections significantly facilitates an ICV's financial and market-based performance measures, such as return on investment, sales growth, and risk reduction in such foreign countries as Japan, Korea, China, Hong Kong, Taiwan, Russia, Eastern Europe, and Southeast Asia.

Market Position

Because a major objective of international expansion is to preempt market opportunities and business potential, a local partner's market power is a key asset. This power is often represented by the partner's industrial and business background, market position, and established marketing and distribution networks. Market power also enables the firm to influence some industry-wide restrictions on output, increase bargaining power, and offer the advantages of economies of scale. A partner's market strength is key to the ICV's financial return and commitment to indigenous market growth. This commitment will make the ICV less inclined to increase exports in its business operations. Furthermore, strong market power can lead to greater bargaining power with the local government. This can help the ICV reduce political risks and business uncertainty.

These benefits have been confirmed in a recent study by Luo (1997), who found that the market power of a Chinese partner is significantly and positively associated with an ICV's profitability, sales growth, and risk reduction in China. Many case studies support the above argument.

Industrial Experience

When operating in a foreign market an ICV seeking efficiency and growth needs an adaptive orientation, a solid supply relationship, comprehensive buyer networks, and a good organizational image. The local partner's market experience and accumulated industrial knowledge are of great value to the realization of these goals. A local partner's established history and strong background in the industry often result in a good reputation or high credibility in the market. Lengthy industrial and market experience signify that the local firm has built an extensive marketing and distribution network, which is a necessary competence for ICV market growth.

In addition, the business activities of ICVs operating in relationship-oriented cultures can be greatly facilitated by the local partner's connections in the domestic business scene. Goodwill and superior contacts constitute country-specific knowledge, or what the resource-based view calls the resource position barrier, which enhances an ICV's competitive advantage, economic efficiency, and risk reduction capability. According to Luo (1997), a local partner's industrial experience has a favorable influence on the ICV's market growth and operational stability.

Strategic Orientation

The degree to which a local firm's strategic orientation (i.e., prospector, analyzer, or defender) matches that of its foreign partner influences inter-partner consistency in terms of strategic goals and behaviors, cooperative culture, and investment commitment. These in turn affect the formulation and implementation of technological, operational, financial, and managerial policies at the corporate, business, functional, and international levels. As strategic orientation determines organizational adaptability and innovativeness, it may affect not only strategic behavior but also organizational aspects, such as managerial philosophy and style and long-term orientation, which in turn influence mutual trust and collaboration between parties.

To reap benefits from market demand in a dynamic market, a defensive orientation (i.e., defender strategy) may be too conservative for firms seeking market expansion. However, it may be unrealistic to orient local firms in a highly proactive direction (i.e., prospector strategy) because this could lead to vast operational and contextual risks and innovative and adaptive costs in a complex, dynamic, and hostile environment. An analyzer orientation fits the environmental traits in a transitional context where environmental sectors are fundamentally complex and dynamic, information is uncodified, and regulations are inexplicit. Under this orientation, the partner candidate should be innovative and adaptive but not extremely aggressive and risk-taking when the market changes. They should allocate most of their resources to a set of reasonably stable environments while conducting somewhat routinized scanning activities in a limited product-market area. They monitor market situations and carefully apply previously developed product and market innovations. This analyzer strategy reduces the likelihood of outright failure and creates upper limits to success. In general, local firms with the analyzer orientation are ideal candidate partners for foreign companies pursuing both profitability and stability.

Corporate Image

A superior corporate image implies a superior product brand, customer loyalty, or organizational reputation. Corporate image may be unusually critical in certain markets where consumers are particularly loyal to products made by the companies maintaining a superior image. For instance, when purchasing household appliances, Chinese people tend to attach more importance to corporate image than to the physical attributes of the products. In deciding whether to buy a joint venture's products, they are used to evaluating not only the reputation of the venture but also the goodwill of local firms in the past. Therefore, it is essential for foreign investors to collaborate with those local businesses that have maintained a good organizational reputation and product image. This selection will significantly benefit the market power and competitive position of the joint venture in the relevant industry. A superior company image also implies better relationships with the local government as well as with suppliers and distributors. These relationships are crucial for firms pursuing a market share and competitive position in the industry.

Organizational Attributes

Leadership

Leadership of a partner firm critically influences the cooperative culture between the two partners, which in turn affects mutual trust. In addition, a partner's ties to the local government in developing countries are largely shaped by interpersonal relationships between its management and government officials. These personal connections can be an important factor in gaining a competitive edge, especially if the venture has to rely upon the local government for acquiring approvals, materials, capital, and other resources or in securing various kinds of support and assistance for dispute resolution, infrastructure access, distribution arrangements, and taxation holidays or allowances.

As a result of continuous industrial decentralization and economic reform in many emerging markets, which further increase the autonomy and authority of corporate-level managers, the effect of local leadership is even more fundamental to joint venture operations today. To evaluate the leadership of Chinese businesses, foreign investors should scrutinize such areas as educational background, relationship with government authorities, innovativeness, international experience, managerial skills, length of previous leadership, and foreign language skills.

Ownership Type

In industrialized countries, ownership type refers to whether the local firm is privately or publicly owned. In many developing countries, economic reforms have given birth to a wider diversity of organizational forms, from state-owned to private and collective businesses. Ownership type influences the firm's motivations for forming an ICV and its commitment and contribution to operations. These in turn affect the ICV's local performance. Publicly or state-owned firms generally have the advantage in gaining access to scarce resources, materials, capital, information, and investment infrastructure. In addition, these organizations usually have greater industrial experience, market power, and production and innovation facilities than private firms. Moreover, it is fairly common for publicly or state-owned enterprises to have privileged access to state-instituted distribution channels. These channels play a dominant role in product distribution in some emerging markets. This ownership form may hence facilitate the market growth in new domains for MNCs. Finally, hierarchical state firms tend to have a better relationship with various governmental institutions. This relationship is expected to result in greater problem-solving capacity. For all these reasons, publicly or state-owned organizations may contribute more to an ICV's local market expansion than privately-owned organizations. The aforementioned advantages of state businesses are certainly among key factors enabling the ventures to dominate their respective markets and become two of the top 60 foreign-invested ventures since 1991.

Private enterprises are typically operated and managed by entrepreneurs. They have fewer principal-agent conflicts and greater strategic flexibility. In many developing countries, the existence of unfulfilled product and market niches increases the chance for survival and growth of private firms. Their simple structure and small size position them for speed and surprise, giving them greater ability to react quickly to opportunities in the environment and proactively outmaneuver more established firms. In addition, privately-owned businesses are pressed by hard budgetary constraints, forcing them to be more efficient and profit oriented. In contrast, publicly or state-owned firms lack self-motivation and operational autonomy while being highly vulnerable to bureaucratic red tape. ICVs with efficiency-oriented privately-owned partners are thus likely to enjoy superior returns on investment.

Learning Ability

Complementary needs create inter-partner fit, which is expected to generate a synergistic effect on ICV performance. However, complementarity is not likely to materialize unless a certain threshold of skills are already in place. Local businesses in the host country generally seek technological, innovational, and managerial skills from MNCs. The success of an ICV's local operations and expansion in a foreign market will largely depend upon its local partner's learning capacity or its ability to acquire, assimilate, integrate, and exploit knowledge and skills. The firm's ability to process, integrate, and deploy an inflow of new knowledge and skills closely depends on how these relate to already established skills. This skill base is expected to influence strategic and organizational fit between ICV partners, which in turn affects financial and operational synergies. As a result, a local partner's learning ability will contribute to an ICV's profitability and sales growth.

International Experience

A local partner's previous foreign experience is critical to the success of intercultural and cross-border ventures. Foreign experience affects the organizational fit between partners in the early stages of the joint venture and how well they remain matched as the venture evolves over time. Because the business atmosphere and commercial practices in the host country can be quite different from those in the outside world, mistrust and opportunism often take place in the course of ICV operations. A local firm's international experience, gained through import and export business or cooperative projects with other foreign investors, proves to be a very desirable attribute because this represents superior knowledge, skills, and values regarding modern management methods (Luo, 1997). Contact with foreign companies and business people can sharpen sensitivity toward competitiveness in the international market. A long history of business dealings with foreign markets can increase receptivity toward maintaining quality standards, customer responsiveness, and product innovation. As international experience includes exposure to foreign values, it increases a local business's ability to effectively communicate with its foreign partner. This acquired knowledge stimulates the trust and collaboration between partners. As a consequence, a local business having international experience will contribute more to the ICV's financial return, risk reduction, and sales growth in the domestic as well as export markets. Many success stories about Western joint ventures in China indicate that local partners' international experience can facilitate interfirm trust, forebearance, commitment, and collaboration, which in turn promote joint venture success.

Human Resource Skills

In an ICV, people with different cultural backgrounds, career goals, compensation systems, and other differences often have to begin working together with little preparation. This people factor can halt the joint venture's progress, sometimes permanently. Because of the existence of cultural barriers, the use of a large workforce, and the reliance on local managers, the possession of human resource management skills by local partners is critical if foreign partners wish to see their goals realized. These skills are reflected not only in the ability to blend cultures and management styles but also in job design, recruitment and staffing, orientation and training, performance appraisal, compensation and benefits, career development, and labor-management relations. Among these attributes, the abilities to overcome cultural barriers, recruit qualified employees, and establish incentive structures are particularly important.

Foreign companies often encounter pressure from local government agencies to hire redundant or unqualified people from trade unions to set minimum or maximum wage rates or from labor departments to implement bureaucratic regulations concerning human resource management. Under these circumstances, a foreign company needs a local partner that is skillful in managing the workforce and dealing with unions while externally handling labor departments and other governmental authorities. It is important to create a corporate culture that contains some aspects of an internationally recognized management style and is, at the same time, acceptable to the local staff. Therefore, a local partner should also be knowledgeable about international practices of human resource management. Several lessons for foreign companies include: avoid taking too many employees from a single source, as this can heighten the risk of hiring a lot of people who will reinforce similar bad habits; practice patience and flexibility when looking for high-quality personnel; find a trustworthy confidante among the local managers who has experience in dealing with the bureaucracy; and mold the right individuals to suit the needs of the company.

Previous Collaboration

As the length of the interaction between partners increases, the economic transactions become increasingly embedded within the social relations of the two partners, which in turn deters opportunism. Previous contact between partners leads to the development of specialized skills and routines adapted to the exchange. These include specific knowledge about the structure and operation of each partner's organization and the abilities of the personnel within the partner firms. Such skills and routines constitute an investment in specific assets adapted to inter-partner cooperation. These are at risk if cooperation breaks down. Hamel, Doz, and Prahalad (1989) assert that the operation and management of ICVs involve daily interactions that can be greatly facilitated if the partners have correctly assessed each other's strengths and weaknesses. Past and existing long-term relationships between partners based on previous import-export experience, investments, or even on private relationships can, therefore, become a fine asset leading to economic efficiency and export growth. Such relations also foster the climate of openness that is essential for discussing behavioral problems that would otherwise be a barrier to learning. The success of many ICVs worldwide, such as alliances between GM and Toyota, Texas Instruments and Hitachi, and IBM, Siemens, and Toshiba, can be partially attributed to previous collaboration between partners.

Financial Attributes

Profitability

A local partner's profitability will directly influence its ability to make a capital contribution, fulfill financial commitments, and disperse financial resources to the joint venture. These in turn affect the joint venture's profit margin, net cash inflow, and wealth accumulation. The profitability attribute will also indirectly influence the joint venture's capital structure, financing costs, and leverage. Less profitable firms usually have to pay higher interest rates or accept shorter terms to attain bank loans. This can even become more exaggerated when the host government adopts a tight monetary policy with increased interest rates, reduced bank lending, and lower money supply.

Viewed from the operational perspective, a less profitable business often implies organizational weaknesses in the technological, operational, and managerial spheres. An unprofitable business normally means poor product quality, poor management, or slow customer responsiveness. Other causes include organizational rigidity, weak competitive advantage, little market power, underdeveloped distribution channels, and the like. In sum, lack of profitability in a prospective local partner can be symbolic of internal weaknesses in financial, technological, operational, organizational, and managerial arenas. Foreign investors should scrutinize indicators of profitability, such as gross profit margin, net profit margin, return on assets, and return on equity.

Liquidity

A local partner's liquidity is critical to ICV operations because it directly affects the venture's ability to pay off short-term financial obligations. In the international business literature, it is commonly understood that foreign investors attain financial synergies from the optimization of operational cash flows. A foreign venture can reduce the default risk and uncertainty of operational cash flow, but this depends on the correlation of pre-cooperation cash flow between the two firms. A larger joint venture will have better access to capital markets and lower financing costs, other things being equal. Given the partial segmentation of national economies and markets, this benefit is even greater in ICVs than in domestic joint ventures. Ideally, to achieve maximum financial and operational synergies, two partners should be complementary in terms of capital structure and financial and competitive strengths. Foreign partners seeking cost and risk sharing or pursuing reduction of operational cash flow uncertainty should be particularly cautious to ensure that they have a thorough grasp of their local partners' liquidity, as reflected in their current ratio, quick ratio, working capital, and so forth.

Leverage

In selecting local partners in the host country, MNCs should choose those that are less vulnerable to outstanding debts and have a strong leverage position. This superior position often implies that the firms are more conscientious about credit screening and investigations and thus have maintained a network of customers and buyers with a superior leverage position, and have better asset management or superior organizational skills. It is essential for firms to establish clear-cut working policies, both internal and external, that will promote the best cash turnover possible and maximize benefits from the economics of accounts receivable. Because these issues significantly influence growth and survival in many countries, foreign investors should attach utmost importance to the leverage level of local firms during the selection process. In doing so, MNCs should examine various leverage ratios of local firms, such as debt-to-assets ratio, debt-to-equity ratio, or long-term debt-to-equity ratio. In some developing countries, the equity structure of firms differs from that in industrialized economies. For example, as a consequence of insufficient equity, the leverage level of most Chinese firms is markedly low. It is well known today that many Chinese firms are encountering a triangular debt problem, whereby the firms owe large sums of money to each other but have no cash with which to settle their accounts. Accounts receivable open more than 180 days are very common, often representing a substantial part of a Chinese company's liquid resources. Apart from credit crunch, this situation can be attributed to cultural factors. Preferential terms of payment, particularly temporal extension of payment deadlines, are widely used in China as a primary marketing tool. In a country where *guanxi* (interpersonal connection) is painstakingly nurtured and the maintenance of harmony is of paramount importance, sellers do their utmost to avoid embarrassing customers who may be temporarily unable to pay.

Asset Efficiency

The asset efficiency of a local partner is critical to the effectiveness of the joint venture because it is a mid-range construct for maximizing return on investment. The net gains from resource contributions depend in large part on the management of assets, especially inventory, accounts receivable, and fixed assets. A partnership with a local firm that manages its total assets skillfully and efficiently is surely beneficial to the foreign investor pursuing either short-term profitability or a long-term competitive position in the market. The level of asset management mirrors the degree of advancement of managerial skills and the extent of effectiveness of corporate administration. Although a large local firm helps the joint venture increase economies of scale and gain better access to capital markets or commercial loans, the net size effect on the firm's financial and market performance relies on asset turnover. Foreign investors should research and analyze a local partner's asset efficiency indicators, such as turnovers in inventory, fixed assets, accounts receivable, and total assets. Additional insights may be obtained by comparing these indicators longitudinally to see how much improvement the local partner has made over time and by comparing the indicators with those of other local firms in the industry to see to what extent the partner outperforms its major competitors.

IMPLICATIONS FOR INTERNATIONAL MANAGERS

To conclude, it is essential to ICV success that the potential partner possess complementary skills and resources and share compatible goals and a cooperative culture. Using reliable sources of information, foreign companies should examine the following attributes of a local candidate: strategic traits, including marketing competence, technological skills, relationship building, market position, industrial experience, strategic orientation, and corporate image; organizational traits, including organizational leadership, ownership type, learning ability, foreign experience, previous collaboration, and human resource skills; and financial traits, including profitability, liquidity, leverage, and asset efficiency. Table 9.1 presents a checklist for partner criteria in the general context. International companies should attach different degrees of importance to each of these criteria based upon goals, internal strengths, and environmental characteristics.

Critical questions that must be asked when assessing a potential partner's six Cs include:

What are you looking for: technology, market access, manufacturing capabilities, distribution channels?

Can an existing relationship be extended?

Have you examined a number of potential candidates?

How will you go about determining compatibility?

Is there any chemistry between your senior and middle management?

Are your corporate cultures compatible? If cultures are significantly different, could you successfully blend the two? How?

Does your partner have previous experience in collaborative ventures? How does its track record stack up?

TABLE 9.1
Checklist of Partner Criteria in the General Context

Strategic Criteria
  Technological and production capability
    Product development and innovation skills
    Process design and innovation skills
    Technological development skills
    Quality control skills
    Transparency of technology transfer
  Market position and power
    Quantity and diversity of customers
    Economy of scale
    Competitiveness in local and international markets
    Market share in local and international markets
    Ability and efficiency of product differentiation
  Marketing skills and expertise
    Distribution channels in local and international markets
    Product promotion skills
    Customer service
    Customer loyalty
    Relations with local and international wholesalers and retailers

Organizational Criteria
  Organizational and managerial skills
    Organizational leadership
    Human resource management skills
    Effectiveness of organizational structure
    Level of employee participation in management
    Managerial and administrative efficiency
  Local and international experience
    Experience in transnational operations
    Experience in the target market
    Experience in international collaborations
    Industrial experience
    Previous cooperation with the firm in question
  Corporate reputation and image
    Reputation in the home country
    Reputation in the host country
    Reputation in the international market
    Reputation in the industry
    Reputation for interfirm cooperation

TABLE 9.1, continued

Financial Criteria
  Ability to make profit
    Cost control ability
    Revenue increase ability
    Tax and expense reduction ability
    Production and operation efficiency
  Ability to allocate and utilize capital
    Ability to allocate and use working capital
    Financing ability
    Ability to use and control debts
    Ability to manage and reduce risks
  Ability to manage assets
    Ability to optimally deploy assets and resources
    Ability to manage accounts receivable and cash flows
    Ability to manage inventory and fixed assets
    Ability to manage intangible assets

Are there any conflicts of interest? Does your partner have any alliances with some of your competitors? Can they affect you? How will you cope with that situation?

Do you and your partner have complementary capabilities in technology, market access, manufacturing, distribution, and so on?

Does the candidate have strengths that might benefit more than one division?

Have you thoroughly researched your partner's capabilities? Is its technology or market prowess as strong as necessary?

How committed will each partner be to the venture? Does the partner appear willing to contribute the resources and skills that are necessary to make the alliance a success?

Is the activity central to both your businesses? If not, what are the chances the venture will be relegated to the sidelines by one of you?

Are you trying to forge too many ICVs at the same time, consequently overlooking critical issues and problems that may disrupt partner relationships? Is your emphasis on the quality, not the quantity, of ICVs?

How difficult will it be for your partner to withdraw from the venture?

What benefits will the partner derive from the venture? Are they greater than yours? How can you keep them equal?

What are the partner's direct costs?

How much can you learn from your partners? How do you plan to transfer any new knowledge, technology, and skills acquired from partners and the venture to the parent company?

How much does the partner need the alliance to meet its tactical or strategic objectives?

Is the venture in a business segment that the partner must have for growth or survival purposes?

How willing and able will the partner be to devote additional resources — capital, human, technologies, time — to the venture?

What alternative strategies are available to your company and to the potential partners?

What are the internal and external barriers to the partner's participation?

What is the price of failure?

To find partners with superior attributes, the following are several suggestions for international managers. First, partner selection should be integrated with the strategic goals of the foreign company. A foreign investor cannot, nor will it need to, find a local partner possessing superior attributes in all of the above. Although superiority in all three categories (strategic, organizational, and financial) would be favorable to the ICV's overall success, the importance of specific attributes within each category is dependent on what the foreign company wants to pursue from the venture. If a foreign company seeks long-term market growth, the importance of a local firm's marketing competence, market position, technological skills, industrial experience, organizational rank, and asset efficiency may outweigh other attributes. If a foreign company seeks cost minimization via export, such attributes as learning ability, foreign experience, and ownership type may be more critical than others. If a foreign company seeks short-term profitability, it should attach a higher value to a local partner's relationship building skills, strategic orientation, profitability, and liquidity. Last, if a foreign company seeks reductions of financial risks and operational uncertainty, more weight may be placed on such attributes as corporate image, organizational leadership, human resource skills, and financial leverage.

Second, obtaining as much information as possible about the potential partner is well advised. Get a copy of its business license, which will tell you about its legal capacity to contract with a foreign investor, its registered capital, its business scope, and the name of the legal representative who is legally authorized to sign any joint venture contract. It is also necessary to obtain a copy of the company's brochure and find out about the industry and the candidate's competitors (this can be another good source for potential partners). If the candidate received any award from upper level government authorities, the foreign investor should get a copy. Such an award may reflect, more or less, the firm's reputation and efficiency.

Third, a good first step when looking for a compatible partner is to examine existing relationships. Forging an ICV with a company with which you have already done business has a number of advantages. The history of the relationship provides proof of how well the two companies can work together; personal ties will already be established. It is often easier to strengthen a relationship with a known entity than to start anew; each company will have a fair idea of the capabilities, business ethics, and culture of the other company; and the partner will be well versed in operating collaborative ventures. On a cautious note, some companies warn of the danger of relying too heavily on extending existing relationships. By restricting one's scope to existing partners, one may not find the optimum partner for a given business venture. Avoiding the grueling process of seeking new partners may lead to a compromise in which you work with a familiar firm that has adequate but not superlative resources. Further, some MNCs fear they could lose their individuality by becoming either too dependent on or too closely associated with just one company. Such a tight bond can diminish a firm's chances of attracting other partners.

Fourth, a site visit is imperative. Reliable information can often be obtained only from such a visit. During the site visit, investors should try to observe employee attitudes and talk to managers, from the lowest to the highest ranks. Do not shy away from asking questions about the operation, employees, finance, technologies, cash flow, and other relevant matters. Social activities, which almost invariably will be pressed on investors during the visit, should be avoided until the deal is signed, sealed, and delivered. During the same trip, international managers should also visit several other candidate firms. This helps a foreign investor maintain bargaining power during ICV negotiation. Further, if the project involves a large amount of investment or has to be ratified by the host country government, managers should pay a visit to governmental authorities in charge of FDI. When several MNCs bid for one project in the host country, a foreign company should strive to demonstrate their distinctive capabilities that are most badly needed by the local project.

Fifth, it is always important to check whether your local partner shares your investment objectives or at least is able to reconcile his objectives to yours. If your partner puts his own interests, benefits, and political advancement above those of the joint venture's, if its management style differs substantially or completely from yours, or if it wishes to base the venture's potential success on its political clout, you have cause for concern. When these priorities are at odds, coordination between the joint venture partners becomes very poor. Beijing Jeep typified one of these clashes over priorities between foreign and Chinese partners. The Chinese felt that AMC had reneged on the terms of their contract, which called for joint design and production of a new Jeep, when exhaust system, noise controls, and speed failed to meet international standards. The breakup between AT&T and Olivetti, one of the most publicized divorces in the ICV arena, also demonstrates how differences in management objectives and styles between partners can impede the ICV's success. Both firms blamed most of the problems in the alliance on differences in these areas.

Last, for both academics and managers alike, several key areas concerning partner selection await further examination necessary for deepening understanding of the requirements for ICV success. First, inter-partner cooperation antecedents and dynamics should be diagnosed. Although partner selection determines the possibility of ICV success or failure, partner collaboration determines the realization of such possibility. Opportunities and threats appearing in the foreign market make this cooperation both of paramount importance and enormously difficult. Those foreign companies pursuing a long-term market position should attach utmost value to the ways their local partners develop, maintain, and improve their evolving collaboration.

Second, the integration of partner selection with other investment strategies, such as location selection, entry timing, and sharing arrangement, needs to be investigated. Given the economic, cultural, and historical diversity of a foreign market, foreign companies cannot use homogenous criteria in evaluating and selecting local firms for projects in different regions. The importance of each criterion to a foreign company may also differ according to timing of investment, given changes in the environment and strategic intent and needs of the investor over time. Because the degree and scope of control needed for a planned venture are important factors underlying partner selection, a local firm's attributes may have different effects on a foreign company's goal accomplishment within different equity arrangements.

Third, more evidence about the evolution of ICVs is needed. Partner cooperation in the operational and managerial process has largely been unexplored. Undoubtedly, many ICVs do not have inter-partner fit in strategic, organizational, and financial areas in the formation stage, but they survive, sustain, and evolve. In other words, we need to examine longitudinally and dynamically how partners maintain fit or adjust misfit over time for the attainment of mutual benefits. We have seen a variety of studies focusing on investment strategies, such as equity control, timing of entry, and industry selection for ICVs, but very little examination of business and operational aspects of interfirm cooperation.

REFERENCES

Beamish, P. W. 1987. Joint ventures in LDCs: Partner selection and performance. *Management International Review*, 27: 23–37.

Buckley, P. J. and M. C. Casson. 1988. The theory of cooperation in international business. In F. Contractor and P. Lorange (Eds.), *Cooperative strategies in international business*, pp. 31–34. Lexington, MA: Lexington Books.

Conference Board, The. 1995. *Making international strategic alliances work*. New York: The Conference Board.

Contractor, F. and P. Lorange. 1988. The strategy and economics basis for cooperative ventures. In F. Contractor and P. Lorange (Eds.), *Cooperative strategies in international business*, pp. 1–28. Lexington, MA: Lexington Books.

Geringer, J. M. 1991. Strategic determinants of partner selection criteria in international joint ventures. *Journal of International Business Studies*, First quarter: 41–62.

Hamel, G. 1991. Competition for competence and inter-partner learning within international strategic alliances. *Strategic Management Journal*, 12 (Special issue): 83–104.

Hamel, G., Y. L. Doz, and C. K. Prahalad. 1989. Collaborate with your competitors — and win. *Harvard Business Review*, 67: 133–139.

Harrigan, K. R. 1988. Joint ventures and competitive strategy. *Strategic Management Journal*, 9: 141–158.

Harrigan, K. R. 1985. *Strategies for joint ventures success*. Lexington, MA: Lexington Books.

Kogut, B. 1988. Joint ventures: Theoretical and empirical perspective. *Strategic Management Journal*, 9: 319–332.

Luo, Y. 1998. Joint venture success in China: How should we select a good partner? *Journal of World Business*, 33(2): 145–166.

Luo, Y. 1997. Partner selection and venturing success: The case of joint ventures with firms in the People's Republic of China. *Organization Science*, 8(6): 648–662.

Parkhe, A. 1991. Interfirm diversity, organizational learning, and longevity in global strategic alliances. *Journal of International Business Studies*, 22: 579–601.

United Nations. 1989. *Joint ventures as a form of international economic cooperation*. New York: Taylor and Francis.

Yan, A. and B. Gray. 1994. Bargaining power, management control, and performance in United States–China joint ventures: A comparative case study. *Academy of Management Journal*, 37: 1478–1517.

Zeira Y. and O. Shenkar. 1990. Interactive and specific parent characteristics: Implications for management and human resources in international joint ventures. *Management International Review*, 30(special issue): 7–22.

FURTHER READINGS

Blodgett, L. L. 1991. Partner contributions as predictors of equity share in international joint ventures. *Journal of International Business Studies*, First Quarter: 63–78.

Brouthers, K. D., L. E. Brouthers, and T. J. Wikinson. 1995. Strategic alliances: Choose your partners. *Long Range Planning*, 28: 18–25.

Goldenberg, S. 1988. *Hands across the ocean: Managing joint ventures*. Boston, MA: Harvard Business School Press.

Hill, C. L. 1990. Cooperation, opportunism, and the invisible hand: Implications for transaction cost theory. *Academy of Management Review*, 15: 500–514.

Kumar, B. N. 1995. Partner selection criteria and success of technology transfer: A model based on learning theory applied to the case of Indo-German technical collaborations. *Management International Review,* special issue (1): 65–78.

Park, S. H. and G. R. Ungson. 1997. The effect of national culture, organizational complementarity, and economic motivation on joint venture dissolution. *Academy of Management Journal,* 40: 279–307.

10

Sharing Arrangement and Control

Sharing arrangements and ownership control have critical implications in risk sharing, resource allocation, knowledge commitment, environment vulnerability, strategic flexibility, and organizational control. This chapter begins with some conceptual background on sharing arrangements and control, followed by a presentation of the antecedents of sharing arrangements. The third section tackles the relationship between equity sharing and control from the mechanism-degree-scope and structure-strategy-operation perspectives. The fourth section illuminates the linkage between control and performance in international equity joint ventures (IJVs) from a dual parent perspective, that is, both foreign and local parents simultaneously.

CONCEPTUAL BACKGROUND

A sharing arrangement concerns the equity distribution and ownership structure established by partners in an IJV. It specifies the proportion of each partner's investment and, in most instances, profit remittance from the IJV. Equity sharing is an important aspect of investment because it is closely tied to the firm's core competency contributions, control over subsidiaries, bargaining power with local partners, globally integrated synergy, and parent-subsidiary relations.

Value-generating assets are increasingly including created assets (e.g., human capital) rather than natural assets. Most of these created assets are intangible and ownership-specific, and often constitute the

major contribution brought by one party to an IJV. Under these conditions, the equity distribution within an IJV is critical, particularly when
the partner firms are pooling core competencies in the venture. Equity
distribution can also affect the ability and propensity of an IJV to influence environmental factors.

An IJV's relative strength within an interdependent, multinational network can reduce its vulnerability to host government intervention. The
reverse is also true. That is, the higher the degree of dependence of the
venture on local relationships, the more the venture is prone to political
or other contextual risks. In general, if an IJV's interaction with the local
environment is high, the parent should decentralize power and disperse
more resources to the venture. Conversely, because the foreign partner's
control over local operations is positively related to its equity status, higher ownership will lead to a lower degree of dependence on local relationships. As a result, it is likely that the greater the portion of equity owned
by foreign investors, the lower the risks and uncertainty assumed by their
IJVs.

Although large multinational enterprises (MNEs) are likely to be able
to bear more risks, empirical evidence indicates that the willingness of
U.S. firms to commit equity in a foreign market is inversely related to the
perception of uncertainty of doing business in the host country (Stopford
& Wells, 1972; Gatignon & Anderson, 1988). However, allowing an
indigenous partner to assume a larger share of an IJV does not only imply
potentially lower switching costs but also ties the interest of the partner to
that of the foreign venture. To the extent that transactional relationships
cannot be separated from contextual ones, the structure of a sharing
arrangement that shifts the economic interests of the party to the venture
lowers contextual as well as transactional uncertainty and risks.

The sharing arrangement can be structured in such a way as to shift
more of the contextual risks of the venture to the local partner, thereby
reducing its propensity to influence changes that might benefit itself to
the detriment of the joint venture or the parent itself. Although having a
larger share may also allow one partner to extract benefits from the venture, it can be possible for a minority partner to keep and exercise control
through carefully structuring the joint venture operations.

In developing countries foreign investors are typically able to exercise
even greater control than their equity levels would suggest. This is
because of the nature of their contributions (e.g., advanced technology)
and more sophisticated knowledge of control mechanisms. Control that
results from competency and managerial efficiency may lead to greater
effectiveness than would be the case elsewhere.

The resource-dependency model states that possession of key
resources by one partner of an IJV can make the other partner(s) of the
IJV dependent on that partner. An entity that has the option either to

contribute or withhold a key resource or input has greater bargaining leverage (Pfeffer & Salancik, 1978). This is especially important if the resource is irreplaceable or non-substitutable in nature. The partner controlling the resource will have more potential partners to choose from than the partner without that resource (Yan & Gray, 1994). The partner that lacks resources will be in a subordinate position during IJV negotiations. Equity ownership is, therefore, unlikely to be symmetric in the event of a dominant partner.

Bargaining power can also be derived from pressures to cooperate, available resources, commitment, and the strengths and weaknesses of each partner (Inkpen & Beamish, 1997). In IJV negotiations, a partner with the greatest bargaining power will generally achieve the highest level of IJV control, which will later allow that partner to dictate the activities of the IJV and hence achieve its own objectives. Goal attainment during the IJV negotiation process can, therefore, be gauged in terms of achievement of control. Following this argument, three kinds of IJV ownership can be identified for an individual firm using equity share as proxy for control (Blodgett, 1991): majority ownership, minority ownership, and split-over ownership (50-50 percent in the case of two partners).

Equity distribution determines ownership structure and relationship of venture partners. A majority equity holding means that the partner has more at stake in the venture than the other partners. Normally, the equity position will be associated with an equivalent level of management control in the venture. In other words, control based upon equity ownership is often direct and effective (Killing, 1983). The correspondence between holding equity and managerial control is not always exact. It is possible for a partner to have a small equity holding but exercise decisive control. Usually, however, management control in general reflects ownership, especially in the international context. For example, in Killing's study of international joint ventures in 1983, 70 percent of dominant-management control ventures were majority owned. Conversely, 76 percent of shared-management control ventures were equally owned (Beamish, 1985). In a field survey of U.S. domestic joint ventures by Harrigan in 1985, management was found to expect a minority (25 percent equity or less) equity partner to be passive (not involved in management). According to the transaction cost explanation, an MNE should try to acquire a majority equity holding of the joint venture whenever possible so as to control the transactional risks effectively (Teece, 1983). In fact, most U.S. firms preferred to hold majority equity and control in their joint ventures (Harrigan, 1985).

When both partners want to be majority equity holders, sharing arrangements often end up equally split. It is not surprising that equal ownership was advocated by Killing for joint ventures in developed countries (Beamish, 1985). As Harrigan (1985) pointed out, a 50-50 percent ownership split ensures that neither partner's interests will be quashed. It best captures the spirit of partnership and is particularly desirable in high technology joint ventures as insurance that both partners will remain involved with the venture's technological development. Equally distributed ownership is the only way that top management from each parent firm will stay interested enough to avert problems in the venture. In fact, the use of equal ownership accounts for 50 percent or more of joint ventures in developed countries (Beamish, 1985).

A 50-50 percent equity sharing arrangement ensures equal commitment from each partner. Decision making must therefore be based on consensus. This often means a prolonged decision process that can lead to deadlocks. The success of 50-50 percent equity ventures relies strongly on the synergy between partners over issues ranging from strategic analyses to daily management of the venture. It is important that partners speak a common language, have similar background knowledge, and share a set of short-term and long-term objectives. In contrast, partners coming from diverse market environments with different business backgrounds and conflicting goals often have a harder time making a 50-50 venture a success. For example, when the partners come from different developed and developing countries, they are more likely to have divergent attitudes that can result in decision-making impasses (Killing, 1983). Such joint ventures have a higher rate of failure than those between two firms from developed countries (Beamish, 1985). A 50-50 percent equity share is more likely to lead to problems in the internal management of the venture when it is necessary to carry out tasks on which the partners do not fully agree. Leadership and coordination systems in general become difficult. Thus, a 50-50 percent equity sharing is often not recommended for these kinds of partnerships. In fact, equal ownership accounts for less than a third of joint ventures between firms from developing and developed countries (Beamish, 1985).

Given that a 50-50 percent equity sharing may not be ideal for joint ventures between firms from developing and developed countries, the next question is whether MNEs should aim for a majority equity holding or a minority position. The issue of which pattern of ownership best ensures joint venture success has been a puzzle to both academics and practitioners. Transaction cost theory suggests that MNEs should assume a majority equity position to gain dominance over joint ventures. Even though MNEs know that majority control does not mean they ignore the importance of goodwill and input from the local partner, many majority holding MNEs cannot refrain from forcing resolution of issues by taking them to a vote. As a result, the commitment of the local partner to the venture is rapidly lost. Although joint ventures with MNEs holding a majority equity often have better coordinated internal management and can respond more quickly to changes in the market, the local partner often becomes passive and does not effectively contribute its local knowledge.

In contrast, transaction cost theory states that a minority equity position is the worst possible arrangement for MNEs entering a developing country. Without dominant control, MNEs cannot run the venture successfully by reducing transactional risks. In short, there is no obvious solution to the question of which type of equity holding position is ideal when MNEs from developed countries are partners with businesses in developing countries.

Each partner contributes different competencies and resources. The partner from the developed country brings technology, capital equipment and machinery, and production and management know-how to the venture. In a minority position, that partner risks opportunism and giving away expertise to the local partner without sufficient returns. When dominant, however, the foreign partner risks losing the local partner's access to land, labor, raw materials, production facilities, and expertise in dealing with the bureaucracy of the developing country. As noted earlier, the 50-50 option presents its own difficulties when differences between the two partners result in managerial problems and impasses.

Instead of arguing for one type of ownership, we maintain that the equity ownership–IJV success relationship is not a simple, linear linkage. Rather, it is a complex, non-linear association in which many factors may affect either IJV ownership and success or moderate their linkage. By the same token, it is difficult to judge whether majority ownership outperforms the other options. Sometimes the question itself does not even make sense. Different MNEs attach varying importance to equity ownership level in IJVs depending upon their strategic goals, integration requirements, resource dependence, firm experience, and alternatives for bargaining power, to name just a few factors. A firm that does not care about equity level because it has many other alternatives for gaining bargaining power and IJV control cannot be analyzed in terms of equity-performance relations.

It is difficult to define properly IJV success and performance. Each parent and IJV management often perceives success differently because they do not share the same goals. Even foreign parent firms may value IJV performance differently because of different motivations for investment in the same host market and idiosyncratic abilities to manipulate transfer pricing within a global network. A large array of factors also affects the equity-performance relationship. Sometimes the factors independently impact equity or performance as predictors, antecedents, suppressor, and exogenous or intervening variables. They could also modify the equity-performance relationship as stimuli or impediments, or as a pure moderator, quasi-moderator, or homologizer. In the course of analysis it is difficult, if not impossible, to control for all these factors.

Recognizing this complexity, we suggest a few approaches to understanding the equity-performance relationship. First, it should be understood that negotiating an appropriate sharing arrangement is an important investment strategy in international expansion. No matter how different this factor is to individual MNEs, it is certainly one of the primary sources of bargaining power, a prominent control mechanism, and a predominant force protecting the firm's proprietary knowledge and strategic resources. As such, the criticality of sharing arrangements should not be underestimated. At the same time, sharing arrangements are not universally important. Both their antecedents and implications are heterogenous among different international firms. This heterogeneity stems from internal goals, capabilities, and strategies as well as external contingencies such as different environments, industries, and partners. Last, the sharing arrangement is not the only contributing factor in bargaining power and managerial control. Of all the control choices available to a firm, it is important to opt for those that will provide the most benefits and, even more importantly, combine them effectively in order to earn the maximum rents at the lowest costs. In addition, each firm should properly assess the importance of the sharing arrangement to the firm. For this purpose, it must first correctly analyze the relevant antecedents and expected effects of such arrangements.

ANTECEDENTS OF SHARING ARRANGEMENTS

Antecedents are the rationales underlying an MNE's choice of sharing arrangement. These antecedents can be broadly categorized into either context-related (external) factors or firm-related (internal) factors. Table 10.1 summarizes the antecedents of sharing arrangements.

Environmental Uncertainty, Complexity, and Hostility

Equity ownership level is associated with the level of risk exposure as perceived by the firm. Joint venture sharing arrangements may be structured to control exposure to uncertainty and mitigate risk taking. The transaction cost implications of the degree of integration or the extent of ownership of productive assets becomes increasingly complicated under conditions of uncertainty. When uncertainty is high, a larger degree of ownership potentially entails greater switching costs should undesirable events occur. The ownership of productive assets may deprive the owner of the flexibility of a low-cost exit from the market. Therefore, firms tend to shun ownership under such conditions. Unlike contractual risks resulting from the exposure of transaction-specific assets, which can be neutralized or mitigated through internalization of intermediate markets,

TABLE 10.1
Antecedents of Sharing Arrangement

Context-Related or External Antecedents
    Expected environmental uncertainty, complexity, and hostility
    Host governmental regulations
    Local partner characteristics

Firm-Related or Internal Antecedents
    Strategic objectives
    Necessity for protection of proprietary competencies
    Available alternatives for bargaining power
    Expected need for a partner's complementary assets
    Firm experience and environmental familiarity
    Expected investment commitment
    Required balance between global integration and local responsiveness

---

uncertainty and risks embodied in the contextual environment are usually beyond the control of the firm. This will also cause the firm to shy away from ownership. When operating in a foreign location, investment in assets that cannot be redeployed is inevitable. When a host environment becomes risky, foreign investors are less likely to invest in such assets. This implies that the MNE would also favor a lower level of equity ownership as risk increases. In light of the above, equity ownership level may be inversely related to expected environmental uncertainty, complexity, and hostility.

Host Government Regulations

Regulations and rules on sharing arrangements enacted by a host government have a direct impact on a firm's choice of ownership level. These regulations and rules are normally manifested in joint venture laws, foreign direct investment (FDI) policies, or industrial policies. FDI in developing countries often encounters more cumbersome treatment and constraints than in developed nations. Today such countries as China, Russia, and most Southeast Asian nations are allowing MNEs to invest in more industries including some previously prohibited or restricted ones (e.g., airline, mining, insurance, healthcare). However, MNEs entering these newly opened industries generally have to accept the joint venture mode and, more importantly, maintain a minority status. On the positive side, minority equity may help the MNE mitigate its vulnerability to environmental uncertainty in these industries, thus reducing its economic exposure to external contingencies. On the negative side, minority equity impedes the MNE's growth potential in these regulated industries.

Local Partner's Bargaining Power

The outcome of ownership arrangements is influenced by the relative bargaining power and resource dependency between parties. When an MNE aims to acquire, or has to depend on, the local firm's strategic assets or distinctive competencies, the MNE may have difficulty increasing the equity level because of lower bargaining power relative to that of the local partner. The factors contributing to a local firm's bargaining power include availability of appropriate partners, strong market power and distribution channels, superior industrial linkages, superlative reputation and product image, and excellence in country-specific knowledge. The foreign company may not need to maintain majority equity control if its intention is merely to secure these distinctive resources and proprietary knowledge.

Strategic Objectives

Any international investment strategy must configure with the firm's strategic motivations. As sharing arrangements are associated with risk-taking propensity and resource commitment, it is natural that MNEs structure equity ownership in IJVs to help realize their strategic goals without taking too many risks or exhausting too many resources. When an MNE targets market entry and expansion or attaining country-specific knowledge, a lower percentage of equity ownership may be acceptable. If an IJV is designed to share financial risks and operational uncertainties with other firms, the MNE will more likely opt for a low level of equity. By so doing, the firm not only lowers its commitment and contribution, thus diversifying more risks, but also creates better ties with its partner, thus mitigating opportunism. In contrast, if an MNE pursues sustained profitability and growth using tacit knowledge and distinctive resources, ownership control is critical unless it has non-equity related bargaining power derived from proprietary competencies. Overall, the greater the importance of local operations to the firm, the higher the equity ownership level is needed.

Protection of Proprietary Competencies

Protecting a firm's proprietary competencies (e.g., technologies, know-how, brand names, trademarks, copyrights, and patents) without leakage to the partner or other local businesses constitutes one of the predominant managerial tasks for venture success. Sharing arrangements serve as one of the major control mechanisms safeguarding a firm's proprietary assets and skills. Everything else being constant, a higher equity percentage or dominant ownership control will better protect a firm's tacit knowledge and strategic resources. The level of equity status is therefore an increasing function of the necessity for protection of such resources and knowledge.

Available Alternatives for Bargaining Power

Bargaining power involves a bargainer's ability to change favorably the bargaining set, win accommodations from the other party, and influence the outcome of a negotiation. Equity share in the venture is only one of many forces propelling bargaining power. Yan and Gray (1994) listed eight alternative sources of bargaining power including: available substitute partners, strategic importance, technology contribution, management expertise, global support, local knowledge, distribution channels, and resource procurement. Because control is positively influenced by bargaining power, each of the above alternatives is able to inflate bargaining power. When these alternatives are strong relative to the local firm, the importance of equity ownership in stimulating bargaining power and organizational control over the IJV can be less significant. In such circumstances, a low equity share or minority status becomes acceptable to some foreign businesses.

Need for a Partner's Complementary Assets

When an MNE greatly needs a local partner's strategic resources, a dependent relationship arises. In this situation, the MNE will have less bargaining power in asking for greater ownership control. This suggests that a foreign firm acquires its local partner's complementary skills at the expense of ownership controls. When the importance of acquiring a local firm's tacit knowledge outweighs that of maintaining high equity control, dominant sharing arrangements may be subordinated to inter-partner learning. The foreign firm will accept a low level of equity distribution if the partner asks for a greater percentage of ownership, *ceteris paribus*.

Firm Experience and Environmental Familiarity

When an MNE enters uncharted waters, it will be less proactive and risk taking in its commitments to local operations. This will be further reflected in its sharing arrangements. Specifically, firms will be more prudent and tactful in undertaking investment and resource dispersal to local ventures when they are unfamiliar with the dynamics of the local environment or have not yet accumulated enough culture-specific experience in the host country. When they still face liabilities of foreignness, circumspect and evolutionary behavior is an appropriate alignment with external contingencies. As equity ownership level is positively associated with investment commitment, discreet behavior will be mirrored in a low equity percentage. Thus, it can also be expected that firm experience and environmental familiarity will be positively linked with equity level. This implies that as an MNE accumulates more host country experience it will increase its equity commitment to the local venture, everything else remaining constant.

Expected Investment Commitment

Expected investment commitment is often manifested in investment size, venture turnover or duration, and capital requirements. When the required commitment is high, the firm is inevitably engaged in greater financial risk and economic exposure. In these circumstances, the foreign company may be more circumspect with respect to equity contribution. Unless the company aims to launch the project at whatever costs (e.g., as in pioneering in the market as the first mover), the firm will usually opt for a low percentage of equity status when the joint venture project is extremely large, has a high capital requirement, or has a long investment turnover. This arrangement decreases the firm's resource commitment, thus reducing its financial risks and operational variabilities. Further, it may make the partner more cooperative and dedicated to the venture as the partner has a bigger stake committed to the joint project.

Required Balance between Global Integration and Local Responsiveness

Sharing arrangements must be subordinated to creating an optimal balance between global integration and local responsiveness. Any investment decisions involving a foreign market must be viewed as an integral part of the MNE's entire global network. Equity control serves as one of the important mid-range mechanisms balancing global integration with local responsiveness; it is one of the major tools used in implementing the MNE's transnational strategies. When a higher degree of global integration is required, greater equity ownership in the IJV becomes necessary, *ceteris paribus*. This sharing strategy gives the firm better control over the venture, thereby better internalizing operations and activities taking place in various nations within an integrated network. If the required integration is low but local responsiveness is high, then the sharing arrangements of a particular IJV do not have to take into consideration integration with headquarters. Therefore, a low level of equity status may be acceptable to the firm, other things being equal. In this event, the firm needs to employ a multi-domestic strategy in international expansion, allowing each individual subunit abroad sufficient autonomy to interact with its indigenous market.

EQUITY SHARING AND CONTROL

Importance of the Issue

The relationship between equity sharing and control of IJVs has been a matter of concern for many years; it is the main focus of work on corporate governance. When joint ventures become international, questions of ownership and control become more complex. For example, companies operating with local overseas partners can encounter significant external interventions in both ownership and control. Some three decades ago, when many commentators and politicians were pitting the interests of MNEs against those of host nations, business concerns about ownership and control focused primarily on potentially hostile government policies. In some cases, such as Bangladesh in the early 1970s, these posed a direct threat to ownership through the nationalization or sequestration of assets. In other cases, such as China in the early 1980s, a series of restrictions was imposed on the use of foreign-owned funds. Moreover, in countries like China historical concepts of equity ownership do not accord with the Western model of legally-protected property rights.

Normally, in IJVs a few companies share ownership, with equity ranging from close to 100 percent to not usually less than 5 percent. In a unified firm with highly dispersed shareholding, 5 percent can constitute a controlling interest, but in an IJV it is definitely a small minority interest. Indeed, a holding of 25 percent or less in an IJV is usually considered a passive investment. Ownership configurations in IJVs can be either a dominant and minority situation or an oligarchic one where two or more significant owners each have relatively equal equity stakes. The interests of IJV owners are usually both complementary and conflictual, so they are always potentially competitive. In the case of an oligarchic ownership configuration, the actions of the few large players are highly interdependent but theoretically unpredictable, just as with the behavior of a few large competitors in an oligopolistic industrial structure. This adds considerable complexity to the relationship between equity sharing and control. Further, in establishing IJVs to exploit complementarity between partners, the dominant firms create foundations for control that derive not from formal ownership but from specific resources, knowledge, and skills they provide. Because these assets are within the possession of the partner firms and have intrinsic value, they amount to ownership factors. These property rights convey powers of control that may be recognized in formal contracts or exercised on an informal, non-contractual basis. The linkage between sharing arrangement and control in IJVs is thus considerably more complex than in either single monolithic firms or wholly owned subsidiaries.

Studies have indicated that there are various problems in managing IJV activities. The efficacy of the collaborative venture should be reevaluated as an organizational mechanism for governing interfirm transactions (Parkhe, 1993). Collaborative ventures fail because of transaction hazards precipitated by one partner's opportunistic behavior or because of the bureaucratic costs involved in coordinating interfirm exchanges. Rivalry among parties attenuates trust building and instigates opportunism, thus generating organizational conflicts between partners. The complexity of coordinating activities for collective goals is difficult and costly. These threats increase the need for control of IJV activities, which in turn influences the success of both the IJV and each of the parent firms.

Control involves the processes by which a firm influences the activities and outcomes of its members and subunits through the use of power, authority, and a wide range of mechanisms. Managerial control of IJVs focuses on the degree of power a parent has vis-à-vis key functions and decisions that are potentially important to the performance of the IJV. It helps the parent firm ensure the most effective and efficient use of its distinctive resources or knowledge, thus optimizing the benefits from these resources. Ineffective or insufficient control over an IJV limits the parent firm's ability to coordinate activities, exploit resources, and implement strategies. Exercising control over some or all IJV activities helps protect the firm from premature exposure of its strategies, technological core, or other proprietary components. Whether from a resource-based view, inter-partner learning, or transaction cost perspective, the key to managing an IJV is the integration, exploitation, and protection of the investor's tacit knowledge or strategic resources.

Control is imperative given the potential for inter-partner conflict during the formation or operation stages. During the formation stage, goal heterogeneity, low trust, resource homogeneity, and ambiguous contracts are endogenous factors driving up subsequent interfirm conflict. During the operation stage, opportunistic behavior, difference in operational policies, emergence of local contingencies, and changes in strategic goals and plans can result in conflict that may impair the creation of expected synergies. Increasing formalization and monitoring of inter-partner relations can also lead to dissent between parties struggling to maintain organizational autonomy in the face of growing interdependence. Moreover, the increase in resource transactions between partners over time implies that their domains will shift from being complementary to more similar. This increases the likelihood of territorial disputes and competition. Cooperation and stability within an IJV require some form of institutionalized mechanisms to control opportunism and guarantee the fair sharing of rewards.

As organizations expand overseas, increasing in both complexity and diversity, the demand for monitoring, coordinating, and integrating their activities and resources increases. When operating in a highly complex, dynamic environment, an interfirm network tends to be more vulnerable to environmental changes and conflict between parties. Environmental change and uncertainty become a serious external threat to the venture. Such vulnerability requires special bonds between the parties if stable and honest transactions are to be sustained. Joint venture management needs to develop institutional control mechanisms because the norms of reciprocity and trust are likely to be insufficient.

Managerial control, as the process and techniques by which parent firms influence IJV operations and work to attain their objectives, enables a firm to reduce transaction costs that would limit a strategy's benefits. Resource-based IJV theory suggests that a parent firm is equipped with firm-specific capabilities that, in turn, require firm-specific controls. Because these capabilities are often intangible, a crucial factor determining the returns a parent can expect is its degree of control over the venture. Controlling resource applications may determine actual rent extractions, and controlling leakages of proprietary knowledge prevents uncompensated transfer of capabilities. Insufficient or ineffective control can limit the parent firm's ability to effectively coordinate activities, utilize resources, and implement strategies. IJV success is a function of the fit between the parent's criteria for success and how well the parent controls activities related to these criteria.

Control incurs costs, both directly and indirectly. This is recognized in the economics of transaction costs, most of which are seen to be incurred in maintaining control so as to avoid opportunism, protect specific-use, high-tech assets, and avoid other risks. Transaction cost economics pays attention to the direct administrative costs that any control mechanism incurs. These are reflected in the over-inflated managerial structures now subject to re-engineering. There are also important indirect costs that arise from the detrimental effects that inappropriate control can have on motivation in subordinate units. Over-control may inhibit the flexibility that IJVs need in order to develop within their own competitive environment.

Equity and Control Relations

Mechanism-Degree-Scope Perspective

Geringer and Hebert (1989) characterized parental control of IJVs as composed of three parts: the extent, scope, and mechanism of control. The extent of control refers to the degree of control achieved by the parent firms. In his study of 23 U.S.-based wholly owned subsidiaries and joint ventures operating in Taiwan and the Philippines, Dang (1977) used a range of 17 items to measure control based on the locus of decision making. He found no relationship between the degree of equity ownership and the degree of parental control over subsidiaries. However, he observed a higher incidence of expatriate managers in joint ventures than in wholly owned subsidiaries, which suggested that the degree of control in these ventures might in fact be higher than that indicated by control indices. Other authors (e.g., Killing, 1983; Beamish, 1985) measured amount of control by examining parental influence over a number of important types of decisions made in IJVs. For example, Killing classified IJVs into three categories: dominant partner IJVs, where only one partner has a dominant influence on decision-making while the other plays a passive role; shared management IJVs, where all parents participate in decision making; and independent IJVs, where the management of the IJV enjoys a high degree of autonomy. Contributing to this perspective in IJV literature was the concept of control as a continuous variable rather than merely an absolute, dichotomous variable representing either total or no control over an IJV.

The scope of control specifies the areas of operations in which control is exercised. In his study, Schaan (1983) found that parental control was exercised only with respect to specific activities or decisions. Schaan suggested that parent firms might seek dominant control only over strategically important activities consistent with their own interests rather than over the entire range of a joint venture's operations. This perspective implies that parents with different strategic objectives and interests in the joint venture will seek control over different activities.

Mechanisms of control refers to the means by which control is exercised. Early studies showed that some firms consider equity ownership to be tantamount to control. They therefore desire high levels of equity ownership (Stopford & Wells, 1972). These researchers also asserted that management control exists for the company that has the majority equity share. We maintain instead that, although a majority equity position ensures some degree of control, as noted above, it is not a strict and automatic consequence of ownership. To ensure joint venture success, international managers should maintain a balance between the desire to control their ventures and the need to have harmonious relations with their partners.

In this regard, it is important to distinguish between de jure control achieved from majority share of ownership and de facto control, which is the effective or managerial control a partner actually exercises. The latter is not necessarily tied to equity position. In general, MNEs may be able to exercise de facto control even with minority equity positions. Such control is exercised when the partner is of some special assistance to the joint venture. For example, the dependence of joint ventures on parent firms for strategic resources, such as capital, technology, management skills, and market access, provides parent firms with means of exerting effective control. The resource dependence approach predicts that firms will be powerful relative to others to the extent that they control resources needed by others and can reduce their dependence on others for resources.

Managerial control can be either positive or negative. Positive control is exercised when a parent firm is in the position to influence activities or decisions in a way consistent with its own interests and expectations. Negative control may be used to prevent the implementation of decisions or activities with which it does not agree.

A variety of control mechanisms other than the equity participation are available to firms, even minority partners. These non-equity mechanisms include the following.

Nomination and Appointment of Key Personnel. Control requires knowledge of events and circumstances. Such knowledge is most readily available to the venture's parents if it supplies key personnel to run or monitor operations or critical functions such as marketing, research and development, or corporate finance (Schaan, 1983). The appointment of key personnel as a control mechanism is especially important to parents in a minority position or geographically remote.

Meetings of Board of Directors. Although a majority equity holder is in an advantageous position in terms of composition and representation on the board, a minority partner has leeway in manipulating the frequency of meetings and agenda coverage. In addition, a majority parent cannot consistently overrule or refuse to compromise with its partner without building significant ill will and risking the long-term survival of the relationship. Further, minority parents can prevent their majority partner from implementing unilateral decisions by negotiating the inclusion in the joint venture contract of veto right over decisions important to their interests. Among the decisions that minority partners want to be able to veto are: dividend policy, exports, approval of major projects, expansion financing, transfer pricing, choice of suppliers, divestment, and selection of key managers. Last, control at the board level is not simply a matter of votes. Control also results from the ability to influence other board members on important issues. This is to a large extent a matter of competence, bargaining power, and negotiation skills. As a result, minority partners have an opportunity to influence IJV management if they are careful to appoint to the board people with a strong grasp of the IJV's operational and strategic issues, good bargaining skills, and empathy for the partner's culture.

Managerial Policies and Procedures. The behavior of executives in an IJV is influenced by various internally regulated managerial policies and procedures devised by the owners. Because a joint venture contract usually does not stipulate or specify these policies and procedures, a minority partner can be more proactive by playing a bigger part in formulating and adjusting such policies and procedures. Reward and report systems are particularly effective for the purpose of control as the former determines the incentive structure and performance evaluations and the latter determines information flow, dissemination, and accuracy.

Budget Control. Five aspects of budget control can be implemented: emphasis on the budget during performance evaluations, that is, using quantitative criteria in evaluating divisional manager performance; participation in the budget setting, that is, the degree of involvement a partner has during budget development; budget incentives, that is, linking pay and promotion prospects to meeting budget goals; budget standard setting difficulty, that is, the difficulty with which budget goals are set; and budget controllability filters, that is, extenuating factors that are brought into the performance evaluation process. In general, minority partners can use all five budget control mechanisms to increase their overall or specific control over IJV operations and management.

Provision of Parent Services. To increase the likelihood that specific tasks in the joint venture will be performed in conformity with their expectations, parent firms may offer staff services and training, sometimes at no cost to the venture. Such services can be provided irrespective of equity ownership level. Increased control thereby accrues to parent firms in the following ways: greater awareness and sensitivity on the part of the parent to conditions within the IJV because of enhanced dialogue with the venture employees, increased loyalty from joint venture employees who identify more with the parent and have assimilated its ethos, and increased predictability of behavior in the IJV because its managers are more likely to use the guidelines within which they have been trained.

Contract Stipulations. As one of the major *ex ante* mechanisms by which conflicts may be overcome and performance enhanced, contract stipulations serve to reduce managerial complexity in coordinating activities for collective goals. It is an institutionalized mechanism for mitigating opportunism and increasing forbearance. A minority partner can maintain greater control over subsequent IJV operations and management if relevant terms and clauses in the contract are more favorable to that firm. Greater bargaining power and superior negotiation skills result in such favorable conditions. Of various terms and conditions, responsibility-rights-benefits, managerial rules, and strategic goals are of particular relevance for the minority party that aims to increase control using this approach.

Resource Allocation and Control. Resource competence leads to bargaining power, and resource allocation and utilization contribute to managerial control. In other words, allocation and control of key resources needed by the IJV are an effective mechanism for a minority party attempting to exert control over the IJV's business activities and management process. This mechanism of control is often powerfully sustained because control of key resources makes both the IJV's success and the partner company's goal accomplishment dependent upon the firm. Blodgett

(1991) also suggests that equity ownership patterns are associated with the nature of expertise that a company contributes to an IJV. According to her study, technology lends dominant equity to the firm that owns it, particularly when its partner supplies marketing channels and other expertise associated with the local environment. Local knowledge is the contribution most consistently associated with a minority share in the original IJV agreement.

Interpersonal Relationship. A minority equity holder can increase its control if it builds and maintains trustworthy, enduring personal relationships with upper level managers representing the partner firm. In fact, this approach has helped many MNEs, as minority parties, to control successfully their IJVs in developing countries. By arranging for managers from local firms to work at foreign headquarters, helping solve personal difficulties they face, or offering favors as needed, foreign companies are able to effectively and efficiently cultivate and solidify relationships with local executives who will, in turn, remain loyal to the foreign company. This will eventually promote the foreign company's managerial effectiveness.

Structural-Strategic-Operational Perspective

Control over the IJV can be exercised at several different levels, including operational (or functional) level, structural level, and strategic level. Correspondingly, as a multi-level construct, control can be classified as strategic, operational, or structural. Equity sharing arrangements significantly affect each of these three types.

Strategic control concerns selected areas that are strategically vital to the parent. Strategic control is crucial to venture success as perceived by the parent because it can better protect contributed core competencies and more efficiently apply key assets and skills, even with a relatively small share of equity or overall control. At times it may be more useful for a parent firm to adopt strategic control over key resources and activities than aim for overall control. The exercise of effective and efficient control measures should focus on those dimensions a parent firm perceives as strategic and critical. Strategic control over areas that the other parent has to depend upon can increase bargaining power and leverage options. When investing in a complex, dynamic environment, the exercise of strategic control over important areas is even more critical to the attainment of expected economic benefits. Strategic control may then be effective in protecting strategic assets, maintaining bargaining power, and reducing vulnerability to contextual changes.

Operational control concerns managerial functions such as marketing, finance, human resource management, and production. Operational control can shape venture operations and management because routinization of management functions is an important element of administrative or bureaucratic control. Through the establishment of a comprehensive system of rules and procedures for directing operations or behavior of divisions, functions, and individuals, bureaucratic control standardizes behavior and makes outcomes predictable, one of the major goals of IJV control. The importance of operational control may differ among various MNEs. This kind of control will be more important to those companies that have greater participation, with respect to either intensity or diversity, in the host market. In other words, when required local responsiveness is high, operational control appears to be more important. Because it is based on managerial functions, operational control can also be applied to the realization of specific operational goals. For example, a parent company concerned with local market expansion may be able to monitor this function via marketing-focused operational control.

Structural control concerns organizational structure and managerial systems. In general, when the management system, decision process, and corporate policies of an IJV are similar in structure to those of one parent, that parent can exercise a higher level of control than its partner. In fact, the ability of a partner to replicate its way of managing the joint venture reflects its level of control over the partnership. A parent firm's structural controls can be enhanced by transplanting its corporate culture, principles, and management styles to the venture. To achieve this goal, the parent company can use its bargaining power or dominant equity position to manipulate the venture's managerial systems and organizational principles, train senior staff of the venture, and make the organizational structure of the venture fit with the parent's stake.

CONTROL-PERFORMANCE RELATIONS: A DUAL PARENT PERSPECTIVE

Overall control implies that the parent firm is concerned with controlling the strategic direction of the combined bundle of complementary resources represented by the IJV. Overall control may influence perceived performance because it not only enhances the benefits realized from the utilization of a partner's strategic resources but also reduces the costs of inter-partner conflict arising from divergent objectives, power sharing, task interdependence, perceived inequality in distribution of costs and benefits, incompatible management styles, and cultural differences. Specific control is crucial for venture success as perceived by the parent because it can better protect contributed core competencies and more efficiently apply key strategic assets and skills, even with a relatively small share of equity or overall control.

The underlying structure of the relationship between overall or specific control and venture success is likely to be similar for all parties, whether foreign or local. Given the potential for conflict, control over an IJV is a critical consideration for every partner. Although partners may have variable objectives, different equity status, and idiosyncratic bargaining power, each requires some overall or specific control in order to protect respective proprietary resources, ensure the implementation of respective strategies, and influence management and operations of the venture. For foreign partners in a dynamic host country, overall control will help shape the strategic movement of the IJV in alignment with long-range goals, such as host market expansion. Specific control will promote the accomplishment of operational objectives that may be heterogenous to those of local counterparts and host governments. For local partners in a host country, selective focus of control is essential because it is a means for maintaining bargaining power over the long run and optimizing benefits from strategic assets, such as distinctive distribution channels, supply networks, and knowledge about local business practices. Local partners must not only achieve their own objectives, such as international market expansion, productivity growth, and product, process, and managerial innovations, but also carry out government-instituted goals, such as export growth and technology absorption. Overall control is hence imperative for them as well. Therefore, both a foreign and local parent's satisfaction with IJV performance is expected to be positively related to the firm's overall or specific controls over the venture.

Although each parent may wish to maintain full control over the IJV, it is obviously impossible for both to achieve this. When one parent maintains a higher degree of overall or specific control, a dependency situation is created. In a cooperative relationship, dependence can be a source of power for the firm controlling key resources because, to some degree, each firm can increase or withhold resources that are attractive to its partner. A firm that has the option of maintaining greater control can use that option as leverage in bargaining with its partner. A parent holding dominant control also increases the dependency of the IJV upon its resources, strategies, and policies. A lack of control and bargaining power over IJV operations and management can be a key factor in the perception of venture performance. If a partner lacks control over some or all strategic resources or activities, it may be perceived as incapable of influencing IJV output and performance. When two parents have different goals, one parent is unlikely to be satisfied with IJV performance if the performance outcome is a function of the other parent's dominant position. This may not hold true, however, when both partners share the same goals or have compatible objectives. High goal congruity not only reduces each parent's opportunism but also alleviates inter-partner conflict in performance perception. Hence, when goal incongruity is high, one parent's satisfaction with IJV performance will be negatively related to the overall control and specific controls exercised by the other parent over the venture. When goal incongruity is low, one parent's satisfaction with IJV performance will not have this negative relationship.

Resource-based theory proposes that sustainable competitive advantages in the global marketplace derive from the unique bundle of resources or competencies that are at the core of global business. These resources are valuable, rare, and cannot be perfectly imitated or substituted. International experience, global reputation, local knowledge, and organizational adaptability are important areas of organizational competence. These ownership advantages determine the success of foreign operations.

The bargaining power perspective in IJV literature argues that the organizational competence of the firm also determines how well it negotiates with its partner, which in turn influences its control over the IJV. Because organizational competence is a predominant determinant of bargaining power, it is not surprising to see that effective control over an IJV is an increasing function of the firm's distinctive competencies but not necessarily of its equity status in the venture (e.g., Mjoen & Tallman, 1997). In summary, stronger organizational competence is expected to increase managerial control via greater bargaining power over the IJV. This in turn improves the firm's satisfaction with the venture's performance. In addition, competence and control are likely to cross-facilitate each other in a dynamic relationship. Control implies that the organizational competence of one parent can be sheltered from casual exposure to the other parent. Effective control of the IJV can ensure that the parent firm will most efficiently utilize its competencies or resources. In such circumstances, a firm's organizational competence may be able to generate more economic benefits or higher satisfaction with the venture. This cross-facilitation effect further strengthens the importance of organizational competence in promoting control-performance relations. Thus, a positive relationship between overall and specific controls and the parent's satisfaction with IJV performance is boosted by the organizational competence the parent brings to the venture.

Inter-partner cultural distance is a particularly potent form of internal uncertainty for IJVs. The greater the cultural distance from the host country, the more unfamiliar a foreign parent will be with the values and operating modes of the local firm. Communications will also be hampered if the parent firms are of different national and corporate cultures. Group homogeneity theory argues that having organizations with socioculturally similar group members prevents losses of coordination and control. Cultural distance between nations has been shown to lead to differences in management practices, values, mindsets, and norms. These differences may lead to cultural ambiguity and process losses when people from different cultures work together. Some researchers further postulate that cultural distance between partners impedes interfirm learning and cooperation (e.g., Geringer & Hebert, 1989). A foreign investor's cultural distance from the host country may be negatively related to its ability to adapt to the host country environment and to local business practices, industrial culture, and business networking. Buckley and Casson (1988) maintain that parental forbearance, commitment, and collaboration are obstructed by social distance. This distance can be a source of conflict, opportunism, mistrust, and instability in many IJVs. Cultural distance may also be an important factor in affecting organizational fit between foreign and local partners, which in turn influences IJV performance. Thus, a positive relationship between overall and specific controls and the foreign parent's satisfaction with IJV performance is hindered by its cultural distance from the host country.

To sum up, Schaan (1983) argues that at times it may be more strategically useful for a parent firm to adopt specific control over key resources and activities of the IJV, rather than aim for overall control. Geringer and Hebert (1989) also suggest that the exercise of effective and efficient control should focus on those dimensions a parent firm perceives as critical, rather than on the entire range of IJV activities. Yan and Gray (1994) postulate that selective control over areas that the other parent has to depend upon can increase bargaining power and leverage options. When investing in a complex, dynamic environment, the exercise of specific control over important areas is even more critical to the attainment of expected economic benefits. Specific control may then be more effective than overall control in protecting strategic assets, maintaining bargaining power, and reducing vulnerability to contextual changes. Moreover, specific control may be more conducive to cooperation because it will make the parent firm seem less overbearing to its partner. Furthermore, because control often incurs managerial costs, specific control may be more cost efficient. Therefore, specific control exercised by a foreign parent may have a stronger positive effect on its satisfaction with IJV performance than does overall control.

REFERENCES

Beamish, P. W. 1985. The characteristics of joint ventures in developed and developing countries. *Columbia Journal of World Business*, Fall: 13–19.

Blodgett, L. L. 1991. Partner contributions as predictors of equity share in international joint ventures. *Journal of International Business Studies*, First Quarter: 63–77.

Buckley, P. J. and M. Casson. 1988. A theory of cooperation in international business. In F. J. Contractor and P. Lorange (Eds.), *Cooperative strategies in international business*, pp. 31–53. Lexington, MA: Lexington Books.

Dang, T. 1977. Ownership, control, and performance of the multinational corporations: A study of U.S. wholly-owned subsidiaries and joint ventures in Philipines and Taiwan. Unpublished doctoral dissertation, University of California, Los Angeles.

Gatignon, H. and E. Anderson. 1988. The multinational corporation's degree of control over foreign subsidiaries: An empirical test of a transaction cost explanation. *Journal of Law, Economics, and Organization*, 4: 305–336.

Geringer, J. M. and L. Hebert. 1989. Control and performance of international joint ventures. *Journal of International Business Studies*, 20: 235–254.

Harrigan, K. R. 1985. *Strategies for joint ventures*. Lexington, MA: D.C. Heath.

Inkpen, A. C. and P. W. Beamish. 1997. Knowledge, bargaining power, and the instability of international joint ventures. *Academy of Management Review*, 22: 177–202.

Killing, J. P. 1983. *Strategies for joint venture success*. New York: Praeger.

Mjoen, H. and S. Tallman. 1997. Control and performance in international joint ventures. *Organization Science*, 8(3): 257–274.

Parkhe, A. 1993. Strategic alliance structuring: A game theoretic and transaction cost examination of interfirm cooperation. *Academy of Management Journal*, 36: 794–829.

Pfeffer, J. and G. Salancik. 1978. *The external control of organizations: A resource dependence perspective*. New York: Harper & Row.

Schaan, J. L. 1983. Partner control and joint venture success: The case of Mexico. Unpublished doctoral dissertation. University of Western Ontario.

Stopford, J. M. and L. T. Wells. 1972. *Managing the multinational enterprise*. New York: Basic Books.

Teece, D. J. 1983. Multinational enterprise, internal governance, and industrial organization. *The American Economic Review*, 75(2): 233–238.

Yan, A. and B. Gray. 1994. Bargaining power, management control, and performance in United States–China joint ventures: A comparative case study. *Academy of Management Journal*, 37: 1478–1517.

FURTHER READINGS

Baliga, B. R. and A. M. Jaeger. 1984. Multinational corporation: Control systems and delegation issues. *Journal of International Business Studies*, Fall: 25–40.

Beamish, P. W. and J. C. Banks. 1987. Equity joint ventures and the theory of the multinational enterprises. *Journal of International Business Studies*, Summer, 1–16.

Bleeke, J. and D. Ernst. 1991. The way to win in cross-border alliances. *Harvard Business Review*, 69(November–December): 127–135.

Contractor, F. and P. Lorange. 1988. The strategy and economics basis for cooperative venture. In F. J. Contractor and P. Lorange (Eds.), *Cooperative strategies in international business*, pp. 1–28. Lexington, MA: Lexington Books.

Fagre, N. and L. T. Wells. 1982. Bargaining power of multinationals and host governments. *Journal of International Business Studies*, Fall: 9–23.

Franko, L. G. 1989. Use of minority and 50-50 joint ventures by United States multinationals during the 1970s: The interaction of host country policies and corporate strategies. *Journal of International Business Studies*, Spring: 19–40.

Hamel, G. 1991. Competition for competence and inter-partner learning within international strategic alliances. *Strategic Management Journal*, 12: 83–103.

Hennart, J. 1988. A transaction costs theory of equity joint ventures. *Strategic Management Journal*, 9: 361–374.

Hill, R. C. and D. Hellriegel. 1994. Critical contingencies in joint venture management: Some lessons from managers. *Organization Science*, 5: 594–607.

Kogut, B. 1988. Joint ventures: Theoretical and empirical perspective. *Strategic Management Journal*, 9: 319–332.

Lecraw, D. J. 1984. Bargaining power, ownership and profitability of transnational corporations in developing countries. *Journal of International Business Studies*, Spring–Summer: 27–43.

Ouchi, W. G. 1977. The relationship between organizational structure and organizational control. *Administrative Science Quarterly*, 22: 95–112.

Pan, Y. 1996. Influence on foreign equity ownership level in joint ventures in China. *Journal of International Business Studies*, 27(1): 1–26.

Schaan, J. L. 1988. How to control a joint venture even as a minority partner. *Journal of General Management*, 14(1): 4–16.

Shan, W. 1991. Environment risks and joint venture sharing arrangements. *Journal of International Business Studies*, Fourth Quarter: 555–578.

Yan, Y., J. Child, and Y. Lu. 1995. Ownership and control in international business: An examination of Sino-foreign international joint ventures. Working Paper No. 6, Research Papers in Management Studies, University of Cambridge.

11

Joint Venture Negotiation, Cooperation, and Termination

Knowledge about determinants, processes, and outcomes of negotiation, cooperation, and termination can help international business managers employ appropriate collaborative strategies that will result in maximum benefits. This chapter tackles the three most prominent issues in the dynamic and evolutionary process of international equity joint venture (IJV) development: negotiation in the formation stage, cooperation in the operational stage, and termination in the concluding stage. The chapter first introduces the conceptual background of IJV negotiation, analyzes antecedents and consequences of negotiation and contractual specificity, presents an integrated framework of IJV negotiation, and illustrates major terms and clauses in a typical IJV contract or agreement. The second section deals with the issue of IJV cooperation. Specifically, it introduces theoretical underpinnings on cooperation, assesses cooperation between foreign and local parental firms and between parents and IJV management, and links cooperation with ownership, competence, culture, trust, commitment, and knowledge acquisition. The final section discusses why, when, and how an IJV should be terminated.

JOINT VENTURE NEGOTIATION

Conceptual Background

Negotiation is a decision-making or problem-solving process, accomplished jointly by two or more people. International interfirm negotiation involves a complex process of deliberate interactions between two or more firms originating in different nations and seeking to define their interdependence. The complexities involved in creating and managing an IJV — a hybrid, multi-ownership organizational form — are reflected in the negotiations leading to its establishment. Inter-partner conflict often arises because of different perceptions, preferences, behavioral styles, and goals, with transaction hazards precipitated by opportunistic behavior in search of private incentives. Cultural differences, legal pluralism, monetary factors, ideological diversity, and greater uncertainty distinguish international business negotiations from domestic ones. National groups employ negotiation behaviors and styles shaped by geography, history, religion, and politics; discussions are often impeded when parties seem to be pursuing different paths of logic.

Negotiations concerning IJV formation are especially daunting. An IJV is typically established by two or more partners undertaking joint investment commitment and risk-benefit sharing according to negotiated terms. From a bargaining perspective, the anticipated need for inter-partner cooperation will influence the negotiation strategies used by the parties. When the parties act in an adversarial manner by holding each other at arm's length, they generally use a distributive strategy in which limited information is exchanged while each party works independently to gain an information-based advantage in the negotiation. Distributive strategies are less likely in IJV negotiations, however, because such ventures involve inter-partner learning and future interdependence. Rather, IJV partners are more likely to utilize integrative strategies that allow the parties to exchange information freely and produce a mutually beneficial outcome. The integrative or problem-solving strategy does not preclude, however, the necessity to define explicitly the relevant conditions for IJV establishment and operations.

When operating in a highly complex, dynamic environment, such as an emerging market, an interfirm network becomes more vulnerable to environmental changes and inter-party conflict. This vulnerability requires strong bonds between the parties to sustain honest transactions. IJV management needs to develop mechanisms for facilitating inter-partner learning and collaboration because the norms of reciprocity and trust are insufficient to control the venture and make best use of its unique benefits.

Inter-partner negotiation on IJV formation is difficult and costly. Each partner's goals and expectations are often incongruent or incompatible. Because an IJV entails mutual commitment of strategic assets in an uncertain, complex environment, transaction costs during formation and subsequent operations are high. Normative specifications and stipulations are necessary for all parties to ensure control of their respective strategic resources and to benefit from possible financial or operational synergies generated from the venture. IJV negotiation is also a social and political process affected by such considerations as cultural distance and government pressure or hindrance.

Given the potential for partner conflict, specifying terms during negotiation is imperative to IJV formation and operation. During the formation stage, goal heterogeneity, low trust, and resource homogeneity are endogenous factors driving subsequent interfirm conflicts. During the operations stage, opportunistic behavior, different operational policies, emergence of local contingencies, and changes in strategic goals and plans by either partner can result in inter-partner conflicts that prevent expected synergies from occurring. Furthermore, the growth of a network through a dynamic cyclical process contains the seeds of disintegration. Increasing monitoring of inter-partner relations may lead to conflict between parties who are struggling to maintain their organizational autonomy in the face of growing interdependence. Moreover, the increase in resource transactions between partners over time implies that their domains will shift from being complementary to being similar, which further increases the likelihood of territorial disputes, conflict, and competition.

Negotiation Specificity

The process of international business negotiation has been extensively addressed. Graham's process model (1985) addresses the importance of successive interactions between negotiators and the impact of context on negotiations. Fayerweather and Kapoor's negotiation framework (1976) highlights the role of the negotiation situation in modifying the negotiation, arguing that environmental and organizational variables affect negotiation patterns. Kochan and Katz's bargaining model (1988) incorporates institutional factors, such as government intervention and interfirm goal congruity, as predictors of negotiation behavior. Tung's conceptual paradigm (1988) explicitly treats contextual political and cultural factors and business characteristics as antecedents affecting negotiation processes and outcomes. Similarly, Thomas's structural model (1976) views behavioral predispositions and incentive structures as determinants of negotiation procedures. Finally, Weiss's relationships-behavior-conditioning perspective (1993) considers conditions (e.g., circumstances, capabilities, culture, and environment) as exogenous factors affecting both negotiation behavior and interfirm relationships. Among a variety of antecedent factors, each may have variable relevance to different negotiation issues.

Comparatively, the contents of transactions have been largely ignored in the literature. A key facet of negotiation content is specificity, namely, the degree to which major terms, clauses, and conditions of transactions are specified during the negotiations and incorporated in the subsequent contract. The specification of major terms during the negotiations and their eventual codification in a contract provide a safeguard against ex post performance problems by mitigating each party's ability to act opportunistically over the course of significant, long-term investments, such as in IJVs.

As one of the major ex ante mechanisms by which conflicts may be overcome and performance enhanced, negotiation specificity serves to reduce managerial complexity in coordinating activities for collective goals. Collaborative ventures can fail because of transaction hazards precipitated by opportunistic behavior on the part of each partner or because of high bureaucratic costs involved in coordinating interfirm exchanges. Where there is rivalry among parties, trust building is attenuated and opportunism instigated, thus generating further conflict. These threats increase the need for ex ante specifications governing each party's rights, duties, and benefits, which are reflected in various binding terms, clauses, and conditions negotiated and agreed upon by all parties. Negotiation ambiguity, in contrast, leaves contractual terms blurred or too general, lacking clear bounds with respect to the benefits and responsibilities of all parties. This ambiguity creates a breeding ground for shirking responsibility and shifting blame, raising the likelihood of conflict between parties. It also hinders each party's ability to coordinate activities, utilize resources, and implement strategies.

Under these circumstances, negotiation specificity serves as an institutionalized mechanism for mitigating opportunism and increasing forbearance. It helps each party ensure the most effective and efficient use of its distinctive resources or knowledge, thus optimizing the benefits from these resources in the IJV. Moreover, negotiation specificity helps protect the firm from premature disclosure of its strategies, technological core, or other proprietary knowledge. Whether from a resource-based view, interpartner learning, or transaction cost perspective, it is clear that the integration, exploitation, and protection of each investor's tacit knowledge or strategic resources are critical management issues in IJVs. Negotiation specificity constitutes the underlying ex ante mechanism for utilizing and protecting such knowledge resources.

According to transaction cost theory, incentives for opportunism are created ex post, once the investments are sunk in anticipation of performance. If a mechanism cannot be devised to mitigate each party's ability to act on these incentives, a cost-minimizing transaction may become unattractive at the contract execution stage. Negotiation specificity works against opportunism and alleviates contract hazards and imperfections. The importance of this specificity is elevated when investment uncertainty is high, duration is long, and commitment is heavy. Thus, negotiation specificity concerning IJV investment in a dynamic emerging market is of paramount value to the success of the partnership.

Although negotiation style, behavior, and strategy typically differ across cultures, negotiation specificity is important to transactions in all cultures. It is not accidental that international business codes and practices have emerged over the past hundred or so years or that there is an International Chamber of Commerce, which provides an impartial point of reference across cultural borders. According to Williamson (1985), economic rationality is likely to outweigh sociocultural contingencies when negotiators commit heavy investments to a long-term venture in an uncertain environment.

Antecedents of Negotiation Specificity

IJVs negotiations are neither easy nor certain. From a social psychological perspective, international business negotiations involve interlocked, sequential antecedent, concurrent, and consequent factors. Graham (1985) contends that situational constraints and bargaining characteristics influence the process of interfirm negotiations, which in turn affect negotiation outcomes.

As proposed below, the antecedents of negotiation specificity in IJVs include cultural distance between partners and differences in their respective goals, as well as contingencies stemming from third parties (e.g., local government authorities) who affect the transaction via introducing the partners and influencing venture management. Finally, the size of the investment is likely to affect how much the partners commit to the venture, which in turn influences their circumspection over transaction terms.

Cultural Distance. Fewer cultural barriers make accurate interpretation of transaction terms and conditions more likely. A narrow cultural distance promotes information exchange, which is conducive to negotiation specificity. Negotiators from similar cultures are less likely to leave a lot of leeway in the contract that can cause future disputes and conflict. In contrast, firms from countries separated by greater cultural distance are likely to negotiate relatively ambiguous contracts initially, planning to make necessary adjustments to these terms over time as they become more familiar with each other. This flexibility is sometimes necessary for parties from culturally distant nations.

Goal Congruity. From a game theory perspective, goal congruence reduces a player's uncertainty about what another player will do, which may in turn facilitate appropriate responses to the predicted strategies of its partners (i.e., Nash equilibrium). When strategic goals between parties diverge, negotiators are more likely to use distributive rather than integrative or cooperative strategies during negotiations. This often gives rise to a negotiation issue that can be referred to as the dilemma of honesty and openness. In this circumstance, negotiators attempt to avoid costly mistakes and possible conflict through information exchange and contract specificity. High specificity of terms and conditions about IJV formation, operations, and management may boost information exchange and transparency and improve the accuracy of interpretation during negotiations. In the presence of goal differences, keeping a certain leeway in negotiating issues may plant the seed for subsequent opportunism and conflict. High negotiation specificity, in contrast, provides rules and procedures that may help IJV partners solve possible disputes or improve interfirm cooperation and coordination.

Third Party Introduction. How the partners are introduced to each other affects expected collaboration in the future, which in turn influences specificity during current negotiations. In most emerging economies, a foreign partner initiates contact with potential local partners either through an introduction by a host government agency, another third party, or by direct inquiry. Because the third party, particularly a government agency, may not know a lot about the potential investor's background and objectives and may have its own motivations behind the introduction, indirect introductions may undermine the stability of the future venture. In such circumstances, partners are likely to be more specific during the contract negotiation as a way of preventing possible controversies and disputes. In contrast, direct inquiry often implies previous involvement or acquaintance with potential partners. A past relationship can foster a climate of openness, which is essential for inter-partner learning and cooperation. Previous contact also leads to the development of specialized skills and routines that are adapted to inter-partner cooperation and are at risk if cooperation breaks down.

Government Intervention. Brouthers and Bamossy (1997) found that in emerging economies, governments are key stakeholders who intervene significantly in IJV negotiations. Such intervention can alter the balance of power and affect the bargaining consequences. For IJVs in emerging economies, the degree of government intervention is often dependent on location, time, industry, local partner, project contribution, export orientation, and technological level. Specificity of contract negotiations can be used as a crucial safeguard against contextual uncertainty, including government intervention. This is in line with the transaction cost argument that specificity of transaction terms and conditions is an increasing function of uncertainty in the environment in which an investment is launched. High negotiation specificity thus performs an important mechanism in reducing possible hindrance from various governmental authorities in the host country. The higher the expected governmental intervention in IJV operations and management, the greater the possibility that negotiating firms will employ more specifications in the negotiation process.

Investment Size. Transaction cost theorists suggest that investors deal more cautiously with transactions that involve greater investment commitment. Higher investments imply higher startup, switching, and exit costs, thus involving greater financial and operational risks. To reduce such transaction costs, firms are usually more circumspect when arranging the terms and conditions of their contracts. Moreover, a partner's commitment is positively related to the expected stakes, that is, the perceived importance of possible gains or losses associated with the commitment. In such an event, firms are likely to negotiate more cautiously because ambiguous regulations in the contract may cause later conflict, hence coordination and resolution costs. These costs may be even higher when arranging project development in emerging economies because of greater contractual and contextual uncertainties. Negotiation specificity concerning transaction terms and conditions is likely to increase further under such conditions.

Consequences of Negotiation Specificity

Both transaction cost and social exchange theorists maintain that negotiation outcomes are determined by negotiation process factors (Rubin & Brown, 1975; Williamson, 1985). As a key concurrent construct in the negotiation process, negotiation specificity, as mirrored in the explicitness of terms and conditions established in the contract, protects a partner's strategic resources, mitigates interfirm opportunism, and reduces operational and financial uncertainties. These benefits in turn reduce transaction costs, enhance economic rents, and improve financial and operational synergies from inter-partner cooperation. Negotiation specificity is, therefore, beneficial to IJV performance, which ideally benefits both parties. From an information exchange perspective, Rubin and Brown (1975), Graham (1985), and O'Connor (1997) suggest that negotiation specificity helps each party get more accurate information regarding each other's duties, needs, and benefits, which allows negotiators to make choices and decisions that boost individual payoffs and joint rewards. In light of the above, IJV performance is expected to be positively associated with negotiation specificity.

It is important to further differentiate specificity into responsibility-rights-benefits (R-R-B) specificity, goal specificity, rule specificity, and solution specificity. My recent study demonstrates that negotiation contingencies collectively have the strongest impact on R-R-B specificity, then goal specificity and rule specificity, and, to a lesser extent, on conflict solution specificity for IJVs investing in China. Further, the study finds that the relation between specificity and process-based performance is stronger than the relationship between specificity and market, financial, and overall performance. These results can be explained in that specificity creates explicit rules for operations and hence has a direct impact on production and management processes. In contrast, market, financial, and overall performances are also influenced by numerous variables unrelated to contract negotiations, such as partner selection and timing of market entry. Of the four areas of specificity, R-R-B specificity, goal specificity, and rule specificity reveal a stronger favorable influence on performance than does solution specificity. Knowledge about exogenous factors underlying negotiation specificity and its performance effects can help international business managers employ appropriate negotiation strategies that will result in a maximum payoff.

An Integrated Model

Specificity in an IJV contract is only one of the major issues in the negotiation process. There exist a large number of antecedents affecting the IJV negotiation process in general, as well as those affecting only specificity. Figure 11.1 delineates an integrated model of IJV negotiations.

Antecedent Factors

Environmental Context. Various contextual factors from the political, regulatory, economic, and sociocultural environments may affect negotiation process. First, possible agreements between parties from two nations must be examined within the context of the political relations that prevail between the countries, such as whether there are normal diplomatic relations between the two countries, technology transfer is constrained, or the material imports and product exports are subject to administrative control. Moreover, possible hindrance from the host country government on the formation and operation of the IJV should be considered during negotiations. In many cases, particularly in developing countries, IJV agreements or contracts cannot take effect unless they are ratified by the government authority in charge of foreign direct investment inflow.

Second, the regulatory environment influences IJV negotiations in two major ways. Primarily, it provides a legal framework by which various terms and conditions specified in the contract must accord. Normally, government regulations have an impact on the following areas: market orientation (export ratio policy), material procurement (localization policy), technology transfer, equipment import (import license policy), project construction (location policy), accounting, finance, taxation, and employee recruitment and compensation (labor, union, and employment policies). Both foreign and local partners must familiarize themselves with any of the host government's foreign direct investment and industrial policies that may impact their project. In addition, it is necessary to review corporate law and joint venture laws enacted and enforced in the host country. Such legalities directly impact how the joint venture should be formed and its contract stipulated.

FIGURE 11.1
An Integrated Model of International Joint Venture Negotiations

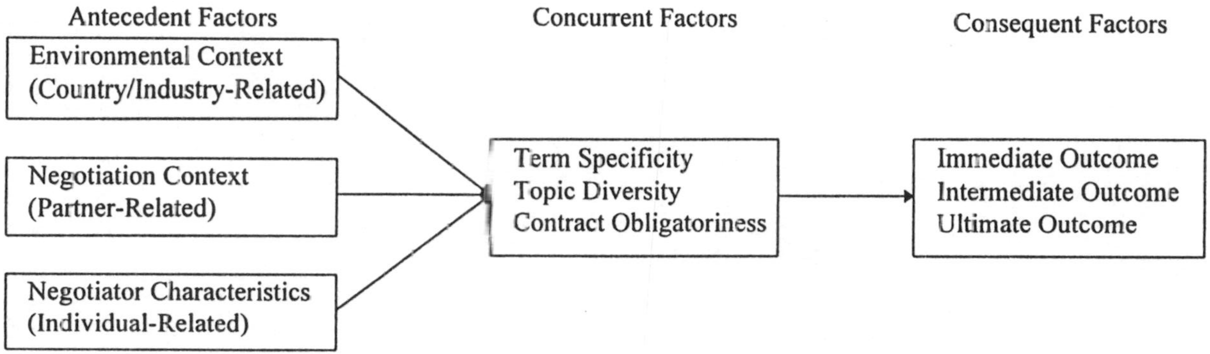

Antecedent Factors	Concurrent Factors	Consequent Factors

Environmental Context
(Country/Industry-Related)

Negotiation Context
(Partner-Related)

Negotiator Characteristics
(Individual-Related)

Term Specificity
Topic Diversity
Contract Obligatoriness

Immediate Outcome
Intermediate Outcome
Ultimate Outcome

The regulatory environment also influences each partner's attitude toward law and litigation. In the United States, for instance, contracts are viewed in legalistic terms; in Japan, contracts are viewed more in the context of the social relationship that exists between the partners. Similarly, in the Japanese context, control (which is of paramount concern to most U.S. enterprises) is viewed in the light of cooperation. These differences in attitude toward law imply that a firm may have to rely upon alternative methods of conflict resolution with partners from different nations.

Third, as political and economic considerations are often inextricably intertwined, the distinctions between the political and economic environments may be fuzzy. The economic focus is on three sets of variables: the type of economic system in a country (e.g., market, centrally-planned, or mixed economies). This determines the nature and form of economic cooperation that can take place; the level of economic development in the country. In general, many less developed countries are chronically short of capital (especially foreign exchange), technological know-how, and skilled labor. Given these circumstances, the partner from the advanced nation must assume much of the responsibility for financing and providing technology and technological capability; and the national objectives or priorities of the host country as defined within five- and ten-year plans and industrial policies. These determine the type and nature of projects that are encouraged in the country at a specific time.

Fourth, culture influences negotiations in several important ways. It affects how people process and interpret information. It also influences people's perception of what is reasonable, right, and acceptable, thus affecting their choice of strategies to pursue in the negotiation process and in the resolution of conflicts. Furthermore, cultural differences are reflected in dissimilarities in decision making, negotiating styles, and choice of methods for conflict resolution. For instance, Tung (1988) found major differences in these respects between the Americans, Japanese, and Chinese. Although the ability to bridge cultural differences does not greatly explain the success of business negotiations, its absence is perceived as a major contributor to failure. That is, ignoring cultural differences often has a detrimental effect on the outcome of negotiations.

Negotiation Context. The negotiation context refers to the structural properties conditioning the course of the negotiation itself, thus affecting the interactions specific to a given situation (Straus, 1978). There are several contextual elements, often firm-related, that may affect the concurrent factors of IJV negotiation. First, the relative balance of power may be influential. The power of a negotiating partner does not reside exclusively within the firm itself but rather in the relationship it has with its external environment. The relative balance of power of the partners determines the extent to which each partner accommodates to the demands of the other.

Second, each partner's stakes may influence the negotiation process. These stakes depend upon the amount of perceived gains or losses associated with particular results. The greater the stakes in the venture, the more important the negotiation process and its outcome. Concurrent factors, such as term specificity and contractual obligations, can serve as ex ante mechanisms protecting the party's stakes. As a result, the partner who commits more to the venture will attach more value to the negotiation process.

Third, repeated negotiations may affect the attitude and commitment of both parties. Negotiators may be more accommodating, cooperative, and honest in repetitive bargaining situations than during one shot transactions because of the prospect of future encounters. Consequently, where the negotiations are expected to be serial, the issues of reciprocity and repercussions become major concerns. Moreover, where negotiations are ongoing, negotiators tend to tread more cautiously because any decision may have implications for subsequent, related negotiations.

Fourth, options for avoiding or discontinuing negotiations will influence the dedication of parties to the negotiations. Where there are available options for discontinuing discussions, either party may be less motivated to work toward an agreement. The selection of strategies and, hence, the progress and outcome of the negotiations are affected. Where one or both parties perceive the cessation of negotiations as detrimental to its or their interests, then either or both partners would become more compromising and more willing to explore other modes of conflict resolution.

Last, the nature and complexity of the transaction may affect the length and process of negotiations. Where the issues under negotiation are numerous and difficult, each party has to make constant tradeoffs while reassessing its priorities and the utility functions of each compromise. This affects the strategy that will be adopted in the negotiation. One party may deliberately magnify the significance of a concession in order to bargain for better terms in other areas. Where the outcome of one resolution is linked with other disputes, one party may make more concessions so as to maximize the outcome during other negotiations.

Negotiator Characteristics. This set of factors consists of individual traits that may influence the process of IJV negotiations. They have a direct bearing on the progress and outcome of negotiations because negotiations are, after all, conducted by individuals. First, the personality of negotiators may affect their strategy and behavior during negotiations. The personality characteristics affecting negotiations include:

introversion versus extroversion (extroversion can have a positive influence on negotiation, *ceteris paribus*);

experience in international business (more experienced individuals may meet with greater success in the negotiation situation);

internationalism versus isolationalism (internationalists tend to be more cooperative than isolationalists in negotiation situations); and

value systems (terminal, instrumental, interpersonal, and intrapersonal) of the negotiators (negotiators' values, in conjunction with the aforementioned personality characteristics, can influence their approach to the situation, choice of strategy, perception of efficacy, and range of possible options).

Interpersonal relationships are also often important to the negotiation success. Choice of strategies is influenced by the relationships that exist between negotiators representing different parties. Where the negotiators trust and respect their counterparts on the opposite team, the issues under discussion can be more easily defined and narrowed, thus facilitating a meeting of minds at the negotiating table (Tung, 1988).

Third, the number of negotiators can have either a favorable or unfavorable influence on negotiations, depending upon the coordination and integration of the group. If the team members from one party coordinate well and prepare their strategies beforehand, having more people on the team may enhance bargaining power or at least put more pressure on the other team. However, if differences in values and opinions abound within the team, having too many people may impair negotiations. To resolve such intra-group differences, trade-offs and compromises will have to be made, thus affecting the selection of strategies to be pursued and the progress and outcome of negotiations.

Last, loyalty of negotiators to the party they represent is deemed to motivate their negotiation behavior. Negotiators who are loyal to their employers will have more zeal and take more initiatives. This leads to more dedication to the process and consequences of negotiations. In fact, one of the widespread strategies used during IJV negotiations is for one side to attempt to reduce the other negotiator's loyalty to his or her firm. This may be fulfilled by strengthening personal relationships, exchanging favors, providing entertainments, and the like.

Concurrent Factors

Concurrent factors during the negotiation process include term specificity, topic diversity, and contract obligatoriness. Term specificity means the degree to which major clauses and conditions of an IJV project are specified during negotiations and incorporated into the IJV contract. Topic diversity refers to the scope of issues that relevant parties discuss and bargain over during negotiations. Contract obligatoriness can be defined as the extent to which each party involved in IJV negotiations is restrained by the binding force of the contract.

The specification of major terms during negotiations and their eventual codification in a contract provide a safeguard against ex post performance problems by mitigating each party's ability to act opportunistically over the course of significant, long-term investments, as in the case of IJVs. Collaborative ventures can fail because of transaction hazards precipitated by opportunistic behavior on the part of each partner or because of high bureaucratic costs involved in coordinating interfirm exchange. These threats necessitate ex ante specifications governing each party's rights, duties, and benefits, which are reflected in various terms, clauses, and conditions negotiated and agreed upon by all parties. Term specificity is a major concurrent factor because it is associated with both antecedent variables and negotiation consequences. Term specificity is likely to be positively propelled by goal differences between IJV partners, degree of host government intervention, and investment size, but negatively linked with culture distance between partners. As a predictor, term specificity positively influences IJV performance.

One of the effective ways to shape the negotiation process and outcome is to control the agenda of the discussions. The party that manipulates the scope of negotiable issues will be in an advantageous position during the formation, operations, and management of the IJV, which will take place later on. Controlling the scope enables the party to avoid discussing issues that may be unfavorable to the firm and to promote those topics and terms that are relatively advantageous to the firm. Thus, topic control facilitates ex post operational and organizational control after the formation of the IJV. This device seems particularly imperative for those who are minority equity holders but need to control local production and operations. Topic diversity represents an ex ante mechanism by which a minority equity holder may dominate IJV operations and growth. Of the macro-level environmental antecedents, political and regulatory factors are relatively more influential in affecting topic diversity because foreign partners are usually left with no choice but to accept host government regulations. Among firm-level antecedents, a party's bargaining power and stake have a strong impact on controlling topic diversity. Although the firm's stake leads to the necessity to take control, its bargaining power makes it possible to implement such controls. Among individual antecedents, personality types and interpersonal relationships between negotiators from different parties are deemed to affect the control of negotiation issues because these two individual traits have a more direct and significant influence on manipulating the negotiation atmosphere and attaining compromise.

Concluding an IJV agreement differs from signing an import-export contract in two primary ways. First, the stipulations of terms in an IJV agreement are more flexible than those in an export sales contract. Second, parties to an IJV agreement are less legally restrained than those in an export contract. In other words, IJV partners have more leeway in stipulating relevant terms and clauses to align with specific needs and interests for both parties. For instance, parties to an export contract must accept certain international rules (e.g., as enacted and published by the International Chamber of Commerce) for the explanation of standardized terms such as letter of credit, documents against payment, and documents against acceptance (three widely used terms of payment) and free on board; cost, insurance, and freight; and cost and freight (three widely used terms of price). In an IJV agreement, however, neither party is constrained by such standards. IJV partners also have the right to ask for revisions after the agreement is concluded. Consequently, IJV negotiators often specify a special clause concerning the degree of obligatoriness defining the terms, which are open to revision, and how the revision would proceed. Different IJV agreements may therefore vary in their rigidity. This is fairly influenced by macro-level environmental antecedents, such as political incidents, economic fluctuations, and institutional changes. Some firm-level antecedents, such as changes in relative bargaining power, stakes, motivations, and strategies, may also affect contract obligatoriness and lead to alteration of certain terms and clauses. The party that has the stronger bargaining position may manage the degree of contractual leeway by controlling contractual obligations so that it can ensure that the terms eventually implemented by both parties will be in its best interest.

Consequent Factors

Broadly, the consequences of IJV negotiations fall into sequentially interrelated categories: immediate effects, intermediate effects, and ultimate effects. Immediate consequences can be used to assess the outcome of IJV negotiations. First, in the event of a successful agreement, the outcome can be measured in terms of negotiator satisfaction. Second, in the event of a stalemate or deadlock, one may examine whether alternative strategies can be devised to help unblock the stalemate. Third, in the event of a complete breakdown between IJV partners, both parties can withdraw and dissolve the negotiations.

The intermediate effects of negotiation consequences rest on the process-based performance of an IJV. Process-based performance dimensions may include technology development, product design, quality control, labor productivity, managerial and administrative efficiency, customer responsiveness, information flow, cost and budget control, and marketing effectiveness. Contract negotiation and specifications create explicit rules for operations, which are necessary for superior efficiency and effectiveness in production and management processes. This effect is intermediate because it links a negotiation's immediate and eventual effects. Sequentially, the immediate effect, that is, the degree of satisfaction with the agreement, implies satisfaction with the specifications of various terms. This will foster performance in production and operation.

Superior efficiency and effectiveness in production and operation processes will in turn boost eventual IJV performance.

The ultimate effects of negotiation consequences reside in financial, market, risk, and the overall performance of IJVs in the host country. Successful negotiation is one of the necessary conditions for IJV success. It provides a sound basis for inter-partner cooperation, managerial rules, conflict resolution, and strategic direction, all of which are critical to the eventual success of the IJV. This success may be reflected in such indicators as profitability, market growth, competitive position, risk reduction, and overall performance. Such ultimate effects are linked with intermediate effects in that the latter serve as predictors of the IJV's eventual performance. Without success in production, operation, and management processes, an IJV cannot attain high financial, market, and overall performance relative to its major rivals.

Major Terms and Clauses during International Equity Joint Venture Negotiation

Following is a brief introduction to the major terms negotiated and stipulated in a greenfield, equity joint venture contract or agreement in which only two parties, one local and one foreign, are involved. A full range of terms and their specifications will be determined by the situation, environment, and firms involved in a given negotiation.

Joint Venture Name, Its Legal Nature, and Legal Address

In most cases, the organizational form of a joint venture is a limited liability company. Each party to the joint venture is liable to the venture company within the limit of the capital subscribed by each party. The profits, risks, and losses of the joint venture company are shared by the parties in proportion to their contributions of registered capital.

Scope and Scale of Production or Operations

When a multinational enterprise invests in a highly regulated industry or country, it is subject to restrictions in terms of business scope. In such an event, the joint venture negotiations and contract should specify the intended scope of business in accordance with the industry's or country's regulations and policies. The stipulation of expected production scale for the beginning period, or for several years after, although approximate and non-binding, can guide the venture and is often required by the host government.

Investment Amount, Unit of Currency, and Equity Distribution

The total amount of investment contributed by all parties is often not the same as that of registered capital. Some host countries may have rules or policies on the amount of registered capital or the maximum difference between the amount of investment and that of registered capital. Investors may also artificially increase or decrease the amount of registered capital to avoid taxes. Because the unit of currency specified in the agreement may not be the same as the one a foreign investor actually remits, timing of cash contribution is also specified. Further, the contract will often specify the payment method, especially for installments (e.g., how many installments are allowed).

Forms of Contribution

Joint venture parties may contribute various forms of assets as their investment. These include, but are not limited to, cash, machines and equipment, technology, land, factories, patents, trademarks, proprietary knowledge or skills, and other industrial or intellectual property rights. The contract should specify explicitly what and when particular forms or combined forms should be contributed. When contributing industrial or intellectual property rights, relevant parties shall include a separate contract regarding these investments as part of the main contract.

Responsibilities of Each Party

These responsibilities are project- and situation-specific. It is hard to provide a standard in this respect. Such responsibilities also differ according to entry mode. In a typical IJV between a developed country investor and a developing country investor, the local partner is generally responsible for: handling approval applications, registration, business licenses, land use, and other formalities concerning the establishment of the joint venture; organizing the design and construction of the project in the case of a greenfield investment; providing cash, machinery and equipment, and facilities in accordance with the stipulations on investment contribution; assisting a foreign party in processing import customs declarations for the machinery and equipment contributed by the firm as investment; assisting the joint venture company in purchasing or leasing equipment, materials, raw materials, office supplies and equipment, means of transportation, communication facilities, and so on; assisting the joint venture in arranging for basic utilities, such as water, electricity, and transportation; assisting in recruiting local management personnel, technical personnel, workers, and other employees for the joint venture; and assisting foreign workers and staff in applying for entry visas, work licenses, and in processing their travel documents. A foreign partner is generally responsible for: providing cash, machinery, equipment, and industrial property in accordance with the stipulations on investment contributions; handling matters relating to foreign markets, such as selecting and purchasing machinery and equipment; providing necessary technical personnel for the installation, testing, and trial runs of equipment, as well as for future production and inspection; and training technical personnel and workers for the joint venture.

Technology or Knowledge Transfer

Both parties in an IJV often agree in advance to exchange skills and technology that each wants from the other, thereby ensuring a chance for equitable gain. Technology transfer agreements are also often signed between the joint venture and a parent firm (or a third party). In addition, contractual safeguards for protecting the parent firm that owns proprietary technology can be written into an IJV agreement. Further, a cross-licensing arrangement may also be specified in the venture agreement.

The following example illustrates a technology transfer arrangement in an IJV contract between a firm from a developed country and one from a developing country. The foreign party guarantees that:

The overall technology, such as the design, technological processes, tests, and inspection of products will be integrated, precise, and reliable. The technology should be sufficient to satisfy the requirements of the joint venture operations and be able to meet the quality standards and production capacity stipulated in the contract.

The technology stipulated in the contract and technology transfer agreement shall be fully transferred to the joint venture company and pledges that the technology provided shall be truly advanced.

It will compile a detailed list of the technology and technological services provided at various stages, as stipulated in the technology transfer agreement, comprising an appendix to the contract.

The drawings, technological conditions, and other detailed information are part of the transferred technology and shall be offered on time.

Within the valid period of the technology transfer agreement, the foreign party shall provide the joint venture company with technological improvements, information, and materials in a timely manner without charging separate fees.

The technological personnel and the workers in the joint venture will master all of the technology transferred within the period stipulated in the technology transfer agreement.

In case the foreign party fails to provide equipment and technology in accordance with the stipulations in the contract and in the technology transfer agreement or in case any deceptions or concealment are discovered, the party shall be responsible for compensating for the resulting direct losses to the joint venture.

The payment of technology transfer fee (i.e., royalties) should be stipulated. The royalty rate is usually a certain percentage of the net sales of the products. The term for the technology transfer agreement signed by the joint venture and the transferrer must also be regulated. After the expiration of the technology transfer agreement, the joint venture usually has the right to continue using, researching, and developing the transferred technology for a stipulated period of time (e.g., no longer than ten years in China).

Marketing Issues

This clause usually specifies market orientation (percentage of sales in local and export markets respectively), marketing channels and approaches (e.g., direct marketing, contracts with sales agents, or setting up sales branches or representative offices in major locations), and the IJV trademark.

Composition of the Board of Directors

This clause generally stipulates: the number of directors in total, and from each party respectively; rights to nominate the chairman and vice chairman of the board; that the highest authority in the joint venture shall be its board of directors, which shall decide all major issues concerning the joint venture. These major issues are often listed in either the body of the contract or a supplemental agreement. A unanimous vote is normally required before any major decisions are made; that the chairman of the board is the legal representative of the joint venture; and the frequency of the board meetings. The chairman may convene an interim meeting based on a proposal made by minimum number of directors (usually one-third of the total).

Nomination and Responsibility of High Level Managers

The agreement should specify which party has the right to nominate the general manager (or president) and several deputy general managers (or vice presidents). The terms of such appointments are usually approved by the board. The responsibility of these top level managers should be generally described. Departmental or divisional managers are usually appointed by the top management. This clause also regulates that in case of graft or serious dereliction of duty on the part of the general manager and/or deputy general managers, the board of directors shall have the power to dismiss them at will.

Project Preparation and Construction

An interim construction office usually needs to be set up to be responsible for the following: examining the project designs; signing project construction contracts; organizing the purchase and inspection of relevant equipment and materials; developing the project construction schedule; preparing the budget; controlling project expenditures and accounting procedures; and maintaining records of documents, drawings, files, and materials during the construction phase of the project. The composition of managers in this office is normally decided by the board of directors. When necessary, this clause may also provide guidance for setting up a technical group under the above office. This group may be in charge of all aspects of the project, including project design, quality control, equipment, materials, and use of technology. After having completed the project, both the office and group shall be dissolved by the board of directors.

Labor Management

The agreement may stipulate that the labor contract covering recruitment, employment, dismissal and resignation, wages, labor insurance, welfare, rewards, penalties, and other matters concerning the office staff and workers in the joint venture shall be drawn up between the joint venture and a trade union or between the venture and individual employees. The appointment of high ranking administrative personnel recommended by both parties, their salaries, social insurance, welfare, and the like may be decided upon by the board of directors.

Accounting, Finance, and Tax Issues

This clause may regulate the fiscal year period, dividend policies, allocation of retained earnings, currency and language used in bookkeeping and financial statements, auditing, financing policies, working capital management, and so on. Some IJV agreements may also specify that venture management should submit the operational plan and financial budget to the board in the early period of each fiscal year and submit a proposal concerning the disposal of profits to the board for examination and approval.

Duration of the Joint Venture

This clause stipulates the duration of the venture in years. The establishment of the joint venture usually starts from the date of issuance of its business license. This duration can be extended, subject to the need of both parties. Usually, an extension is proposed by one party and unanimously approved by the board of directors.

Disposal of Assets after Expiration

Upon the expiration of the joint venture agreement or termination before the date of expiration, liquidation will be carried out according to relevant laws in the host country. The liquidated assets will be distributed in accordance with the proportions of investment contributed by respective parties. In case any party of the joint venture intends to assign all or part of its investment to a third party, consent shall be obtained from the other party of the venture. In this case, the other party usually has preemptive rights to buy the ownership.

Amendments, Alterations, and Discharge of the Agreement

Amendments of the contract usually come into force only after a written agreement is signed by both parties and approved by the board. In case of an inability to fulfill the contract or to continue operations because of heavy losses for successive years as a result of a force majeure, the duration of the joint venture and the contract may be terminated prior to the time of expiration after unanimous agreement by the board of directors. Should the joint venture be unable to continue operations or achieve the business purpose stipulated in its contract because one of the contracting parties fails to fulfill its contractual obligations or seriously violates stipulations of the contract and articles of association, that party shall be deemed in breach of contract. The other party shall have the right to terminate the contract and claim damages in accordance with the provisions of the contract. If both parties agree to continue operations, the party that fails to fulfill obligations shall be liable for economic losses suffered by the joint venture.

Liabilities for Breach of Contract or Agreement

Should all or part of the contract and its appendices go unfulfilled, owing to the fault of one party, the party in breach shall bear the responsibility. Should it be the fault of both parties, they shall bear their respective responsibilities accordingly. To guarantee the performance of the contract and its appendices, both parties usually provide each other with bank guarantees for their respective contributions according to the contract. If one party fails to pay contributions on schedule, the other party may have the right to terminate the contract and claim damages from the party in breach.

Force Majeure

Should either of the parties to the contract be prevented from executing the contract by force majeure, such as an earthquake, typhoon, flood, fire, war, or other unforeseen events, this party shall notify the other party by cable without delay within 15 days, and thereafter provide detailed information of the events and a notarized document explaining the reason for the delay or inability to execute all or part of the contract. Both parties shall decide through negotiation whether to terminate the contract, exempt some of the obligations necessitated for implementation of the contract, or delay the execution of the contract, according to the effect of the force majeure on the performance of the parties in carrying out the stipulations of the contract.

Applicable Law

The formation of the joint venture contract or agreement, its validity, interpretation, execution, and settlement of disputes shall be governed by the relevant laws of the host country.

Settlement of Disputes

This term specifies the settlement method if any disputes arise. This method may include consultation, arbitration, and lawsuits. The term may regulate the combination and sequence of these methods (e.g., start with consultation, follow with arbitration, and end with lawsuits). Firms often strive to settle disputes with negotiation and consultation in the first place. If no settlement can be reached, the dispute may be submitted for arbitration to an impartial, professional, and authoritative arbitration institution, agreed upon by both parties and stipulated in the contract. The arbitral award is final and binding upon both parties.

Effectiveness of the Contract and
Miscellaneous Concerns

The relevant appendices may be specified as an integral part of the joint venture contract. The contract and its appendices generally come into force on the date of signature by both parties or the date of approval by relevant host government authorities if such approval is needed. Once the contract takes effect, two parties should be obligated to the contract. This binding force should be explicitly specified in the contract.

JOINT VENTURE COOPERATION

Conceptual Background

Negotiation success is important to both parties of an IJV. However, it only offers the written basis on which an IJV is formed and operates. An IJV contract or agreement cannot stipulate all aspects of managerial policies and procedures, strategic goals, forms of conflict resolution, and R-R-B for all parties. More importantly, IJV operation is an ongoing, dynamic, and evolutionary process. Many events cannot be foreseen by IJV negotiators. When an IJV contract or agreement is successfully reached, venture success will largely depend on inter-partner cooperation during subsequent operations and management. The negotiated IJV agreement serves as a static mechanism governing the formation and development of an IJV, but cooperation ensures the survival and growth of an IJV.

Interfirm cooperation is a core concept in the study of IJVs. It has been shown to correlate positively with joint venture longevity, effectiveness, and performance (Parkhe, 1993). Cooperation, however, does not emerge automatically. As Buckley and Casson note, "all the parties involved in a venture have an inalienable de facto right to pursue their own interests at the expense of others" (1988: 34). Consequently, IJVs are often character- ized by instability arising from uncertainty regarding the partner's future behavior and the absence of a higher authority to ensure compliance. To make an IJV stable and profitable, parental firms need to adjust their behavior to the preferences of their partners. The mutual dependence involved in an IJV makes interfirm cooperation necessary if the compa- nies are to achieve their goals.

Joint venture success is dependent on not only inter-partner coopera- tion but also collaborations between IJV management and the parent firms. An IJV occurs when two or more firms pool a portion of their resources into a common legal, independent organization. Managers in such organizations direct the ventures to accomplish goals that may or may not correlate with those of one or both parental companies. As inde- pendent agencies, these managers may have their own incentives to behave opportunistically in dealing with the parent firms. A minority parent may dominate the venture if it can convince the IJV managers to be more cooperative and supportive than they are with its partner. When partners' objectives diverge, a parent's relationship with venture man- agers becomes even more important.

The problem of cooperation arises in situations of conflict and interde- pendence. Conflict stems from the fact that individuals and organizations may have incongruent goals or goals that are mutually exclusive. Inter- dependence requires mutual accommodation if all parties are to meet oth- erwise incompatible goals. Transaction cost economics conceives the problem of cooperation as present in transactions involving a high degree of asset specificity, given uncertainty and bounded rationality (Williamson, 1985). When two parties engage in a transaction, a bilateral monopoly is created. The party contributing specific assets runs the risk of these rents being expropriated if the other party behaves opportunisti- cally. Opportunism can be governed by mechanisms that mitigate risk by the exchange of "hostages that equalize the exposure of the partners" (Williamson, 1985: 531) and reduce incentives to "cheat" (Buckley & Cas- son, 1988).

According to the prisoner's dilemma, cooperation is not automatic because it is not in the interest of each player to behave cooperatively if there are no guarantees that the other player will reciprocate. Individual behavior leading to maximum joint payoffs does not necessarily result in the maximum individual payoffs. If both partners try to maximize their own payoffs, however, then neither individual nor joint payoffs will be maximized. Cooperation can be achieved by altering the incentive structure so that behavior that maximizes the individual payoffs also maximizes the joint payoff. Promises and threats are devices that modify the incentive structure. A rational second player can be constrained by the knowledge that the first player has altered its own incentive structure. When more players are engaged in the game, collusion, opportunism, and information imperfection are normally intensified, which will compound the difficulties involved in achieving subgame-perfect Nash equilibrium for all parties (Gibbons, 1992).

In economic theory, a transaction is ideally designed so as to align the interests of the transacting parties. This should lead to cooperative behavior because what is in the interest of the first party is also in the interest of the other party. Therefore, the parties have an economic basis for expecting reciprocity. In contrast to economic theory, the sociological perspective maintains that social norms are partly exogenous and partly endogenous to the transaction. They are exogenous insofar as social mechanisms are embedded within the broader societal context; they are endogenous to the extent that there exist mechanisms within a joint venture that favor the creation of an internal social norm of reciprocity. Social exchange theory suggests that the expectation that the party initially receiving some benefit will reciprocate in a comparable way at some time in the future is conductive to cooperation. Cooperative behavior is thus based on the general consensus that an individual who rewards another obligates him or her to return the favor. In fact, he or she will return the reward received because of his or her basic need to continue other social exchanges in the future; these would not take place if the individual did not behave reciprocally. Thus the parties have a social basis for expecting reciprocity.

According to Ouchi (1980), if the goals of the transacting parties are highly incongruent but tasks are unambiguous, transactions are mediated by the market, where the price mechanism guarantees that the transaction will be equitable. If the goals of the transacting parties are highly incongruent and tasks are ambiguous, transactions are mediated by bureaucracies; the existence of a central authority assumed to compensate each party fairly guarantees that the transaction will be equitable. Last, if goal incongruence is low and tasks are ambiguous, transactions are mediated by the clan mechanism, where goal congruence and the trust it generates guarantee that the transaction will be equitable.

The need for cooperation arises where both interdependence and conflict are simultaneously present. IJVs combine several types of resources not belonging to any one firm. Each company lacks some of the other's resources; each would be unable to gain the benefits of the IJV independently. Each firm depends on its partner to achieve its goals for the joint venture. Thus, each firm needs to take into account how its partner may respond to its behavior and how this response will affect the outcome of the IJV.

Inter-party conflicts may occur in both formation and operations stages. During the formation stage, goal heterogeneity, low trust, resource homogeneity, and ambiguous contracts are endogenous factors driving subsequent interfirm conflict. During the operations stage, opportunistic behavior, difference in operational policy, emergence of local contingencies, and changes of strategic goals and plans will result in inter-partner conflict that may impair the creation of expected synergies. Also, the growth of a network through a dynamic cyclical process contains the seeds of disintegration. Increasing formalization and monitoring of inter-partner relations leads to conflict and lack of consensus among parties who are struggling to maintain their organizational autonomy in the face of growing interdependence. Moreover, the increase in resource transactions among partners over time implies that their domains will shift from being complementary to being similar, which increases the likelihood of territorial disputes, conflict, and competition. Thus, even a long surviving IJV with improved norms of equity and trust can experience some inter-partner conflict.

Cooperation between Foreign and Local Parent Firms

Reciprocal forbearance is the essence of cooperation. Cooperation is defined by Buckley and Casson as a "special type of coordination effected through mutual forbearance while coordination affects a Pareto-improvement in the allocation of resources" (1988: 32). Cooperation cannot be assumed for IJVs, however. Because all parties have the right to pursue their own interests, both forbearance and cheating can take place. When only the immediate consequences of an action are considered, it often seems best to cheat. When the indirect effects are considered, forbearance may seem more desirable. This implies that forbearance appeals most to those investors who take a long-term view of the situation. As foreign businesses in a dynamic foreign market tend to pursue long-range goals, such as a sustained market share and competitive position, forbearance appears to be imperative for the goal accomplishment of partners.

A small amount of mutual forbearance can be transformed into a large amount of trust and cooperative efficiency within a venture. Cooperatively efficient IJVs accord all parties an opportunity to reciprocate forbearance within an observable sequence of decisions that calls for increasing levels of loyalty. A cooperative environment provides ample opportunity for overt positive behavior and only limited opportunity for covert behavior. Positive behavior in turn facilitates the efficiency and effectiveness of cooperation. In the language of transaction cost theory, a composite quasi-rent is only maximized when actors who are prepared to cooperate and trust actually meet each other. The invisible hand of the market also favors cooperation over time. Hill (1990) maintains that the emergence of a cooperative, trusting relationship generates more superior economic rents than does internalization involving substantial asset investments.

Some transaction cost theorists argue that cooperation may not necessarily lead to superior venture performance if outcomes are highly uncertain or the payoff from opportunism in the present period outweighs the discounted present value of future cooperation that is put in jeopardy by such action (e.g., Buckley & Casson, 1988; Hill, 1990). According to social exchange theory, however, within the context of dynamic markets, this assertion may not hold. In a dynamic society where the role of informal social networks outweighs that of formal mechanisms or even legal frameworks (e.g., in the Chinese society), cooperation is initiated because of the expectation that this behavior will be reciprocated in the future. An individual who rewards another obligates him or her to return the favor. A receptor who fails to make such a return loses social status. Once their reputation is lost individuals or organizations, whether local or foreign, will then lose everything. Cooperative behavior is, therefore, a surprisingly effective way of maintaining survival and growth of the firm. The importance of cooperation is magnified when future relations are critical to the firm, which is often the case for international IJVs in dynamic foreign markets.

Cooperation between foreign and local parents leads to superior performance of IJVs as perceived by not only the joint venture management but also both parent companies. Cooperation means that each partner is well adapted to helping the other and also to learning the values that inspire the other partner to make an unreserved commitment to the venture. In general, superior cooperation is acquired when there exists goal congruity or compatibility between the parties. This means that both parties will be satisfied if the IJV succeeds. According to social exchange theory, cooperation will lead to both parties being better off (Ouchi, 1980).

Cooperation between Parent Firms and International Equity Joint Venture Management

IJV literature remains silent concerning the influence of cooperation between parent firms and IJV management on venture performance. This is an important gap because IJV managers are legally responsible for the ventures themselves. There are three players in the game, not two. Because of agency costs, venture managers seek their own benefits or, at best, those of the venture. Such goals may be heterogenous with those of the foreign or local parents. Agency costs are often high because it is difficult for the board of directors of an IJV to convene frequent meetings and make spot examinations aimed at overseeing IJV management. In the absence of agency costs, IJV management may still have objectives at variance with those of a particular parent because the goals of two parents may conflict. This variance becomes even larger when the external environment is more uncertain, complex, and hostile and the host government intervenes in IJV operations.

According to game theory, the more players involved, the more likely it becomes that collusion and opportunism will increase (Gibbons, 1992). Collusion emphasizes the covert rather than overt dimensions of behavior. It therefore generates little trust and creates incentives to cheat. Even when IJV management remains neutral, it may be regarded as a weak form of cheating because they have failed to perform for the benefit of either of the parent firms. In general, strong cheating involves disruptive actions, and weak cheating means making a minimal amount of effort. Forbearance, by contrast, involves providing a maximum effort. The attainment of cooperation and forbearance from the venture managers is key to achieving benefits for each parent firm.

Because of the legal independence of IJVs, it is easy for one of the parent firms to collude with IJV management. Although joint venture management is often controlled by the parent that possesses majority ownership, the minority parent can take control of the venture by maintaining bargaining power derived from distinctive capabilities and strategic resources upon which the venture or other parent must rely. These resources may include advanced technologies, international distribution, managerial skills, process innovations, and organizational image. Even without these proprietary resources, the minority parent may still be able to control and collude with venture management. For instance, many foreign investors, despite minority status, entice key local managers with opportunities to work at the foreign headquarters. Local parents, on the other hand, may promise managers political promotions.

Cooperation between a parent firm and IJV management may lead to greater satisfaction for that parent firm, but not necessarily for the other. This depends on whether the strategic goals between parents are consistent or compatible with each other. Goal congruence reduces one player's uncertainty about what another player will do, which may in turn facilitate one player's response to the predicted strategies of the other players (i.e., Nash equilibrium). However, goal congruence cannot ensure the satisfaction of one parent if the other parent cooperates too well with IJV management. In game theory, having more information (or, more precisely, having the other players believe that one has more information) about goals can make a player worse off. This problem is enlarged when one parent holds the majority ownership (i.e., Stackelberg's sequential game rather than Cournot's simultaneous model) (see Gibbons, 1992). This suggests that cooperation between one parent and the joint venture managers may not be positively related to the satisfaction of the other parent. Cooperation with only one parent may not represent the best strategy for IJV management either. In the *n*-players ($n > 2$) normal-form game, cooperation with only one other player suffers from the inability to achieve the Nash equilibrium that contributes to the best payoff for the player. If the goals are incongruent or incompatible, one parent will very likely suffer if another parent cooperates with venture managers. Cooperation between two players will make the third player worse off if the former have different goals from the latter and the former know this difference before playing the game. Thus, cooperation between the foreign parent and IJV management is expected to be positively associated with IJV performance as perceived by the foreign parent but negatively associated with IJV performance as perceived by the local parent if the goal difference between parents is high.

Cooperation and Ownership

The perceived importance of cooperation by one partner of an IJV depends upon the vulnerability of that party. A party is vulnerable if some course of action that might be chosen by another party would significantly reduce its welfare. Vulnerability encourages a party to think through how its own actions affect the incentives facing others. The more vulnerable the party is, the more important it is to avoid stimulating an adverse response from other agents. Each party can, to some extent, induce long-term thinking in other parties by emphasizing their vulnerability to its actions.

The ownership status of one party determines its vulnerability to another party's responses, actions, and forbearance. The majority owner has a greater stake in the IJV than does the minority owner. The survival and growth of the joint venture provide more fundamental benefits to the majority owner. Although IJV performance also affects the minority owner, the perceived importance of this performance is not as significant as it is for the majority party. The two parties are not equally exposed to the venture's activities. This inequality is likely to create the incentive to cheat and carries the risk of opportunism. Because the majority owner contributes more strategic resources, involving a higher degree of asset specificity, it runs a greater risk of having its economic rents expropriated if the other party behaves opportunistically. Thus, cooperation with the other parent firm is more crucial to venture success as perceived by the majority owner than by the minority party.

Cooperation with joint venture management is also more important for the majority holder. This cooperation can help the majority parent control the venture's activities, increase bargaining power over the partner firm, and facilitate the implementation of its corporate and business strategies. Moreover, cooperation boosts information transparency and flow between the venture and the majority parent. This in turn enables the latter to have a better strategic position than the other parent firm (Gibbons, 1992). As a consequence, cooperation with the partner firm and IJV management is more important to joint venture performance as perceived by the parent who maintains majority ownership than the one who maintains minority ownership.

Cooperation, Trust, and Commitment

Trust and cooperation have at times been treated as synonymous. They are different but correlated concepts. Trust refers to the willingness of a party to be vulnerable to the actions of another party based on the expectation that the other will perform a particular action important to the trusting party, irrespective of the ability to monitor or control that other party. Trust frequently leads to cooperative behavior. Nevertheless, in theoretical terms, trust is not a necessary condition for cooperation to occur, because cooperation does not necessarily put a party at risk. In the short term, a firm can cooperate with a company it does not really trust as long as the expected benefits from cooperation outweigh corresponding costs.

Trust is critical to propelling IJV profitability and stability over the long run, particularly in a dynamic context. Two firms may cooperate without trust in the short run or for a single transaction. IJVs, by contrast, are often long-term collaborative arrangements aimed at securing mutual benefits. Trust and commitment are, therefore, fundamental to the survival and growth of IJVs. In successful IJVs that share long-term common goals, cooperation is often perceived as an end rather than a means. To fulfill this end, trust appears to be a necessary condition for sustained long-term cooperation.

Trustworthiness is determined by several factors, particularly a party's ability, benevolence, and integrity. Ability is a party's skills, competencies, and characteristics that enable it to have influence within some specific domain. If such abilities are complementary to those of the partner firm, their contribution to trustworthiness will be higher. Benevolence is the extent to which a firm is believed to want to do good to the trusting party, setting aside any profit motive. Benevolence suggests that the trusted party has some specific attachment to the trusting party. The relationship between integrity and trust involves the trusting party's perception that the other party adheres to a set of principles that the former finds acceptable. Acceptability precludes a party committed solely to the principle of profit-seeking from being judged high in integrity. Such issues as the consistency of the party's past actions, credible communications about that party from other sources, belief that the party has a strong sense of justice, the degree to which the party is concerned with the other party's needs, and the extent to which the party's actions are congruent with its commitment all affect the degree to which the party is judged to have integrity.

It should be noted that all three interrelated determinants are necessary conditions for high trustworthiness. In other words, if ability, benevolence, and integrity are all perceived to be high, the party will be deemed quite trustworthy. Trustworthiness, however, should be thought of as a continuum, rather than a dichotomy (i.e., either high or low). Each of the three determinants can vary along the continuum.

The degree of commitment to an IJV is likely to be conditional upon certain characteristics of the joint venture (Buckley & Casson, 1988). The commitment of the partners is likely to be higher, for example, the more socially meritorious or strategically important the output is deemed to be. Commitment will also tend to be higher if the distribution of rewards from the venture, when it is successfully completed, is deemed equitable to all parties. Envy of the share of gains appropriated by another partner can not only diminish motivation but also encourage cheating. The psychology of commitment, if understood correctly, can be used by one party to manipulate another. Securing commitment through manipulation is a dangerous strategy for a party, however, because it will lead to some form of reprisal from the other party.

Cooperation and Knowledge Acquisition

Acquisition of a partner firm's knowledge is recognized as one of the major rationales underlying IJV formation. Once one partner has acquired the other partner's knowledge, unless the latter is contributing other valuable skills to the IJV, the rationale for interfirm cooperation is eliminated. In other words, if one partner attaches a high value to the acquisition of its partner's knowledge and has the ability to acquire that knowledge, the probability of IJV instability increases. This suggests that the acquisition of knowledge enables firm autonomy. If two partners of an IJV are only motivated to acquire each other's knowledge, cooperation serves merely as a means rather than an end. In this event, an IJV is very likely to be unstable and short lived, which may not necessarily be an undesirable consequence. If there are other important concerns and objectives for both parties, cooperation turns out to be a stabilizing mechanism. A party may take steps to ensure that its role encompasses more than simply contributing knowledge. The other party may choose access to a partner's knowledge rather than acquisition of the knowledge in order to promote stability (Inkpen & Beamish, 1997).

When a partner contributing knowledge to a foreign company is concerned with IJV stability, it should consider minimizing the foreign partner's acquisition of local knowledge. Local knowledge here refers to established local infrastructure including sales force, plants, market intelligence, and local marketing presence. It is also related to cultural traditions, business practices, norms, values, and institutional differences. Unlike technological know-how, which can be protected by several contractual safeguards, such as cross-licensing, wall-off structure, and access constraints, firms have more difficulties controlling their local knowledge if they want to make the IJVs profitable and sustainable. Nevertheless, a local partner may wish to discourage a foreign firm from sending large numbers of managers to the venture because knowledge acquisition by organizations begins with individuals (Inkpen & Beamish, 1997). The greater the number of managers from the foreign partner, the greater the foreign partner's access to local knowledge. In addition, the local firm can continue to invest actively in local knowledge or bargain for greater responsibility in managing the IJV. In effect, it can increase the importance of its role to the venture's success.

JOINT VENTURE TERMINATION

Why Terminate

Although partners usually establish long-term objectives, IJVs are more often terminated than not. Clearly, it is important to be alert to conditions that can lead to the demise of the venture. These may be hidden at the start but become more evident over time. A number of conditions have been identified as the source of major disputes threatening the IJV. Gates (1996) highlighted problems ranging from disagreements over capital and management decisions to the venture's or alliance's failure to meet shifting targets.

Exploit versus Invest

Partners may disagree over whether they should exploit their original investment or continue to invest capital or technology in the venture instead. The initial shared perspective could easily fall apart because of inequalities in partner size or capabilities (industrial versus financial). Moreover, one of the partners may decide that it has obtained enough knowledge or access from the alliance to be able to go it alone.

Replicate or Adapt Operation

One partner may prefer to replicate its operational procedures within the alliance, whereas the other stresses the need to adapt to new markets, technologies, or products. Conflict is likely to ensue.

Fight versus Cooperate

If the basic stance of one partner is to win by confrontation, the other partner could feel that this puts too much strain on the venture. Issues and problems that should be raised are likely to be avoided because they provoke combative behavior.

Management

The partners may be incapable of reaching an agreement on management appointments. If the IJV is not equally shared, the dominant partner may impose its own management choices. However, if both partners seek to avoid any conflict over the appointment, they may end up giving management more free rein than either wishes. In this instance, the parents become dependent on a small number of managers who, with time, become irreplaceable. When future problems arise, disagreement over management selection becomes even more severe.

Internal Focus

Once the venture or alliance is underway, there is a tendency to view it as a set of coordination problems. This internal focus can also take the form of politicking. In this case, managers within the venture may begin taking credit for results that have yet to materialize. It is important to redirect management's attention externally to the competition.

Inability to Meet Shifting Targets

Non-performance can doom an IJV to failure. Targets cannot be met because of inadequate resources, time, or effort, or perhaps because of unrealistically ambitious goals. Rather than signal the end, non-performance should be seen as an opportunity to reset goals or evaluate inadequacies more closely. The targets set for the venture may be shifting because of rapid market developments, changing strategies, or even a change in ownership at one of the firms. In practice, there may be a number of reasons why the partners' interests have diverged.

Apart from the above reasons, an IJV may be terminated because: a partner needs to exit the joint venture because of financial difficulties or to take advantage of financial opportunities, the joint venture has already met its goals, differences and incompatibilities between partners intensify, there is a breach of agreement, or the venture no longer fits the goals or strategies of a partner.

How to Terminate

Serapio and Cascio (1996) list three possible divorce scenarios and three possible outcomes of the termination of an IJV or alliance. The first scenario concerns planned or unplanned terminations. Planned terminations are, however, the exception rather than the rule. Divorces in IJVs are typically unanticipated. Most companies enter an IJV without really knowing how long it will last.

The second scenario concerns whether the termination is friendly. Friendly separations are typically handled through negotiated settlements. In contrast, unfriendly divorces are often contested in courts or end up in arbitration.

The third scenario concerns whether all parties have agreed to the termination. Having a partner that refuses to terminate presents one of the most complex scenarios.

In general, there are three forms of termination, namely, termination by acquisition, termination by dissolution, and termination by redefinition of the alliance. In the first case, the alliance is terminated with one of the partners acquiring the stake of the other partner. Termination by acquisition could also take the form of one partner selling its equity stake in the joint venture to another company, or both partners selling their shares to a third company. Termination by acquisition is most common in international equity joint ventures. Termination may also occur by the redefinition of the IJV agreement. In lieu of termination, partners to an international alliance may agree to redefine or restructure their original agreement.

Regardless of which condition has provoked termination or which type of termination is occurring, the process should be managed in accordance with procedures stipulated in the initial IJV contract or its supplements. These procedures generally include conditions of termination, timing, disposition of assets, disposition of liabilities, and dispute resolution mechanisms.

First, partners in an IJV must agree on the circumstances that would allow each partner to exit or call for the dissolution of the IJV. Events such as the following might trigger such a call: material breach of agreement, breach of law, repeated (two or more) deadlocks among the members of the board of directors, changes in the laws and regulations of the home or host country, failure to meet a specific target, or a set period has lapsed. In addition, the partners must agree on voting rights and procedures for dissolving an alliance. For example, termination may require either a majority or unanimous approval by the board of directors.

Second, the timing of a possible termination establishes from the outset the amount of commitment or flexibility each party has with respect to the joint venture. If two companies have mutually agreed not to retract their participation in the joint activity, then they have sent a strong signal to each other indicating their level of dedication to the project. A benchmark event may be set, such as only allowing termination of the venture when it has reached a stage of self-sufficiency that does not leave either partner vulnerable.

Third, the partners should specify the methods to be used in valuing assets. Partners should negotiate how the IJV will liquidate its assets and how the partners will share in the assets. Asset valuation or pricing is a

major source of disagreement during a divorce. The contract should stipulate whether one partner will be given the opportunity to bid on the
equity share of the other. The basis for asset valuation should also be clarified. It may be based on the actual amounts invested by the partners, the
findings of an independent appraiser, or an offer from one of the partners
or an external buyer.

Fourth, a clause needs to stipulate liabilities disposition. How partners
deal with the liabilities of the IJV and how the venture deals with contingent liabilities should be clarified. For example, terminating a venture in
host countries such as Italy, Spain, or Belgium can be very expensive
because of significant severance benefits that the governments of these
countries require employers to pay terminated employees. To illustrate,
terminating a 45-year-old manager with 20 years of service who is earn-
ing $50,000 (U.S.) per year costs about $130,000 in Italy, $125,000 in Spain,
and $94,000 in Belgium, compared to an average $19,000 in the United
States. Partners to an IJV must be prepared to address these and other
types of liabilities related to termination.

Last, the contract should regulate the dispute resolution methods. Disputes may be resolved judicially or through arbitration. Partners to an IJV
should be aware of the advantages and disadvantages of each alternative
before selecting a particular mode of dispute resolution. If the partners
agree to resolve disputes judicially, they are usually free to specify which
country's laws will govern any dispute.

An additional step in this process is to reach an agreement on what
must be accomplished in order to allow one of the partners to continue
operating the venture. This is an operational definition of what the joint
venture requires to survive, if not to prosper. It may include specifying a
target market penetration or a milestone in the transfer or development of
a given technology.

Partners to an international distributorship alliance should specify the
rights and obligations of the manufacturer and distributor in the event
that the partnership is dissolved. Many countries provide distributors
with protection against termination approaching those offered to terminated employees. Terminating a distributor in such countries can require
substantial payments designed to compensate the distributor for expenses that it has incurred and for the goodwill that it has developed for the
manufacturer.

Protection of proprietary information and property is also an important factor in the termination decision. In alliances that involve an
exchange of intellectual property (e.g., patents, know-how, trademarks,
copyrights, tradenames) the partners have to weigh the impact of termination on proprietary information and property. Questions such as the
following must be addressed: What intellectual property rights will

belong to the exiting partner(s)? What will remain in the alliance? How will licenses be handled?

Rights over sales territories and obligations to customers also should be considered. Upon termination of an alliance, it is important to specify who will have responsibility over various sales territories and who will support the IJV's customers. Such long-term considerations should not be left unaddressed until the partnership is on the brink of dissolution. Rather, they should comprise integral parts of early planning.

In addition to the legal considerations, the partners to an international alliance must be prepared to address other important business issues related to termination. First, partners to an alliance should know at what point they are willing and prepared to exit. For example, a major U.S. computer company uses a scorecard to monitor the performance of its international alliances. If an alliance falls below expectations, the company will consider exiting the alliance. In addition, relations with the host government should be taken into account. The host government of a partner may be unwilling to permit the alliance to terminate. It could object to the termination in an overt way, such as not permitting a foreign partner to sell its interest in the alliance. There are also subtle ways to discourage a partner from leaving an alliance, such as blocking the repatriation of the foreign partner's investments in the alliance. Finally, it is important to consider carefully the long-term effects of terminating an alliance on the ability of the company to do business in the same host country in the future.

Although partners should consider all these issues, occasionally it is better to be less specific in anticipating the outcome during negotiations. A precise formula for valuation in the event of termination may actually facilitate the breakdown of an IJV. If two partners recognize that they will face difficult future negotiations in determining the value of their shares, they may tolerate the agreement longer or even work harder toward success of the venture. Another reason it can be dangerous to negotiate specific separation procedures initially is that too much detail about termination places an emphasis on mistrust when the opposite should be nurtured.

REFERENCES

Brouthers, K. D. and G. J. Bamossy. 1997. The role of key stakeholders in international joint venture negotiations: Case studies from Eastern Europe. *Journal of International Business Studies*, 28: 285–308.

Buckley, P. and M. Casson. 1988. The theory of cooperation in international business. In F. J. Contractor and P. Lorange (Eds.), *Cooperative strategies in international business*, pp. 31–34. Lexington, MA: Lexington Books.

Fayerweather, J. and A. Kapoor. 1976. *Strategy and negotiation for the international corporation*. Cambridge, MA: Ballinger.

Gates, S. 1996. Strategic alliances: Guidelines for successful management. *The Conference Board*, Report No. 1028.

Gibbons, R. 1992. Game theory for applied economists. Princeton, NJ: Princeton University Press.

Graham, J. 1985. The influence of culture on the process of business negotiations: An exploratory study. *Journal of International Business Studies*, Spring: 81–94.

Hill, C.W.L. 1990. Cooperation, opportunism, and the invisible hand: Implications for transaction cost theory. *Academy of Management Review*, 15: 500–513.

Inkpen, A. C. and P. W. Beamish. 1997. Knowledge, bargaining power, and the instability of international joint ventures. *Academy of Management Review*, 22(1): 177–202.

Kochan, T. A. and H. C. Katz. 1988. *Collective bargaining and industrial relations*, 2d ed. Homewood, IL: Irwin.

O'Connor, K. M. 1997. Motives and cognitions in negotiation: A theoretical integration and an empirical test. *The International Journal of Conflict Management*, 8: 114–131.

Ouchi, W. G. 1980. Markets, bureaucracies, and clans. *Administrative Science Quarterly*, 25: 124–141.

Parkhe, A. 1993. Strategic alliance structuring: A game theoretic and transaction cost examination of interfirm cooperation. *Academy of Management Journal*, 36: 794–829.

Rubin, J. Z. and B. R. Brown. 1975. *The social psychology of bargaining and negotiation*. New York: Academic Press.

Serapio, M. G. and W. F. Cascio. 1996. End-games in international alliances. *Academy of Management Executive*, 10(1): 62–73.

Straus, A. L. 1978. Negotiations: Varieties, contexts, process, and social order. San Francisco, CA: Jossey Bass.

Thomas, K. W. 1976. Conflict and conflict management. In M. Dunnett (Ed.), *Handbook of Industrial and organizational psychology*, pp. 039–935. Chicago, IL: Rand McNally.

Tung, R. L. 1988. Toward a conceptual paradigm of international business negotiations. *Advances in International Comparative Management*, 3: 203–219.

Weiss, S. E. 1993. Analysis of complex negotiations in international business: The RBC perspective. *Organization Science*, 4: 269–600.

Williamson, O. E. 1985. *The economic institutions of capitalism*. New York: Free Press.

FURTHER READINGS

Adler, N. J., R. Brahm, and J. L. Graham. 1992. Strategy implementation: A comparison of face-to-face negotiations in the People's Republic of China and the United States. *Strategic Management Journal*, 13: 449–466.

Contractor, F. J. and P. Lorange. 1988. The strategy and economics basis for cooperative venture. In F. J. Contractor and P. Lorange (Eds.), *Cooperative strategies in international business*, pp. 1–28. Lexington, MA: Lexington Books.

Fisher, G. 1980. *International negotiations: A cross-cultural perspective*. Chicago, IL: Intercultural Press.

Frances, J.N.P. 1991. When in Rome? The effects of cultural adaptation on inter-cultural business negotiations. *Journal of International Business Studies*, 22: 403–428.

Graham, J. L., L. I. Evenko, and M. N. Rajan. 1992. An empirical comparison of Soviet and American business negotiations. *Journal of International Business Studies*, 23: 387–418.

Hamel, G. 1991. Competition for competence and interpartner learning within international strategic alliances. *Strategic Management Journal*, 12: 83–103.

Moran R. T. and W. G. Stripp. 1991. *Successful international business negotiations*. Houston, TX: Gulf Publishing.

Park, S. H. 1996. Managing an interorganizational network: A framework of the institutional mechanism for network control. *Organization Studies*, 17: 795–824.

Pye, L. 1982. *Chinese commercial negotiation style*. Cambridge, MA: Oelgeschlager, Gunn, and Hain.

Ring, P. S. and A. H. Van de Ven. 1994. Developmental processes of cooperative interorganizational relationships. *Academy of Management Review*, 19: 90–118.

Salacuse, J. W. 1991. *Making global deals: Negotiating in the international marketplace*. Boston, MA: Houghton Mifflin.

Index

ABOUT THE AUTHOR

YADONG LUO is Associate Professor of International Management at
the University of Hawaii, Manoa, where he is a Teaching Excellence
Award recipient. He has published more than 60 journal articles on international business. Before coming to the United States, Dr. Luo taught at
leading universities in China and served as a provincial official in charge
of international business in China for six years.

ISBN 1-56720-161-X

9 781567 201611
HARDCOVER BAR CODE